154

THAT DESPICABLE RACE

★ ★

That Despicable Race

A History of the
British Acting Tradition

BRYAN FORBES

ELM TREE BOOKS LONDON

★ ★

This book would not have seen the light of day had it not been for the foresight, knowledge and expertise of John Knight. Mr Knight is a distinguished producer in the archives department of BBC Radio. It was his original idea to produce a series of broadcasts, written and narrated by myself, utilising some of the historical material which, in its wisdom, the BBC has carefully stored for posterity.

In order that proper recognition is given to Mr Knight's invaluable help throughout, I would like to dedicate this volume to him in gratitude and affection.

BRYAN FORBES

First published in Great Britain 1980 by
Elm Tree Books/Hamish Hamilton Ltd
Garden House 57–59 Long Acre London WC2E 9JZ

Copyright © 1980 by Bryan Forbes Ltd

Design by Patrick Leeson

British Library Cataloguing in Publication Data

Forbes, Bryan
    That despicable race.
      1. Theatre—Great Britain—History
      2. Acting—History
      I. Title
    792'.028'0941   PN2581
    ISBN 0-241-10164-6

Filmset by BAS Printers Limited, Over Wallop, Hampshire
Printed in Hong Kong

CONTENTS

COLOUR PLATES

BLACK AND WHITE ILLUSTRATIONS

Sources of black and white illustrations are listed on page 310

FOREWORD:
IN DEFENCE OF A TITLE

'Women, and Englishmen, are actors by nature.'

Such was the verdict of George Jean Nathan who for so many years enlivened the American cultural scene, dispensing his trenchant wit and wisdom in the manner of Oscar Wilde disguised as Malcolm Muggeridge.

It is always comforting to have the blessing of such a distinguished Colonial, for as a nation we are excessively given to periodic bouts of self-disparagement, never more content than when we are acclaiming foreign talents and misprizing our own. We take our pleasures cautiously, paddling where others swim, and make a virtue of under-valuing our glories for fear the conceits betray us. Yet the glory of the English acting tradition is such that it demands a few tunes played in its honour.

Like so much that Nathan wrote, his casual aside conceals more truth than flesh is usually heir to. You will note that he said, *Women, and Englishmen,* and in tracing our theatre back to its origins we find that at the time we were proud to have a Queen on the throne, but rampant male chauvinism excluded female players on the stage, thus probably giving rise to the first theatrical jokes. For nearly a hundred years after James Burbage established the first real theatre in Europe the stages of England were denied women. His actor son Richard, a leading member of *'the strolling tribe, the despicable race'* as Charles Churchill put it, was no effete or mincing player, but a true Elizabethan. One has only to look at his portrait (which is a poor enough painting to be accurate) to appreciate that he was a man of strong character, for the eyes and mouth hint of arrogance. Together with other *'peel'd, patch'd and piebald, linsey-woolsey brothers, Grave mummers, sleeveless some shirtless'* he shaped our theatrical heritage, creating a tradition which is still, at its best, without rival in the world. Burbage lived in a flamboyant, violent age and England at that time was more noted for her plundering ambitions than for excellence in the Arts—the European Renaissance had not crossed the Channel intact, and whilst the Tudors swaggered across the scene, painting the canvas of history in lurid and sometimes terrifying colours, local talent in the Arts was not as highly regarded as the venal adventurers.

In seeking the origins of the English acting tradition, I felt it would be a mistake to approach my subject in academic fashion, for once the historian separates the theatre from living people he starts to squeeze the life from it. My main qualification is that I write as an insider, for I started my professional life as an actor and pursued that calling

9

for the best part of twenty years. I know only too well the justice of Hazlitt's damning summing up of my original vocation. Giving no quarter to his own generation of players, he wrote: *They live from hand to mouth. They plunge from want into luxury . . . chilled with poverty, steeped in contempt, they sometimes pass into the sunshine of fortune and are lifted to the very pinnacle of public favour. They have no means of making money breed and all professions that do not live by turning money into money . . . spend it.*

The majority of my contemporary colleagues still spend the greater part of their lives living from hand to mouth, for acting is not a profession noted for its automatic justice— talent, alas, holds out no guarantee of recognition or success. The true actor despises security: he may outwardly profess that he yearns for it, but in his heart he acknowledges it is the worm within the bud. His instincts, which led him to make his choice in the first place, also lead him away from the deadening routine that is the lot of most. In many mysterious ways, not always self-acknowledged, the lack of continuity of employment provides the adrenalin so necessary for the vitality of his performance when luck favours him. If, transiently, he passes into the sunshine of fortune, it is not surprising he makes the most of it, living his life to the full and in the process providing endless copy for Grub Street, since his freedom provokes envy in others. Look at me, he seems to say, rattle your chains and envy me as you trudge towards the testimonial dinner and the statutory gold watch. Tolerance of the foibles of others is the hallmark of the actor and in the circumscribed age we now endure he remains healthily aloof from most of the anxieties that politicians would have us believe are necessary to the human condition as 1984 approaches. Racial and ethnic considerations seldom enter into his reckoning; he does not judge his colleagues by their religion, race or colour, only by their talents, and if from time to time certain factions within his crowded profession press him to take up a particular political stance he is likely to regard their efforts as an irritating and unpardonable encroachment on his basic neutrality. When he has money he is easily parted from it, most of his excursions into the jungle of commerce ending in disaster. He is not one of Nature's willing tax-payers, nor does he respond kindly to regimentation. Charity, on the other hand, often begins at an actor's home.

His sexual habits, I have observed, differ little from those of stockbrokers, Members of Parliament, airline pilots, trade union officials, dramatic critics or the clergy, yet they are invariably given an exaggerated prominence in the popular Press, which over the years has succeeded in depicting him as an unbridled lecher, deflowering all in his path. Homosexuality, once naively thought to be a patented invention of the theatrical profession has, since Wolfenden, emerged from so many closets that even the most bigoted detractors now hesitate to accord the actor a monopoly.

Given the nature of acting, given that an actor is 'a sculptor who carves in snow', given that, despite all evidence to the contrary, the public in general, perhaps mindful of the dullness of everyday life, clings to the illusion that the acting profession is saturated with glamour, it is hardly surprising that the actor makes the most of his brief span. He is more Caliban than Adonis, constantly exploited even at the height of his fame and seldom wanders far from the precipice of obscurity (and nowadays television, that glutton eater of reputations, that devourer of careers, daily pushes him closer to the edge). I would not

RICHARD BURBAGE
Supposedly a self-
portrait

wish to conceal his many faults and conceits, but in fairness he never sets out to sell reality
and in a world that survives on make-believe it is inevitable that some of the fantasy rubs
off on him. He is a gigolo of the Arts and must resign himself to that central role. That is
his calling, that is what the patrons demand, and at every single performance he must
break the mould of his own personality and cast another.

You may well ask, why, if a title needs defending, did you choose it in the first place?

I present my case on the evidence of irony mixed with compassion. I am not, as others
before me have sometimes chosen to do, fouling my own doorstep. I do not think my
fellow actors *are* despicable, but they derive a certain inner satisfaction from allowing
others to continue in the belief. Personally I never cease to find the majority of actors very
engaging company. They may be much maligned as to their personal habits, but pound
for·pound I have found them much better value than the average businessman or
politician. For one thing they don't take themselves so seriously. Politics, the Bar and the
clergy are allied trades to the acting fraternity and all three have taken great care to

surround themselves with a bogus mystique that fools most of the people most of the time. Actors, on the other hand, have managed to survive without benefit of entrance exams or legally-defined privileges. Possessed of little dignity to begin with, they have happily never felt the need to protect what remains. Any impartial observer will admit that the laws of slander and libel are frequently bent when it comes to actors.

Now I admit actors are insular and talk shop whenever possible, communicating in a private language that baffles outsiders. But then so do golfers, bank managers, taxi drivers, school teachers and farmers; and since I have been exposed to the table talk of most other professions and trades, I have found that the average actor has more natural wit than most and is certainly better company when the slings and arrows are falling fast. Since few actors are strangers to poverty, humiliation or failure, they seem to me to have a keener appreciation of what life is all about and view the worst that civilisation hurls at us with a certain detachment coupled with an ability to duck at the last moment. Paragons of virtue they are not, but unlike certain sections of the community they can seldom be bothered to conceal their peccadillos and therefore suffer out of all proportion for their frankness. Their saving grace is that they have few saving graces, for as Billy Wilder the distinguished film director once remarked, the public won't pay good money to see the girl next door.

In most cases the self-confidence that an actor displays is a facade. Behind the public mask one can usually be sure of finding another—strip away the tinsel, as the saying goes, and you get down to the real tinsel underneath, and the last layer, when stripped away, reveals the face of insecurity. That is why I view an actor's conceits with tolerance, that is why what some find despicable, I find strangely human. Curiously, actors enjoy being set apart; it is another form of protection, another means of survival. To be found ordinary is to be found wanting, a verdict that will hasten the journey towards the scrapheap. The public does not demand perfection from its heroes, it demands excitement and to satisfy that demand the actor has to remain defiant. That is why most theatrical humour has a streak of cruelty in it—we feast upon the failure of our brothers because we know that our turn will come. On with the jolly old motley, eat, drink and be merry because tomorrow the notice goes up. Humour in the theatre abounds in self-mockery and is seldom if ever concerned with success. It is sad, often in bad taste, but not particularly obscene. Much of it is built around the reality of an actor's life rather than a fantasy fiction of that life. Example: the landlady asks an actor if he has a good memory for faces. When, slightly puzzled, he says yes, she replies: 'Oh, that's good because there's no mirror in the bathroom.'

The theatre squanders, abuses and, worst of all, ignores talent as often as it extols it, and the actor is never, for a single moment of his existence, other than at the mercy of the entrepreneur. The attributes that an actor has to sell never show up on a balance sheet, cannot be treated as the software to be fed into the computer; they are not constant and, once worn out, can never be replaced. Theatre rents can be raised, the price of admission can be trebled within a decade, the pensions for the front of house staff secured against inflation while the actor is lucky if he gets an armchair to sit in whilst making-up in his squalid dressing room. Ergo, it is all irony. Television, that great boon to mankind, has widened the scope of employment for the actor but at the same time drastically reduced his artistic boundaries. Beamed into every living room, he becomes ordinary, a member of the family, sold like a detergent, discarded like a beer can when the ever-increasing poverty of his material falls below the tolerance level of the lowest common denominator. Television, the cheapest spectator sport, closed the repertory theatres and the cinemas, and substituted the quiz game, the formula series, the glorification of the amateur. Give the people something for free, as the old adage has it, and they'll always turn up. A goodly proportion of them will resent paying even a nominal sum for the television licence, which denial sets in motion a chain of excuses finally explained in the actors' pay packet. We no longer pelt members of the despicable race with rotten vegetables as was once the custom, we condemn them to the slavery of the long-running serial or mediocre plays that outlast the original casts, enabling the actors to be replaced like battery hens, debeaked of all creative ambition.

This book is an attempt to correct the balance, to evoke a whiff of that artistic gunpowder which used to surround our players, however humble their aspirations or performances. They were not all giants, but they shared the common danger of their daily lot and in the process evolved a theatrical tradition second to none. It is a biased account, for that is the nature of a defence, just as on the other side of the court a critical prosecution is also biased. It would seem to me that in an age when our cultural heritage is threatened on all sides, when this country spends less on the arts than it does to prop up the bloody regimes of Third World dictators, such a defence is an honourable necessity. An actor takes little from society, but

When the Actors sinks to rest,
And the turf lies upon his breast,
A poor traditionary fame
Is all that's left to grace his name.

Let these brief chronicles of their times be well used, for the participants, though named despicable, had but one arrogance—the conceit of wishing to give others pleasure.

The play is done; the curtain drops,
  Slow falling to the prompter's bell:
A moment yet the actor stops,
  And looks around, to say farewell.
It is an irksome word and task:
  And, when he's laughed and said his say,
He shows, as he removes the mask,
  A face that's anything but gay.

THACKERAY, *The End of The Play.*

[[1]]

LONDON
THE FOUNT OF BRITISH ACTING

I
T is entirely in keeping with the rest of this story that the origins of our acting tradition should have rooted outside the City of London boundaries—literally beyond the pale. Most hands, whether blessed or otherwise, seem to have been against the actors. Although one of our earliest theatrical managers was a monk—the venerable Geoffrey, Abbot of St Albans, who briefly flourished his dual personality in the twelfth century— by the time Edward VI was crowned king, the actors and the clergy were in direct conflict, for having used the Drama as a means to spread the Gospel through the alliterative Morality, Miracle and Mystery plays, the Church now decided that the competition was outselling the original product. One imagines that some of the early strolling preachers (who numbered amongst them one saint—St Adhelm) must have been a combination of Billy Graham and George Formby, since when St Adhelm *found his audience growing weary of too much serious exposition, he would take his small harp from under his robes, and would strike up a narrative song that would render his hearers hilarious.* Saints, it would seem, ain't what they used to be.

An official directive went out in the first half of the sixteenth century to the effect that religious drama, unless divinely inspired, could not be the work of minds sufficiently heavenly and spiritual and would risk bringing God down to man, instead of raising man to Him. Princes of the church found the activities of roystering players 'pestiferous', Bishop Gardiner of Winchester once ordering an entire audience to be examined one by one to determine if any member could or would remember whether he had heard or seen anything slanderous or licentious: an extreme form of dramatic criticism which, happily, never caught on. Another prelate, the Reverend 'Bilious' Bale, a one-time Roman Catholic priest who decided he preferred leading roles to walk-ons, and became a Protestant bishop as well as taking a wife, fancied himself as a man of the world and wrote 'religious comedies'. The churches had no scruples about joining those they could not lick.

All this left our actors dispossessed, prohibited by the sovereign's decree from strolling through the kingdom, since they were pre-judged to be disseminators of seditions and heresies. In London, then as now the hub of any dramatic innovations, they were harried to a lesser extent, and during the reigns of Mary and Edward VI certain minor concessions were made. It was finally allowed that they could exercise their vocation 'between All Saints and Shrovetide' but were still subjected to the most stringent censorship our stage has ever known. It was not until Elizabeth I succeeded to the throne that James Burbage, the joiner-turned-actor and father of Cuthbert and Richard, obtained a licence to build a threatre on the Northeast side of the Thames in one of those areas outside the jurisdiction of the all-powerful London Council. These were known as 'liberties' and the site chosen by Burbage had once been church land that had passed to the Crown at the time of the Reformation. It was situated east of Finsbury Fields in the liberty of Holywell and consisted of five slum tenements and a decrepit barn that had seen service as a slaughter house. It was here on the vacant plot between the tenements and what remained of a Benedictine priory that Burbage and his workmen began to erect his first playhouse. Since he had no right-of-way from the main thoroughfare of Holywell Lane, his future patrons would have to cross Finsbury Fields with its uncharacteristic windmills, then bridge an open sewer before sampling his entertainment. Of necessity, theatregoers had to be keen!

James Burbage was not a rich man, and although possessed of a vision, tempered this with caution. He borrowed a not inconsiderable sum from his brother-in-law, John Brayne, a prosperous grocer. He signed the lease in April 1576, the month of Shakespeare's twelfth birthday, and proceeded to bankrupt Mr Brayne, the partnership leading, inevitably, to a stormy lawsuit in later years. The edifice he eventually built he called quite simply and fittingly The Theatre.

His first vocation as a master joiner enabled him to construct the building with more care than was usually lavished on the surrounding dwellings, for Elizabethan London was still a medieval city, and whole sections of it resembled something akin to a modern shanty town. An understanding of the environment in which the early professional actors lived is important not only to an appreciation of their characters, but also of the forces that shaped the dramas they enacted; the theatre traditionally and justifiably mirrors the civilisations that spawn it, and actors cannot be judged in isolation from their fellow citizens.

The London of Elizabeth I was a city of violent contrasts and life was a vale of tears for the majority of its inhabitants. It was a true capital city, but a city that had grown too fast—a great shifting mass spreading in all directions from the malodorous, sewage-choked Thames where dead animals and other carrion floated on the surface. Emblems of brutality were everywhere. 'Brave London Bridge', the only span crossing the river, sported the severed heads of executed criminals and pirates, and those who were so dispatched were sometimes considered the lucky ones, for the visitor could observe other felons chained to the river banks 'there to be washed by three tides'. Permanent gibbets stood behind the Tower and at Tyburn, the rotting corpses of hanged men food for the scavenging kites—birds that were afforded more protection than most of the teeming multitudes existing below them. The term 'hanged, drawn and quartered' is so far removed from current enlightened thought as to be almost incomprehensible, and yet it was no abstract verdict, but an actual ceremony. The hangman at Tyburn prided himself on his gruesome skills, for in order to comply faithfully with the judges' directions, the heart of the partially-hanged victim had to be cut out and shown to him before his eyes were mercifully closed for good. The third and last act of the ritual murder was then carried out on the steaming corpse with the expertise of a master chef. This was entertainment for the masses, alongside the bear and bull baiting—the bears, sometimes blinded, sometimes enjoying the dubious fame of being nicknamed by their fans (Harry Hunks and George Stone were two of the favourites), were either whipped by groups of men or else pitted against dogs 'of enormous size'. A foreign tourist of the period, one Paul Hentzner, noted in his commonplace book *at these spectacles, and every where else, the English are constantly smoking tobacco.* He might also have noted that the English consumed ale on a scale only equalled by the American introduction of Coca Cola in this century. According to Anthony Burgess in one of his erudite explorations of the Elizabethan period, *everybody was, by our standards, tipsy. Nobody drank water* [and for good reason] *and tea had not yet come in. Ale was the standard tipple, and it was strong. . . . It was not what we could call a sober city.* Cruelty was as endemic as the black rat, that permanent lodger in so many of the hovels within sight and smell of the more affluent inner city. Open sewers, filth, pestilence, careless reminders of man's inhumanity to man and beast—these were some of the Elizabethan 'glories' to be set beside the pomp and elegance of the virgin queen's court and the more vaunted exploits of her captains. They released the odours of despair amongst the majority of her London citizens and it was small wonder that, in the circumstances, when occasional pleasures came they took them seriously. If poverty did not dispatch them prematurely, then the plague was close behind—life, anybody's life, was held cheaply and the harshest justice was not withheld from the mightiest in the land: the chance of violent death was open to all.

This then was the setting for Burbage's circular jewel. The design of his theatre was borrowed from various sources. He took the classic shape of the Roman amphitheatre and adapted it to his own requirements, grafting on the galleries copied from those inn yards where he had played in his itinerant days. Despite difficulties with his mortgage, he was an astute businessman in matters theatrical and he knew the public he was aiming for. He was determined not to price-out his main audience and from the start catered for the 'penny trade'—the backbone of any repertory enterprise. His auditorium, although open to the skies, had good acoustics, for this was an age when scenery played little part and therefore the spoken word was all important. Audiences demanded their money's worth in no uncertain terms, and they liked to eat and drink throughout the performance, the sale of such refreshments being an extra source of revenue which Burbage was quick to monopolise. Although highly combustible like the rest of London, his theatre was soundly built, the final cost running to several hundred pounds, and before long he had been imitated by a competitor—reputed to have been one Henry Laneman—the second house taking its name from an adjacent quarter to the Theatre, Curtain Close, and being known as The Curtain. Laneman's enterprise was not as successful, for he lacked any theatrical know-how, being what today would be termed a property speculator, and around 1585 he admitted defeat and joined forces with Burbage, the arrangement being that they would pool their profits and not act in opposition to each other.

And what of this first generation of actors—brought in out of the cold and given a semi-permanent home? Previously the only security they had known had been provided by the patronage of the nobility. The royal licence of 1572 had granted certain favours to those troupes of actors connected with noble houses. James Burbage had enjoyed the patronage of the Earl of Leicester, and since everybody sensible enough or wealthy enough quit the reeking city during those hot summer months when the plague was most likely to strike, once his enterprise at the Theatre was firmly established he and his company took to the road again for provincial tours. There is evidence to substantiate that Burbage's company, as well as those of the Queen's men, Essex's and Lord Stafford's, visited Shakespeare's birthplace during 1586–1587. The exact date of Shakespeare's birth remains a mystery, but painstaking scholarship by a series of distinguished historians over the centuries has narrowed the conjecture to one of three days—either 21st, 22nd or 23rd of April 1564. To satisfy popular romantic taste the date officially celebrated is St George's Day—April 23rd, though the only written record that exists is the entry for his christening, dated April 26th 1564. The plague visited Stratford-on-Avon that year, wiping out nearly one-seventh of the inhabitants, and the infant Shakespeare can therefore be counted lucky to have survived. By the time Burbage and his men came to perform, he would have been 22 years old, married and the father of three children and his fabled 'lost years'—the period between 1585 and 1592—begun. There have been many attempts to penetrate the mystery of these years, the most popular legend being that he was forced to leave his birthplace rather than risk arrest and imprisonment for poaching deer in the grounds of Charlecote Park, ancestral home of the Lucy family. Others have it that he served an apprenticeship to a local butcher, others still that he was for a time employed by a country attorney, a printer, a barber-surgeon— the choice is wide; yet another theory, favoured by Aubrey, is that Shakespeare was a schoolmaster. Whatever the truth of those lost years, we do know that shortly before 1592 he had found his way to London, though once again we have no exact record of how he made the acquaintance of the Burbage family, or gained entry to the Theatre.

It was to be a period of great innovation in the drama, for from the pens of the great Elizabethan playwrights, with Shakespeare at the pinnacle, came the plays that allowed the British acting tradition to flower. It is worth while examining the day to day habits of those theatrical pioneers and ridding ourselves of certain misconceptions. There was an order and discipline of sorts, but it bore no resemblance to the more regulated atmosphere of the theatre in later centuries. It was the age of gifted plagiarism; plots were purloined, dialogue was improvised, inspiration was handed down by unreliable memories, and into this free-for-all came the injections of genius from Marlowe, Ben Jonson, Robert Greene and, of course, Shakespeare himself. We have seen the violent age they lived in and it would be foolish to imagine that any of these men, including Shakespeare, somehow lived apart from the mainstream of Elizabethan life, writing the new drama of heroic dimensions in a sublime and peaceful vacuum. They were part and parcel of the whole, and what they saw, how they ate, drank and whored, those cruelties they witnessed at first hand, the filth they trod in the streets, their knowledge of the corruption and intrigue surrounding the Queen's court, and above all their awareness of the transience of life helped shape their professional and personal actions and guided their pens. One cannot say 'it was ever thus' for equally revolutionary periods in history have not thrown up another Shakespeare. In all the annals of dramatic history his supremacy

BEN JONSON
Engraving by G. Vertue from
the painting by Gerard
Honthurst

has so far not been challenged, and as *Time* magazine reported in December 1978 'the British lion may be muted, but Shakespeare still roars'.

Again, in the absence of corroborated fact, we can make the reasonable assumption that Shakespeare, arriving unknown and unheralded into London, made a sufficiently favourable impression on the Burbage family to be taken under their wing. He may even have been an early 'car-park attendant' as some historians contend, holding horses for the wealthier patrons of the Theatre, or he may have started his new career as a prompter-cum-small-part-actor. We know that he eventually played one or two minor roles in his own plays, but his acting career was obviously not distinguished and it could well be that he quickly abandoned all ambition in that direction when his superb gifts as a playwright became obvious to all. Since this is not a life of Shakespeare, I will make no attempt to enter the age-old controversy which surrounds the plays, but Shakespeare's name commands pride of place in this account if for no other reason that he is the unquestioned genesis of our classical acting tradition. His works provide the frame on which succeeding generations of our actors have hung their hats. Other dramatists have given us single works of genius, and some have given us several, but nobody has approached Shakespeare's total of thirty-seven, amongst which, as a personal selection, I could name a dozen as possessing those qualities that signify genius.

Richard Burbage, then. Shakespeare started to provide, Burbage met the flow of new

NED ALLEYN

challenges. Slightly younger than Shakespeare, a pupil of Ned Alleyn and the *natural* successor to Alleyn—for he gave the public less rhetoric and attempted more realistic portrayals, had more comedy talent than his mentor and used his secondary talent—that of a painter—to achieve innovations in make-up. He became in due course the most famous and popular player of his day, his performances eagerly awaited and exhibited to packed houses. It would not be an exaggeration to accord him the title of the first matinee idol, since most performances were given in the afternoons. *Thus every day around two o'clock in the afternoon in the city of London*, wrote Thomas Platter, *two and sometimes three plays are performed at different places, in order to make the people merry. The play-actors are dressed most exquisitely and elegantly, because of the custom in England that when men of rank or knights die they give and bequeath almost their finest apparel to their servants, who, since it does not befit them, do not wear such garments, but afterwards let the play-actors buy them for a few pence.*

Certain of the actors—who from the above report seem to have acquired their wardrobes remarkably cheaply—became rich, notably Alleyn, who climbed a few notches up the social scale and on his retirement moved 'to his country estate', having married well, and was sufficiently in funds to endow the charmingly named College of God's Gift at Dulwich.

Burbage the elder having shown the way, the number of theatres multiplied. His original building eventually lost favour in the teeth of competition and ended its days as a prize-fight arena. He next moved to Blackfriars before his family became associated with the most famous Elizabethan theatre of them all, the Globe. This is the building we always couple with Shakespeare's name and it was built on the south, or Surrey, side of the Thames in what became, in colloquial terms, the first 'Broadway'—a veritable theatreland still celebrated today by the collection of South Bank buildings which include the Royal Festival Hall, a television studio complex and the National Theatre. The area is close to Southwark Cathedral where Shakespeare's brother is buried in front of the altar and is a district with many historical associations (shady and otherwise, embracing the site of the old debtors' prison in Clink Street which gave rise to the slang term). The Globe was not the first theatre to be built in this colourful district. It was preceded by two others in what was then known as the Manor of Paris (or Paradise) Garden. These were the Swan and the Rose which opened their doors towards the end of the sixteenth century (the Rose under Alleyn's partnership with the builder Philip Henslowe, whose daughter he eventually married). Shakespeare was undoubtedly connected with the Rose, for in 1594 there is a record of Sussex's men giving a performance there of his *Titus Andronicus*. The Swan, built four years after the Rose, was an equally ambitious structure and again we find that Shakespeare was acquainted with the management—in this case a money-lender called Francis Langley. Johannes de Witt makes mention of no less than five places of public amusement at this time, one being a building *devoted to the baiting of beasts, where are maintained in separate cages and enclosures many bears and dogs of stupendous size, which are kept for fighting, furnishing thereby a most delightful spectacle to men*. We talk now of living in a 'permissive age' but one can imagine the furore that would attend any attempt to bring back such 'delightful spectacles' to amuse present day audiences. The fact that playwrights had to compete with such public 'entertainments' may account for the fact that many of the plays written by Shakespeare and his contemporaries seem to have an excess of dramatic blood and gore. We know that Burbage and others strove to give their audiences many spectacular effects and made liberal use of stage blood. Despite the fact that young boys and pretty men took the female roles, it would be a mistake to think of the Elizabethan actors as posturing mummers. They might strut as peacocks in their cheaply-acquired finery on the boards, but in real life they were required to drink and fight for survival. It was not an age noted for pacifists.

De Witt also noted that the Swan could accommodate three thousand people and that its wooden columns were cunningly painted to resemble marble. But for all this architectural magnificence, the actors still laboured under difficulties and were periodically harried by officialdom and subjected to much abuse whenever some alderman wished to gain cheap, political publicity for himself. Students of contemporary history will doubtless be aware that criticism and censorship of the arts is still the easiest game for the lazy politician.

One of the most celebrated tracts of the times was written by a pamphleteer named Stephen Gosson. In 1579 he *first nibbled his pen and made it fly furiously over paper in a wordy war against the stage and stage-players*. A prejudiced rabble-rouser, Gosson did not water down his vitriol, and claimed that when Britons ate acorns and drank water they were giants and heroes; but that once the actors had appeared on the scene his compatriots had dwindled into a puny race, incapable of any noble or patriotic achievements. He seems to have been singularly out of touch with contemporary events in view of the successes of Drake and others.

Others grubbers asserted that plays were invented by heathens in order to appease false gods. The author of *A Short Treatise against Stage Plays* was in no doubt as to consequences of attending such pagan spectacles. His argument was that while parents enjoyed themselves shamefully at the theatre, seducers were at work on their daughters at home. As the estimable Dr Doran pointed out in his *Annals of The English Stage* such pleading would seem to indicate that if you wish your daughters to escape seduction, take them to the theatre with you. In this continuing diatribe there are echoes of current thinking with regard to football crowd violence, since the unknown author asks his readers to remember how many royal and noble men have been slain when in the theatre, on their way thither, or returning thence. He goes on to relate that theatres have caught fire and audiences suffocated, that stages have been swept down by storm and spectators trampled to death in the rush for the exits. I can only surmise that he was possibly a rejected playwright or else attended too many of his own flops.

The heyday of Bankside was comparatively short-lived and in the year 1647 the actors were decreed to be *incorrigible and vicious offenders who will now be compelled by whip, and stocks, and gyves, and prison fare, to obey ordinances which hitherto they have treated with contempt*. The legislators of both Houses fully intended to crush the actors for ever, and they achieved a certain measure of inglorious success. Many of the persecuted members of the profession literally took up arms, entering military service on the royalist side. Alleyn himself served as quartermaster-general to Charles I's army at Oxford. Another actor named Mohun served in Flanders and returned with the rank of major, therafter insisting that his military rank be included in his billing. Charles Hart, Will Robinson, Pollard, 'Lusty' Lowen, and Taylor are other names recorded as having gone to war during this turbulent period of civil strife. The theatres stood empty, the distress was severe, but as Doran puts it, 'the profession had to abide it'. With the beheading of the King the situation grew worse. During the time of Puritan suppression those actors bold enough to test authority made an effort to circumvent the laws. Amongst these was one Richard Cox who cunningly side-stepped the words *play* and *player* and devised an entertainment that appears to have approximated to present day cabaret. Others, bolder still, performed in open defiance and enjoyed three days of their old freedoms at the Cockpit in 1648 before the theatre was attacked by the Puritan army. The audience was savagely dispersed, the actors arrested and the seats and stage wantonly destroyed.

Enter a true English eccentric, who came to the aid of the players. This was Lord Hatton, whom Doran describes as a man who 'devoted much time to the preparation of a Book of Psalms and the ill-treatment of his wife'. These hobbies apart, Hatton proved to be a supreme patron of the actors and organised discreet venues in the houses of his friends where performances could once more be given. Holland House in Kensington was frequently used for such illegal purposes and the entire operation seems to have been conducted in much the same way as gambling in this century before new laws made it passably respectable. The widow of Holland House must have been a lady of some courage, for her husband the Earl of Holland had been beheaded in March 1649 and she ran a considerable risk in affording the players a temporary home under her roof. We are told that after such performances a collection was made and the money divided between the players 'according to the measure of their merits'. Cromwell could not tolerate Shakespeare's plays, though he shared with succeeding generations of politicians a liking

THOMAS BETTERTON
Engraving by Gucht from the
painting by Sir Godfrey
Kneller

for buffoonery and low comedy. But the plays and the memories of the actors who had performed them were kept alive by word of mouth, certain stage effects, bits of 'business', the manufacture of props—all these were carefully preserved and passed along the line. The memories of actors are as suspect as any but what gives their anecdotes an extra verisimilitude is their sense of the *colour* of events. Actors are capably expressing themselves in more than one dimension, and therefore their remembered accounts often have a dramatic value lacking in the reminiscences of other professional men.

With the downfall of Cromwell the actors' lot improved. Most periods of repression are followed by a violent swing of the pendulum in the opposite direction, and the Restoration revived public gaiety as well as the monarchy. The first name to emerge out of the darkness is Thomas Betterton—'incomparable' Betterton as he was later called— the son of a man who once worked as an under-chef in Charles I's kitchens. His mentor was that intriguing character Sir William Davenant, a fervent Royalist who was imprisoned under Cromwell and rescued from the scaffold through the efforts of Milton, among others. It is sometimes rumoured that he was Shakespeare's son, but this fascinating suggestion does not stand up to detailed examination. Davenant was a minor dramatist and eventually a theatre manager, but it is his friendship towards and encouragement of Betterton that claims our gratitude.

Betterton swiftly became the leader of his now less-tarnished profession and held that position for fifty-one years, creating in that time no less than one hundred and thirty new characters in addition to his performances in such favoured roles as Falstaff and Hamlet. Unlike some of his predecessors he cultivated respectability, was liked for himself as well as for his undoubted talents as an actor, being *as good a country gentleman on his farm in Berkshire as he was perfect actor in town; pursuing with his excellent wife the even tenor of his way; not tempted by the vices of his time, nor disturbed by its politics,* and was accorded a royal funeral in Westminster Abbey. During his long career he did much to restore the image of the actor as a useful member of society and by his own example convinced many that the old prejudices should be set aside. There was no overnight change and many of his colleagues, scorning his lead, did their best to impede his moral crusade.

We shall follow Betterton and his friends across the river, for the South bank gradually lost favour as the rallying point for the theatrical community; the emphasis shifted to the 'sacred ground' of English drama—Drury Lane—enduring until the present century as the focal point for the highest and lowest aspirations.

⟦2⟧

TO DRURY LANE . . .
AND THE LADIES

THE ill-fated Cockpit theatre was sited in Drury Lane and was said to have demoralised the surrounding district. It was also known as the Phoenix, and with good cause, for it several times rose again from the ashes of riot. As the original name implies it had first been designed for the exhibition of cock-fighting; there is a reference to its notoriety in Ben Jonson's *Volpone*. On Shrove Tuesday 1617 it was sacked by the apprentices of London who, by tradition, claimed the dubious privilege of demolishing houses of ill fame on that day. It was subsequently repaired and converted to a schoolhouse before reverting to its role as a place of public entertainment, but was afterwards sacked a second time. Damage was so extensive on this occasion that a third building was erected on the same site and Sir William Davenant reappears as part of the management, being responsible for producing a diversion with the unpromising title *The Cruelty of the Spaniards in Peru, exprest by instrumental and vocal music, and by the art of perspective in Scenes*. Evelyn went to one of the performances in May 1659, describing it as 'an opera after the Italian manner . . . much inferior to the Italian composure and magnificence; but it was prodigious that in a time of such public consternation such a vanity should be kept up or permitted. I being engaged with such company could not decently resist the going to see it, though my heart smote me for it.' Evelyn's self-justification smacks of those members of watch committees who feel compelled to expose themselves to exhibitions likely to 'deprave or corrupt' others, but which, miraculously, always seem to leave the reformers unscathed and untainted.

A year later a company under Rhodes, the old prompter of Blackfriars turned bookseller who first fired Betterton's ambition to become an actor, assumed residence and gave a number of performances. It is obvious that the Cockpit saw more bad days than good, though it bears the distinction of having housed the first performance of Massinger's *A New Way to Pay Old Debts*. Rhodes' company was then dispossessed by Thomas Killigrew and his partner Herbert, now operating under royal patent, as was Davenant, Charles II having decided that two companies were sufficient for London's needs. Davenant's troupe were called the Duke's Servants and included Betterton, and they took over the Cockpit while Killigrew and his King's Servants moved in to the new theatre in Drury Lane. The many comings and goings bear some resemblance to a French farce, and there was no Historic Buildings Commission to protect what fire and mob violence spared. Killigrew's first home in Drury Lane perished by fire. It was built at a

THOMAS KILLIGREW
Engraving by W. Faithorne
from the painting by
W. Sheppard

cost of £1,500 in 1663 and opened with Beaumont and Fletcher's *The Humorous Lieutenant*. Pepys paid his first visit on the second day of its being opened. He found some faults in the construction and from his and other accounts it does not appear to have been entirely weatherproof. In the event it only stood nine years. The second Drury Lane theatre was designed by Wren and cost the inflationary figure of £4,000. Dryden pronounced Wren's effort 'mean and ungilded'.

The King having first decided that two theatres were more than enough to satisfy the public, it was now found that this could be reduced to one, and in November 1682 Killigrew's and Davenant's companies came together under Wren's roof. Davenant himself had not lived to see the union, and Killigrew died the following year.

The principal actors of the joint company included Betterton's brother, William (who was drowned at Wallingford), Kynaston, the before-mentioned Major Mohun, 'Scum' Goodman, Robert Nokes and the Shatterel brothers, William and Robert. Betterton's young brother was one of six lads 'of tender years' employed to represent female characters, though within a short space of time, aping the new French fashion of using women to play women, the company was enlarged to include such as Mrs Corey, Mrs Davenport, Miss Saunderson (whom Betterton married) and the most celebrated of all, Nell Gwyn.

The ladies were not immediately accepted. Tradition had been outraged and various puritans such as Prynne and Thomas Brand were 'justly offended' though in such a lusty age one wonders why, since some of the 'lads' who frisked about the stage disguised as wenches of fifteen were in fact men past forty. (I like Doran's description of real kings

EDWARD KYNASTON

being kept waiting 'because theatrical queens had not yet shaved'.) In or out of petticoats, some of the boy-actresses achieved great fame, the most notable trio being Hart, Burt and Clun, with Hart as the undisputed star. All three were members of Killigrew's original King's Company, and Hart went on to become a much-praised Othello—'his dignity therein was said to convey a lesson even to kings'—and was one of Pepys' favourites. Kynaston was apparently 'the loveliest lady' ever beheld by Pepys and several authorities insist that 'it was a frequent custom of the ladies of quality to carry him in his female dress, after the performances, in their coaches to Hyde Park.' Despite being severely beaten on one occasion for daring to impersonate a certain Sir Charles Sedley, Kynaston apparently kept his looks to a ripe old age. Cibber tells us that 'even at past sixty, his teeth were all sound, white and even as one would wish to see in a reigning toast of twenty'. His reputation in female roles was such that following his death one of his obituaries declared 'it is disputable among the judicious whether any woman that succeeded him so sensibly touched the audience as he'.

His success as a female impersonator extracted a price, however, for over the years the effort of representing the fairer sex affected his voice in 'some disagreeable way'. An apocryphal story has it that Kynaston one sympathised with a fellow actor, Powell, who was suffering from a monstrous hangover. 'What makes you still feel so sick?' he asked and got the reply: 'How can I feel otherwise when I hear your voice?'

Kynaston died in his own bed a rich man, and was buried in 'the actors' church', St Paul's, Covent Garden, where so many of our distinguished players have since found a last resting place. He was more fortunate than poor Clun, who was 'most cruelly butchered' though he apparently met his tragic end 'with a lady hanging on his arm and some liquor lying under his belt'. Hart retired on a pension of half his salary (said to have been, at most, three pounds a week) but only lived to enjoy it for a few months before succumbing to a 'painful inward complaint'.

It was the king himself—'Old Rowley' to use his nickname—who legalised the employment of women in the English theatre, spelling it out in a Royal Charter: *And wee doe likewise permit and give leave that all the women's part to be acted in either of the two said companies for the time to come may be performed by women soe long as their recreacones, which by reason of the abuse aforesaid were scandalous and offensive, may by such reformation be esteemed not onely harmless delight, but useful and instructive representations of humane life, to such of our good subjects as shall resort to the same* . . . The king's motives may have been suspect, but the deed was done in the name of a moral crusade, done allegedly to prevent his subjects being corrupted by the sight of men dressed as women—a typical act of British hypocrisy, of course, but nevertheless a milestone, a minor social revolution.

One wonders how Killigrew went about the selection of his first leading lady? Did he hold auditions? Did he advertise? Was he besieged by a multitude of female hopefuls desperate for the honour? Did he, by chance, inaugurate the legend of the casting couch? Where did she come from, this first lady of the English stage? And who was she? There are two principal contenders—Anne Marshall and Mistress Margaret Hughes—and although most sources narrow it down to Mrs Hughes there is a surprising lack of documentary evidence surrounding her first appearance which took place on Saturday December 8, 1660 in a tennis court converted into a playhouse (two more years were to elapse before Killigrew built Drury Lane) on a site now known as Kingsway. Curiously, it would appear that King Charles did not attend this most notable gala performance. Whereas we have chapter and verse for many lesser occasions no handbills survive and therefore although Mrs Hughes is usually given the credit there is no absolute proof of her claim.

We do know that the play selected was a version of Shakespeare's *Othello* with the text heavily doctored. Killigrew had commissioned a special prologue from a well-known writer of such things, Thomas Jordan. It was to be the literary equivalent of the red flag that preceded the first steam locomotives, just in case any members of the audience were frightened by the spectacle about to be revealed. There was to be no further subterfuge. Jordan's effort was baldly stated for what it was: 'A Prologue, to introduce the first Woman that came to act on the Stage, in the Tragedy called *The Moor of Venice*'.

I come unknown to any of the rest
to tell the news; I saw the lady drest
The woman plays today; mistake me not
No man in gown, or page in petticoat
A woman to my knowledge, yet I can't
If I should die, make affidavit on't.
Do you not twitter, gentlemen? I know
You will be censuring; do it fairly though.

'Tis possible a virtuous woman may
Abhor all sorts of looseness, and yet play;
Play on the stage—where all eyes are upon her;
Shall we count that a crime France counts an honour?
In other kingdoms husbands safely trust 'em;
The difference lies only in the custom.

It continued for another twenty-four lines in the same vein and was hardly worthy of the occasion, but perhaps it was not a time for subtlety. Before the event Killigrew may have had second thoughts: audiences were notoriously disrespectful, not to say dangerous, and he must have had some anxious moments. Thomas Jordan had also prepared an Epilogue, a tactless piece of doggerel which began:

And how do you like her?
Come, what is't ye drive at?
She's the same thing in public as in private,
As far from being what you call a whore
As Desdemona injured by the Moor . . .

This may have been the quickest review ever accorded to an actress, and one doubts whether Mrs Hughes could have had it read to her in advance. She went on to join Killigrew's original company at the Lane, played a great number of roles and apparently played them well. At some later date she transferred her talents to the rival theatre which Davenant had founded, becoming in due course the mistress of the celebrated Prince Rupert who had distinguished himself by leading the Royalist charges against Cromwell's forces. Perhaps remembering Jordan's scarcely flattering Epilogue, she led the dashing Prince a dance until she obtained what she wanted. He paid a high price for her favours—some £25,000, the cost of Brandenburgh House in Hammersmith. In return she presented him with a daughter and eventually beggared him. After his death she proceeded to gamble away the fortune she had amassed. 'A mighty pretty woman', was Pepys' verdict. 'She seems, but is not, modest', he wrote. Other sources make mention of the fact that she was once the mistress of the same Sir Charles Sedley who arranged for Kynaston to be mugged and throughout this whole period one is conscious that an endless game of sexual Monopoly was being played, the players exchanging partners and possessions, buying favours, trading them, shifting residences, extracting emotional rents, following each other around the board in a daisy-chain of intrigue and promiscuity.

Despite the importance of Mrs Hughes' debut there was no overnight revolution and the boy-actresses continued to perform for some years after she had shown the way. In order to simulate feminine grace the boys wore a platform shoe (a forerunner of the elevators still in use to give stature to leading men lacking in height) which, we are told, sometimes gave them as much as an extra twelve inches and must have made balancing very difficult. Female costumes were of course elaborate, and stage lighting primitive, so that the more obvious male attributes could be easily concealed and thus were no hindrance to the illusion. (Female impersonation continues to fascinate present day audiences and in the last two decades we have seen a great increase in the number of 'drag' acts.) This is not the place to fully explore the sexual undertones that condition both players and audiences to this popular form of entertainment, but it is worth noting that one of the best-loved comedies of all time—Brandon Thomas' *Charley's Aunt*—continues to enthral people of all ages and in many languages. It has been the origin of at least three film versions, a stage musical which in turn became a film musical (*Where's Charley?*) and is based around a particularly crude female impersonation. I once witnessed a German production in which 'the aunt' gave a performance of such flagrant outrageousness as to make Danny La Rue seem like the heartiest of rugby players. The description 'outrageous' seems apposite, since this was the title of the first full-length drag film made with serious intent in 1978, the Canadian producers of the film being apparently quite willing to acknowledge that the desire to shock is inherent in such displays. So in a sense the cause has become the effect. What began in the Elizabethan theatre as an incongruous piece of prudery has been reversed; the use of men dressed as women on the stage is no longer an act of respect towards the female sex, but must be seen, in most cases, as a direct affront to convention. Female sexual attributes are invariably exaggerated by male performers in drag (the Ugly Sisters in pantomime, a form of entertainment primarily aimed at children, usually parade grotesque breasts and behave lewdly) and it is curious that their appeal is often largely to women. The paradox of men aping the less attractive aspects of the opposite sex—the humour is always bitchy—and being admired by the subjects they are parodying is worthy of a detailed clinical study. We also have the further development in the current pop world, with self-acknowledged homosexuals, ablaze with rainbow finery, screaming banal and often obscene lyrics at audiences composed of teeny-boppers who, one must assume, are unaware of the many sexual contradictions they are being exposed to.

All this is a far cry from Margaret Hughes, the professional origin of the female of the species, and yet in tracing the careers of those leading ladies who followed her we can discern a pattern which endures to the present day. It may offend some purists, but the name of the game is commercialism. Most great art stems from the artist's need to earn a living rather than a desire for immortality. Acting being the most ephemeral of all the arts it is small wonder that those who attempt it as a career are often forced into predatory acts of desperation in order to survive. Margaret Hughes had blazed the trail and thereafter many pass in review, adding rich and tempestuous legends to the annals of our stage history. In researching this book, I found myself amazed by the number and variety of actresses who overnight appeared on the scene. One day the males were supreme and then, it seems, that supremacy was challenged overnight—a long list of ladies, some distinguished, some scarcely remembered, but all contributing to their new profession in some manner. Downes, Davenant's industrious prompter and valuable historian, has given us many of those early pioneers—Mrs Davenport, Ann Gibbs, Mrs Saunderson, Mrs Davies, Mrs Holden, Mrs Jennings and Mrs Long. We can select Mrs Davenport for the first honours, not because she was the most consummate actress of the bunch, but because she created the most excitement and was the victim of a cruel hoax—persuaded by Aubrey de Vere, twentieth Earl of Oxford, to enter into a bogus marriage performed by one of his trumpeters masquerading as a parson.

Mrs Long was the mistress of the Duke of Richmond, and earns her place in history by being the first actress to appear in male attire—a swift reversal of previous events. Her appearance on stage in breeches caused a furore and is a prime example of the necessary commercialism I have already mentioned. Downes acknowledged this: . . . 'the first time she appeared in Man's habit prov'd as Beneficial to the Company as several succeeding new plays'. Pepys, in many respects the average male audience, closely followed the progress of these ladies. The first time he ever saw 'women come upon the stage' was in January 1661 during a performance of Beaumont and Fletcher's *Beggar's Bush*, but he mentions no names. He admired Mrs Davenport, pronouncing her 'very handsome' and maintaining that she was the best Roxalana (a character from Davenport's popular *Siege of Rhodes*) he ever saw. There is an amusing reference of Downes', who recorded the deaths as well as the triumphs of his players, in which he describes the loss to the theatre of Mrs Davenport, Mrs Davies and Mrs Kennings 'by Force of Love', a sympathetic way of explaining their loss to the stage through the marriage.

Some of the ladies went against tradition by being thoroughly respectable, in certain cases respectability being forced upon them, for as Macqueen-Pope noted in a characteristic aside, 'Mrs Norris was probably plain, which was another inducement to respectability in Restoration times'. However the most distinguished 'woman of an unblemished and sober life' was Mary Saunderson, whom Betterton married in 1662. They were the first married couple to act leading roles opposite each other, forming a partnership which flourished on and off stage for over thirty years. They must have been an extraordinary couple, for Betterton was a great actor and his wife, who had beauty, a lovely voice and perfect diction, complemented him in many of the classical roles. Pepys judged Betterton's Hamlet to be 'the best acted part ever done by man' and writing of the same production, Downes' comment was 'no succeeding Tragedy for several years got more Reputation, or Money, to the Company than this'. Mary succeeded as Lady Macbeth, the acid test for any actress before or since, Cibber's verdict on this occasion being that she was 'so great a mistress of nature that even Mrs Barry who acted the Lady Macbeth after her, could not in that part, with all her superior strength and melody of voice, throw out those quick and careless strokes of terror, from the disorder of a guilty mind, which the other gave us with a facility in her manner that rendered them at once tremendous and delightful'. Together she and Betterton were a constant box office attraction, their lives unsullied by scandal, adoring and adored and faithful unto death. Betterton's departure from the stage was a painful one, but dignified by his courage, so often the hallmark of a great actor. In his final years he was crippled with gout, his life savings swallowed up overnight by a disastrous business speculation, and his farewell appearance at a remarkable benefit performance at the Theatre Royal, Drury Lane, in 1710 can, without exaggeration, be said to have been the death of him. His physical condition on the actual day of the benefit was such that most men would have sworn off. But that was not Betterton's character. Taking leave of his wife at their home in Russell Street,

Covent Garden, he went by coach to the theatre and there was carried into his dressing room. He had chosen one of his great roles, that of Melantius in *The Maid's Tragedy*. He was seventy-five and he had been a popular favourite for fifty-one years. His helpers started to dress him in his costume, but when he came to put on his boots they could only manage to fit one. His other foot, monstrously swollen with the gout—that hideously painful disease which, curiously, is frequently used as a comic device—was swathed in bandages. A slipper was tried in place of the boot, but again to no avail. Betterton still refused to be defeated. By now the auditorium was packed, the last call of Overture and Beginners had been given, and he resorted to desperate measures, plunging his deformed foot into a bowl of cold water in an effort to reduce the swelling. This drastic treatment succeeded. He hobbled on stage to be greeted by an audience which cheered him almost continuously, obliterating his pain and spurring him to one last consummate performance. Perhaps it was a price he was willing to pay, for the cold water expedient proved fatal—the gout travelled to his stomach. He lingered for fifteen days and died on April 28, 1710, being buried in Westminster Abbey with all due honours. Mary Betterton survived him for two years, but for much of that time her mind was unhinged. She had once coached Princess Anne, now the Queen, in some amateur theatricals at Court, and after Betterton's death the Queen remembered and granted her a pension of £100 a year. Nothing could compensate for the loss of her beloved husband and on April 13, 1712 she joined him again, being buried in the same grave in the Abbey.

True female beauty has always been one of the most potent forces in the theatre and the presence of a beautiful actress has saved many a bad play. The most evocative name to come down to us from this period of transition, and one associated in the public's memory with such beauty, is of course Nell Gwyn. We have to fight a way through the tangle of romantic distortions that have cluttered around her legend over the centuries in order to arrive at anything approaching the probable truth. Royal paramours have always inflamed the popular imagination and 'pretty, witty Nell' remains England's chief rival to Madame de Pompadour as an instigator of puerile fictions.

Nell Gwyn's origins are obscure. The city of Hereford has staked its claim as her birthplace, likewise Oxford, but there is more substantial evidence pointing to Coal Yard, Drury Lane, a dismal address which later accommodated two notable criminals— Jonathan Wild and Jack Sheppard. There are various claimants to her paternity, but none that can be substantiated. We can be fairly certain that her mother was a common prostitute at the lower end of that ancient profession, and that she had a sister named Rose. Both girls had to struggle to survive in such an environment. Despite the more glamorous aspects of the term 'orange-seller' the chances are that Nell's first occupation was that of a hawker of herrings in the filthy streets leading off Coal Yard. In any case 'orange-girls' was merely a kinder description of the precocious whores who nightly sold fruit and riper favours to Killigrew's playgoers. They were marshalled by an engaging old doxy called Mary Meggs, nicknamed 'Orange Moll' who had secured the valuable franchise for £100 down and 6s. 8d. a night for a period of thirty-nine years and who was on intimate terms with many of the regular patrons whilst also enjoying the confidence of the actors backstage. Doubtless Nell was acquainted with her, but further evidence is sparse, although it it true to say that most people demand that their heroines be portrayed in the most attractive light and the fantasy is harmless enough. I will admit that the mental picture of a nubile red-head cheerfully holding an apron-full of bright oranges is immediately more pleasing than the fishy alternative.

It is abundantly clear that Moll was a woman of many parts—procuress, gossip, a mischief-maker and an avaricious businesswoman. Mrs Knipp (or Knepp) used Moll to carry messages to her great admirer, Pepys, and she crops up in many other contemporary diaries, being an established 'character' of the Drury Lane scene. Perhaps one could best describe her troupe of young assistants as early Playboy Bunny girls since they served the same dual function for the management: they dispensed the refreshments demanded by the patrons and also gave an extra, blatantly sexual reason for the young blades to attend. As with Mr Hefner's most celebrated inventions, the costumes they wore were designed to draw attention to and prominently display their breasts. It was a debauched period in English history, a Restoration not only of the monarchy but also of unbridled licentiousness. Charles II was a rooster king who presided over a barn-yard court, and what was good enough for the King was good enough for his subjects; and what was good enough for his subjects became, in due course, good enough for his queen. Casting aside the rigid conventions of her Portuguese upbringing in an effort to retain the interest of her ever-erring husband, the Queen took to going about the town masked, sometimes disguised as such an orange-girl, wearing clothes which 'exposed her breasts and shoulders without even the slightest gauze'—her dresses cut so low that the nipples were visible.*

At such a time and in such an atmosphere of general depravity, when from the King downwards men doted upon women 'beyond all shame', it requires but little imagination to chart the jubilant progress of Nell Gwyn from nymphet to actress to royal mistress, but we must still attempt to separate the ordinary truths of that permissive age from the sentimental embroidery stitched on by later generations, in particular the Victorians. Pepys, Evelyn, Cibber and Madame de Sévigné, although not innocent of certain exaggerations, have all set down the day to day intrigues characteristic of that era, and I prefer to draw upon their accounts than other more fanciful chronicles. Nell Gwyn, like Emma Hamilton, is always in danger of being smothered by layers of cloying prose, both ladies being burdened with near-sainthood by a series of over-enthusiastic biographers. The fictions that surround them are not necessarily stranger than the truths.

Let us consider a few of the probabilities. Nell must have made audacious use of her precocious charms at an early age, for she attracted the attention of actor John Lacey before she was fifteen. He is alleged to have 'instructed' her in the elementary dramatic arts, but as Graham Greene revealed in his long-delayed biography of the notorious Earl of Rochester, a poem attributed to Rochester begins with the words 'Nelly, my life, tho' now thou'rt full fifteen' and goes on to describe Nell's body and the author's intimate knowledge of it in explicit and obscene terms. We do know that Nell regarded Rochester as a friend. In her only surviving letter she expresses regret for his enforced absence from the Court and it is not beyond the bounds of possibility that she was, briefly, his mistress.

* Evelyn *Diaries*

33

What is certain is that she quickly passed from Lacey to Charles Hart, and that it was under his patronage that she made her stage debut in Dryden's *Indian Emperor* at the King's Theatre. From all accounts she was unfitted for tragedy and it was not until she assumed comic roles and stamped 'the smallest foot in England' on the boards that she carried the town, enslaving both nobility and commoners. She must have been what we call a 'natural'—one of those rare creatures who have the nerve to seize luck by the throat, who require no formal training and who catapult themselves into the popular imagination by a combination of physical beauty and the ability to make people laugh. I do not believe that she was the dedicated actress that certain historians have claimed. I think she merely took the easiest escape route available to her from the squalor of Coal Yard. A talent to amuse is perhaps the most formidable weapon in a mistress's armoury and when eventually she attracted the royal, roving eye, it was this quick cockney sense of humour—turned on herself as readily as on others—that ensured her success.

One reason why I do not subscribe to her alleged dedication to the stage is the fact that she was easily persuaded to relinquish her career. Two years after her debut, at the age of nineteen, she took herself off with 'clever Lord Buckhurst' 'to keep mad house at Epsom' (then a fashionable spa). Pope assures us that Buckhurst was 'the grace of courts, the muses' pride' but this may be an overgenerous summing up. Nell's affair with him burnt itself out in the space of six summer weeks, during which time the Dutch fleet brazenly carried war up the Thames in a rare and humiliating challenge to Pepys' department. Nell returned to Drury Lane in August 1667 to resume her career in a variety of roles, to some of which she was ill-suited.

Pepys was frequently on hand to record this critical period in her career. *26. Aug., 1667. To the King's playhouse and saw 'The Surprisal', a very mean play I thought, or else it was because I was out of humour, and but little company in the house. Sir W. Penn and I had a great deal of discourse with Orange Moll, who tells us that Nell is already left by my Lord Buckhurst, and that he makes sport of her, and swears she hath had all she could get of him; and Hart, her great admirer, now hates her; and that she is very poor, and hath lost my Lady Castlemaine, who was her great friend, also; but she is come to the house, but is neglected by them all.'*

Again, on October 5th 1667: *To the King's House and there going in met Knepp, and she took us up to the tiring rooms; and to the woman's shift, where Nell was dressing herself, and was all unready, and is very pretty, prettier than I thought. And into the scene* room, and there sat down, and she gave us fruit; and here I read the questions to Knepp, while she answered me through all the part of 'Flora's Vagaries', which was acted today. But, Lord! to see how they were both painted would make a man mad, and did make me loathe them, and how lewdly they talk, and how poor the men are in clothes, and yet what a show they make on stage by candlelight, is very observable. But to see how Nell cursed for having so few people in the pit was pretty; the other house carrying away all the people at the new play, and is said now-a-days to have generally most company, as being better players.*

A strange mixture, Mr Pepys, and in this instance aptly named! Fascinated, yet repelled by certain aspects of theatrical society, he was torn between a love-hate relationship; on

---

* This would be what we call the Green Room. Pepys' reference that he 'read the questions' to Mrs Knepp, undoubtedly means that he gave her the cues and helped her remember her lines for the role she was playing that afternoon.

the one hand wanting to be accounted an intimate, sharing the glamour at second-hand, with easy access to the back-stage tiring rooms where he could observe the actresses in a state of undress, and yet when he got there commenting on them in insulting terms. He writes of 'loathing' them because they wore heavy make-up, though one would have thought he was an experienced enough playgoer to have realised that with the poor stage lighting the actors were forced to exaggerate their features, otherwise people sitting far back would have seen only blobs instead of faces. He is also indiscriminate in his use of the word 'pretty'. The most fascinating aspect of this particular passage is the comparison between the casual, disorganised atmosphere of Nell's and Mrs Knepp's dressing room (obviously shared) and the mannered calm of present-day dressing rooms. Back-stage visits immediately prior to a performance are not commonly welcome.

We are searching for the origins of the English acting tradition, yet we can see that it was very much a hit and miss affair. There was no acting school as such. Killigrew did attempt to train young ladies for the profession immediately following the King's Charter, but the enterprise folded after a few months. One must remember that there were no directors in the sense that the term is used today. There were prompters, like Downes, who would supervise the basic moves and stage directions handed down from previous performances, but the star actors often disregarded these if it suited them and moved as the fancy took them on the night. Scenery was virtually non-existent, the stages being draped, though there might be some rough and ready structure for, say, the balcony scene in *Romeo and Juliet*. But from Pepys' account we observe that anybody could lend a hand, dropping in on the spur of the moment and picking up a copy of the script, which illustrates that there was very little back-stage discipline.

The ladies quickly established themselves as a force in the theatre, challenging the supremacy of the male stars in many cases, yet the revolution seems to have been accomplished without open warfare. Most of the temperaments displayed seem to have been reserved for off-stage activities and where the ladies are concerned, their histrionics and feuds were carried into the bedchambers rather than exhibited for public approbation.

Pepys' reference to Barbara Villiers, Lady Castlemaine, brings us closer to Nell's liaison with the King. Lady Castlemaine, one of Charles' many concubines, whom he created Duchess of Cleveland in 1670 and who was the acknowledged mother of six of his illegitimate children, was Nell's main rival at this time. Nell's great strength where the King was concerned (leaving aside her performances in his bed) was that she was never politically ambitious and was seemingly devoid of conventional petty jealousies. She retained her sense of humour and was not self-deluded by her sudden elevation. Her cockney sense of proportion about such transient matters must have given her the edge over many of her competitors. A libertine such as Charles must have been relieved to find such rare honesty when self-advancement was a full-time occupation for many. The public at large did not resent Nell's progress because she resolutely refused to give herself airs. She had a basic effrontery that met most situations, took life as it came and belongs to that select band of ladies who crop up throughout history to bring kings down to earth. If they also possess talents outside the royal sheets, as in Nell's case, so much the better; if they can in addition, give credence to the Cinderella legend then, until their beauty fades, their careers flourish. Nell Gwyn was spared the ravages of old age, for she died of apoplexy at thirty-eight, her looks and fairy-tale existence intact. I am not convinced that she was a great actress—a superb performer, yes, able to move and dance well, with an instinctive sense of comedy and the ability (like Vesta Tilley and Marie Lloyd in later years) to persuade audiences that although set apart from them, she did not consider herself superior. It is best described as 'the common touch' and it is a totally different talent from that possessed by a great classical actor. An important talent, and the theatre would be immeasurably impoverished if, at regular intervals, it did not manifest itself, and it has provided us with some of the most colourful characters ever to grace our stages. Nell Gwyn endures in the popular imagination because she embodied many cherished ideals. Her fame has travelled down through the centuries while many other worthier names have disappeared completely because she was the very stuff of legends. Perhaps she knew it and acted it to the full, giving in real life her greatest performance.

She bore Charles II two sons. By calling them 'bastards' in his presence she persuaded him to create her eldest boy Earl of Burford and later Duke of St Albans, which line still survives. The second son died at the age of nine. Charles was generous to her and when she retired from the stage he provided her with a fine house and intended to confer on her the title of Countess of Greenwich, but died before this could be put into effect.

Cibber summed her up thus: *If we consider her in all the disadvantages of her rank and education, she does not appear to have had any criminal errors more remarkable than her sex's frailty to answer for . . . Yet if the common fame of her may be believed, which in my memory was not doubted, she had less to be laid at her charge than any other of those ladies who were in the same state of preferment. She never meddled in matters of serious moment, or was the tool of working politicians; never broke into those amorous infidelities in which others are accused of; but was as visibly distinguished by her personal inclination for the King as her rivals were by their titles and grandeur.*

It would be difficult to improve on that.

⟦ 3 ⟧

'OUR SISTER MRS BRACEGIRDLE'

AS an early example of the way in which actors are exploited by unscrupulous managers, let us take a look at Christopher Rich who in 1690 acquired the Drury Lane Company from a descendant of Sir William Davenant for the meagre sum of £80. Rich was described as a 'waspish, ignorant pettifogger'. He was a lawyer by profession, noted for his sharp practices, and according to Cibber *as sly a tyrant as ever was set at the head of a theatre; for he gave the actors more liberty and fewer days pay than any of his predecessors; he would laugh with them over a bottle, and bite them in their bargains . . . He kept them poor that they might not rebel, and sometimes merry that they might not think of it. All their articles of agreement had a clause in them that he was sure to creep out at.*

Under Rich's management actors of the first rank such as Verbruggen and Powell received only £2 a week, and it was Rich's custom to give them benefit performances rather than rises in salary, thus making the public pay for his meanness. It is small wonder that some of the actors resorted to crime. Among these, the best actor and the greatest rogue was Cardell Goodman, or 'Scum' Goodman, as he was called by his enemies. He had a short but eventful career, beginning as he apparently intended to continue, being sent down from Cambridge University for slashing a portrait of the Duke of Monmouth. He lodged with a fellow actor, Griffin, and they are described as an odd couple sharing one shirt between them, an arrangement which inevitably led to many complications. Kept in penury by the ghastly Mr Rich, Goodman took to moonlighting as a highwayman, and did well at both careers until apprehended. He was imprisoned at Newgate and would have swung from the gallows at Tyburn, but was pardoned at the eleventh hour by King James and returned to the stage with his reputation enhanced. He tested his luck yet again, by entering into a plot to poison two of the Duchess of Cleveland's children, to whom he had taken a violent dislike. He was yet another of the Duchess's lovers, an ardent one by all accounts, and frequently dedicated his performances in the theatre to her, refusing to go on stage until she was in the house. Although his plot was discovered before he could dispatch the unfortunate children, he again escaped the rope (one can only assume he had unlimited charm), was later, and ungratefully, involved in the Fenwick and Charnock plot to kill King William and eventually fled the country. After his departure we lose track of him, but it is worth recording that amongst his many crimes he is alleged to have been the first forger of bank-notes.

JAMES QUIN

Joseph 'Count' Haines was another amiable rogue, accounted a splendid low comedian and a great practical joker. He created the role of Sparkish in *The Country Wife*, gave a much admired performance as Captain Bluff in Congreve's *The Old Bachelor* and crowned his career with his Tom Errand in Farquhar's *The Constant Couple*. Powell, another player kept on the breadline by Rich, who was referred to as 'Haughty George Powell', was a brilliant but idle performer who seldom bothered to learn his lines. We are told that his memory often failed him at the most important crisis of a play, and he was much reviled by audiences and the rest of the cast. One contemporary source states that in the end *he fell into such degradation that his example was a wholesome terror to young actors willing to follow it, but fearful of the consequences*. Reading between the lines we are forced to the verdict that he was a ferocious drunk since the same source remarks that on the first night of *The Relapse*, in which he played Worthy, *he was so fired by his libations, that Mrs Rogers, as Amanda, was frightened out of her wits by his tempestuous love-making*.

Into this gallery of colourful portraits of the period we should include poor Mathew Medbourne, a young actor of merit arrested on the testimony of Titus Oates for his participation in the Popish Plot and who died 'of the Newgate rigour'. His claim to fame rests on the fact that he introduced Molière's *Tartuffe* to the English stage. To him we can add the name of Little Bowman who was severely wounded on stage during a fencing bout and as a result tragically *lost power not only of action but of speech*—a terrible end for any actor. There was James Quin who instructed George III in elocution, was proclaimed the first tragedian of his day, acted with Garrick during the course of a long career and on his death bed consumed two bottles of claret in an effort to hasten the end of his agonies. And of course we have to include that accomplished performer Harris, Betterton's contemporary who in certain lightweight roles was considered Betterton's equal; a man noted for his intelligence who could hold his own against the best wits in town, but moody, threatening and discontented with his lot, possessed of that dangerous talent in an actor—a charming voice but with too great a love for displaying it regardless of the character he was playing.

These, then, are some of the portraits of the age, chosen to illustrate the great diversity of talent that was on show at that time—few of them men of substance, most of them flawed, some of them near-criminals, others openly so; men who flouted conventions, brash and flamboyant in their private lives, perhaps because to be dull off stage reduced their popular appeal on stage. The places of entertainment had changed since Burbage's day, but the public still demanded more than an ordinary jot of excitement from the performers, they wanted their favourites to be larger than life, and in order to survive the actors had to satisfy that need. There was a seething restlessness about the theatre—we get the impression that the whole scene was constantly on the boil. It was an age of great activity amongst the playwrights, and many of the performers turned their own hand to writing, creating star roles for themselves rather than wait for something to be handed to them—mostly inferior pieces of plagiarism culled from a variety of sources which they pushed onto the stage with the minimum of rehearsal. But there was vitality, energy, a constant movement, reminding us of a host of soldier ants, that species forever on the move. There was a swaggering quality to the life these players led, perhaps not wholly genuine, but forced on them by circumstances, by the bleakness of their day to day existence off stage, an awareness that they were a luxury the public could so easily discard.

It is time to include the ladies again, since they were just as colourful as the men, in many cases more so. There was Moll Davies who had won an infamous distinction at King Charles II's hands by her singing of the old song, 'My lodging is on the cold ground'. She performed it so charmingly that, according to Downes *not long after it rais'd her from her Bed on the Cold Ground, to a Bed Royal.* But it is the 'great Mrs Barry' we must turn to next. Elizabeth Barry was the daughter of a barrister who raised a regiment for the King during the time of the Rebellion and ruined himself in the process. She was taken into Davenant's house with the idea of training her for the stage, but she proved of such dull disposition that Davenant despaired. Once again familiar names criss-cross. Doran has it that Rochester, that same James Wilmot the second Earl who figures in the story of Nell Gwyn, was the man who willed intelligence into Mrs Barry. When others had despaired of ever making her into a passable actress, Rochester stepped in and wagered that he would accomplish the miracle within six months. One can safely assume that when he anticipated the role of Svengali his motives were not divorced from self interest. Mrs Barry was the passion of his life, but in schooling her for a profession for which, in the beginning, she had no great enthusiasm, he sowed the seeds of misfortune. Rochester won his wager, his pupil went on to establish herself as the most formidable actress of her time who so excelled *in the art of exciting pity*, said Cibber, *she had a power beyond all the actresses I have yet seen, or what your imagination can conceive.* Unfortunately for Rochester she also became a cold-hearted whore, certainly exciting no pity as she chose her lovers with a combination of wantonness and avarice. *That mercenary prostituting dame,* wrote Tom Brown, *should you lie with her all night, she would not know you next morning, unless you had another five pounds at her service.*

Looking at Kneller's portrait of her and taking it for a realistic likeness, we see a bold, full face, with fine hair drawn back from a long forehead, the nose strong—the whole effect is one of a woman used to getting her own way. It is a somewhat Byronic face with more than a hint of the poet's romantic, hermaphrodite quality: a glint of that steely imperiousness characteristic of a personality in which traces of either sex are intermingled. She obviously became an actress of great power and endeared herself to her public. Back-stage she was given to frequent and violent feuds with rival actresses. On one occasion, exasperated at failing to get the costume she demanded for a performance of *Rival Queens, or the Death of Alexander the Great* (a curiously muddled title, one would think), she took the opportunity during the play to plunge her dagger through the stiff armour of her rival's, Mrs Boutell's, stays. No lasting damage was done and with that brazenness for which she was justly acclaimed, Mrs Barry excused her behaviour on artistic grounds.

Following the general pattern, she bore two illegitimate daughters fathered by Sir

ELIZABETH BARRY
from the painting by Sir Godfrey Kneller
Reproduced by courtesy of the Garrick Club

MRS BRACEGIRDLE

George Etherege and Lord Rochester and had a long career lasting thirty-seven years. It is worth nothing that a future great actress—'our sister Mrs Bracegirdle' as Sir John Gielgud so charmingly describes her—played a small role of a page with Mrs Barry in one of Otway's tragedies. Mrs Bracegirdle was approaching six years old at the time. In her industry and in the number and variety of the roles she played, Mrs Barry was as indefatigable as Betterton and we are told that she originated no less than one hundred and twelve characters which, taken over the span of her career, averages three a year, and this in addition to the many classical roles she also attempted. Coupled with her equally impressive list of lovers we are left with a feeling of respect for her prodigious energies. She did not die in harness but on her retirement withdrew to the pleasant village of Acton. Contrary to the *Handbook of London* which falsely gives her final resting place as Westminster Cloisters, diligent searches by later historians established that she was buried close to 'one of the ugliest village churches' in Acton Vale where it is recorded that she 'departed this life the 7th of November 1713, aged 55 years'. Throughout her life she inspired many men to worship her, notably Rochester who belied his reputation as a hellfire rake in many of his tender letters to her. *I thank God,* he once wrote, *I can distinguish, I can see very woman in you, and from yourself am convinc'd I have never been in the wrong in my opinion of women: 'Tis impossible for me to curse you; but give me leave to pity myself, which is more than ever you will do for me.* Their love child died at the age of fourteen and was buried close to where her mother was later interred at Acton. It is interesting to note that Mrs

Boutell was also one of Rochester's mistresses, which leads one to believe that the stage dagger which pierced her stays was thrust home more in jealousy than in an excess of artistic fervour!

From that chance appearance as a page standing in Elizabeth Barry's shadow, Mrs Bracegirdle went on to carve her own distinguished and equally long career. Unlike Mrs Barry she was a model of discreet decorum. *Her virtuous discretion*, writes Cibber, *rendered her the delight of the town.* She so enthralled her audiences with her happy graces of manner that it is said she never made an exit without her fans feeling as if they had moulded their faces into an imitation of hers, which is a delightfully quaint and period way of expressing those qualities which, in this century, with the mass appeal of the Hollywood idols, persuaded many a shop girl that they, too, could look like Joan Crawford or Mary Pickford.

Like Mrs Mountford, to whom she was favourably compared by many, Mrs Bracegirdle had a pleasing and musical voice—a 'laughing voice' as it is sometimes termed, which was much commented upon by contemporary critics. She was a superb Millamant and for her Congreve wrote his Araminta, his Cynthia, his Angelica and Almeria, as well as that elusive enchantress of *The Way of The World* who was the cornerstone of Dame Edith Evans' career two and a half centuries later. Many men as well as Congreve lost their hearts to her and laid siege to her affection. On one occasion a bevy of peers, including my Lords Dorset, Devonshire and Halifax, slightly in their cups, were so concerned to out-eulogise each other in praise of her virtues that, led by Halifax, they subscribed the considerable sum of eight hundred pounds which they presented to her as a 'homage to the rectitude of her private character'. So on the one hand we have Mrs Barry universally admired for her wantonness and on the other we have Mrs Bracegirdle extolled for her serenity. Perhaps there is some truth to the theory that their names play an important part in determing the success or otherwise between purity and passion. 'Bracegirdle' has an unattractive, almost comical ring to it when set alongside a name such as Mme de Pompadour, for instance.

Once again we find the characters in this history constantly weaving in and out of each other's lives. Naturally the fact that the circle they moved in was strictly confined has much to do with it, but there is fascination to be found in tracing the maze. We have the tragedy of that fine actor, the luckless Will Mountfort, of whose violent death at the hands of Captain Richard Hill, companion of Lord Mohun, the beauty of Mrs Bracegirdle was the unintentional cause. The villainous Captain Hill, greatly infatuated with Mrs Bracegirdle, devised a plot to kidnap her with the aid of Mohun. The plot misfired and in the ensuing mêlée Mountfort, arriving innocent upon the scene of the attempted crime, was run through by Hill's sword. Mountfort's widow became the wife of Verbruggen, and so the maze winds on.

Mrs Bracegirdle's chastity was a source of amazement at a time and in a profession where most of the ladies bestowed as many favours as they could, without damage to their health, accommodate. This, as much as her undoubted prowess as a leading lady, has ensured her a place in theatrical history. She lived to beyond the age of eighty and 'to the last was visited by much of the wit, the worth, and some of the folly of the town'. She was the exception. Most accounts of this period chronicle the feuds, the brawls, sometimes the violent deaths of the protagonists who peopled the stage.

One of the most intriguing, and to an extent mysterious, incidents concerns the actors Bowen, Johnson and Quin, for all three were curiously embroiled in a storm in a tea cup which resulted in the death of Bowen and the trial of Quin. It all started with a fairly mild assertion that Johnson played the role of Jacomo in *The Libertine* in a superior fashion to Bowen. This resulted in a tavern fight between Quin and Bowen, instigated by the latter who worked himself into such a state of fury that he killed himself by falling on Quin's weapon. Quin was said to have been acquitted at the subsequent trial and returned to the stage, but a newspaper report of the day gives a different version. This states that *Quin and Bowen fought on the question which was the honester man. The coroner's inquest found it 'Se Defendendo'; but an Old Bailey jury returned a verdict of Manslaughter, and at the end of the Session it is found that, amongst the names of malefactors sent to Tyburn, or otherwise punished, 'Mr Quin, the comedian, burnt in the hand'.*

There were others, equally colourful, some possessed of nicknames that might have been invented by Dickens for his more fanciful characters: 'Jubilee Dicky' for instance, the name by which the comic actor, Norris, was known; Dogget, who always acted Shylock as a ferociously comic character in defiance of convention, and for whom Congreve wrote several roles, notably Fondlewife in *The Old Bachelor* and Ben in *Love for Love*. This same Dogget died sufficiently rich to leave funds for a boat race to be rowed annually from London Bridge to Chelsea by six watermen whose apprenticeship had expired during the preceding year. Then there was Pinkethman, who took liberties with the texts and with his audiences and who established the Richmond Theatre. And after 'Pinky', young Hildebrand Horden who met his end in another bar-room fight and was much mourned by a bevy of loving women who went in masks to weep over his handsome, shrouded corpse.

The turbulent century ended on a familiar note. Despite the entry of the ladies as conquering gladiators at last, despite Betterton and his wife, and Mrs Bracegirdle, the theatre and its inhabitants were still held in contempt by many. A grand jury in Middlesex found no distinction between the two main playhouses and the remaining bear-garden, describing them under the same heading as *nuisances and riotous and disorderly assemblies.* Others inform us that the theatres were *pestered with tumblers, rope-dancers, and dancing men and dogs from France*, the chauvinism of the last item being doubly offensive. It was a rude time, using the word in its traditional sense—something violent and unrestrained; a time in which wit was frequently made to sleep with coarseness and few men cared a jot for conventions or laws. There were spectacles at Tyburn as well as Drury Lane and sometimes only a thin veneer of taste separated them. The plots our actors performed with such panache were often crude and complicated, matched by the plots hatched in the changing world outside and which, doubtless, they reflected, for the living drama always mirrors the age it lives in. And as the century ended and some of the same cast went forward into the next we can dimly discern the genesis of what was to become the classical tradition of English acting—a shedding of old skins during that extraordinary and prolonged process whereby the grubs become butterflies.

⟦ 4 ⟧

THE START OF TWO LEGENDS

LET us jump ahead to Act II of the eighteenth century. The year is 1737. We are in Lichfield in the County of Staffordshire.

Two young men share a common resolve to leave their homes and strike out for London. One is 20 and the other 26. The elder has been tutor to the younger. Lacking sufficient funds for the coach fares, they decide to make the journey by hiring one horse and taking turns in riding it. The name of the tutor is Samuel Johnson and his younger companion is David Garrick. It is the start of two legends.

In charting the parallel lives of these two giants it is necessary once again to push a pathway through the tangle of myths which inevitably surrounds the lives of great men, even though in Johnson's case we have Boswell to guide us. Garrick's first biographer, Tom Davies, states that he had already been taken to the capital city on several previous occasions by affluent friends of his father in order that *he might feast his appetite at the playhouse*. I am inclined to accept later doubts as to the truth of this, for it seems odd that in his numerous letters to his father he never makes mention of what would obviously have been momentous occasions in his young life.

What appetites could he have satisfied had he made such journeys as a schoolboy? The theatre was still in a state of flux, with the Lord Chamberlain once again wielding despotic powers over the players and playwrights. The amazingly prolific and often reviled Cibber who was to enrich posterity with his autobiographic *Apology* to which we owe so much, was for all his faults one of the most dominating influences. Although savagely ridiculed by critics of the time (including Johnson in due course) and doubtless deserving of some of the abuse heaped upon him, he cannot be loosely dismissed. His energy was prodigious and during the course of his long career he sampled many of the roles that the theatre has to offer. The greater part of his life was spent at Drury Lane and he seems to have cultivated a personality that nowadays is vulgarly termed 'arsecrawler', finding grace with the miserly Mr Rich and eventually becoming Poet Laureate, an appointment which drove Fielding to publish a bitter denunciation. The award of this particular honour continues to arouse the intensest emotions to the present day, and while poor Cibber lacked any discernible poetic talents, his predecessors and indeed many of his successors displayed the same shining mediocrity.

My own view is that Cibber has been harshly treated. He was never a great actor, though his Justice Shallow was much praised, and he undoubtedly behaved in somewhat cavalier

COLLEY CIBBER
Engraving by I. Simon from
the painting by Grisoni

fashion towards many of his humbler colleagues, but at the same time he did, by devious means, bring about a minor revolution, helping *to fix standards of gentility and politeness which were profoundly to influence comic writing throughout most of the 18th century*. As far as we can check he was as reliable a critic as any when judging his contemporaries and at least he had the foresight to leave a detailed record of the day to day happenings in the theatre of that period. His efforts as a playwright were and are dismissed as pedestrian when not being attacked as 'revolting', and his fame as a dramatist mostly rests on his celebrated 'interference' with Shakespeare's *Richard III* which Hazlitt dubbed 'a vile jumble'. Cibber stole with fine abandon from *Henry IV, Part 2, Henry V, Henry VI, Part 3* and *Richard II*, but it is hypocritical as well as historically incorrect to lambast him as the most notorious plagiarist in the history of our theatre. As we have seen, everybody stole to the extent they could get away with it, and in fact Cibber gave to his version two of the best known 'Shakespearean' quotations: 'Off with his head! so much for Buckingham' and 'Richard's himself again'. They are exactly the sort of telling lines that dramatists through the ages have been glad of and do not hesitate to claim for their own. Many and more grosser liberties have been taken with Shakespeare's texts in later centuries—including a few hippy versions that I have suffered through myself—and some of our present day stage directors make a fetish out of distorting Shakespeare's originals, sanctifying their often misguided efforts in the name of progress. The majority of modern dress Shakespearean productions I have witnessed sit uneasily on our stages, and there are few critics willing to admit that such conceptions are ludicrous in the extreme. At least Agate had the perception and the authority to give Cibber his due and observed that *Richard III* is 'really a boy's play—a play for one boy to write and another to see'. It was this refreshing attitude that fashioned Olivier's great performance in the title role during the memorable 1944–45 season at the re-vitalised Old Vic, when he played it as melodrama rather than genuine tragedy.

When his version of *Richard III* was first produced at Drury Lane in the opening year of the new century, Cibber played the title role with scant success. We are told that he 'screamed through four acts without dignity or decency . . . and when he was killed by Richmond, one might plainly perceive that the good people were not better pleased that so execrable a tyrant was destroyed, than that so execrable an actor was silent'. His performance may have invited such damning reviews, but his text survived both in Europe and later in America and was not driven from the stage until the end of the nineteenth century.

Cibber, like Mark Twain, can also claim the distinction of reading his own premature obituaries. This occurred after the first performance of one of his rare successes during the 1717–18 season at the Lane—an adaptation of *Tartuffe* which Cibber entitled *The Non-Juror* and which he had turned into a slavish championship of the Hanoverian cause with little regard for Molière's original. It found immediate favour with the King and Cibber—with an eye to obtaining the post of Poet Laureate—dedicated the play to his monarch in his most craven mood, addressing the King as 'dread Sir' and calling himself 'the lowest of your subjects from the theatre'.

——The then Poet Laureate, Rowe, who also held the post of Land Surveyor of Customs in

BARTON BOOTH

the Port of London (a curiously unpoetic combination one would have thought) wrote a prologue for the occasion. We are assured that the play was admirably acted by Barton Booth, Mills, Wilks, Cibber, Mrs Porter, Mrs Oldfield and Walker, the last named shortly to be famous as Captain Macheath. Contemporaries described it as 'the purest comedy on the stage' with 'farce enough for the gallery . . . suggestions and didactic phrases for the rest of the house'. Cibber's success was greatly resented by his many enemies and the hatred he aroused was kept alive for a period of fifteen years by one of his most implacable foes, the editor of *Mist's Journal.* Soon after the first night, that publication inserted a short paragraph to the effect that 'yesterday died Mr Colley Cibber, late comedian of the Theatre Royal, notorious for writing *The Non-Juror*'. But Cibber was thick-skinned, endured this and the 'few smiles of silent contempt' and eventually achieved his ambition by succeeding Rowe as Poet Laureate. For all his unlikeable qualities (and he had more critics than friends) he must be accounted a major figure and fathered a minor dynasty in that two of his children added lustre to the annals of eccentricity. I shall be dealing with the career of his son Theophilus later in this narrative, but one of his daughters, Charlotte, is sufficiently interesting to be dealt with in isolation, a footnote as it were to her father's life.

She married at an early age, her husband being a violinist at Drury Lane named Richard Charke. It seems probable that the marriage was forced upon her against her own inclinations, since we are told that she was intensely masculine, spent most of her time in the company of stable boys and despised all pursuits except hunting and shooting. She went on the stage briefly, quarrelled with everybody in a manner that suggests she was her father's girl, ran away from her husband and then engaged in a variety of odd occupations often disguising herself as a man—conjuror's assistant, puppet master, tavern keeper and finally authoress, publishing an extraordinary autobiography called *The Narrative of the Life of Mrs Charlotte Charke.*

Before moving on to the next illustrious name—Barton Booth, who inherited Betterton's mantle—we should perhaps take note of a few lesser players if for no other reason than to emphasise that the British stage has never lacked supporting actors of calibre.

There was Richard Escourt, for example, according to Cibber, a great Falstaff, who left the stage (possibly because of lack of proper recognition) to become a wine merchant and who obtained the appointment as *Providore* to the famous Beef Steak Club which survives to this day. Then long-nosed Tom Durfey 'poor enough to be grateful for a benefit given in his behalf'; Will Peer whose career stretched back to Cromwellian times; Mrs Bradshaw who, we are told, was as dear to the age as Queen Anne; Mrs Horton who never achieved the fame of some of her sisters but was described as 'one of the most beautiful women that ever trod the stage'; the two Bullocks, Pack, Cory, Mrs Rogers and Mrs Knight—the list stretches on and although we learn that 'they none of them had more than a negative merit' I yet prefer Cibber's perceptive summing up *for, though the best of them could not support a play, the worst of them, by their absence, could maim it—as the loss of the least pin in a watch may obstruct its motion.*

Barton Booth is not to be confused with any member of the later and ill-starred family of Booths who included the assassin of President Lincoln, John Wilkes Booth. Barton came from good Lancastrian stock and was educated at Westminster School where his talents as an actor were early displayed in the *Andria* of Terence. Like many a theatrical aspirant, before and since, his family disapproved of his ambitions and he was compelled to go to Dublin for his apprenticeship before returning to London and attracting the attention of Betterton. He was given a place in Betterton's Lincoln's Inn Fields Theatre and later moved on to the company's new home in the Haymarket. He had no overnight success, but gradually imposed himself on the public, having first to surmount the jealousy of his fellow actor Wilkes. (A strange coincidence in view of later events.) At the start of his career he was self-confessed 'too frank a lover of the bottle' but he conquered this with 'an uncommon act of philosophy in a young man' and never again allowed drink to hinder his progress. He became sober of thought as well as of habit, transforming himself into an intellectual actor as opposed to one of those who thought of his profession as a purely emotional calling. Booth desired perfection from himself and was seldom self-deluded even when showered with praise. 'The longest life', he was fond of repeating, 'is not long enough to enable an actor to be perfect in his art'. Some idea of the concentration he must have applied to his work can be illustrated by the fact that his performance as the Ghost in *Hamlet* was judged to be 'of such extraordinary power, such a supernatural effect, so solemn, so majestic and so affecting' that it challenged the supremacy of Betterton in the title role.

But it is in the role of Cato that his lasting fame rests. He was fortunate in that the production of Addison's play coincided with a changing political climate which favoured such a timely spectacle. In company with Harley and Bolingbroke many of the Tories felt that Marlborough's demand to be appointed commander-in-chief for life was an attempt to establish a dictatorship. It so happened that the action and sentiment of Addison's work was antagonistic to such a move, and the play therefore took on added significance. It must be assumed that Booth was well aware of the coincidence and capitalised on it in his own performance. It was a rare piece of luck, since the play had been in Addison's desk for many years yet had never been performed or printed.

Johnson penned an account of the first night, although it was patently not an eyewitness account since he was only two at the time. His version has it that *the Whigs applauded every line in which liberty was mentioned, as a satire on the Tories; and the Tories echoed every clap, to show that the satire was unfelt*, which is in strict contrast to Dr Doran's who maintains that the Tories were depicted as the principal supporters of liberty. History would indicate that Doran is the more reliable. However, diarists and historians were united in their praise of Booth's portrayal. The production enjoyed an exceptionally long consecutive run and the managers of the theatre, Wilks, Cibber and Dogget, shared a profit of £1,350 at the end of the season. In today's terms this represents a very handsome return. The play was then taken to Oxford where it proved 'an uncommon curiosity in that place', attracted crowds big enough to fill the theatre for three days, made a further £450 profit which in turn enabled the actors to be granted double pay and the managers to give a contribution of £50 towards the repairs of St Mary's Church. Honour was satisfied on all sides.

Others dared to follow Booth in such a money-making role but none approached his success. 'Booth with the silver tongue' who had such a talent for 'discovering the passions where they lay hid in some celebrated parts by the injudicious practice of other actors' was also an early exponent of the art of listening on the stage—setting an example often studiously ignored by other star performers more intent on their own glories. Perhaps, in Booth, we can discern more noticeably than in others the beginning of that elusive 'tradition' which carries forward to our own great age: an ability to delve beneath the surface of the role he was playing, coupled with a lack of pettiness towards his fellow members of the cast which has so often marred an otherwise great actor. The habit of 'upstaging' or of deliberately engaging in some distracting piece of business during another actor's speech has given birth to many an apocryphal theatrical story, but no matter how amusing such tales may appear to the uninformed the fact remains that only selfish and unsure performers use these devices in the furtherance of their own careers.

Not that Booth was without his own faults. He was lazy and extremely sensitive to restless audiences, thereby breaking another unwritten law of the theatre which, with justification, says that the audience is seldom at fault. If he felt he was confronting a public he could not respect, Booth pulled back from his best. In his personal life he experienced his measure of unhappiness, for his first wife died at an early age. For a time he lived with Susan Mountfort, the younger daughter of the actor, and when she left him to become the mistress of another man, Booth passed over her life savings which he had carefully guarded—£3,200, a small fortune resulting from a lucky sweepstake ticket—but these were quickly dissipated by her new lover. The young lady went insane as a result of this incident, though it is credibly asserted that, while demented, '*she one night went through the part of Ophelia with a melancholy wildness which rendered many of her hearers almost as distraught as herself*'. She died shortly afterwards and Booth went on to marry a former ballet dancer, a Miss Santlow. Curiously enough, remembering the background to *Cato*, Miss Santlow had once been the mistress of Marlborough. This previous liaison does not seem to have worried Booth; perhaps he enjoyed the irony, since the marriage was an exceedingly happy one, though like his career it was not greatly prolonged.

He had a miserable end at the hands of the medical profession. After being misguided enough to perform in Theobald's wretched Shakespearean forgery, justly titled *The Double Falsehood*, his health started to fail. He first tried the cure at Bath, then when that failed travelled to various places on the Continent, visiting Ostend and Antwerp before journeying on to Holland to consult a noted physician called Boerhaave who made the extraordinary pronouncement that since Booth lived in England he should never leave off his winter clothing until midsummer day, and then resume it the day after. The invalid returned home to Hampstead and later into London where he was prostrated with bouts of fever, jaundice and other maladies. At which point he came under the care of a quack who persuaded him that his only hope was a course of crude mercury. Within five days the unfortunate Booth 'took within two ounces of two pounds weight of mercury' and then, *in extremis*, summoned the noted physician Sir Hans Sloane to his bedside, but, alas, not to his rescue. The rest of the story is, in Doran's words, like reading the details of an assassination. *As if two pounds minus two ounces of mercury were not enough, poor Booth was bled profusely at the jugular, his feet were plastered and his scalp was blistered; he was assailed in various ways with cathartics, and mocked, I may so call it, by emulsions; the* Daily Post *announced that he lay a-dying at his house in Hart Street, other notices pronounced him moribund in Charles Street; but he was alive on the morning of the 10th May 1733, when a triad of prescriptions being applied against him, Cato at length happily succumbed. But the surgeons would not let the dead actor rest; they opened his body, and dived into its recesses, and called things by strong names, and avoided technicalities; and, after declaring everything to be very much worse than the state of Denmark, as briefly described by Hamlet, Alexander Small, the especial examiner, signing the report, added a postscript thereto, implying that 'There was no fault in any part of his body, but what is here mentioned.'*

This most evocative piece of writing brings us back to the point when Garrick and Johnson were contemplating their journey to London. With Betterton and Booth both dead, the stage was cleared for Garrick's entrance.

〚 5 〛

GARRICK: A NEW AGE IN THE THEATRE

D AVID Garrick, the *beau idéal* of all players, was not born into the profession he later adorned with such distinction. He was intended for the Law but first made his living as a wine merchant, setting up in business with his elder brother, Peter, with £1,000 capital left to him by an uncle. It was a modest and not very profitable enterprise which had its London 'headquarters' in Durham Yard close by the Strand. David took care of this branch while his brother ran the branch in Lichfield, though Peter frequently came to London, was well thought of by Johnson and in advance of David's debut as an actor had many friends and connections in the theatre.

But before examining the phenomenon that was Garrick we should remind ourselves of what he was destined to replace. When the critics of the day were praising those actors we have already discussed, they were praising a *style* of acting that nowadays would be ridiculed as unbelievable 'ham'. Since the time of Dryden most English actors had aped the French model. They did not walk about the stage so much as they struck attitudes, frequently coming down to the floats and declaiming their lines with flamboyant gestures. Today we might say 'they put on a voice', what in Victorian times was known as 'an actor laddie's voice', a method of speaking that was deliberately artificial, a voice moreover that had little light or shade in it, that produced a sort of all-purpose sound. The public accepted it for the simple reason they were seldom offered an alternative. Since, as we have seen, there was little or no formal training for the stage, most of the performers jumping in at the deep end and surviving as best they could, it is not surprising that the imported French style was left undisturbed. Few members of the profession thought of it as an Art—acting was and always will be a pleasant way of earning a living despite the many pitfalls and uncertainties, and even in those days some of the star actors earned quite handsome salaries compared to, say, a professional soldier. I suspect that many women went on the stage purely because it was the most obvious way of acquiring an affluent husband. They certainly did their best to improve the bloodlines of the English aristocracy and are to be congratulated in this respect.

Upon his arrival in London, Garrick, who was patently stage-struck from an early age, made it his business to haunt those coffee houses in the immediate vicinity of Covent Garden where he could observe and eventually introduce himself to many of his idols. It was in such establishments that he first made the acquaintance of Margaret 'Peg' Woffington, the most sprightly charmer of her day. Like many a young man in such a situation he first tried to express his admiration in poetry and also tried his hand at writing sketches, occupations which easily distracted him from the more mundane business of selling his stocks of Malmsey and Red Port. The market centre of Covent Garden with its proliferation of flower, fruit and vegetable stalls standing amongst the taverns, coffee houses and luxury shops gave it a deceptive air of country innocence. It was in fact an oasis of quasi-respectability in a sea of corruption, for the area surrounding the 'garden' housed little else but brothels and gaming houses of the lowest repute. Those houses that had been abandoned by the nobility when the tone of the place went down were now exclusively occupied by actors and artists, the former choosing the address for the advantage of being close to the two great theatres, Drury Lane and the Garden itself. They were mustered for rehearsals by the beat of a drum and the spectacle of stage-favourites strolling across the sanded market square was a daily attraction for fans such as Garrick. This and other distractions ensured that his career as a wine merchant did not prosper and within a very short period he was writing to his brother that 'I have run out nearly four hundred pounds . . . almost half of my fortune.' I get the impression that he was not unduly dismayed by this, that in fact it helped concentrate his mind on the real goal.

At this time the two main theatres were in the hands of Rich (John Rich, not the Christopher Rich previously noted), who managed the Garden, and Fleetwood who now owned Drury Lane. Rich was an engaging illiterate who had delusions of grandeur and believed himself to be an actor of quality. He often treated his audiences to unrehearsed pieces of action, and once struck an over-anxious prompter to the ground, coming back from the wings to step out of character and tell his audience 'The fellow interrupted me in my Grand Pause'. Quin had many feuds with him and their violent exchanges provided much amusement to outside observers.

Fleetwood, on the other hand, seems to have been a character who anticipated P. G. Wodehouse. He came of an old family, was easy going and somewhat bumbling in his business activities, and was never happier than when dissipating what remained of his fortune at the gaming houses. We are told that the actor Macklin—'Wicked Charlie'— was frequently his companion on such ill-advised excursions, and it was this same Macklin who became Garrick's boon-companion and greatly influenced his thinking. Macklin was a stage name. His real name was McLaughlin and in keeping with his Irish ancestry he enjoyed, at times unfairly, a notorious reputation. The principal reason for this was the fact that he had once, by accident, killed a fellow-actor in the green room. But he also suffered because of his villainous 'nutcracker' appearance which, although an asset in certain roles, was a liability in real life. Fundamentally he was not an unpleasant man and throughout his career made a great effort to conquer a violent temper. Often kind and helpful to younger colleagues, he was essentially a serious actor with a more intellectual approach than the majority of his contemporaries. He sensed that the techniques of acting would have to change if the theatre was ever to progress and he made early attempts to bring about such a revolution. These ended in his dismissal by Rich who saw no reason to rock a profitable boat and was not, in any event, capable of grasping Macklin's theories. There was a flaw in Macklin's character, one that he was born with.

He was in advance of his time but lacked the personality to become a true star actor. This was his tragedy. He was reaching out for a more naturalistic method of acting, a breaking away from the imported, stylized rigidity which had such an ossifying effect on the English stage—the men declaiming every role with ponderous sameness, the women adopting a curiously unattractive sing-song delivery. Macklin was impatient and offended, he felt his profession had fallen into a rut and he anxiously sought converts to his way of thinking.

Garrick not only came fully equipped to the profession he graced for so many years, but began his career, under Macklin's influence, with a natural aptitude for the new school of acting. His powers to attract an audience had always been there, ever since, as a schoolboy, he had assumed the star role of actor-manager when giving amateur

CHARLES MACKLIN as Shylock, MRS POPE as Portia, Covent Garden, 1792.
Engraving by Nutter from the painting by I. Boyne

performances of *The Recruiting Officer* at the home of his mentor Mr Walmesley in Lichfield. He had discovered a cruel talent for mimicry which he used, with the unthinking callousness of the young, to parody Johnson's bedroom techniques with his new wife, Tetty. Garrick later described her as 'very fat, with a bosom of more than ordinary protuberance, with swelled cheeks of a florid red, produced by thick painting and increased by the liberal use of cordials'. Tetty was twenty years older than Johnson, and that in itself must have been an invitation for mockery. Garrick, perfected the impersonation, and it became his set-piece during those years when Johnson was his tutor, revealing a side of his character that Johnson, amongst others, found unattractive. It also gave him the taste for public performance, an awareness of his own powers that, increasingly, he was anxious to test in front of larger audiences. When Macklin became an intimate, Garrick was a willing convert to his theories, and in many ways this was a brave decision because in his desperation to become a professional actor he could have chosen the more conventional, and thus easier, route. But he did not. He embraced Macklin's new concept and put it into practice at the earliest opportunity. He had the arrogance of youth combined with a tremendous natural talent and the combination was formidable. He was the quiet revolutionary who crept up on the acting establishment and stole their old clothes as surely as he claimed his share of their thunder.

Macklin pointed the way, the first leading actor to play Shylock as somebody other than a low-comedy figure, having persuaded his gambling companion Fleetwood to let him attempt what was—before the event—a distinct commercial risk. It may have been the uneasy age of transition, but the old guard was still in command, ready to resist any changes that challenged their supremacy. Macklin's unique conception of Shylock deeply impressed Garrick, and he was not alone in applauding his friend's courage. It would be more dramatic to report that Macklin had to fight his way to success on the first night, but history records that almost from his first entrance—wearing a piqued beard, a red hat and a loose gabardine cloak, items he had carefully researched as being authentic for the role—the audience responded with a generosity that did them credit. They were amazed, but they did not mock, and accorded Macklin a triumph at the end of the play. He had banished all traces of burlesque from his portrait of the Jew, and appears to have startled his fellow actors as much as the paying customers. Being nervous of the effect he was going to create, he had kept the rest of the cast in ignorance of his true intentions during the rehearsals, so that they discovered the innovations at the same time as the audience. Kitty Clive, we are told, was greatly shaken, but such was the power of Macklin's new conception of the central role that she did not dare cut across it with the comic turn which she sometimes interpolated in the third act, but pulled her own performance up to his level. With Garrick in the audience on that first night was the 'wasp of Twickenham', Pope, never noted for his charity with the pen, but he too stayed to approve. George II with his well-known distaste for 'blays and boetry' was persuaded to pay a visit and stayed to be frightened. The uniqueness of Macklin's portrayal was not confined to the innovations of his appearance, the great change was his naturalistic delivery of the lines, and this was the lesson that Garrick took to heart. So with this one isolated incident, given by an actor who never scaled the heights or achieved anything like the fame that

PEG WOFFINGTON
from the painting by
Van Loo

Garrick attracted and who, today, is scarcely remembered, the whole style of English acting was changed overnight. Although Garrick was the most avid disciple, others also took note and began to alter their approach. Quin, for example, was very impressed and began to question his own abilities. Had Macklin been a more romantic figure his own career might have been quite different from this point. It was Garrick's great good fortune that he arrived on the scene at this particular moment, armed not only with ruthless ambition, but with youth and good looks and—most important of all—uncluttered with historical precedent. He had no debris to sweep away before striding across a clean deck.

Macklin's triumph was the fillip Garrick needed finally to divorce himself from his family and the conventions of his upbringing. Again, although luck favoured him, he proceeded with caution. There was an unlicensed theatre in Goodman's Fields, run by a man called Giffard, and it was there, not long after Macklin's triumph, that Garrick made his first, anonymous, appearance as a professional actor. Hiding behind the borrowed mask of the announced player, Dick Yates, who had been taken suddenly ill, Garrick performed as Harlequin. One taste was enough to commit him for life.

Let us suspend Garrick there, behind the mask of Harlequin, while we pick up the threads of another career that ran parallel with his for a number of years and provided the first romantic frame for his enduring legend. The name of Margaret 'Peg' Woffington must always be coupled with Garrick's during that early period of his professional life.

'Lovely Peggy' came to the London of *Tom Jones* from Dublin where she had enjoyed early success as a precocious star performer in a troupe of children organised by an ex-rope-walker who styled herself Madame Violante. The children were all said to be under ten years of age, though it would be a mistake to think of them as exploited. They were probably fortunate in escaping from the poverty of their surroundings. Madame Violante's youthful players acted out a pirated version of *The Beggar's Opera* with notable success, and Peg created a minor sensation as Polly Peachum. The troupe was known as the 'Lilliputians' and Madame Violante brought them to London in 1732 where they gave their all at the new theatre in the Haymarket, performing Gay's celebrated piece 'after the Irish manner, which was given 96 times in Dublin with great applause'. On this occasion the part of Macheath was taken by 'the celebrated Miss Woffington' according to an advertisement in *The Daily Post* which seems to indicate that she was already enjoying a certain notoriety. Despite such an auspicious introduction to the London scene, the nubile Miss Woffington attracted little local attention and returned to her native Dublin. The next four years are nowhere documented and when next we hear of her she is playing Ophelia in a new Dublin playhouse in Aungier Street which lay in the more fashionable quarter of the town. By then she had progressed to an adult's salary of thirty shillings a week and had become something of a celebrity with her portrayal of Sir Harry Wildair in Farquhar's *The Constant Couple*. To have a very personable young actress don the *breeches* and impersonate the fashionable *beau* held a particular fascination for eighteenth century audiences, and whilst this is the genesis of the Principal Boy tradition in pantomime, one should not take the comparison any further. Principal Boys have a singular lack of sexuality in keeping with the neutered atmosphere of most pantomimes, but the male impersonations of Peg Woffington's era were deliberately aimed at creating an aura of risqué sex; audiences liked nothing more than to be treated to the spectacle of one of their favourite actresses revealing her figure in such costumes.

Scandal and innuendo surrounded Peg Woffington from an early age and her seamy reputation preceded her return to London in 1740. She made the journey with a shadowy male companion that history has not positively identified, though we are left in no doubt that she had enjoyed several lovers prior to this time. Throughout her life she provided good copy for the gossips, most of it prurient and a great deal of it pure invention. Not that one should attempt to whitewash her reputation. She was promiscuous and she enjoyed it. One source, admittedly not a reliable one, has it that she was first seduced at the age of eleven, though perhaps it is not so improbable if, by then, she was already portraying Polly Peachum. Children who are thrust into such limelight are not unaware of their sexual attractions and it was, after all, an age when few eyebrows were raised at such precocity. It would be wrong, however, to think of her as a child prostitute. Throughout her life she chose her lovers carefully, even fastidiously, and there is reason to believe that she started as she meant to continue.

Nearly all her biographers mention that she laid siege to John Rich when she arrived back in London, one account stating that she called no less than nineteen times at his house in Bloomsbury Square before gaining admittance. There are colourful descriptions of her finding him sprawled on a sofa nibbling toast and almost obliterated by twenty-seven cats 'in different attitudes of repose or play'. If this sight (and possibly smell) startled her, her effect on the slovenly Rich was equally dramatic. We must assume that advance notice of her beauty and talent had not reached his ears, otherwise he would have received her the first time she called, but once she had introduced herself he became immediately smitten. At a later date he stated piously: 'It was fortunate for my wife that I was not of a susceptible temperament' but against this there is ample evidence to show that though eager to repeat her Dublin successes in London she would never have entertained the illiterate Rich as a stepping-stone lover.

Her first adult appearance in London took place on November 6th 1740 and was announced as being 'by command of His Royal Highness The Prince of Wales'. The Company of Comedians presented Farquhar's thirty-year-old favourite *The Recruiting Officer* at Covent Garden with the Irish actress Margaret Woffington in the role of Sylvia. Expectations were high, most regular theatregoers being anxious to get their first look at the new import. Garrick and Macklin were amongst the opening night audience and shared the general approval of her debut, Macklin being especially taken with her since she was living proof that his theories worked: Peg spoke and moved with a refreshing naturalness that impressed Macklin as surely as her physical beauty enslaved Garrick.

Shortly afterwards she made an even greater impact when she repeated her portrayal of Sir Harry Wildair. The role had originally been written for Robert Wilks and for nearly fifty years no one but Wilks had been considered equal to it. Peg Woffington changed all that. She was described as 'perfection' and memories of Wilks were immediately effaced. The revival became an overnight sensation with the town flocking to obtain seats. At a time when plays seldom ran for more than three nights, Peg was required to repeat her performance twenty times during that season, her entrances being greeted with such prolonged applause that the action of the play was held up for minutes on end.

Garrick had yet to make his own name and at this time was merely one admirer amongst many. The man with first claim to her affections during this period was Sir Charles Hanbury-Williams, the author of the famed 'Curl-paper' verses which she treasured to the end of her days. The portrait of Peg painted by J. B. Vanloo in 1742 was in the possession of Sir Charles' family until this century, and she undoubtedly numbered him amongst her lovers. Not all her admirers were as young or as socially presentable as Hanbury-Williams (he was in his thirties, a Member of Parliament and married to the youngest daughter of the Earl of Coningsby). We are told that her green room was nightly thronged with suitors, including one senile libertine who craved nothing more than to be allowed to comb her hair. Various descriptions of her beauty have been handed down to us. One talked of her being as majestic as Juno, while another extolled her charms in a somewhat muddled piece of purple prose, stating that she had 'a head of beautiful form perched like a bird upon a throat massive yet shapely and smooth as a column of alabaster'. The chances are that she epitomised that generation's conception of ideal beauty, having a most engaging and Irish personality, a ready wit and the sort of impudence that success early in life often encourages. She came to prominence at a time when audiences were looking for change—Macklin proved that, and Garrick was to consolidate Macklin's pioneer experiments. Instead of yet another sonorous leading lady, theatregoers were suddenly presented with a comedy actress as talented as she was beautiful and the combination proved irresistible. Garrick knew he had found his ideal, but he was to wait over a year before he could claim her.

Following his anonymous first appearance in Goodman's Fields, Garrick travelled to Ipswich with Giffard's company during the summer of 1741, this time using an assumed name—Mr. Lydall. It was in Ipswich on July 21st 1741 that he first revealed his face to an audience, playing the role of Captain Duretete in a comedy entitled *The Inconstant, or The Way to Win Him*. It is true that he had given one previous performance with the company, as a black-faced noble savage in a feeble piece called *Oroonoko*, but this later appearance as Captain Duretete was the first time he showed himself without mask or burnt cork.

He had no illusions about the importance of his Ipswich engagement. He had gone there, as he later remarked, in the firm resolve to swim or sink. He would convince himself and others of his talent or else forever renounce an acting career. It was a peculiar age when time and time again we find totally inexperienced players attempting major roles the first time out and apparently acquitting themselves with honour. As we shall shortly see, when eventually Garrick came to London to make his debut there, he had no intention of sliding into history by the backdoor: he introduced himself by playing Richard III. Even today with our greater emphasis on stage training, voice production, mime, improvisation, our numerous classical companies where a young actor can observe the techniques of his more exalted elders and profit by them, it is doubtful whether any commercial management would be bold enough to allow an unknown and untried performer to appear in a role as complex as Richard III in his first season.

Garrick, on the other hand, returned to London from Ipswich convinced of his own destiny. Perhaps such arrogance is a necessary attribute of the star actor, for it is seldom that the meek inherit the centre of the stage. Most actors are immediate addicts to the drug of applause, and Garrick sped back to London in the conceit that his talents were exactly what Fleetwood and Rich were looking for. Unfortunately such was not the case. He offered his services to both in turn, and both refused him. It was the last thing he had expected.

Even so, though doubtless disturbed by their lack of enthusiasm, he had no intention of giving up. He convinced himself that their stupidity in refusing him was really a blessing in disguise. In later years he confided that had he been accepted in one of the two main theatres it might well have blighted his career, since he would have been merely a small fish in either of those two great ponds, compelled to accept minor roles for which he had no liking. With Giffard he had a better chance to shine, and it was to Giffard he once more returned. He was frank enough to acknowledge that it was stardom he craved rather than just a place of employment. Perhaps something of Johnson's personality had rubbed off on him during the days when the great man had tutored him, for there was ice as well as genius in Johnson's make-up.

So we turn to the playbill for October 19, 1741 which announced that:

At the late Theatre in Goodman's fields, this
day will be performed a Concert of Vocal
and Instrumental Music, divided into Two Parts.
   Tickets at three, two and one shilling.
   Places for Boxes to be taken at The
   Fleece Tavern, next to the Theatre.
N.B. Between the two parts of the Concert,
will be presented an Historical Play, called
   THE LIFE AND DEATH OF KING RICHARD III
Containing the distress of K. Henry VI
The artful acquisition of the Crown by King Richard
The murder of young King Edward V and his brother
in the Tower
The landing of the Earl of Richmond; and the death of King Richard in the memorable battle of
Bosworth-field; being the last that was fought between the houses of York and Lancaster.
With many other true Historical passages.
The part of King Richard by a Gentleman
   (who never appeared on any stage).

The last piece of information was false and presumably only included as an added inducement for the curious. The reason for the play being sandwiched between a vocal and instrumental concert was to circumvent the law, since Giffard's theatre was unlicensed and Giffard had to resort to such obvious, but effective, subterfuges.

The announcement did not set the town alight. We are told that the house that awaited Garrick's first appearance in London was 'cold, thin and unexpectant'. This is hardly surprising, since those people who had come to enjoy vocal and instrumental pleasures wold be a different mixture from those prepared to sit through a ranting tragedy, and vice versa. They were also in for a very long evening.

Garrick was extremely nervous before his first entrance—we have this from Macklin, who naturally attended his friend's debut. It is worth reminding ourselves that the play opens with a soliloquy from Richard, so the actor playing the title role is plunged into 'Now is the winter of our discontent' without further ado. There is no easing into the play—the curtain goes up and Richard enters, solus. The actor must make an immediate impression. Macklin described Garrick as 'faltering' and I take this to mean that he came on, momentarily lost his nerve and dried. Any actor will tell you that the more famous the speech the quicker it vanishes from memory in such testing circumstances. Luckily the moment of terror was brief, Garrick recovered and went on to confound all present with a performance that owed nothing to previous impersonations of the crook-back king. He had studied the role thoroughly (it was Cibber's version still) and brought to his attempt as much of Macklin's new theory as his limited experience allowed. The effect would have been doubly startling to that 'unexpectant' audience. Not only were they witnessing an unknown player, but they were also being treated to a totally new conception of the role. We have Hogarth's portrait to tell us what he looked like, and it is a romantic young face that stares out from the canvas. There is no withered arm or nose distorted by putty. Contemporary reports compliment Garrick for his lack of strutting, mincing and 'unnecessary spitting'—which gives some indication of the habits of those predecessors he set out to obliterate. Accounts of that first night are, on the whole, somewhat fatuous. Doran, for instance, tells us that Garrick seemed unconscious of the audience 'speaking not as an orator but as King Richard himself might have spoken in like circumstances', which is a meaningless observation. Arthur Murphy, a minor actor and dramatist who was also present, states that Garrick's performance was a strange mixture: 'all was rage, fury, almost reality'. This is in total contrast to other observers who tell us that in place of the usual rage and fury Garrick spoke the lines calmly. We do have Garrick's own word for the fact that by the end of the second act he had almost lost his voice and had to take the juice of an orange in order to continue, so perhaps Murphy was closer to the truth than others, yet the phrase 'almost reality' makes little sense in this context. It is feasible that nerves, a lack of voice training and the sheer length of the role all combined to strain Garrick's vocal cords, and we lack any reliable evidence as to the acoustic of the theatre, an all-important consideration.

Whatever the truth of the various accounts one thing is certain. Garrick's debut heralded the beginning of a new age in the theatre, and nothing was ever quite the same again. He played Richard III on the following two nights, then reverted to the role of the noble savage, Aboan, in *Oroonoko*—on the face of it a surprising choice, but probably explained by the fact that he had no time to study another role and wanted to give an immediate demonstration of his versatility. Doran states that for the first seven nights the receipts only averaged £30, which does not substantiate the legend that 'the whole town flocked to Goodman's Fields'. Pope journeyed forth from Twickenham again and was in the house when Garrick once again reverted to Richard III. Pope's verdict: 'That young man never had his equal and never will have a rival.' His praise was not unqualified, since he added the caution that he hoped Garrick would not become vain 'and be ruined by applause'.

By the end of November Garrick was playing to full houses and had added four other plays to his growing repertoire. I have not been able to discover whether Giffard had to resort to the ploy of sandwiching the performances between vocal and instrumental concerts every night, but perhaps in view of Garrick's spectacular success the Lord Chamberlain and his officials turned a blind eye. 'Good God! what will he be in time?' declaimed the formidable Mrs Porter, one of the most respected *grandes dames* of the green room who had achieved fame both as an actress and as the heroine of a real-life adventure when she successfully challenged a highwayman, a piece of heroism that cost her dear— her horse bolted after the encounter, overturning her chaise and she was left with a permanently injured hip. Mrs Bracegirdle, then in her seventieth year, also pronounced her approval of the newcomer, but there were others, notably Cibber, who were not so generous.

Quin's mixed feelings were entirely understandable. 'If this young fellow be right', he said, 'then we have all been wrong'. He compared Garrick to George Whitfield, the evangelist leader of the Calvinistic Methodists: 'Garrick is a new religion. Whitfield was followed for a time, but they will all come to church again.' It is the voice of the eternal reactionary who can never accept that change will upturn the old order. One can sympathise with Quin and the other established players, for they must have been bewildered by this overnight revolution. They were too old and too set in their ways to adapt to the new style. I like Doran's description of Quin at this time—'he felt his laurels shaking on his brow'. But Quin still had his supporters who doubted the staying power of Garrick, dismissing him as a mere passing fancy that the public would soon grow tired of. Gray and Walpole added their measure of censure. 'Did I tell you about Mr Garrick, that the town are horn-mad after?' Gray wrote to a friend. 'There are a dozen dukes of a night at Goodman's Fields, sometimes; and yet I am stiff in the opposition.' Walpole likewise: 'All the run is now after Garrick, a wine-merchant, who is turned player at Goodman's Fields. He plays all parts, and is a very good mimic. His acting I have seen, and may say to you, who will not tell it again here, I see nothing wonderful in it; but it is heresy to say so.'

What Walpole called mimicry we might describe as versatility. The great difference between Garrick and those he was in the process of supplanting is that he took pains to change his appearance and mannerisms with every fresh role he played. It was said of Cibber, Foote and Quin that they were always recognizable from the moment they stepped out from the wings, a school of acting that more or less died out until the advent of the Hollywood star system in this century when popular favourites were encouraged to remain stoically the same whatever role they attempted.

Although he had made such an impact as Richard III, Garrick was greatly attracted to comedy roles and on the whole excelled in them. He often presented a double bill of tragedy and farce on the same night, an innovation which evokes memories of Olivier's great season for the Vic when he gave us Oedipus and Mr Puff with only an interval between them. I feel that there are more than passing similarities between Garrick and Olivier, even a certain physical resemblance and certainly numerous parallels in their approach to the art of acting. It would seem that Garrick, like Olivier, was a tragic actor who always had to suppress his gift for comedy when satisfying his audiences' demands to see him in the major classical roles. Olivier's well-known fascination with nose putty, his painstaking and elaborate disguises (he even polished the soles of his feet for his Othello) that have always been hallmarks of his career, are likewise characteristic of Garrick and when I think of Olivier, Garrick comes alive to me.

The first London season continued at Goodman's Fields until the end of May 1742. During this time Garrick advanced his salary from £1 a night to a half share of the profits. What was good for Giffard was disastrous for Fleetwood and Rich: whenever Garrick was playing the two patent theatres were emptied. After threatening to take action in law in support of their privileges, Fleetwood, the more intelligent of the two, sensibly came to terms and Garrick was brought to Drury Lane at a salary guaranteed to put poor Quin's nose further out of joint; Garrick was to receive £600 per annum, the highest sum ever paid to any player and £100 more than Quin had been receiving. He had played for a total of eighty nights for Giffard and he did not forget his debt, stipulating that Giffard and his wife should also be offered an engagement at the Lane. His great leap into the unknown had changed his life and the face of the English theatre. By now he had widened his repertoire, having played nineteen different roles, including Lear—not Shakespeare's king, but the version by Nahum Tate which first found favour during the Restoration. In all these ventures he had closely consulted Macklin and it was their joint resolve to form a dramatic academy to propagate the new acting theory, an enterprise which never got off the ground though at a later date they included Peg Woffington as the third member of the 'faculty'.

Garrick was learning all the time and took note of his critics, which speaks well for him. He was not satisfied with his Lear and worked hard to improve it. After six performances in the role he felt he was getting steadily worse, perhaps failing to realise that Tate's distortion of the original had completely unbalanced the play by giving it a happy ending. In mid-April of the season he challenged himself anew, giving both Lear and Cibber's *The Schoolboy or The Comical Rival* on the same bill, and contrasting his mad king with an oafish boy of fifteen. Years later he revealed how hard he had studied to find the key to Lear, a role that has defeated many a fine actor, just as Lady Macbeth has eluded some of the best of our player queens. Garrick made it his business to closely observe an actual madman, a neighbour in nearby Leman Street, who had been driven insane by accidentally killing his small daughter. It was Garrick's proud boast that he owed his eventual success as Lear by copying nature, and it is a further instance of his original approach to the whole problem of acting. Acting, by definition, is an imitation of life, selective at its best, but still an imitation. Garrick had the perception to recognise this truth early in his career; to acknowledge that so-called 'realistic' acting is a basic contradiction, it being the actor's task to simulate realism by being larger than life since ordinary everyday behaviour is too shapeless and lacking in dramatic form. The playwright indicates and the actor enlarges, projecting a physical force across the footlights sufficiently powerful to move those sitting at the back of the gallery—a basic requirement too often neglected in our modern theatre where, conditioned by films and television, many actors cannot project themselves beyond the first few rows of front stalls. The art of projection has nothing to do with brute vocal power, but is solely concerned with the actor's ability to impose his presence on the whole house by a combination of personality and technique. Mere shouting only blurs the outline of a performance.

In exploring Garrick's early years, it is also instructive to compare the 'work-rate' of leading players with their modern counterparts. Garrick played nineteen different characters during his initial season, a prodigious record which puts me in mind of those numerous vast canvases painted by Goya and El Greco. Energy is a prime requirement in any great actor's make-up—the ability nightly to recharge exhausted batteries; to be able to play one major role while at the same time studying another major role, rehearsing, playing, rehearsing, an endless cycle of effort with the added burden that the results have to be displayed to an ever-critical public. The novelist and the painter can work in isolation, but the actor has to create in full view and, what is more, re-create time and time again. Few great painters repeat their major canvases, a novelist would commit professional suicide if he told the same story in every new book, but no matter how

DAVID GARRICK as King Lear

brilliant his technique, the actor must bring a degree of originality to every performance he gives—even if he is subjected to the deadening routine of a long run (as is so often the case in the modern commercial theatre) the onus is on him to give each new audience their money's worth. Most great actors that I have known possess extraordinary physical stamina: absenteeism is all but unknown in the theatre, most actors preferring to crawl to their dressing rooms rather than admit defeat. Contrary to popular belief, they are not, as a race, indolent except when indolence is forced on them by lack of employment.

When Garrick signed his contract with Fleetwood it carried the stipulation that he should make three appearances at the Lane before the season ended. In addition to the stiff competition from Goodman's Fields, Fleetwood's company had been decimated by an, as yet, undiagnosed plague, which was later to be identified as a virulent strain of 'influenza'. Peg Woffington had been amongst those struck down, though happily she did not die of it like so many others. Fleetwood therefore thought it imperative to display his new leading man as soon as possible, and Garrick agreed to play Bayes in George Villiers' famous satire, *The Rehearsal*, a role that allowed him to exercise his cutting powers of mimicry to the full. He followed this with Lear and Richard III, all within the space of five days at the end of May 1742. His first appearance at Drury Lane took place on May 11, when he performed without salary in a benefit for the widow of an actor named Harper, taking the role of Chamont in a play called *The Orphan*.

It was now that his professional association with Peg Woffington blossomed, although it is reasonable to assume that they had become lovers some time before. Following his

63

brief introduction to life at Drury Lane, Garrick accompanied Peg to Dublin. On arrival there he was very much the junior partner, since her fame as a local star was very much greater than his own, but he quickly achieved the same success in Dublin as he had in London. The weather was perfection, too good in fact, and during the very hot summer that followed the packed and ill-ventilated theatre became a breeding ground of an epidemic that became known as 'the Garrick fever'.

Their first season together opened at the Smock Alley* theatre with Peg repeating her popular success as Sir Harry Wildair according to one source, though other accounts differ. In the opposite camp, at the Aungier Street theatre, Quin, Mrs Cibber and Mr Delane were playing in competition, but the match proved uneven and after Delane had attempted his Richard III with humiliating results, Aungier Street was forced to close while Duval, the manager of Smock Alley, was turning away more people than he admitted. It was here that Garrick first attempted Hamlet with Peg playing Ophelia. Again he flouted tradition, dispensing with certain bits of 'business', edited out any word that might give offence to Dublin ears and from all accounts affected a strange accent. Although the evening—a monstrously hot one—was judged a success, it was generally felt that he had room to improve in the role.

Only one unpleasant incident marred this riotous and happy season. It occurred during a performance of *Lear*, in the last scene of Act IV where the king is discovered asleep in a tent in the French camp, his head in the lap of Cordelia. A drunken member of the audience made his way onto the stage and attempted an assault of 'incredible depravity' on Peg who was playing Cordelia. We have an eye-witness account from a young man called Thomas Sheridan: '. . . a Gentleman threw himself down on the other side of the fair Princess, and without the least regard to her Rank, began to treat her with the utmost Indecency: Resentment followed on her part, and Abuse on his. Mr Garrick was silent but could not help casting an Eye of Indignation at so brutal a scene.'

I should explain that Garrick's behaviour was not as cowardly as it seems. Despite the fact that he was a much admired leading man, he still dared not assume the privileges of a 'gentleman'. He was a mere player with few rights and it would have been more than his life was worth to challenge any of the arrogant *beaux*, even more insolent in Dublin than their counterparts in London, who treated the stage as an extension of their own homes. As it was the 'eye of indignation' was considered insult enough, as Sheridan goes on to explain: '. . . after the Play was over, he and two of his Comrades searched the House, vowing with dreadful Imprecations that they would put him' (Garrick) 'to Death'. It must have been a particularly hideous moment for Garrick, to see the woman he loved abused so publicly and yet be powerless to prevent it.

Although Mr Sheridan makes no direct reference to Peg Woffington's feelings in the matter, it would appear that actresses had to tolerate such outrages as a normal occupational hazard. (I know of no such indecent assaults in recent times, but performers are still at the mercy of the lunatic fringe. Dame Cicely Courtneidge told me of one occasion when a man wandered up from the audience and took a seat on stage during a performance, helped himself to a cigarette and joined in the dialogue from time to time

* so called because of the brazen whores who frequented the area

64

until forcibly removed by the police at the end of the act.)

The season in Dublin consolidated Garrick's growing reputation and cemented his domestic arrangements with Peg. On their return to London they attempted to set up their Dramatic Triumvirate with Macklin under the same roof at Macklin's house, No. 6 Bow Street. It was an arrangement that raised eyebrows even in that permissive age, though most of the gossip was jealous conjecture. We lack informative documentation about this period in Garrick's life, and Macklin's later memoirs are not reliable, for by the time he related them his bitterness towards Garrick was too transparent. The chances are that Macklin's wife and small daughter also lived at Bow Street during this time and rumours of a bawdy house were probably without foundation. We know of one incident when one of Peg's former lovers—almost certainly the Earl of Darnley—paid an unexpected visit and was incensed to find Garrick's wig on Peg's dressing table. She wormed her way out of the situation by insisting that the wig was her own that she used in one of her male impersonations. I think the real importance of this incident is that it demonstrates that she must have been a considerable actress to convince the Earl that his jealousy was unfounded. Macklin made use of the story to demean Garrick, suggesting that he was the true cuckold, and also did his best to perpetuate the legend that Garrick was basically mean. This is something that Johnson also commented upon, but we have to turn to Garrick's admirable biographer, Carola Oman, to redress the balance. Carola Oman has the perception to point out that at this time in his career Garrick suffered, like many actors before and since, from a management reluctant to pay him a regular salary. Although Fleetwood had contracted to give him a larger sum than ever before offered to a leading player, the 'ghost' did not walk every pay day. Garrick had new responsibilities, a new standing in society to uphold, and the chances are that he could not compete with some of Peg's more affluent titled admirers. Macklin became jealous of Garrick's greater success and as the years went by they quarrelled more frequently till in the end the early friendship had rotted into malice.

But if we return to those first halcyon days when all three enjoyed each other's company, we can trace the enthusiasms that led them to believe they could make a success of their projected 'dramatic academy'. They had agreed to share everything; all the household expenses were to be divided equally out of their pooled salaries, augmented, or so they fondly imagined, by fees from the students. Alas, there is no evidence that anybody enrolled and the enterprise collapsed after six months. It is difficult to imagine how it could ever have succeeded, given the life they led.

During the season of 1742–1743 Garrick played fourteen roles, seven of which were new to London. He presented his Dublin *Hamlet* and repeated his triumph. There is a painstakingly detailed and dull account of this performance written by a contemporary German critic, done with Teutonic thoroughness in an excess of adulation which regrettably achieves the reverse of what the author obviously intended. When set alongside Johnson's barbed comment (Boswell asks him what he felt about Garrick's confrontation of the Ghost in *Hamlet*, and the Doctor replies that if he reacted as Garrick did the chances are he would frighten the ghost!) we get the impression that Garrick's performance was 'over the top'.

This question of how taste travels through the centuries is an interesting one and seldom explored in any great detail. History shows that yesterday's heroes frequently become today's comedians, obvious targets for parody and satire. This is not confined to the acting profession, being equally applied to generals, politicians and the great majority of dead authors. But where acting and actors are concerned the historian has to be particularly wary of accepting contemporary accounts at face value. We have little or no visual evidence, and since acting is so ephemeral and memories of any performance so unreliable, the best we can do is to try and extract the probable truth from the mass of conflicting evidence. The role of the critic, even the few that can be said to have real perception of the art of acting, is a difficult one. He witnesses a particular performance on a particular night and such are the demands of his calling that he is required to pronounce instant judgement. Although the artist frequently thinks otherwise, the critic is human too, his views conditioned by his mental and physical state at the time he makes up his mind. Great critics have never been thick on the ground and the timing of their occasional emergence does not always coincide with the life span of a great artist. It is my belief that the over-riding function of the critic is to anticipate future developments in the arts rather than merely to record current events. Shaw could see the way ahead, so could Hazlitt and so could Agate: they were often in advance of public taste and had the courage to say so in no uncertain terms.

Garrick was an innovator, of that there can be no doubt. It is also abundantly clear that he had great natural gifts, was a facile mimic, and had a profound belief in his own destiny. Armed with such formidable attributes from the very beginning, and given his immediate success, the chances are he became very conceited. He was young, he was in love and loved by a lady who had no shortage of admirers, he had queue-jumped from obscurity to the leading position at Drury Lane where he could more or less dictate, and the public were flocking to see him: it is a situation that would have turned most heads. In addition he was hastily learning and rehearsing a variety of new roles, and we should once again remind ourselves that he had no regular producer to guide and correct him, or give objective advice. Having arrived like a meteor he was expected to flash across the sky night after night. The playwright Richard Cumberland talks of 'little Garrick' as 'young and light and active in every muscle and feature' bounding onto the stage. 'It seemed', Cumberland says, 'as if a whole century had been stepped over in the transition of a single scene'. This description gives flesh to my own conjectures. It is not my intention to reduce Garrick's reputation, but to attempt to humanise it.

The failure of the Macklin-Garrick-Woffington dramatic academy becomes more understandable when we appreciate their separate and turbulent professional lives. They had the resolve, but they simply did not have the time to put it into effect. Some idea of the daily scramble is indicated by what happened on the first occasion that Garrick acted with Peg at Drury Lane. They had selected Fielding's *Wedding Day* as the vehicle for the occasion. This was a play written some twelve years previously for Wilks and Mrs Oldfield, but curiously the leading female role was not suitable for Peg and she was cast as the ingénue with one good scene opposite Garrick. As a general rule it is seldom a good idea for a leading actor to offer his mistress a secondary role, and this may have been a

KITTY CLIVE

contributing factor to the squabbles which followed. Nothing, it seems, went right. Poor Fielding was crippled with the gout, had a favourite child dying in one bed and his wife 'in a condition very little better in another' and the bailiffs on the doorstep. He was also being badgered to make changes in the script by the Lord Chamberlain. During rehearsals Kitty Clive quit in a huff, declining to continue in the role of Mrs Useful because she considered herself above playing whores. The unfortunate Fielding also had to contend with Garrick who was demanding a rewrite of his role and by the time the opening night arrived the whole production was in turmoil. A packed house was treated to an impromptu announcement from Macklin, thrust on stage to explain and apologise for what was to come.

Macklin craved their indulgence (never lightly given in those days) and informed them that 'an accident' had happened. He wisely prefaced everything by offering to return their money if they so wished, and went on to give the news that 'Mr Garrick . . . who performs a principal character in the play, unfortunately has sent word, 'twill be impossible, having so long a part, to speak the Prologue: he hasn't had time to get it by heart.'

Back-stage Garrick was in a blue funk. He had not succeeded in his attempts to persuade Fielding to rewrite a key scene and was convinced he would get the bird. He was right. Once an audience scents the possibility of failure (and Macklin's speech had forewarned of this) the collective cruelty is heartless. Garrick was hissed. It was his first experience of public disapproval and by the time the Act One curtain came down he was so unnerved he wanted to retire. It is doubtful whether anybody other than a fellow actor can fully appreciate the horror of such a nightmare. He was persuaded to continue but there was no way he could retrieve the situation. The production was withdrawn after six performances and we are told that audiences dwindled away to nothing; on the final night there were only five ladies in the house.

He made a further strange decision a few weeks later when he presented *The Constant Couple* and awarded himself the role of Sir Harry Wildair, despite the fact that this was to be a benefit for Peg and Wildair was her most famous role to date. Again the production seems to have been thrown together without sufficient rehearsal and Garrick frequently 'dried'. Doubtless enjoying his discomfort, Peg prompted him loud enough for the audience to hear. He never repeated the experiment.

On the credit side, he was intelligent enough to profit by these mistakes and it was now that he gave what was to become one of his most celebrated portrayals, that of Abel Drugger, the tobacconist's sly assistant in Ben Jonson's *The Alchemist*. It proved to be the next turning point in his career, for most contemporary observers agree that although he excelled in many classical roles, his true forte lay in comedy. He prepared carefully, determined that he would never again go before the public with his lines half-learnt, becoming the only pupil in his own dramatic academy and rehearsed privately with Macklin. From the moment he started studying the role he concentrated on removing all traces of his own personality. Instead of *acting* the oafish Abel Drugger, he wanted to *be* Abel Drugger and this is a further indication of those qualities which set him apart from his fellows. Traditionally, comic roles were crudely drawn in the broadest strokes, most players getting their laughs with exaggerated grimaces and reactions, often abandoning any attempt at reality. There is a modern expression for this: we talk of performers 'selling programmes' which, interpreted, means that they are over-acting to the extent that they completely step out of character.

Garrick was experimenting with naturalism and when, finally, he exhibited his version of Drugger the result was apparently a revelation. Fanny Burney wrote: 'Never could I have imagined such a metamorphose as I saw, the extreme meanness, the vulgarity, the

GARRICK as Abel Drugger (*right*) with Burton and Palmer as Subtle
and Face in Ben Jonson's *The Alchemist*, 1743. Engraving by J. Dixon after Zoffany

low wit, the vacancy of countenance, the appearance of *unlicked nature* in all his motions.'
Arthur Murphy added his mote: 'He seemed to be a new man' and as Richard Findlater
remarks with his usual perception of these matters, 'Here was an example of that
transubstantiation which marks one kind of greatness in acting: the visible erasure of one
identity by another, the radical change of being.'

Publicly all seemed to be going well, but behind the scenes there was private as well as
professional dissent. Garrick's love affair with Peg was to be short-lived and Fleetwood's
management of the Lane was verging on bankruptcy. By the end of the season he owed
Garrick six hundred pounds salary and desperate remedies were called for. Garrick's
domestic situation had altered; he was no longer living under the same roof as Macklin
and indeed their relationship was not as amicable as before. Garrick believed that
Macklin was in cahoots with Fleetwood (his suspicions were largely unfounded) and set
about organising a revolt of the actors. He held meetings in his new lodgings in James
Street, Covent Garden, after first nailing his own colours to the mast by refusing to
appear at the theatre for a period of three weeks. Fleetwood took refuge in drink during
all this, for by now his debts were beyond him and the bailiffs came knocking.

Garrick's actions constitute a rare instance of the actors going on strike. He persuaded
certain other members of the company to join with him in signing a document that
announced their intention of withdrawing their services from Fleetwood. It was then

Garrick's plan to approach the Lord Chamberlain for permission to open a new theatre. Significantly, Peg Woffington did not attend the meeting or sign the declaration, and Macklin, who was present, argued strongly against it which further convinced Garrick that Macklin's sympathies were with Fleetwood.

The Lord Chamberlain at that time was Charles Fitzroy, second Duke of Grafton and like many holders of that office did not care overmuch for the players. He felt that Garrick was giving himself airs, and when the deputation came to see him, received them coldly and would not yield to their suggestion. He questioned Garrick as to his salary at Drury Lane, conveniently ignoring the fact that Garrick was still waiting for it. On being told the sum, he was offended, stating that he had a son presently serving the Crown and risking his life for half that amount. The deputation went away empty handed.

Actors are not very adept at organising themselves and Garrick's leadership began to falter. It would appear that Fleetwood somehow managed to extricate himself from debt, because he offered to forgive and forget. Garrick was willing, Macklin was not. One possible explanation for Fleetwood's attitude towards Macklin (allowing for the irrational behaviour of habitual drunkards) could be that, having stood by Macklin at the time of his murder trial, he considered the betrayal too heinous to forgive. Peg Woffington wisely refused to take sides and when the next season opened at the Lane she was the star attraction and Garrick was still absent. Most of the other members of the rebellion had been taken back, some on reduced salaries, but no doubt grateful for small mercies.

Garrick held out for a further two months, but an actor is always looking over his shoulder for the potential rivals that inevitably appear, and it was increasingly obvious that unless his own blossoming career was to wither and die, he had to make his peace with Fleetwood even at the risk of further alienating Macklin. He was trapped between honour and ambition. He wavered, made desperate last minute attempts, but in the end he abandoned Macklin. One should not judge him too harshly; he had also to take into account the plight of the humbler members of the company who by now were staring penury in the face. The revolt collapsed. Garrick returned to the Lane.

We next come to what Sherlock Holmes might have called 'The Curious Case of Charles Macklin, Comedian'. Poor Macklin lashed out in all directions. With the help of others he composed and published his version of recent events, violently denouncing Garrick for his treachery. Then as now, the public enjoyed a good old spat between two such well-known figures. Garrick replied with handbills asking his fans to reserve judgement until he could prepare a full defence to the scurrilous charges. He had to move swiftly because Macklin had published his attack on the morning of Garrick's return to the Lane.

By the time the curtain went up it was obvious that Macklin had the advantage. The pit was packed with his cronies, hastily recruited and well armed with quantities of rotten fruit and eggs. The moment Garrick made his first appearance he was shouted down and pelted with rubbish. This was not the first time that the stage of Drury Lane had been fouled with garbage; disgruntled spectators frequently made it impossible for the actors to walk in the slime. But this was certainly one of the rare occasions when an actor of

Garrick's stature had been so abused. The tumult was so great that none of the actors could make themselves heard, though with considerable courage, and taking their lead from Garrick, they attempted to carry on. The barrage of shouted and actual abuse continued unabated; the situation accelerated towards riot and the curtain had to be rung down. Nothing like it had ever been seen before.

This was on December 5th 1743. By December 7th Garrick with the assistance of a professional hack called William Guthrie had written his defence. Somewhat boldly he announced that he would make another attempt to present *The Rehearsal* with himself in the role of Bayes on the evening of December 9th. Macklin needed no further provocation and once again drummed his army into the pit. But on this occasion Fleetwood had taken precautions and recruited some thirty bruisers who were under instructions to move in at the first sign of any disturbance. They didn't have long to wait. Before the overture had finished the house was once again in uproar. Battle was joined and Macklin's rowdies were defeated. The curtain rose and Garrick was able to perform without further interruption.

Still Macklin felt he had been refused satisfaction. By December 12th he had issued a *Reply* to Garrick's Vindication. But the steam had gone out of it; the public had had their fun and Macklin's attempts to prolong the debate had become a bore. His career now non-existent, he tried to set up his own Dramatic Academy. This failed and he eventually became a tavern keeper. It was not a workable or profitable solution to his problems and he went bankrupt. The lure of the stage was always there and he made various attempts to win back a public and was still performing, a pathetic wreck of his former self, at the age of eighty-nine. Some say that, miraculously, he lived to be a hundred. We do know that when Garrick became manager of Drury Lane he tried to patch up the quarrel and invited Macklin to join his company. Macklin's wounds were still raw and he declined the offer. In later years he cobbled together his memoirs with the aid of his biographer William Cooke, and the old animosity towards Garrick bubbled out of him—stale beer that left an unpleasant taste. Garrick went on to forge his legends, yet it was Macklin who showed the way, Macklin who first gave the young hopeful from Lichfield encouragement and guidance, Macklin who introduced naturalism to the English stage with his revolutionary Shylock—a role that, sadly, he carried over into real life, demanding a pound of flesh that finally he had to cut from his own body.

ORDER, DECENCY, DECORUM
—AND SHAKESPEARE

LTHOUGH the Age of Garrick was to last for over thirty years until his death in
1779, his position as the star actor of his day was frequently challenged by new
talents as well as the more established players of his generation. The ubiquitous Quin was
always lurking in the wings anxious to prove his superiority; the rivalry between the two
was good for business and perhaps they encouraged it. Quin was puzzled by Garrick;
puzzled when Garrick chose to present *Macbeth* and the newspapers informed him that
the play was to be given 'as written by Shakespeare'. 'What does it mean?' asked Quin.
'Don't I play it as written by Shakespeare?' He had no idea, apparently, that the version
he was accustomed to had been done over by Sir William Davenant.

Garrick and Quin acted together for the first time in 1746, the same year that the
splendidly named Spranger Barry arrived from Dublin, twenty-seven years old, bushy-
tailed and raring to test Garrick on his home ground. The Quin-Garrick duet was played
in *The Fair Penitent*, Rich having persuaded them to join forces at Covent Garden. It must
have been a fascinating evening to see the most popular leading exponents of the old and
new styles pitted against each other, but it proved an uneasy artistic truce, the audience
being well aware of the undercurrents of passion. Both men were thrown by repeated
advice shouted up at them from the pit. The cast also included the ultimately tragic Mrs
Cibber—Susannah Cibber, wife of Theophilus, Colley's unattractive son. She is said to
have 'recitatived' her role, while Quin delivered his lines in his customary monotonous
fashion.

Yet it would be false to make the comparison between the two men a reason for
dismissing Quin. He was by all accounts a most powerful personality and no mean actor
in the right part—Falstaff, for instance, which he played with a full bottle of claret in his
hand (no solution of cold tea for him!). It could well be that Garrick, anxious to keep the
peace after his experiences with Macklin, was being tactful, but he is reported as judging
Quin's Falstaff to be 'the perfection of acting'. I am inclined to the belief that his praise
was genuine, for he played Hotspur without great acclaim in the same production and
relinquished the role to another actor, Havard, after five performances and never
attempted it again. Garrick was consistently aware of his physical limitations, being
extremely sensitive about his lack of height.

Macklin's name crops up again in connection with young Barry. We are told by Doran
that he tutored Barry in the role of Othello, playing Iago to Barry's Moor at the

SPRANGER BARRY as Macbeth,
Drury Lane, 1746.
Mezzotint by M. Jack

SUSANNAH CIBBER as Cordelia in Nahum Tate's version
of *King Lear*

Irishman's first appearance at Drury Lane. This connection between Macklin and Barry smacks of revenge: it would be consistent with the rest of the story for Macklin to try and further Barry's career at Garrick's expense. So at this period Garrick was fighting on two fronts: appearing with Quin at Covent Garden in what has to be taken as a deliberate move to prove his new style superior to the old, while at the same time being challenged by the newcomer Barry at the Lane.

Fleetwood's patent at Drury Lane came to an end and it eventually passed to Lacy, an Irish businessman who had previously served as Rich's assistant. It was a small, confined world and always turbulent with intrigue. Garrick quarrelled with Lacy, exchanging acrimonious letters with him. Money was once again the cause of Garrick's anger and Lacy responded by calling him avaricious, arrogant and dishonest. It was a golden opportunity for Rich to step in and secure Garrick for life. He was fully aware of Garrick's desire to become part of management rather than fight it all the time, and he knew at first hand Garrick's undoubted drawing power, for his theatre had prospered as never before during Garrick's stay there. Yet for some reason he made no move. The truth is he loathed actors; eccentric, inarticulate and his own worst enemy. Even a full house depressed him—he would peer through a hole in the curtains before the start of a performance and mutter: 'What? Are you there? Much good may it do ye.' Lacy, the man he had trained, became his rival at the Lane, and yet he still did nothing. The golden opportunity came and went.

It was hardly the most propitious time for any kind of financial gamble. There had been two runs on the Bank of England as Prince Charles Edward Stuart began his march south and although the Rebellion was now over and the last of the rebels had been executed on Tower Hill, the City financiers were still acting scared, chary of investing in such highly speculative ventures as theatres. Fleetwood, who always seemed to land on his unsteady feet, had been bought off and departed to France though debts of twelve thousand pounds still remained. In spite of all this Garrick was still determined to become his own master. He was exhausted and in ill health, his affair with Peg Woffington had ended because of his reluctance to give her the wedding band she craved, and he could see his position as a star attraction being eroded by Barry. So he made his peace with Lacy and on April 9, 1747 entered into an agreement which gave them joint-ownership of the Lane. Lacy was to provide four thousand pounds, Garrick eight thousand. In addition he was to receive five hundred pounds a year as his acting salary plus a further five hundred as one of the two patentees. Like many an actor he neglected to read the fine print and the agreement did not give Garrick the freedom he sought in matters of artistic control. His initial neglect of these matters led to niggling differences between him and Lacy. Despite meeting every day they resorted to writing each other abusive letters and finally an arbitrator had to be called in.

For as long as there has been an acting profession the basic and for the most part inescapable conflict between management and performer has existed. At best there is an armed truce, with differences held in check while the business is good, but liable to blaze afresh the moment the box office returns fall off. Lacking any organised protection of their interests until the first quarter of this century, the majority of actors, and indeed variety artists, circus performers and the like, were at the mercy of their employers. Back-stage conditions were intolerable and even today can hardly be described as ideal: cramped dressing rooms, even for the stars, usually furnished without taste or comfort, inadequate toilet facilities, bad ventilation, lack of any form of heating. Even when the Industrial Revolution spurred the early reformers they ignored the actors, despite the fact that their conditions of employment were often as ghastly as for those working in factories. It is a fact that an actor is for the most part indifferent to his surroundings. This and the built-in transient nature of an actor's life, which he accepts to the amazement of others, are the prime factors that managements have exploited throughout the centuries. There have been few periods in our history when the world wanted to owe the actor a living. It is not surprising then that leading figures like Garrick have frequently attempted to improve their lot by joining or competing with those who treat the theatre as just a means of making money. Alas, such crusader intentions are no guarantee of success, and the most exalted in the profession are just as likely to fail as the humblest beginner. Dame Edith Evans lost her entire life savings with a single venture into management and there are many other names just as distinguished as hers who have seen their fondest hopes crumble and their capital disappear overnight. For nearly a century it was devoutly hoped that when our National Theatre was finally able to open its doors a new reign of milk and honey would dawn for the actor. Well, we now have a National Theatre at long last and it attracts the best actors, directors and designers that the profession has to offer, but from certain angles and on certain occasions it more closely resembles an adjunct to British Leyland than a temple of the arts. The dressing rooms are no more comfortable than a field hospital and are so far removed from the stages they might as well be in another building. Sir Peter Hall, the present and most able Supremo of the National, must sometimes believe he is running an industrial complex rather than the hoped-for box of delights.

Yet the world of Garrick's Drury Lane had many similarities with the world that currently exists on the South Bank where Burbage first raised his flag. It was confined, insular, often petty, dependent on the public whim, but always reaching out for new perfections. There was Garrick, freshly ordained as an actor-manager, bursting to put his innovations into practice, convinced that he could succeed where others had failed. His thrift, that Macklin, Johnson and others made mock of and labelled meanness, had proved worthwhile—he was now half-owner of his own theatre. Furthermore he was in love again: the worst, he thought, was behind him.

But when he and Lacy took a closer look at the building they had acquired (and Garrick was forced to see it with a keener eye than when he had entered its doors as a mere actor) they found that Wren's seventy-three years old edifice was shabby and badly in need of renovation. They had inherited a formidable army of permanent staff: dressers, doorkeepers, sweepers, porters, messengers, a barber, property master, scene-shifters, candlewomen, laundry-hands and, most amazingly, a troop of soldiers (ever since the Lincolns Inn riots of 1721 the militia were required to mount guard outside the theatre at every performance). All were on the payroll whether the theatre was dark or open to the public. (Again a curious aspect of the theatrical scene. The actors accept that they will never enjoy security, but are willing to grant it to others). Garrick must have walked amongst them with mixed feelings. They were familiar faces to him, but now he was no longer a fellow employee but their employer, responsible for their continued well-being.

Together with Lacy he discussed the alterations he wanted made to the fabric of the building. He had no love for the 'apron' design of the existing stage, which he felt shattered all illusions by allowing the actors to approach too closely to the audience. In view of past experiences he might also have felt that such intimacy exposed the actors to added dangers from the pit mobs. Plans were drawn up to incorporate the changes he felt imperative and the painters and carpenters set to work.

Of even greater importance to Garrick were the plans he had to change attitudes back-stage. He intended to introduce stringent disciplines. Visitors were to be barred from the dressing rooms and wings, a courtesy that over the years had become so abused that often the players had difficulty making their stage entrances through the crush of rubberneckers. 'Order, decency and decorum', he told his company. There was to be no slackness and unpunctuality at rehearsals. Again, and doubtless recalling his own shame when he had failed to memorise his entire role in *Wedding Day*, he would insist that everybody be word perfect. They would not, he instructed, 'supply the defect by a bold front and forging matter of their own.' He intended to search out and go back to Shakespeare's original texts for his revivals and make the name of Garrick synonymous with all that was best in the Bard. He would engage the finest players in the land and wanted to avoid all feuds. The play was to be the thing, and he, Garrick, would set the example (true to his word, he did extend the olive branch to Macklin).

He was soon in trouble. However well intentioned, no manager can afford to overlook the guile of his various leading ladies. Garrick and Peg Woffington had severed their personal relationship, but she had parted from him with the words 'from this hour I separate myself from you except in the course of professional business' and he still held her in high regard as an actress. His new favourite, however, was Mrs Cibber, though their relationship was strictly professional—that unfortunate lady was in no need of any further emotional entanglement. He had to keep the peace between four leading ladies, all of whom he wished to see in his new company. In addition to Peg and Mrs Cibber, there was Kitty Clive to deal with and Mrs Pritchard. Mr Pritchard, always quick to take offence on his wife's behalf, wrote to Garrick before the theatre reopened and the gist of his letter was that under no circumstances could his dearly beloved play second fiddle to Mrs Cibber, as had been rumoured to him. Garrick was an inveterate letter writer and also kept copies, so that we have detailed and accurate volumes of his correspondence to draw upon. On this occasion he was diplomatic, but firm. 'I have a great stake, Mr Pritchard, and must endeavour to secure my property and my friends to the best of my judgement. I shall engage the best company in England, if I can, and think it to the interest of the best actors to be together. I shall to the best of my ability do justice to all, and I hope Mr Pritchard and his friends will be the last to impeach my conduct.' Having dealt with that he sensibly retired to take the waters at Tunbridge Wells and get himself in trim for the coming rigours of management. 'I go to bed at eleven', he wrote to a friend, 'rise at seven, drink no malt liquor, and think of nothing. Old Cibber is here, and very merry we are ... I don't dance but I sleep without my cold sweats and eat like a ploughman.'

Garrick's mention of 'old Cibber' is a timely reminder of that industrious man's nefarious son and the woman he married and made so miserable. A recent biography of Susannah Cibber was titled *The Provoked Wife** and it is apposite. She was the daughter of Thomas and Anne Arne, one of eight children born to the couple, of whom only three survived—which was better than the national average for those times. The Arnes were upholsterers and undertakers and had a flourishing business in Covent Garden where their services for both trades were in great demand. She had a brother, also named Thomas, an accomplished musician who went on to find lasting fame as the composer of 'Rule Britannia' and 'The Lass of Richmond Hill' amongst other works. Her uncle had perished in horrifying circumstances in the notorious Fleet prison dungeons, mirroring the fate of her paternal grandfather who had suffered a like fate as a debtor in the Marshalsea prison. It could therefore be said that her inheritance was not too

* by Mary Nash (Hutchinson, London, 1977: Little Brown, Boston)

SHAKESPEARE, The Chandos Portrait
National Portrait Gallery

THE GLOBE THEATRE
Based on Visscher's Long View of London 1618
Ehrlich/Tweedy Archive, British Museum

encouraging, though her parents seem to have accepted these tragedies without too much concern.

She was never a beauty, but was well educated, as was her brother, who went to Eton, and she spent her childhood quietly in an atmosphere closely concerned with all aspects of birth and death: while her father made a good living as an undertaker, her mother dealt with the other end of the human spectrum—she was a midwife. Susannah was brought up in her parents' faith as a Catholic, which is probably the prime reason why she led a sheltered childhood and was not encouraged to mix with the children of other Covent Garden tradespeople, since Papists were still regarded with distrust.

Extravagance being an enduring family failing, by the time Susannah was fifteen her father's previously flourishing business was in financial difficulties. Economies had to be made and Susannah was the first to suffer. She was denied the singing lessons she had so greatly enjoyed and at which she had excelled. Always a willing and diligent scholar she was proud of her education and to the end of her days liked to be referred to as 'the learned Mrs Cibber' in glaring contrast to the majority of her rivals.

Casting around to find some novel way of retrieving his fortunes, her father devised a scheme whereby he could capitalise on his children's musical talents. The jump from undertaker to theatrical impresario is a large one but Thomas Arne, Snr apparently took it in his stride. He entered into an arrangement with two acquaintances—one a man called Lampe, who had been introduced to him by his son's violin teacher, Michael Festing, and the other the bastard son of Lord Eland, Henry Carey. These gentlemen had been searching for a patron who would further their ambitions (they had both dabbled in the theatre), for they had an eye to try and cash in on the current popularity of Gay's *The Beggar's Opera* by producing something of their own. Lampe had written the music and Carey the libretto. Although personally impoverished, Thomas Arne, Snr somehow raised the necessary cash. He does not seem to have worried overmuch whether his only daughter actually wanted to embark on a stage career and she, for her part, was apparently so under his thumb that she never questioned the wisdom of such a move. Another curious aspect of this venture is that Arne arranged for his son to be a general dogsbody in the enterprise, ignoring the fact that, compared to Mr Lampe, Thomas Jnr had musical genius.

Handel was then the reigning monarch of English music and his works were presented in a magnificent Opera House in the Haymarket. On the opposite side of the street was a small theatre which was rented out on an ad hoc basis to anybody bold enough to mount a theatrical event. So it was on March 13, 1732, five years before young Garrick set out from Lichfield, that Susannah Cibber made her debut playing the title role in *Amelia*, described as 'a new English opera to be performed after the Italian manner'. In the great tradition of stage success stories, she triumphed beyond all expectation, so much so that Lampe and Carey burnt the midnight oil to hastily produce extra songs for her. Success went to her father's head rather than to Susannah's; he became so enamoured of his new status that, to the dismay of his partners, he announced plans for a production of Handel's *Acis and Galatea* with Susannah singing the role of Galatea.

One can search a long time for a stranger genesis to a great career—an undertaker turned theatrical impresario compelling his daughter to pursue a career which was still far from being considered respectable and becoming in the process fanatical about his own imagined importance.

And from such a beginning Susannah Cibber went on to become Garrick's 'perfect complement; his twin, his female counterpart ... In their playing they warmed and animated each other to such a degree that they were both carried beyond themselves'. When she died Garrick proclaimed 'Tragedy has died with her'. She was not unfamiliar with tragedy in her personal life, her marriage to Theophilus Cibber being another of her father's coercions, one that brought her the least joy. Physically repulsive, Theophilus Cibber was hardly the bridegroom a good Catholic girl would have chosen for herself. He had none of his father's graces but instead, a sadistic streak that he practised on his long-suffering wife—some of the things he forced her to do to save him from a debtor's prison anticipated Krafft-Ebing. When she became a leading force in the theatre he pocketed her salary, removed her clothes, humiliated her to the point of illness and contrived that she should enter into a seamy relationship with a married man and a member of the landed gentry, William Sloper. And when this did not go the way he wanted, he resorted to law and brought about a suit alleging that Sloper had alienated his wife's affections in a most lascivious fashion. To substantiate his case he employed witnesses to supply evidence of the goings on in the Sloper-Susannah love nest—an early example of 'bugging' as it were, for the couple were said to have been observed through a hole in the wainscot. The trial, sensational in its day, permanently ruined Susannah's health and social reputation, but as is often the case with performers, when eventually she was persuaded to return to the stage, she found her public had remained faithful and it was this sympathy which more than anything else enabled her to find a new belief and authority in her undoubted talents.

When she became one of Garrick's 'family of froward children', after he had assumed the role of actor-manager at the Lane, she quickly and devoutly embraced the new disciplines he insisted upon. He called her 'one of Milton's faithful angels' and her influence in the theatre, her kindness towards minor players, became a byword. After her death Garrick was to say she was 'the greatest female player belonging to my house. I could easily parry the artless thrusts, and despise the coarse language of some of my other heroines; but whatever was Cibber's object, she was sure to carry by the acuteness and steadiness of her perseverance.'

They had acted together before Garrick joined forces with Lacy, when she had been a notable Constance to his shaky King John in Shakespeare's play of the same name during the 1745 season. He had engaged her then on Quin's recommendation. 'That woman', Quin said, 'can do anything where passion is concerned'. Perhaps it is not too fanciful to imagine that Susannah, pushed from pillar to post, first by her father and later by her husband, could only find fulfilment in her acting; that those emotions she was compelled to stifle in real life, or else were stifled for her, surfaced on the stage. The story of her career is another example of the divers ways in which the English acting tradition was forced. Unlike the French and Italians we had no formalised school of acting. Most of our great players seem to have worked from instinct rather than training. Some achieved fame almost by accident and some, like Susannah, were pushed into the limelight to satisfy the ambition of others.

Susannah Cibber served Garrick well and there was an enduring affection between them, the stronger for being platonic. Although the usually accurate Carola Oman states that Garrick wrote to her from Dublin that 'he sadly wanted to make love to her again' I can find little to substantiate the theory that they were ever lovers. Garrick left nothing in his papers that could compromise his memory; he preserved only those letters that presented him to posterity in a favourable light, and if he ever exchanged tokens of passion with Peg Woffington, they have not survived. It is true that an undated letter exists from Lord Rochford to Garrick which has been interpreted by some biographers as confirming a closer relationship with Mrs Cibber than a mere stage partnership. Likewise it is also true that Mrs Cibber wrote Garrick letters of a playful nature which again have been taken as evidence that they were lovers. I am inclined to doubt this. Mrs Cibber heaped enough on her own plate by committing adultery with William Sloper, and she does not suggest herself to be a promiscuous woman; flirtatious perhaps, certainly lonely and often unhappy. Equally Garrick was much too ambitious and too careful to expose himself to such obvious complications. He was determined to become a respected pillar of society as well as a great actor-manager. And when he married, he married for life. It would have been out of character for him to introduce a second ex-mistress as one of his leading ladies. Given the jealousies that existed between the leading ladies of that time, it would have been an act of madness on his part, and Garrick did not take such chances where his own career was concerned.

After Peg Woffington, scandal did not touch Garrick. He courted and within a few months married a young lady who had arrived in England under mysterious circumstances. Legend has it that his future wife was smuggled from Holland disguised as a boy. Another version contends that she was compelled to leave Austria at the pointed suggestion of the Empress Maria Theresa because she had too closely engaged the attentions of the Emperor. Although known as Mlle Violette when first she attracted Garrick's eye, her real name was Eva Maria Veigel, and shortly after her unorthodox entry into England she resumed her career as a ballet dancer at the Opera House. We are told that she created a sensation during this engagement by revealing, as she kicked up her legs, black velvet breeches and rolled stockings. The Prince of Wales was amongst those who found such things to his liking, and arranged for her to have tuition from his private dancing master, the celebrated Desnoyer. She declined such exalted patronage and the Prince, no doubt put out by her refusal, took no further interest. Even so, her progress through London society was spectacular, and she was soon to be seen at Drury Lane (where almost certainly Garrick first spotted her, since it coincided with his engagement at Covent Garden) and had been taken under the wing of Lord and Lady Burlington. She became their surrogate daughter and not surprisingly the rumour spread that she must in fact be Lord Burlington's natural child by a Florentine mistress.

Although they had no professional contact, Garrick and Eva Maria met socially and fell in love. This development did not meet with Lady Burlington's approval, for she had set her sights higher than a common actor as a prospective husband for her adopted daughter. Their early courtship had to be conducted discreetly (one story has it that

Garrick went to the lengths of disguising himself as a woman in order to succeed in an assignation). Eva Maria was certainly a child of mystery, the very stuff of romantic legend. In the end Lady Burlington bowed to the inevitable and the young couple were married in Bloomsbury on June 22, 1749, a second Catholic ceremony taking place later the same day to respect the bride's faith. Their first home was at No. 27 Southampton Street, within walking distance of Drury Lane and here the stage was first set for a fairy-tale happy marriage. There is no reason to dispute the pleasing story that in their thirty years of married bliss they never spent a night apart.

Once married, Mrs Garrick renounced all personal ambition and 'the finest and most admired dancer in the world' (Horace Walpole's absurdly exaggerated compliment) never resumed her career. Instead she became the perfect complement to Garrick, content to remain in the background and exert her considerable influence on him in the privacy of their various homes. Garrick relied on her judgement, so much so that Johnson and others insisted that she ruled him. This was not true; their relationship was based on mutual respect. She had all the attributes of an Austrian hausfrau, but was not a shrew. As befitted the wife of England's leading actor, she was a gracious hostess with exquisite manners, able to advance his career off-stage as surely as he consolidated it in public. An amazing number of fictions surround her life, and probably these began with the fact that, inexplicably, Garrick's early biographer Tom Davies made no mention of the marriage when he published *The Memoirs of the Life of David Garrick Esq*, in 1780. A few years later another and even more fanciful account came from the pen of Charles Lee Lewes ('He is a great liar', Mrs Garrick pronounced when she read Lewes' book). What is truly remarkable about Garrick's wife is that she never regretted her retirement: if we are to believe the opinion of Walpole and others, she relinquished what might have been a career as outstanding as Garrick's own, and the lure of the footlights is as strong as an addiction to drink—few can give it up, especially if they have tasted success. 'Retirements' are seldom other than temporary, but Mrs Garrick is a shining exception to the general rule.

If Garrick's domestic life was now settled and happy, he had much to contend with at the Lane. Lewes put forward another dubious piece of gossip that Spranger Barry was also passionately in love with La Violette and pursued her even after her marriage. Barry was an exceedingly vain young man, boringly temperamental, and did his best to disrupt the smooth running of Garrick's company. Garrick seems to have behaved with remarkable constraint in his efforts to keep the peace, relinquishing Othello and other favourite roles when Barry made life too difficult. Mrs Cibber was also 'acting up' at this period, and he always had Kitty Clive and Mrs Pritchard to contend with. Since his health was never too robust he came more and more to rely upon his wife's calm disposition. He needed her wise counsel, for before too long there was open warfare. Barry and Mrs Cibber defected from Garrick to join Rich. Rival productions of *Romeo and Juliet* were hastily mounted, with Garrick appearing opposite a new female partner—the strangely named George Anne Bellamy. She was younger and prettier than Susannah Cibber, but lacked experience. Barry was a matinee idol to the ladies, more passionate than Garrick in the role, though many found his reading devoid of intellectual content. The

MRS DAVID GARRICK
Attributed to Zoffany Reproduced by courtesy of the Garrick Club

town flocked to see both productions and make comparisons. The most quoted *bon mot* came from a lady of the town: she appears to have had the same kind of wit as Coral Browne in this century, saying that as far as she was concerned Mr Garrick could climb up to her balcony any time he wished, but she herself would jump down to meet Mr Barry. There were jealousies everywhere, with Macklin—who was playing Mercutio in the Barry-Cibber *Romeo*—still fermenting trouble and branding Garrick 'a little tyrant'. It was a turbulent period, with London suffering a rare earthquake that sent a good proportion of the population into panic and flight, and the theatres being closed in peremptory fashion by the Lord Chamberlain on the death of the Prince of Wales from pleurisy. Garrick took the opportunity to depart for Bath with his wife.

Such petty rivalries may have been spasmodically good for business, but they thwarted Garrick's great plan for a unified company of players that would raise the whole status of the profession. More energy was being expended on this unproductive competition than on his avowed mission in life. As Margaret Barton, one of Garrick's many biographers, put it when describing the various rivalries: 'Mrs Cibber and Mrs Woffington had a long-standing contempt of each other; Quin disliked Barry; Barry disliked Quin, they all despised Rich, and Rich hated the whole lot of them.' When we add to this unsavoury list Macklin's well-documented hatred of Garrick and the difficulties Garrick encountered keeping the peace between Bellamy and Mrs Cibber, it is small wonder that he welcomed, however callously, the Prince of Wales' untimely death.

In the seasons that followed once Drury Lane had been reopened Garrick found a new right-hand man in an actor called Harry Woodward who was accounted one of the finest Harlequins, and settled down to several years of tranquil prosperity. Woodward was also an accomplished comedian (some said he even surpassed Garrick in certain roles) and Garrick apparently thought so highly of his talents that, alone among his actors, he permitted him to interpret his roles without interference. He also paid him handsomely but over the years Woodward became increasingly disenchanted and resented Garrick's greater affluence. When he left Garrick he did not prosper.

The average reader can have no real comprehension of the tensions that always exist back-stage even in the best regulated companies. All good actors feel insecure; only the untalented are spared such necessary fears. For all his undoubted genius, and despite the increasing power he wielded, Garrick was never a stranger to those doubts that troubled the humblest member of his company. Public acclaim foisted certain vanities on him, but he was not ungenerous towards his fellow actors. He had a vision and worked tirelessly to convert others, coaching, rehearsing, trying to infuse his colleagues with his own burning enthusiasms and raise them to the standard he felt was needed. When, as often happened, they repaid his concern with ingratitude, he engaged new blood and started again. During the latter half of 1751 he brought over three young actors from Dublin—David Ross, Dexter and, most notably, Henry Mossop. Under Garrick's tutelage Mossop proved to be a tragedian of note, excelling in character roles such as Richard III which Garrick made over to him in another example of his generosity.

Although he concentrated on restoring many of Shakespeare's bowdlerised texts, he also realised that the theatre could only prosper if new playwrights were encouraged to come forward. In the four years 1751–1755 he presented eight new plays, incurring losses on seven of them, which could not have pleased his partner Lacy. There is a story, possibly apocryphal, that during this period, despairing of finding a popular comedy he approached the aged Colley Cibber and asked if he had anything tucked away. 'Who have you to act it?' Cibber is said to have enquired. 'Clive, Pritchard and myself', was Garrick's reported answer. 'No', old Cibber is made to answer. 'No, it won't do'.

It is worth exploring the theory that Shakespeare's overpowering genius has in fact been a blight as well as a glory to the English stage, in that his brilliance emasculated all other challengers. The sheer volume of his achievement has always proved daunting. The Restoration brought forth many superb comedies (and few will quarrel with the verdict that Shakespare's comedies do not weather as well as the tragedies) but nobody ever approached Shakespeare's innate sense of dramatic construction. The proof is surely in the pudding. Shakespeare's many detractors over the centuries cannot challenge the record. They can put forward their own favourites, argue at length regarding the authorship of certain plays, compare and dissemble, but in the end they must retire defeated by the unsassailable facts. To be merely popular, even overwhelmingly so for certain periods, is patently not enough to ensure immortality. If this were not so our stages would be even more cluttered with puerile revivals of minor works than they sometimes appear to be. It must be true that no other dramatist who has ever lived has been performed more frequently than Shakespeare. He has held sway over four centuries, and when, as we shall subsequently show, he has been temporarily pushed to one side we have always come back to him. That there is an English acting tradition we owe primarily to Shakespeare, which is not the same as saying that there would never have been such a tradition without him. But when we examine and compare our own stage history with that of other nations we find that, apart from isolated festivals, there is no such unbroken line, nor any foreign dramatist (if we exclude the Greek school) who has been exported as Shakespeare has been exported. The very fact that he can be successfully translated and performed in other languages speaks volumes. And if we follow the basic argument through we have to acknowledge that few dramatists can have survived so many execrable productions over the centuries and still be regarded as the master. He has even survived being taught in our schools, surely the worst fate that can ever befall a writer of genius.

Garrick was the first of our great actors to place Shakespeare in the proper perspective and attempt to correct the worse abuses done to the texts. From his first performance in Goodman's Fields he shook off the old order of things and, tipping his cap towards Macklin, melded his genius with that of Shakespeare's in such a way that the style of English acting was never quite the same again. Cutting through all the other legends that surround his name, this seems to me to be his most auspicious achievement.

'THE GREATEST, GRANDEST
GENIUS EVER BORN'

T HE actors may not have appeared gentlemen in some people's eyes, but they were certainly given decent burials, and Garrick was no exception. He was interred in Westminster Abbey following one of the most magnificent funerals that London had ever seen. The route from Adelphi Terrace (his last home) to the Abbey was chocked with people who had come to pay their last respects. A detachment of cavalry stood by in case the crowds got out of hand, but we are told that although their numbers were so great that some were forced to watch the cortege pass by from rooftops it was an orderly gathering, 'the most evident demonstration being their woe'.

There was no hint of the despicability that had been ascribed to so many of his predecessors. He numbered a duke and many lords and notables amongst his pall-bearers; six coaches carrying Gentlemen of the Literary Club followed the coffin and there were eleven more for 'intimate friends'. The chief mourner, Sheridan, bade farewell in style, having two attendants to lift his black velvet train. Johnson was bathed in tears at the loss of his old companion and Burke sobbed audibly as the coffin was lowered at the foot of Shakespeare's monument in Poets' Corner.

This was February 1st, 1779, forty-two years after he had set out from Lichfield and in the interim the theatre had undergone profound changes. Not only had the status of the actor been elevated in society but many of the petty restrictions surrounding the profession had been removed. Garrick died an immensely rich man; probably no actor before or since enjoyed such enormous success. At one point in his life he had a house at Hampton Court, designed by Adam, the furniture hand-made by Chippendale, the paintings on his walls by artists such as Reynolds and Zoffany, as well as his London home in Adelphi Terrace. Estimates as to his fortune range from fifty to one hundred thousand pounds, which if true would make him a pound millionaire by today's standards. The exact total is shrouded in some mystery, and there were the inevitable squabbles and disagreements that always seem to attend the breaking up of such an estate. The undertaker responsible for the elaborate funeral went bankrupt, for instance, while awaiting payment for his services, valued at one thousand five hundred pounds. Garrick's widow was burdened by conditions in the will that stipulated that she must keep up both homes, and popular conjecture had it that Garrick had made a will very much exceeding his real fortune. Even so it cannot be denied that he was no pauper, a much respected and highly respectable member of the upper echelons of English society

David Garrick's villa at Hampton with the Temple of Shakespeare

The Apotheosis of DAVID GARRICK

who had demonstrated throughout his career that the actor had no need to fear comparison with others.

Almost dead centre of Garrick's span came the birth of 'the greatest, grandest genius that ever was born'—the description is Haydon's—Mrs Siddons. Her mother was Sally Kemble, and on July 5th, 1755, at an inn called The Shoulder of Mutton in Brecon, she was safely delivered of a daughter—the first of twelve children, four of whom died at an early age. The child was baptized Sarah, the church register giving her father as 'George Kemble a Comedian'.* Sarah was born into an extraordinary family. Her mother was the more dominant of her parents, her father being of amiable disposition while Sally was described as a tartar, 'strong minded as a wife and despotic as an employer'. They had inherited a theatrical company from Mrs Kemble's parents who curiously having first refused permission for their daughter to marry into their own profession learnt to live with the situation in their fashion. After seeing her new husband perform Sally's father, John Ward, accepted defeat in some style. 'I forbade you to marry an actor', he told her. 'You have not disobeyed me since the man you have married neither is nor ever can be an actor.' Delivered of this scathing verdict, her father behaved with contradictory generosity and handed over his own company to the young couple—a belated and possibly cynical dowry from a man who combined the strictest Methodist principles with an acting career. He had once managed the Dublin theatre where Peg Woffington made her early appearances and it was his harsh disciplines that were said to have driven her away to seek fame elsewhere. The Wards seem to have had no regrets at quitting the profession so abruptly.

Roger Kemble accepted the unexpected bounty and was content to let his formidable wife take charge of things. Under her supervision the company swiftly acquired a high reputation in the provinces, and once she had got it running smoothly Sally Kemble set about producing her astonishing brood.

Sarah appears to have had no qualms about following an acting career and as a child took life as it came. Her parents wanted her to act, she would act, albeit without too much effort or enthusiasm. She was exhibited as a child prodigy at Kington and found herself in the forefront of an isolated protest against child exploitation which, as one of her biographers remarks, was 'a curious occurrence for Georgian England'. Her mother was more than equal to the occasion. She quelled the rowdy mob by taking her child down to the footlights and plonking her there. Possibly as much in awe of her mother as she was scared of the audience, Sarah dutifully launched into a recitation of a poem called 'The Boy and The Frogs'. The audience quietened and listened. It was her first taste of the authority she used to such devastating effect in the years to come, and the lesson was not wasted on her. She displayed like courage at a much older age when confronted with an openly hostile crowd at Drury Lane.

The Kemble troupe flourished and was more successful and better thought of than most, although the spectre of failure and poverty was never too far away. As Sarah grew into her early teens she developed a dark, almost Semitic beauty which attracted many would-be suitors. While still adolescent she was greatly smitten with a one-time-

* His real name was Roger.

SARAH SIDDONS, 1793
From the painting by Sir W.
Beechey

hairdresser turned indifferent actor called William Siddons. History swiftly repeated itself, for when her parents became aware of her infatuation they reacted in much the same way as the Wards had done when Roger and Sally fell in love. Kemble thought William Siddons a mediocre actor and told him so. Given his notice, the young man made a bold attempt to present his side of the story in some wretched doggerel he had composed and which, without warning, he addressed to the audience at the end of his last appearance with the company. Mrs Kemble was waiting for him in the wings at the end of this impertinence and soundly boxed his ears. She and her husband refused permission for the young couple to marry and although William flirted with the idea of eloping, nothing came of it and Sarah was removed from the scene and placed in service with the widow of a member of Parliament, Lady Mary Greatheed. This move, far from enslaving her, liberated her. She was treated more like a friend of the family than a servant and was given an intimacy with a cultured style of life which otherwise she would never have known, and at an age that mattered. It shaped the rest of her life and certainly saved her from acquiring those bad habits she would have been forced to employ had she remained on the grinding repertory circuit. She enjoyed new freedoms and was able to develop her considerable natural intelligence in an atmosphere divorced from the frenzies of a travelling theatrical company. She remained in love with and was faithful to William and, from time to time, they were allowed to meet. Her resolve never weakened and in due course her parents withdrew their opposition, possibly remembering their own experiences. Sarah married 'Sid', as she called him, in 1773 when she was eighteen. She took his name and gave it immortality. Their marriage was a strange one, but it lasted. Overshadowed from the start by his young bride, William was nevertheless her first love and her last and she must have seen in him qualities that few others ever discerned. He never made any outstanding contribution to her career, and as she became more famous he attempted to manage her business affairs, but was just as inefficient at this task as he was indifferent as an actor. The sexual side of their marriage seems to have anticipated a Henry James plot; all the evidence points to deep repressions on her part, Victorian in their intensity, though she bore him seven children. It has been said that he infected her with a venereal disease, and there is more substance to the theory than mere rumour. She was certainly plagued with ill health for the greater part of her career and many of the symptoms of her most recurring ailment (terrible headaches and deterioration of the central nervous system) have a medical validity to support the contention that they were caused by one of two major venereal scourges. William is reputed to have had at least one affair during their thirty-five-year marriage, though his adultery would seem to have been as discreetly concealed as his other talents. No doubt he was too aware of his main meal ticket to give open provocation, since everything his wife earned—and during the course of her career she earned a great deal—was legally his.

I particularly like Roger Manvell's description that Sarah 'was as starved of private affection as she was overwhelmed by public admiration' for it is close to her own valuation of her life. To 'Sid' she proved 'too grand a thing' and one can sympathise with him for she must have had an obliterating personality sufficient to have emasculated a much stronger man than he was. For her part she confessed that her husband had 'checked my tongue and chilled my heart in every occurrence of importance through our lives' but in this instance he is easier to believe than she, for she was greatly given to exaggeration when it served her purpose. Repressed she may have been, disappointed and unfulfilled sexually, but to cast herself in the role of the misunderstood, weaker partner was a feat of considerable imagination. Her capacity for self-dramatisation was too well known; she lived with an intensity that no human frame could sustain without damage. 'I have worked harder', she wrote, 'than any body ever did before' and it was probably true. Apart from that brief interval spent at Guy's Cliffe in the tranquil company of Lady Mary Greatheed, she worked all her life and despite her often repeated protestations of weariness, her many threats to retire, she could not contemplate the idea of living without acting.

After her marriage she took the sensible course of leaving her parents' company. She and William found spasmodic employment with various other travelling groups though without much material or artistic success. Eventually they joined a barnstorming troupe run by two gentlemen of dubious reputation named Chamberlain and Crump, better described by their nicknames—Fox and Bruin. Their travels eventually brought them to Cheltenham, then a small town which was just beginning to attract the attention of the well-to-do as a watering-place. In theatrical parlance it would have been known as a 'good date', a cut above the average, though it boasted only one wretched theatre.

The company put on a performance of *Venice Preserved* and amongst those summer visitors who thought they would relieve the tedium of their stay by an evening's 'slumming'—convinced that they could enjoy themselves at the expense of third-rate players—was the Hon. Henrietta Boyle. She and her friends went to scorn and stayed to admire. Sarah Siddons, heavily pregnant, perhaps aware of the Hon. Henrietta's intentions, pulled out all the stops and gave a performance that reduced the visitors to a state of admiring hysteria. So much so that they sent word the following day that they had been unable to leave their rooms since they were still 'disfigured with weeping'. In an effort to atone for her intended bad manners, Henrietta—who was an intelligent young lady and well versed in the arts—immediately set about giving Sarah what advice and material help she could. Thus began a friendship that was to endure to the end of their lives. Henrietta supplied Sarah with a new wardrobe and other necessities and made sure that news of her 'discovery' reached the right ears in London.

Before long word had filtered through to Garrick himself and he dispatched a talent scout—a fellow actor Tom King—to Cheltenham to observe and report back. King was equally impressed and urged Garrick to engage Mrs Siddons. For some reason Garrick ignored his colleague's recommendation and left the matter in abeyance, though he continued to enquire after Sarah, and one of his letters to a touring friend asks: 'Have you heard of a woman Siddons who is strolling about somewhere near you?' but did nothing further at the time.

When Garrick was finally persuaded to take her into his company he was a sick man, his energies and enthusiasms greatly diminished. In the interim Sarah was forced to fend for herself. After Cheltenham she moved on to Liverpool, had her first child, and with the inheritance of her mother's astounding energy set about enlarging her repertoire as well as running a family. She was quickly pregnant again but by the summer of 1775 she was familiar with such roles as Portia, Imogen, Jane Shore, Rosalind and Euphrasia amongst others. More than one person endorsed King's opinion of her to Garrick, but he still hesitated, despite being assured that her Rosalind was the best to be seen.

She was acting by instinct, driven forward by necessity and had acquired few of the derided 'strolling habits' that perhaps concerned Garrick. He knew he had somehow to replenish his company with a new young leading lady, but, unable to go into the provinces to see for himself, hesitated to take anybody else's word for her excellence. The delay was unfortunate for both of them. When he finally plunged—having accepted the testimonial written by yet another delegate, the self-opinionated Rev. Henry Bate, sporting parson, proprietor of the *Morning Post* and would-be theatre critic—he had almost left it too late. Reports of Sarah's talent had also reached his rival at Covent Garden, and indeed for a while there was a distinct danger that the Siddons would fall between two stools and lose both chances. Garrick won in the end and Sarah and William were engaged at the paltry salary of £5 a week, divided between them (nobody was too keen to have William). They journeyed to London shortly after the birth of their second child, William having successfully petitioned Garrick for an advance of salary. Garrick sent £20 and studied the list of possible roles which Sarah had submitted. She had included no less than twenty-three, and indicated that of these she considered her London debut should be picked from seven she had underlined. It is curious that at this stage in her career she was convinced that her future lay in comedy, and it was mainly as a comic actress that Garrick employed her.

The worst thing an ambitious actor has to contemplate—and Garrick remained ambitious, socially and professionally, to the end of his days—is the want of something to leave behind him that shall carry down an idea of his talents to posterity. I believe that this partly explains his initial hesitation. When he took from the depth of the provinces, on the say-so of acquaintances and without benefit of his own prior evaluation, this 'untutored genius', this 'raw girl', he could not admit of possible failure. There were many circumstances that conspired against him and the timing of her debut was not propitious. She misjudged herself, he was ill and liable to make rash judgements. In Sarah's case she was rushed into making her London debut far too soon after her confinement, and Garrick decided that, from the list she had supplied, Portia was the right choice for her first appearance. It was not a happy situation, but the two young people, with no experience of the politics of the theatre and certainly in no position to question Garrick's decision, did as they were told.

She stepped on to the stage at the Lane on 29th December 1775; Tom King, the very man who had gone to Cheltenham to report on her abilities, was cast as Shylock. Sarah was billed merely as 'A Young Lady', a curious decision on Garrick's part. It proved to be a nightmare experience. She was bewildered by the size of Drury Lane, she was under-rehearsed, physically weak and rendered almost incapable by nerves. Condemnation was almost universal. She was called clumsy, tremulous, inaudible, ugly, vulgar—they damned her without pity. The only faint voice raised in her defence was a prejudiced one: the Rev. Henry Bate, seeking to justify his original recommendation, wrote that 'allowing for her great natural diffidence, we see no unpromising presage of her future excellence'. It was scarcely enough.

The old guard of leading ladies could not conceal their delight—the three termagants Garrick had to contend with at this time were Mrs Abington, Miss Younge and Mrs Yates, individually and collectively monsters. All three had wearied him to the point of no return with their endless petty bickerings. When Sarah Siddons appeared on the scene these three closed ranks against the new common enemy. Naturally her resounding failure as Portia delighted them, but to their continued fury Sarah was not removed from Garrick's patronage as they expected. On the contrary he went out of his way to afford her special courtesies in their presence. After years of enduring their tantrums he probably enjoyed the situation and played off Sarah against them in order to get some of his own back. Sarah eventually saw through this ploy and never forgave him, but at the time she accepted his choice of Portia for her debut in good faith, believing the great man to be utterly sincere when he explained that he dare not introduce her London audiences in a more prominent role for fear that one of the outraged trio would do her actual physical harm. It is not difficult to imagine the situation from Sarah's point of view, nor should we be surprised that she swallowed the tale he told her. She was weak from childbirth, desperately scared, in strange and august surroundings, thrust into an intimacy with the greatest living actor and—most of all—she and William needed the money. Garrick's vastly superior sophistication must have made him a god in her eyes, and one does not argue with gods.

The courage she had displayed as a child had not deserted her and four nights after the first agony she again played Portia. In fiction most novelists would accord her a triumph the second time around, but alas the initial failure was compounded. Where she found the will to continue is something to marvel at, but continue she did and remained until the end of that season. Success never approached her. Garrick persisted (and I cannot subscribe to the theory that he pursued this course merely to thwart the other three leading ladies) casting Sarah in a series of roles and even, at the very end of his career, reviving his famous *Richard III* for his penultimate appearance with Sarah as his Lady Anne. She was pronounced 'pathetic', 'lamentable'. By now her nerve had gone completely; she could do nothing right. Five nights later after bidding farewell to his public as Don Felix in *The Wonder* (a strange choice for a swan song) Garrick handed over the management of the Lane to Sheridan, Forde and Linley. One of Mrs Siddons' biographers, Yvonne ffrench* caught this moment perfectly when she wrote: 'The two greatest players in the nation's history had thus for a few weeks appeared, like stars, in conjunction. Nobody was aware of the event.'

When he took his leave of Sarah and William, Garrick lacked the courage to tell them what he must have known—namely the new management would not be renewing their contract. The young couple had taken off for a tour of the provinces when the Lane season ended, convinced that they would be given a second chance. When they received the bitter news in Birmingham Sarah became seriously ill, a spiritual and physical decline that lasted for eighteen months. Even so she was forced to keep working, albeit in comparative obscurity. I believe she could have forgiven Garrick for his initial deviousness, his unhappy choices of roles and all the other disappointments that attended her first season at the Lane, but she could not forgive him his cowardice. Outwardly he had befriended her and taken pains with her (he insisted that she watch his performances from one of the boxes on those nights when she was not playing). He had defended her against the malice of others and shown his faith in her in the teeth of public indifference, but in the end she felt that he had betrayed her. She took refuge in hatred of him, and perhaps that was the only thing left to her if she was to survive. In later years she tempered this with a profound respect for his professional gifts, but she separated this from the personal hurt in her mind and the wound never healed completely.

Fortunately for her, news of her abject failure at Drury Lane had not blanketed the country. In many of the provincial towns she visited during this period she was the young actress who had recently played opposite the great Garrick and that was more than enough. She joined up with Henderson, another actor who felt he had a grievance against Garrick, and it was Henderson who was responsible for the next fillip to her career. He attempted to push her cause with Palmer the manager of the flourishing theatre in Bath. Palmer did not act upon the recommendation immediately, but the seed had been sown.

(There is a revealing footnote to Sarah's departure from the Lane. Despite all that had gone before, alone amongst those who gloated at Sarah's downfall, Mrs Abington

* *Mrs Siddons, Tragic Actress*, pub. 1936; subsequently republished by Verschoyle 1954.

anticipated the verdict of posterity. While others were congratulating each other over the dismissal of the 'lamentable' Mrs Siddons, the voice of experience cut through the malice. 'You are all fools', Mrs Abington said, and her perception, not to mention her generosity, deserves recording.)

Sarah and William resumed their provincial wandering, journeying further north to Liverpool when Palmer declined to act on Henderson's suggestion. In Liverpool Sarah rejoined her old manager Younger and gave her *Hamlet*—the idea of a woman playing the Dane being entirely acceptable to past audiences. Contemporary observers of this period in her career talk of her 'frail appearance' which makes strange reading in the light of the rest of her life, and contrasts strongly with the portraits that have come down to us. Her self-pity gradually diluted as she began to find more and more public acceptance and her reputation increased. The provincial audiences echoed Mrs Abington's sentiments and felt that they had scored over London in having such a jewel in their midst. The rising middle-class wanted to make their new superiority felt, and one way of expressing this was to challenge the capital's patronage of the theatre. It is an attitude which persists to this day. Brighton theatregoers pride themselves on their ability to pick the winners before the London critics—Brighton being traditionally the last stop before a West End opening.

The rising bourgeoisie weren't yet prepared to accept the actors within their ranks and were quick to react against anything they took to be an insult to their standing in society. In 1778 when Sarah was appearing in Liverpool the management apologised for presenting a company that had not been given the accolade of appearing before the King. Fulfilling his mission in life, the unfortunate William—Sarah's 'Sid'—was given the job of carrying the placarded apology on stage. He was pelted to flight while Mrs Kniveton, another actress in the company, went into convulsions at the uproar. We are told that Sarah viewed the happening with contempt and possibly some of that contempt was heaped upon her husband for exposing himself to such ridicule.

The experience she was gaining convinced Sarah that she had been wrong in her first evaluation of her own talents. She steered herself away from comedy and began an intensive study of the classical tragic roles. Her single-mindedness was impressive. It even impressed her in retrospect, for many years later, remembering those early times she wrote: 'That I had strength and courage to get through all this labour of mind and body, interrupted too by the cares and childish sports of my poor children who were (most unwillingly often) hushed to silence for interrupting my studies, I look back with wonder.' Possessed of a remarkable memory (a vital piece of the actors' armoury) she had seldom bothered to *study* a role in advance. She learnt them between household chores and then played them by instinct, a method which can work admirably with certain roles when one is young, but does not commend itself to the great classical characters such as Lady Macbeth. Her attempt to apply this hit-and-miss technique to Lady Macbeth finally cured her of the habit. We have her own account of the calamitous occasion. 'As the character is very short, I thought I should soon accomplish it.' She had not really applied herself to Shakespeare's text until the night before she played Macbeth's wife for the first time! As she read it carefully 'the horror of the scene rose to a degree that made it

NELL GWYN
From the painting by Sir Peter Lely
National Portrait Gallery

DAVID GARRICK as Richard III
From the painting by Hogarth
Walker Art Gallery, Liverpool

impossible for me to get farther'. Rising from her chair in the manner of the character she was about to play, she fled to her bedroom in a 'paroxysm of terror', and the lesson was well learnt.

When Palmer finally invited her to go to Bath and she accepted, she had travelled a long way from the raw fledgling that Garrick employed. Bath was the first provincial city to have a Theatre Royal, the letters patent being granted in 1768. From the very beginning Palmer had been determined to establish and maintain the highest standards. He had made his money as a brewer, but had a compulsion to spend his wealth on the theatre. Shortly after he invited Sarah to join his company he acquired a second theatre in neighbouring Bristol and alternated his company between the two, transporting them the twelve miles in fast coaches. He offered Sarah £3 a week, the same salary as she had received from Garrick, and allotted her the Thursday night performance which was well-known as being the dullest and least attended of the week. As at the Lane she came into the company to find other leading ladies already established and she was once again prey to their petty jealousies.

So here we have this truly remarkable woman who had somehow picked herself up off the floor, taught herself, disciplined herself, coped with a family and an ineffectual husband, endured long months touring around England and had somehow remained sane. Now she found herself in a reputable theatre, but starting at the bottom of another ladder. At first she was given subordinate roles in comedy—Lady Townley in *The Provoked Husband*, for her Bath debut. It did not lure the patrons away from their customary Thursday night Cotillon Ball. And then, surprisingly, her luck changed. After being with the company a month she appeared as Elwina in Hannah More's tragedy, *Percy*, and her whole career was transformed. Bath's most influential critic pronounced her 'the most capital actress that has performed here these many years'. Palmer had the perception to see what Garrick hadn't—namely that she could make people weep. For the next thirty years she demonstrated these extraordinary powers, the effects of which, if we are to believe many contemporary reports, can only be compared with the sort of hysteria the Beatles created two centuries later. She literally frightened her audiences into hysterics and fainting fits, she cowered them, she reduced them to jelly. One of the greatest critics of that or any other age was not immune: Hazlitt sobbed his way through her Isabella in *The Fatal Marriage* and went home to write that he felt 'as if a being of a superior order had dropped from another sphere to awe the world with the majesty of her appearance . . . It was something above nature. We can conceive of nothing grander. She was not less than a goddess, or than a prophetess inspired by the gods. Power was seated on her brow, passion emanated from her breast as from a shrine. She was Tragedy personified.' In this century Richard Findlater gathered together the threads of his long years of research and penned an equally evocative passage: 'She struck them into submission with the savageness of her contempt, the fury of her rage, the profundity of her despair, the magnitude of the wrongs she endured at the hands of men, as she went mad, or was murdered, or committed suicide.'

She exercised and increased these unique powers week by week during her four seasons in Palmer's company, becoming in the process his leading attraction. Thursday was no longer the loneliest night of the week in the theatre at Orchard Street; the dancers were seduced away from the Cotillon Balls in ever greater numbers. Her new fame travelled back to Garrick, but he was too ill to care. And while she added role after new role to her repertoire, acting now in Bristol, now back in Bath, learning, rehearsing, travelling—while undertaking such a heroic schedule, she also became pregnant again and gave birth to her third child, another daughter. Apart from his initial assistance in this domestic matter, her husband appears to have done little else. He was occasionally given minor roles to play, and played them badly, but did not hesitate to give his brilliant wife advice on her own performances. From this we must believe that she was not capable of making *him* submit to the savageness of her contempt, but reserved all her fury for the stage. Although her salary was steadily increased and she received useful lump sums from her benefits, as a dutiful wife she handed it all to William. He doled out a quarterly allowance and the paradox of the situation is beguiling. Here we have this towering presence on the stage, capable of reducing strong men to sobbing wrecks, yet docile and malleable at home, accepting William's pocket money paid from moneys *she* had earned. On the strength of her success Palmer was able to carry out further renovations and improvements to his theatre and raise his prices. In the past the cost of admission had been closely watched by the patrons and many an attempt to increase prices had been met with riots. With Sarah Siddons on the bill, Palmer had no such problems, and this, as much as Hazlitt's eulogy, demonstrates her extraordinary hold over the audiences of the day.

It was inevitable that the London theatres would attempt to woo her back, and it was inevitable that, after a proper show of reluctance, she would go. She had conquered Bath and Bristol, now she could not refuse herself the chance to erase forever the memory of that first season with Garrick. Sheridan laid siege to her and it was Sheridan who finally claimed the prize. I have no doubt in my own mind that it was not Sheridan's flattery that tipped the scale, but the fact that he managed Drury Lane. She did not want to go back to London per se, she wanted to go back to the Lane, and there triumph.

She was given three farewell benefits, two in Bath and one in Bristol, which some people felt was overdoing it. On the second occasion at Bath she stage-managed her own dramatic curtain call—bringing on her three children from the wings, holding the youngest in her arms while she declaimed a specially written Epilogue. The effect on her admirers must have been heightened by the fact that she was yet again in an advanced stage of pregnancy. This was her fifth child, the fourth having died in infancy. Her very last performance at Bath was given on June 19th 1782 when she played Mrs Belville in *The School for Wives*, only seventeen days after her confinement, when she had been safely delivered of another daughter. Her stamina is something to be wondered at.

[[8]]

FROM THE LANE
TO COVENT GARDEN

LET us clear the stage for Sarah Siddons' return to London in 1782. Garrick had been dead nearly three years; Kitty Clive had retired; old Cibber and his daughter were both gone and the theatre was once more in a state of transition.

When she journeyed from Bath with William and the family to take up lodgings at 149 The Strand, she brought with her an enviable reputation and a growing sense of panic. It had been decided that she would make her return appearance in the play that was to cause Hazlitt such pleasurable agony—*The Fatal Marriage*, in which she took the role of Isabella. She began rehearsals in the daunting vastness of Drury Lane and immediately many of the old fears returned. Nothing destroys a voice quicker than nerves, and by the time the last rehearsal was over she could hardly speak. She went back to their lodgings and slept the clock round. When she awoke the sun was shining and her voice was back to normal. Like many actors she was superstitious and a believer in omens: the reappearance of the sun after a number of overcast days seemed auspicious.

In an account such as this, spanning four centuries and with an ever-changing cast of characters all intent upon the same end, nothing could be more self-defeating than constant descriptions of individual triumphs. But there are certain landmarks in the theatre that demand to be recorded in some detail, and 10th October 1782 was one of them.

First-night audiences are a peculiar breed and can be divided into three distinct groups. There are the professional critics, the friends and relatives of the performers, and those who go in a state of mind that allows them to enjoy disaster. This third group are also to be seen at other blood sports—such as boxing, Grand Prix motor racing and at the bottom of Olympic ski jumps, anywhere in fact where there is a reasonable chance of the participants coming to grief. It is a basic part of the mob instinct for the many to find satisfaction in the humiliation of the few.

Sarah was no stranger to the 'many-headed monster of the pit' as Pope described that section of the audience, and she knew that it could turn either way. Her return to the Lane had aroused the keenest interest, but it would be a mistake to imagine that the whole house was for her before the curtain rose. I am sure that Sarah was under no such misapprehension, and we know that when she entered her dressing room on that first night her heart was in her boots. The rest of the cast wisely gave her a wide berth, for she had gone into one of her 'desperate tranquillities'. She got into her costume without a

SARAH SIDDONS in *Isabella, or The Fatal Marriage*, 1782

word to her attendants 'though often sighing most profoundly'. The actor, like the gladiator or duellist, is totally alone on such occasions and given to embracing the direst thoughts. A quick death often seems preferable. The face that stares back at us from the dressing room mirror seems that of a demented stranger, a lunatic who for reasons now incomprehensible chose to follow a career for which he is patently unfitted.

In writing of that moment Sarah describes going into the wings for her first entrance, then finally coming face to face with the 'awful consciousness that one is the sole object of attention in that vast space, lined as it were with human intellect from top to bottom, and all around.' But this proved one occasion when the gods—mythically and literally, if we use the word in its colloquial sense for the topmost layer of 'human intellect'— were with her. In her twenty-seventh year, after six years of waiting, she gave what must have been one of the most staggering performances in the history of the British theatre. Her new manager, Sheridan, sobbed audibly in his box, while all around him the house became possessed. People fainted, shrieked and carried on as though they were witness to intense personal grief. Even allowing for the exaggerations that history grafts on to every major event, and mindful of the fact that such exhibitions of mass hysteria are not necessarily true barometers, Sarah's triumph was patently conclusive.

Long before the final curtain the actors were having difficulty in making themselves heard above the tumult. But this was the tumult of success, the most gratifying noise an actor can hear. We are told that at the climax of her performance Mrs Siddons plunged a dagger into her breast and then gave a great cry of laughter—something so unexpected, so original that it tore the house apart, 'the greater part of the spectators were too ill themselves to use their hands in her applause'.

Afterwards she went home with her father and her amazed husband and ate a 'frugal neat supper'. She had done it and there was no need, in her mind, for further celebration.

The triumph was no fluke. She repeated her success on the second night and once again the great auditorium was the scene of unparalleled public adulation. She was to give her Isabella twenty-four times in the eight months to June 1783. The King, who was no lover of tragedy, came five times in the month of January alone, 'vainly endeavouring to conceal his tears behind his eyeglass'. He was not alone. The Prince of Wales, the Duke of Cumberland, in fact all the notables of the town flocked to use their handkerchiefs and pay homage. The Queen was so overcome that she had to turn her back upon the stage to control her emotions.

Sarah's meagre salary was immediately doubled and she was allowed two benefits which produced more than she had earned in four years at Bath. Perhaps the crowning moment came when she was given Garrick's old dressing room. 'It is impossible to imagine my gratification when I saw my own figure in the self same glass which had so often reflected the face and form of that unequalled genius.' Gratification which was, I am sure, tinged with a little malicious regret that Garrick had not lived to see his 'raw, untutored girl' become his rightful successor.

The diaries of Henry Crabb Robinson, which span the London theatre from 1811–1866 (the twilight of Mrs Siddons to the first glimpses of the juvenile Ellen Terry) are an invaluable source of unprofessional reporting. Crabb Robinson, an inveterate theatre-lover, abandoned what might have been a distinguished career in literature in favour of a mediocre one in law. He was much travelled and before he died at the ripe old age of ninety-two spoke of his happiness at having 'met Goethe, been a friend of Wordsworth and seen Mrs Siddons act'.

He was one of those Mrs Siddons reduced to hysteria and vividly describes his behaviour when she gave a benefit performance of *Fatal Curiosity*.

In the scene in which, her son having put into her hands a casket to keep, and she having touched a spring, it opens and she sees jewels—Her husband (Kemble) enters and in despair exclaims 'Where shall we get bread?' With her eyes fixed on the jewels she runs to him, knocks the casket against her breast and exclaims 'Here, here'—In Mrs Siddons tone and in her look there was an anticipation of the murder which was to take place. I burst into a loud laugh—which occasioned a cry of 'Turn him out'—I was in the pit with Naylor—This frightened me but I could not refrain—A good natured woman near me cried out 'Poor young man he cannot help it'—She gave me a smelling bottle which recovered me, but I was quite shaken and could not relish the little comedy of *The Deuce is in Him*.

The theatre had been turned on its head. Comedy was ousted and tragedy all the vogue. Garrick's efforts to bring the players back to naturalism now suffered a reverse. When Sarah Siddons brought her genius to the new style of acting she transformed dross, but one shudders to think what some of her less-talented imitators did with the same material. Not that such diversity of excellence was peculiar to the era in which she reigned. The moment any great actor bursts upon the scene with a revolutionary style it is inevitable that others will attempt to emulate him, but, lacking that spark that sets him apart, they gradually reduce his impact. And so the revolution dies away gradually until the next innovator comes along. What is fascinating about Sarah Siddons is that she took the drama by the scruff of its neck and shook life into the corpse. It was not always great drama, for it was not the age of great drama—the dramatists did not rise to her levels, but she often raised their work to hers. And although there had been many exceedingly fine actresses since the time when Margaret Hughes had first shown the way, no leading actress before Mrs Siddons had so completely dominated the stage. Garrick would have been difficult enough for the men to follow, but Mrs Siddons was impossible. For the next twenty years, carefully rationing her appearances (for she realised the value of making her public want for more), she was a power in the land. She became increasingly rich and was responsible for furthering her brother's career: John Philip Kemble joined her, and made his London debut in the autumn of 1783 as Hamlet. Intended for holy orders by his father, he had renounced the church for a more spectacular pulpit. His success in no way approached that of his sister, but in the next three decades he became the pillar of the British stage: not the grandest of edifices, for he was a somewhat dull and ponderous man, but a pillar nevertheless.

Raymund FitzSimons, the theatre historian and biographer of Edmund Kean, tells us that 'Kemble was aiming at an interpretation, a psychological interpretation, of character. The classical school behaved heroically, they behaved regally not only in the enunciation of the words, but even in the arrangement of their garments, the way they moved and sat. When Kemble sat on a throne he would arrange his garments around him so that his entire appearance was statuesque. Every action, every movement was precise—the way he 'killed' a man: he would stick a dagger with the precision of a lady darning or knitting. Every speech was given with an absolute reverence to the verse. He was obsessed by the meaning, by the interpretation, by whether his reading was, as he put it, 'sensible'. Towards the end of his career he became so absorbed in this that his performances were deadly dull.'

This was not a description that could ever be applied to his sister. As the years progressed she became something of a national monument and appears to have carried her stage histrionics into everyday life. Sadly we have no means of telling what she really sounded like, but we do know that on one occasion when shopping for material she confronted the draper's assistant with the question: *Will it wash?*, in such a way that the poor assistant promptly fainted. Certain experiments have been carried out, notably by Professor David Abercrombie, Professor of Phonetics at Edinburgh University, in an attempt to reproduce the probable sound of Garrick's voice. After a prolonged study of Garrick's diaries and leters in which he noted the pattern of words used, how often they

JOHN PHILIP KEMBLE as
Hamlet with QUICK (as
Osric?)
from the painting by Sir W.
Beechey

were used and the emphasis they were given, Professor Abercrombie constructed a voice pattern. To this was added the probable local colour of Garrick's accent, which apparently he never lost completely, and a modern actor was then recruited to recreate how Garrick might have spoken the most famous of Hamlet's soliloquies. A most interesting recording of this exists and has been broadcast by the BBC. The truth of course remains a matter of conjecture, though it is fairly obvious that the actors of this period in no way approached the sound or patterns of speech employed today.

We cannot leave Mrs Siddons without mention of her Lady Macbeth—that graveyard for so many leading ladies through the ages. We have read how the role affected her when first she studied it, and for a long time she refused to entertain the idea of playing it. She pronounced Lady Macbeth 'not female' and it is interesting to record that Dame Edith Evans felt the same way a hundred and fifty years later. Unlike Edith, Mrs Siddons changed her mind and thrust herself into a conception of sublime evil, flaunting traditions of utterance and action. She was the first to use the 'handwashing business' in the sleep-walking scene, which has become standard practice ever since. One contemporary report talks of her 'rushing from the stage' at the end of this notorious passage, and this puzzled others who came after. John Philip Kemble supplied the answer. He said, 'She never moved'. In this century Donald Sinden, who has made a deep study of the period, took the explanation further. 'It's exciting to pick up these two things. If she did the hand-washing scene with little or no physical movement, then however she left the stage would have seemed like rushing.' It is a most perceptive comment and one that makes great sense to me. Mr Sinden, like many other fine actors, knows the value of stillness on the stage. In the right hands it is much more effective than a flurry of movement.

Mrs Siddons' break with tradition in her interpretation of Lady Macbeth alarmed many of her admirers. Sheridan ignored her unwritten law and invaded her dressing room prior to the first performance and begged her to reconsider. Mrs Pritchard, he told her, had always played it in a certain way and to change such hallowed business as the carrying of the candle would offend her audiences. It can hardly have been a timely or welcome piece of advice to give to a leading lady; Mrs Siddons rejected it and went her own way. In addition to the physical changes she introduced, she also gave her interpretation much deeper intellectual and psychological insights, and we are in no position to quarrel with the verdict of Professor G. J. Bell who in 1809 devotedly collected a mass of material, eventually published in three volumes, which embraced every aspect of her career. It was his contention that nobody would ever surpass her in the role, and it is a verdict that has probably stood the test of time. Opinions varied as to many of her other performances, but praise for her Lady Macbeth is, from all reliable sources, unanimous. Perhaps only somebody like Sarah Siddons, no stranger to repressions, possessed of an intuitive sense of human tragedy, gifted with a unique voice, can do full justice to Shakespeare's incomplete woman. Like real ale, she fermented slowly, producing in the end the perfection of an absolute original. Gainsborough may have said that there was 'no end' to her nose when she sat for him, but succeeding generations have never questioned the verdict of her contemporaries: 'The stateliest ornament of the public mind.'

Like Garrick before her, and stateliest ornament or not, Sarah suffered at the hands of management. 'Uncertainty personified', as she called Sheridan, consistently cheated her and other members of the company and on several occasions she felt compelled to withhold her services. Sheridan with his great gifts as a dramatist and his even greater charm managed to placate her time and time again, though he did not mend his ways. He enjoyed practical jokes and found it impossible to take Sarah as seriously as she took herself. His opinion of her was 'a magnificent and appalling creature to whom I would as soon have thought of making love as to the Archbishop of Canterbury', Perhaps word of this reached Sarah's ears, because eventually she and her brother decided enough was enough and removed themselves to his rival theatre, Covent Garden. As Madeleine Bingham states in her excellent biography of Sheridan 'it is hard to understand why a man who wrote so well for the theatre, and who understood so instinctively the feelings of the players, and the interest they took in the smallest points of staging, could have killed the talents he so clearly had'. Sarah still had another nine years of professional life ahead of her, and although her drawing power fluctuated, it never disappeared. When she left him, Sheridan still owed her £1,500, and for any manager to make an enemy of such a star attraction must be commercial foolishness. Madeleine Bingham offers a valid explanation: his consuming fault was vanity and in Sarah Siddons he found that vanity challenged and could not stomach it.

Part of the inducement for Sarah and John Philip Kemble to move over to Covent Garden was that Kemble was allowed to buy in as part-owner of the theatre. He had one sixth and could thus further his ambitions as actor-manager. During those last nine years she spent at Covent Garden Sarah was seriously challenged only by the child prodigy, Master Betty. Like W. C. Fields in the twentieth century she wisely decided not to compete with infants and deliberately retired herself for the season of 1804–5. Kemble joined her.

Who was Master Betty? The name has comic undertones, but there is no disputing his amazing early success. He was thirteen years old when he arrived in London and set the town alight, and had already made his mark in Ireland and Scotland. Quite apart from the obvious curiosity value of his tender years, he must have possessed precocious talents of the highest order. Just to *learn* Hamlet at the age of thirteen commands respect* and there were some who judged him better than Garrick in the role. Whoever engineered his debut in London must have been conscious that the time was ripe for change. The public was bored with Kemble and his school, they wanted new excitements and Master Betty, known as the Young Roscius, supplied them. For four months, during which time he played many of the great tragic roles, the Betty craze wafted him to dizzy heights. In twenty three nights they paid £17,000 to see him and he took home £50 a night, which contrasts sharply with Sarah's first salary at the same theatre. Drury Lane and Covent Garden shared him in a rare instance of co-operation and the mania persisted for four months. Doran tells us that 'if the overtaxed boy fell ill, as he did more than once, the public forgot the general social distress, the threats of invasion, war abroad and sedition at home, and evinced such painful anxiety, that bulletins were daily issued, as though the lad were king-regnant or heir-apparent.'

On one occasion the House of Commons, on a motion of the younger Pitt, adjourned in order that members might not miss his performance as Hamlet. There were frenzied scenes at both theatres and patrons fought each other to gain the best seats. 'Gentlemen who knew there were no places untaken in the boxes, and who could not get up the pit avenues, paid for admission into the lower boxes, and poured from them into the pit, in twenties and thirties at a time. The ladies were occupied almost the whole night in fanning the gentlemen who were beneath them in the pit. Upwards of twenty gentlemen, who had fainted, were dragged up into the boxes. Several more raised their hands as if in the act of supplication for mercy and pity.' Master Betty, we are told, 'was not disturbed by the uproar of applause which welcomed him and answered the universal expectation'. Whether all this hysteria went to his head is not recorded, though it would seem likely to corrupt any child of that age.

I have not been able to discover whether Sarah or her brother ever witnessed any of

* He is reputed to have memorised it in four days.

Master Betty's triumphs, and perhaps the whole experience was too galling for them: no actor enjoys being reminded of the public's fickleness. Their turn came round again, for Master Betty burnt himself out very quickly. Not even the most seasoned of players could have sustained the pace that greedy managements and a demanding public required of him; after four brief months of glory the hysteria died away as abruptly as it had first appeared. The rest of his career was spent in semi-obscurity, although he continued to be a spasmodic attraction up and down the country on the strength of his early fame. His father squandered most of the money he had earned and for a time he enlisted in the North Shropshire Yeomanry Cavalry and obtained the rank of Captain. Following his father's death he attempted a come-back, but London no longer asked for him, or thought of him. He went to Edinburgh and there played with Macready and took his final farewell in Southampton on August 9, 1824 at the age of thirty-two. He lived on to well over eighty and of those intervening fifty years we know little. He stands almost alone, a rare phenomenon, undoubtedly gifted beyond his years when first he claimed attention— a prime example of all that is best and worst in the theatre. Exploited by managements, extravagantly admired and then cruelly ignored by the public, denied the ordinary path to maturity, he was ultimately an object for pity. Few child stars survive the squandering of their immature energies and unless they retire completely and make serious attempts to live normal lives, the years beyond their childhood frequently contain nothing but tragedy.

John Philip Kemble remained at Covent Garden until his retirement in 1817, at the close of the season in which Macready made his first appearance and Lucius Junius Booth (a wonderfully grandiose stage name!) 'flashed promise for a moment and straightway died out.' Doran describes Kemble as having a 'Cervantic' gravity and this seems to fit with other opinions of his character. Like Cervantes' hero he was not lacking in courage and bore his misfortunes manfully. When Covent Garden burnt down a few years after he had taken up residence he was 'not much moved' although the fire virtually bankrupted him and he had to start again from scratch. Rich's old theatre with the royal arms in the centre of the curtain (taken from the old curtain at Lincoln's Inn Fields) blazed to rubble in four hours. Twenty-two people perished in the fire which took with it most of the stock of scenery, costumes (including all his sister's dresses and jewels carefully collected over thirty years), manuscripts and records. Also lost was Handel's great organ and some of the Arne scores. Lesser men would have been totally crushed by such a disaster, but Kemble found the necessary resolve to continue despite the fact that the cost of rebuilding the Garden was put at £300,000. A public appeal was successfully launched, the Duke of Northumberland heading the list of donors with a bond for £100,000 which he gallantly burnt at a dinner to celebrate the reopening. In order to cover the capital expenditure Kemble and his associates unwisely decided to raise the prices, precipitating what came to be known as the O.P. (Old Prices) Riots: a well organised and prolonged campaign by a public that was not prepared to tolerate such extortion. It must be said that the increases were steep, taken in the context of the time and the value of money set against the earning power of the average patron. Admission to the boxes went from six shillings to seven and the pit seats advanced sixpence to four shillings, proportionately one sixth and one seventh. It is worth remembering that the theatre was the main source of public entertainment—there was no comparable alternative. Since there is always something beyond the surface evidence, account must also be taken of Kemble's personal relationship with his audience. Like some minor, icy Everest he was there: they respected him, but they did not like him; he appeared as autocratic, indifferent to the needs of those who provided him with a living.

The riots reduced the opening night's performance of *Macbeth* to near farce, since few could hear what Kemble and Mrs Siddons were saying. They ploughed on, as the expression goes, acting to a sea of angry faces. If they thought they had survived an isolated protest, they were wrong. The demonstrations continued every night, week after week, no doubt becoming more and more a popular substitute for normal theatregoing. No physical violence was aimed at the players, but the protesters were well drilled, arriving with placards, dancing a special O.P. dance, wearing O.P. hats and badges, armed with every variety of gongs, bells, horns and whistles with which to obliterate the unfortunate actors. They could also claim support for their cause in the press, and *The Times* added its own measure of thunder, condemning Kemble's intransigence. Inevitably he soon bore the brunt of the abuse and a smear-campaign directed against him personally was added to the general protest. It became increasingly vicious; his house was attacked and his wife went in fear. When an independent committee failed to convince the public that the increases were justified, Kemble was forced to admit defeat. The old prices were restored, but the battle had cost him dear. He never recovered his lost fortunes and the humiliation he had suffered made his final years in the theatre a misery. He retired an embittered and ailing man, passing on the dubious legacy to his brother Charles, while he quit his homeland to die in Lausanne.

Kemble presents an interesting example of the 'manufactured' actor, a man who never found the key to release all those stored-up talents he undoubtedly possessed. The most closely documented of all the male Kembles, he aroused strongly conflicting emotions amongst his critics and admirers and the result is a maze of contradictions. Leigh Hunt, his most destructive critic, insisted that he was not an actor at all, merely 'a teacher of elocution' which is manifestly unjust, a prime example of those sweeping dismissals few critics can resist from time to time. We know only too well that audiences did not tolerate mediocrity for long, and Kemble held sway for thirty years. During that time he made heroic efforts to overcome his acknowledged deficiencies. A chronic sufferer from asthma, his deliberate enunciation that so many of his detractors commented upon was undoubtedly his method of combating the illness in public. He lacked his sister's genius and suffered from the family comparisons, but he did not merit the scathing comment of the playwright Colman, author of *The Iron Chest* (a sad title in view of Kemble's complaint) who held Kemble solely responsible for the play's initial failure. 'Frogs in a marsh, flies in a bottle, wind in a crevice, a preacher in a field, the drone of a bagpipe, all—all yielded to the inimitable soporific monotony of Mr Kemble!' Against this we can balance Hazlitt, who called him 'the only great and truly impressive actor I remember, who rose to his stately height by the interposition of art and graduations of merit.' If we pick our way through the rubble of criticism that surrounds his career we can, with a keen eye, select those separate pieces which made up the whole man. He had dignity and he had presence: most are agreed on that. Sometimes brave to the point of stupidity, he lacked the imagination of Garrick or Barry (and sometimes bravery stems from a lack of imagination as to the consequences of one's actions) but had few of Barry's conceits, and did not devote so much of his time to social climbing as Garrick. Such success as he did achieve had to come from application and hard work. His range was narrow and to his credit he had the self-honesty to acknowledge this; at the end of his days he said with regret: 'I am only just beginning thoroughly to understand my art.' Turning again to Hazlitt he was at his best 'in the development of some one solitary sentiment or exclusive passion . . . where all the passions move round a central point and are governed by one master key.' In roles such as Cato and Coriolanus, he was unrivalled in his time. 'Intensity' was the world Hazlitt used to illustrate the distinguishing excellence of his acting, and the picture comes to me over the years of a well-meaning man who consistently attempted to give nobility to his life and profession, always seeking to serve an aesthetic ideal, and not always understood by his fellows. If we go back to the riots that accompanied the price increases, it could well be that what kept him from the heights was his inability to communicate on a popular level. There have been many lesser talents who succeeded where he failed simply because they had that quality—which defies intellectual analysis—traditionally known as 'the common touch'.

One of the saddest aspects of the theatre is the spectacle of a great artist compelled by either pride or necessity to continue beyond his prime. It is a fate, alas, that many have experienced. Crabb Robinson records towards the end Mrs Siddons' 'voice appeared to have lost its brilliancy (like a beautiful face through a veil)'. He was writing of her performance in *The Gamester* on April 21, 1812. The following month he made another entry in his diary: 'in the expression of plaintive sorrow and in pathos her voice has lost its power. And she labours.' Then in June, at a performance of *Comus* at Covent Garden: '. . . for the first time in my life I saw Mrs Siddons without any pleasure. She was dressed most unbecomingly with a low gypsy hat and feathers hanging down one side—She looked old and I had almost said ugly—her fine features were lost in the distance. And her disadvantage of years and bulk made as prominent as possible.'

It makes painful reading. And so, as the awesome talents of Edmund Kean make their appearance, so yesterday's giants exit into the wings. The 'disadvantage of years' finally take their toll. As for poor Kemble, he was forced to dispose of his beloved library and, eventually, to take himself off to die in Lausanne. Even those who mourned his passing were quick to shift allegiance. The little man with the Italian face and the fatal eye was waiting impatiently for his first entrance and was not to be denied his chance to shatter old reputations and launch new legends.

[[9]]

KEAN . . .
THE THUNDER'S ROLL

London, January 26th, 1814.

IT is the perfect setting for the opening of a novel by Dickens. The city is shrouded in snow and fog. We pick out the figure of a young man leaving his squalid lodgings in Cecil Street and making his way through the slush in the direction of Covent Garden. He wears a second-hand great coat with many capes to conceal his shabby attire; had he the money he would wear mourning, for his beloved eldest son has recently died from malnutrition, aged five. He carries with him a small bundle—a few stage properties bound in a poor handkerchief. When he arrives at the stage door of Drury Lane theatre he is admitted, somewhat surprisingly, and makes his way to a dressing room shared with two or three other actors. They ignore him. He takes his place at a dressing table and from the knotted handkerchief he produced a black wig, which he shakes and begins to fit on his head. Still none of the others speak to him. To them it is just another night; because of the weather there is a thin house out front, less than a sixth full. They have no great enthusiasm for the performance of *The Merchant of Venice* they will shortly give. From time to time they exchange condescending looks. Their new companion, a provincial actor recently arrived from Exeter, engaged for want of anybody better, has already chafed them at the scant rehearsals and now they have no time for him. To them he is like the weather—something to be endured and then forgotten as soon as possible.

The young man completes his make-up and dons a black gabardine, then leaves the dressing room to take up his position in the wings. He is beyond nerves. Rae, the stage manager of the Lane, who has pretensions to be a leading man himself, is also in the wings, dressed to play the role of Bassanio. As with other members of the company he has nothing but contempt for this provincial nobody.

The play begins to a house as cold as the streets outside. The two players await their cue. There is no exchange between them, no polite expressions of good luck—even insincerity is denied the young actor. He listens, the cue comes, and he makes his first entrance.

On stage he leans over his crutched stick, using both hands and when he judges the moment right he turns to fix Bassanio with his restless eyes. Beyond the gutting candles of the footlights the sparse audience is prepared to be indifferent, though the first glimpse of the new man has aroused some comment. Shylock in a black wig, neat and tidy? What is this?

'Three thousand ducats?'

Then a pause, longer than they are accustomed to. The Jew seems to gather his thoughts, drawing out the next word as though he as suddenly chanced upon the solution to a problem . . . 'Well?' . . . And Rae, his fellow actor, who came prepared to walk through a performance, feels the first touch of steel. He gives his response.

'Aye, sir, for three months.'

And Shylock ponders this, stretching his next reply, giving added weight to the repetition of the word 'well' which ends his first three speeches. There is a smouldering humour in his voice, a feeling that at any moment fierce and long-stored resentments will explode. The young actor draws on long years of deprivation as he shapes his characterisation; he has everything to lose and therefore he fears nothing or nobody. His fellow actors may ignore him off stage but in front of the audience they must fight him for professional survival. He is possessed and he colours the Jew's search for revenge with his own experience. And the house rises to him; by the time he has played the first scene the alchemy has taken hold. They are no longer indifferent. They have caught the edge in his voice and seen the flash in his eye. For the first time they have been in the presence of Edmund Kean.

Yes, it is pure Dickens, something larger than life and with all the off-stage trappings.

He did not need to study long to play the outcast, it is a role he had been familiar with from birth. Some said he was the bastard son of the Duke of Norfolk,* others that he was the illegitimate son of 'Nance' Carey and Aaron Kean, a tailor. Or was it Edmund Kean, a builder, or his brother Moses Kean? The birth took place in an 'unoccupied chamber' or Gray's Inn; or possibly some hovel in Castle Street, Leicester Square. Then again, it could have been a garret in Ewer Street, there are many locations to choose from, and he seems to have had a narrow escape from being born in the streets. Whatever the truth his mother's pitiless neglect of him can be said to have begun before his birth.

She farmed him out at an early age to a poor actress called Miss Tidswell (pure Dickens

---

* 'I was born in the year 1787, and if anybody asks you who was my mother, say Miss Tidswell, the actress; my father was the late Duke of Norfolk, whom they called *Jockey*. I am not the son of Moses Kean, the mimic, nor of his brother, as some people are pleased to assert, though I bear the same name. I had the honour of being brought up at Arundel Castle till I was seven years old, and there they sometimes, I do not know why, called me Duncan! After I quitted Arundel Castle, I was soon put upon the stage by my mother. The very first part in which I appeared was the Robber's Boy in *The Iron Chest*, when it was originally brought out at Drury Lane in 1796 . . . I was at Arundel Castle a few years ago, and, as I showed to the people who had charge of it, I knew every room, passage, winding and turning in it. In one of the large apartments hung a portrait of the old Duke of Norfolk and the man who was with me said, "You are very like the old Duke, sir". And well he might. I am his son!'

This is said to have been taken down from Kean's words by a gentleman who showed it to Payne Collier. Kean named his first boy, the one who died just before his debut as Shylock, *Howard*, which was supposed to have been in support of the Norfolk legend. Whereas it is always possible that he was the bastard son of the Duke (though in which case it would appear that the Duke consorted with near-whores) the childhood spent in Arundel Castle does not stand up to scrutiny. Kean was at some pains to throw dust in his biographers' eyes. The twenty-seven years he spent in obscurity before triumphing at Drury Lane bit into his soul and he deliberately cloaked his origins in mystery.

in name and character) who lodged in Vinegar-yard, Drury Lane. He called his surrogate mother 'Aunt Tid' and his real mother disappeared to resume her Hogarthian progress to a drunkard's grave. The only love, charity and schooling he received came from 'Aunt Tid', but even she could not tame him. He was dragooned into work 'almost before he could well walk' and appeared as Cupid in one of Noverre's ballets at the Opera House when he was barely three years old. At seven he was an imp dancing with others round the witches' cauldron in Kemble's *Macbeth* and was dismissed for bad behaviour. It would appear that he suffered from that common complaint of the neglected, starved child—rickets, since several of his early biographers mention his legs being in 'irons'. This is not easy to reconcile with other accounts of his childhood which tell of him dancing and tumbling at fairs and in taverns, but what seems certain is that he only survived by his wits and realised that he could best earn his crusts as an entertainer. Perhaps this was a heritage from one of his alleged 'fathers', Moses Kean, an orator and mimic.

Again legend has it that at this point the plot takes another Dickensian twist. 'Nance' Carey is supposed to have returned and claimed him once word got out that he had proved a breadwinner. She forced him to accompany her as a strolling player, according to Doran: 'she is a vagabond still; tramps the country with pomatums, and perfumes, and falbalas, and her son is her pack-horse—and the bird, to boot, that shall lay golden eggs for her.' Even the kindly figure of 'Aunt Tid' seems to have had a darker side to her moon, for some sources have it that she was Moses Kean's mistress. Eventually Edmund escaped his mother's clutches and possibly went to sea for a time, hired as a cabin boy on a collier plying between England and Madeira. Edward Stirling's *Old Drury Lane*, a pot-pourri of anecdotes published in 1881, states that his naval career was short-lived and that 'for a time a vague report was in circulation that some considerate gentleman, struck by his abilities, had sent him to Eton' but there is nothing to support this, unless he was enrolled under a false name. A lady called Mrs Clarke then took him into her care (according to Stirling). 'In her house his wild erratic temperament received a check for the first time in his life. Education dawned upon him, he saw and profited by the chance from want to opulence, from coarseness to refinement.' I have been unable to ascertain the truth of this, but what does seem certain is that by 1801 he was being billed as 'The Celebrated Theatrical Child' and that in 1802, when he would have been in his middle teens, assuming his date of birth was 1787, he gave a programme of recitations at Covent Garden appearing as 'the celebrated Master Carey'. By 1804 he was on the treadmill of the provincial circuit, starting in Sheerness and visiting such towns as Durham, Shields and Sunderland. We can also trace him to Garrick's home town, Lichfield and to Cheltenham, where some say he met and married a young actress called Mary Chambers. Doran has them meeting in Gloucester, and others give the place as Sunderland. They were married at Gloucester in 1808; the bride and her sister Susan, who witnessed the ceremony, both signing their names as Chambres. The wedding over, they were fired* and resumed their

* Beverley, the manager of the company, is said to have told Kean: 'You know I like you but my rules must not be broken. Married folks are not attractive in a playbill. Single men draw single lassies; single women, if pretty, turn the heads of all the young fellows. You must go; a fortnight's notice. Good-day.'

touring. Their first son, the ill-fated Howard, was born in Swansea the following year.

'A hard coming they had of it', in the words of Eliot's poem,* for Kean's journey to London took many years, and by the time he arrived he had sown the seeds of his own eventual destruction. When he and his family left Beverley's company they obtained an engagement in Birmingham at a guinea a week to each of them, but when that ended they were reduced to walking from Birmingham to Swansea, some two hundred miles. Swansea did not take to him and they were forced to try their luck in Ireland, joining a company in Waterford. We have an account of his performance in Hannah More's tragedy *Percy*, in which he played the hero and his wife took the role of Edwina and 'was applauded to her heart's content'. After the play Kean apparently gave an exhibition of tight-rope dancing and then sparred with a professional pugilist, topped that with a musical interlude, 'and finished with Chimpanzee, the monkey, in the melo-dramatic pantomime of La Perouse, and in this *character* he showed agility scarcely since surpassed by Mazurier or Gouffe, and touches of deep tragedy in the monkey's death scene, which made the audience shed tears.'** It was an age when the strolling player had to resort to all manner of things to attract and hold his audiences, and quite obviously they demanded value for money! It is worth reproducing a long playbill intact to give some indication of the length and variety of a single evening's entertainment.

I have no idea how long such a programme lasted, but it is certainly a good half crown's worth and gives us a startling glimpse of an actor's lot. As can be seen the material was mostly second-rate and it must have been particularly humiliating for an actor of Kean's stature to be condemned to this galley-slave existence in the provinces. He thirsted for London and proper recognition, and when that thirst was not satisfied he quenched his frustration in alcohol.

A second son was born in Waterford, then they once again took to the road. We find traces of them in Dumfries where Kean was forced to give an 'entertainment' at a tavern in return for food and shelter. Mrs Kean prayed for death to release her and the two small children for the purgatory of their lives. Yet through it all Kean never lost sight of his own unique talents. He must have been possessed of an incredible will to have survived such years of deprivation, to have soldiered on in the most degrading circumstances, denied the recognition he so obviously deserved. There is no other instance in our theatrical history of such a giant being treated with such indifference for so long. It is small wonder that when he did reach London and triumph there he brought with him a rage to live the remainder of his life at full tilt.

It was in Exeter that he was finally 'discovered'. Seen by a gentleman with the coincidental name of Dr Drury who reported back to the Drury Lane Committee in favourable terms, Kean expected to be signed on the spot, but this did not happen; even at this late stage there was no instant, fairy-tale ending. His first son, Howard, died before

---

* *The Journey of the Magi*
** Grattan

UNDER PATRONAGE

Ball Room, Minster-yard, York

Thursday evening, October—1811

MR KEAN

(late of the Theatres Royal, Haymarket and Edinburgh, and author of 'The Cottage Foundling, or Robbers of Ancona', now preparing for immediate representation at the Theatre Lyceum), and

MRS KEAN

(late of the Theatres Cheltenham and Birmingham), respectfully inform the inhabitants of York and its vicinity, that they will stop

FOR ONE NIGHT ONLY

on their way to London; and present such entertainments that have never failed of giving satisfaction, humbly requesting the support of the public.

Part First

Scenes from the celebrated comedy of

'THE HONEY MOON;
or
HOW TO RULE A WIFE.'

DUKE ARANZA   Mr. Kean.
JULIANA   Mrs. Kean.

Favourite comic song, 'Beggars and Ballad Singers,' in which Mr. Kean will display his powers of mimicry in the well-known characters of London beggars.

IMITATIONS

of the London Performers, viz.: Kemble, Cooke, Braham, Incledon, Munden, Fawcett and The Young Roscius.

Part Second

The African Slave's appeal to Liberty!!! Scenes from the laughable farce,

'THE WATERMAN;
or
THE FIRST OF AUGUST.'

TOM TUG (with the song, 'Did you not hear of a Jolly Young Waterman,' and the pathetic ballad of 'Then Farewell my trim-built Wherry'),
                                    Mr. Kean.

MISS WILHELMINA   Mrs. Kean.

After which, Mr. Kean will sing in character, George Alexander Stevens's description of a

STORM.

Part Third

Scenes from the popular Drama of

'THE CASTLE SPECTRE'

EARL OSMOND   Mr. Kean.
ANGELA   Mrs. Kean.

Favourite comic song of 'The Cosmetic Doctor;' to conclude with the laughable farce of

'SYLVESTER DAGGERWOOD;
or
THE DUNSTABLE ACTOR.'

FEMALE AUTHOR   Mrs. Kean.
SYLVESTER DAGGERWOOD Mr. Kean.

(In which he will read the celebrated playbill, written by G. Colman, Esq., and sing the 'Four-and-twenty Puppet-shows,' originally sung by him at the Theatre Royal, Haymarket).

Each character to be personated in their appropriate dresses, made by the principal theatrical dressmakers of London, viz., Brooks and Heath, Martin, etc.

Front Seats, 2s 6d; Back Seats, 1s. Doors to be open at six, and begin at seven, precisely.
Tickets to be had at the Printer's.

negotiations were concluded and they made the journey to London at the end of the year 1813 to take the cheapest lodgings they could find in Cecil Street. Kean did the only thing left to him. He went and stood in the hall at Drury Lane day after day waiting to be given an audition. Doran states that 'Rae, handsome and a fool, affected not to know him, though they had played together . . . Arnold* treated him superciliously, with a *'young man!'*—when he condescended to address Kean. Other new actors obtained trial parts, but there was none for that chafed, hungry, restless little man in the capes. Even drunken Tokely, like himself, from Exeter, could obtain a "first appearance", but Kean was put off.'

The fortunes of Drury Lane at that time were at a low ebb. They could be revived only by a genius, and the genius was there, waiting in the hall, ignored by all. He saw others like Stephen Kemble attempt Shylock and fail. Then a Mr Huddart, from Dublin, was given his chance, went on as Shylock and was never heard of again.

Finally, and in a manner designed to remind him of the wretchedness of his position, the Committee offered Kean Richard III. And it was then that Kean showed his true mettle. He refused their offer. He would play Shylock, or nothing. Most actors in his position would have accepted anything, even a walk-on. Not Kean. He had waited too long and they had misjudged his character as much as they had misjudged his talents. He persisted and they capitulated.

Apparently he was given one rehearsal only. His conception of the role offended the regulars and scared the management.

'Sir! this will never do', the acting manager, Raymond, told him. 'It is quite an innovation and cannot be permitted.'

'I wish it to be so', Kean replied, and again he carried the day.

After the rehearsal which took place on the day of the first performance, he allowed himself the luxury of a square meal, and then he went back to the theatre and put on the black wig to claim his rightful place in history. The years of obscurity were over.

Contemporary accounts tell us that before the end of that first performance news of this provincial thunderbolt travelled across the piazza to the rival theatre; actors and spectators hurried through the fog and snow from Covent Garden to the Lane to catch the last act and join in the general acclamation. He had entered the theatre that night as an unknown; he left it as a legend.

Hazlitt was the first to recognise Kean in print, writing as the dramatic critic of the *Morning Chronicle*, and was well in advance of his colleagues. The collective verdict was withheld until Kean gave his Richard III some two weeks later, by which time the town was ablaze with talk of his extraordinary mastery. Byron paid his homage and Hazlitt, in a second adulatory piece, pronounced that Kean had 'destroyed the Kemble "religion" '. How Kean must have savoured those first weeks of triumph. Those who had previously ignored him, now fawned. Arnold, the stage manager, brought him negus—hot sweetened wine and water—where previously he had proffered vinegar. They called him 'sir' and upped his salary. He was not taken in by their sudden changes of heart, he knew that he alone had saved the theatre from ruin, and he did not forgive them. There is a

* One of the stage managers

EDMUND KEAN as Richard III

pleasing, if apocryphal story, that he returned home to his wife and child to make the prediction: 'Mary, you shall ride in your carriage yet and Charley shall go to Eton!' One hopes that the story is true.

Status in the theatre was very important, and the divisions sharply defined. For instance, only actors in receipt of ten pounds a week or more were permitted to use the First green room. Those lower in the pecking order were relegated to the Second room. When Kean 'arrived' he naturally claimed the privilege of the upper chamber. An old strolling companion, an actor called Hughes who was receiving three pounds a week was refused admission to the First room and this enraged Kean. He sent for Rae and insisted that his old friend be allowed to join him. Rae would not yield, whereupon Kean played his trump card: 'Very well, then it'll be Richard without Gloster tonight.' There was no adequate answer to that, and Kean had his way.

If he remembered old friends in this way, he also found he had plenty of new ones who appeared out of the woodwork 'as they are wont to do where there is an opportunity of basking in pleasant sunshine, imparted by genius'.* One of these visitors proved to be his mother, who claimed more than sunshine. She exacted £50 a year from her now affluent son and introduced him to a Henry Darnley who addressed Kean as 'dear brother'.

* Doran

Having brought down Kemble's temple by surpassing the memory of Macklin in the role of Shylock, and having shown himself the worthy successor of Garrick as Richard III, he enjoyed 'the honeymoon of criticism' when to the majority he could do no wrong, and enlarged his repertoire with Hamlet, Othello *and* Iago (alternating with Pope and Sowerby). Garrick's widow came to see him as Hamlet and was most generous in her praise, although she did offer some advice as to how he might improve his playing of the closet scene. 'More sternness', she suggested then, being an actor's wife, probably thought that she had been presumptuous; she sent him fruit from Hampton and presented him with Garrick's stage jewels.

During this first season he played Shylock fifteen times, Richard twenty-five, Hamlet, eight, Othello ten and Iago four. Prior to his arrival Drury Lane had been sliding towards bankruptcy with one hundred and thirty-nine nights of continual loss: this Kean reversed into a profit of some £20,000.

After an understandable show of reluctance, Kemble was at last persuaded to view this commanding rival and occupied a box for one of the performances of Othello. When asked by a friend: 'Did you see the little man, Kean?' Kemble replied, 'No, sir, I did not see Mr Kean. I saw Othello; and further I shall never act the part again.' Poor Kemble attempted to stand his ground, but Kean had youth as well as a new acting style on his side and the contest was one-sided. When Kean eventually played Sir Giles Overreach, a role Kemble felt he had a prior claim to, he was unwisely tempted to play it in competition. Once again Kean took the honours, Kemble being hissed for his efforts. What Kean was doing in the sudden joy of his liberation was to sweep away 'the usual solemn pedantry of the stage'. Byron summed him up as 'truth without exaggeration' and regretted that he (Byron) did not have the talent for the drama, 'else I would write a tragedy now'. Kean played Shakespeare in the Byronic manner, the theatrical incarnation of the poet's radical and romantic vision. 'He burst forth with the fury of the thunderstorm', wrote John Cole, 'making everything give way to his tremendous touches'. We are told that 'the greatest asset of Kean was that he had some tremendous physical presence, some great animal magnetism that could connect with the audience even before he had spoken. He had no purity of style, he depended upon certain 'points' and would hurry through a scene to get to one of them, to one of his 'shocks'. For example he would go right through the First Act of *Othello*, right through the Second, Just getting towards the Third—the great scenes with Iago and Desdemona. Up to then his acting would have been patchy, hurried; he was getting to his 'points'. As Hazlitt said, 'You cannot say that Kean has a style. You can only judge his performance by the number of electrical shocks in it.'

'Some people towards the end of his career would go to the theatre to laugh at him. They would count the number of steps he took before he spoke. He would deliver the speech and then the audience would go '2, 3, 4, 5, 6,' . . . . Kean would stop and then deliver the speech. I am talking now of the time when he had become a picturesque ruin. People went to mock, a horrifying thing for so great an artist. But the whole of Drury Lane would be packed with people who had merely come to jeer. Kean half-drunk, his memory half-gone, tottering, with a big pot-belly and the spindly legs of the alcoholic, would come on and go through one of his great masterpieces . . . To be laughed at, perhaps, but the masterpiece never altered and the great electrical shocks still came.'*

We owe our most detailed and intimate glimpses of Kean to the industry of a New York merchant, James Henry Hackett. He was born in the year 1800 and survived to 1871. A gifted amateur actor and mimic, he was celebrated for a remarkably faithful imitation of Kean as Richard III, once giving himself a benefit during which he performed the entire play in the manner of Kean! A newspaper report of this event stated that he achieved 'a success which exceeded even the anticipation of his friends. He had evidently studied the peculiarities of Kean with great closeness of observation'.

Just how closely was later revealed when he made a bequest (which eventually found its way to the Victoria and Albert Museum in the Enthoven Collection) of a copy of Oxberry's edition of *Richard III*, published in Boston in 1822. Inside Hackett's copy was a comment in his own hand: 'I have noted all of the *business* and *readings* of Mr Kean in this play, during at least a dozen of his performances of Richard.' It was mostly Cibber's text with later additions by Kemble, subsequently done over yet again by Kean himself. A facsimile was published in London by the Society for Theatre Research in 1959 and I have used a copy of this from Dame Edith Evans' library for my own research. It is a fascinating document of the greatest interest to any student of acting and I will quote two passages to give an indication of its uniqueness.

* Raymund FitzSimons

The first is Hackett's description of Richard's entrance (given as Act I, Scene II in this version) prior to the 'Now is the winter of our discontent' soliloquy:

> *Gloster enters hastily—head low—arms*
> *folded. At the words 'ocean buried' unfolds*
> *his arms and walks the stage till 'And now'*
> *(grins and frets) 'But I' (stands and pulls*
> *on his gauntlet tighter and keeps the centre*
> *writhing his body R and L and using his right*
> *hand. 'Deformed' (vehement—plays with his*
> *sword belt—starts and X's L) 'Then since'*
> *starts up—'Why then'—swings his right arm*
> *'This mis-shapen trunk'—strikes his breast*
> *3 times and points to his forehead—'be*
> *circled'—pauses—chuckles and X's toward*
> *R.H. (exit hastily).*

From this first entrance to the last scene when he fights Richmond to the death:

> *fights furiously back and forth—in*
> *turning loses balance, falls on his knee*
> *& fights up—in turning receives Richmond's*
> *thrust—lunges at him feebly after it—*
> *clinching is shoved from him—staggers—*
> *drops the sword—grasps blindly at him—*
> *staggers backwards and falls—head to R.H.*
> *turns upon right side—writhing rests on*
> *his hands—gnashes his teeth at him (L.H.)*
> *as he utters his last words—blinks and*
> *expires rolling on his back.*

The death scene was one of Kean's great 'points' and my mind flashes forward to this century and Olivier's interpretation; developed during his stage performance it was brought to perfection in his filmed version, and there can be few of his admirers who will ever forget the overhead shot of Richard writhing like some black reptile, clawing at the earth and grass as he died. It is transparently clear from the many accounts which have come down to us that Kean excelled in this scene. Hazlitt describes it thus: 'He at first held out his hands in a way which can only be conceived by those who saw him—in motionless despair—or as if there were some preternatural power in the mere manifestation of his will: he now actually fights with his double fists, after his sword is taken from him, like some helpless infant.' Echoing Hackett's observations, Brougham tells us that Kean 'continued pushing with his hand after he had received his wounds' and Phippen also makes note of this: 'When the loss of blood had exhausted almost every faculty, and while yet his eyes were glaring in all the horrors of unexpected death, he dropped the sword, and, in staggering to the ground, made many pushes with his half-lifted arm, meditating revenge in the last agonies of death.'

Amateur detectives will observe that there are minor variations in all these accounts, for no stage fight or fall can be duplicated exactly night after night, and in Kean's case he was often fighting with different Richmonds, both here and in America.

When he went on tour he would send his manager in advance with instructions to tell the rest of the cast to give Mr Kean good clearance in all directions, and it would not be unusual for Kean to meet the actors for the first time during the performance and without benefit of any prior rehearsals. He was not a great believer in ensemble playing; he was the star, he was what the audience had paid to see, and he wasn't going to be upstaged by anybody. Describing a performance of *Richard III* given in Bath in 1815, Genest is critical of Kean's technique. 'Richard was Kean's best part—but he overdid his death—he came up close to Richmond, after he had lost his sword, as if he would have attacked him with his fists—Richmond, to please Kean, was obliged to stand like a fool, with a drawn sword in his hand, and without daring to use it.'

The long years Kean spent in the wilderness undoubtedly affected his attitude towards managements and audiences. He was one of the damned who once said of himself that success would drive him mad. Drink, rather than success hastened his descent into near-madness, but even towards the end of his career when only sacred and profane fragments of his former self remained, he still exercised a profound control over his audiences. The sight of a once great performer blurred by alcohol is something that evokes pity rather than contempt. I can think of many careers that have been blighted from want of timely recognition: when it comes—if it comes at all—the pressures are often too great. I have acted with drunks and it is an unnerving experience, yet in certain cases I can bear personal witness to the fact that, unable to stand off-stage, they are yet able to dredge up credible—sometimes incredible—performances from a mixture of technique and instinct. They provoke legendary stories* and achieve, after death, a different kind of fame, admiration coloured by regret for what might have been. In attempting to bring Kean back to life for modern readers I can only liken him to the noise of a distant storm, a

---

* Anecdotes about Kean abound, though many are difficult to trace back to their source. One of the most popular is that he required sexual stimulation before a performance, and on one occasion is reputed to have satisfied three whores in his dressing room before going on as Richard III. There seems to be some truth to this; an entry in James Winston's Drury Lane Diary for August 16th 1820 states, 'The play (*Venice Preserved*) waited a few minutes at the commencement for Kean. His reply was, "I always take a shag before the play begins".' 'Shag' is of course slang for copulation.

Again from Winston's Diary: 'March 16th 1825. Kean, about three o'clock in the morning, ordered a hackney coach to his door, took a lighted candle, got in, and rode off. He was not heard of till the Thursday noon when they found him in his room at the theatre fast asleep wrapt in a large white greatcoat. He then sent for a potence, some ginger, etc, and said, 'Send me Lewis or the other woman. I must have a fuck, and then I shall do it." He had it. They let him sleep until about six, when they awoke him, dressed him, and he acted but was not very sober. After the play we got to supper at Sigel's lodgings and got him to a bedroom and locked him up till the morning.'

'August 6th 1825. Kean came to the theatre this morning at six o'clock with two women. He forced his way by the watchman and firemen, etc., and remained with the women till one o'clock when Dunn and Winston sent word that the women must leave the theatre. They did, and Kean came to Dunn soon after, was very abusive on the subject, said the town would call him a great blackguard and he gloried in being one.'

storm that will never reach us, but which we hear from afar and respect. There is a couplet on Byron by Matthew Arnold which seems to fit Kean equally well:

He taught us little,
But our soul had felt him, like the thunder's roll.

In many ways Kean inhibited the development of our acting tradition. He was too big, outside all schools, acting out his private fantasies until in the end he destroyed himself. His death was fittingly dramatic. He was playing Othello with his son Charles as Iago on March 25th 1833. The setting was Covent Garden, not the Lane where he had first taken London by the throat. Genius was no longer traceable in his bloated face; the intellect was all but quenched in those once matchless eyes; all nerve ends were exposed. He got as far as 'Villain, be sure thou prove my love a whore . . .' when he fell into his son's arms and cried: 'Oh, God! I am dying . . . speak to them for me'. He was carried off stage for the last time and died on May 15th, aged forty-three or thereabouts. It was said of him that he was a man 'trained upon blows, curses, starvation and the charity of strangers' but he used those mixed blessings and scourges to transform life into art, reaching out into the ugliness of the world for vagrant beauty.

‖ 10 ‖

MORAL, GRAVE,
SUBLIME MACREADY

I T is perhaps a sad reflection on human nature that the renegade is often more cherished than the reformer. Dissipated genius, talents squandered, beauty ravaged have always held a peculiar and sometimes morbid fascination for succeeding generations. I must immediately confess that in approaching two men as widely different as Kean and William Charles Macready I was already biased in favour of Kean. Now I feel this to have been a mistake. It is 'moral, grave, sublime' Macready who ultimately proved the more rewarding study.

In seeking out the origins of our acting tradition a meteor like Kean flares our judgement, blinding us to the less spectacular but more solid achievements of a Macready. Actors such as Kean do not establish traditions, they demolish them. Those who come after may impersonate them, or attempt to recreate their great set pieces, but imitation without the divine spark is a poor substitute, at best only a reminder of what we have lost. It is on the valley slopes rather than the mountain peaks that traditions are established, just as there are guides and mountaineers. If everybody could scale Everest the challenge would disappear and yet we do not dismiss as of no consequence those who fail in the attempt to reach the very summit. Perhaps Macready did not plant a flag in that rarefied air at the very top, for that requires a special kind of madness that was missing from his personality; but he climbed steadily and always with courage. I find him one of the most fascinating and paradoxical talents ever to grace our stages and I am curious as to why history has treated him so casually.

There have been few leading members of our theatre further removed from the labels 'rogue and vagabond'. Scandal of the kind that sells tickets did not touch him. Contrasted with Kean's profligacy, his cultivated respectability appears plodding; his noted scorn for certain aspects of the profession he led for so many years seems petty when set against Kean's lifelong contempt for convention; his tortured zeal a mere pose when compared to the torture of Kean's whole life. But a little knowledge of Macready is a dangerous thing, leading us away from the truth of the matter. It has been fashionable to suggest that he was dull in both public and private life—a solemn, ungiving man too concerned with personal dignity to be of lasting interest. But a closer look at his life and personality (never better revealed than in his copious journals—often spoken about, as J.C. Trewin remarks, but seldom read) yields a different picture. The portrait that emerges is infinitely more complex than Kean, Kemble or Garrick, but because he did not readily fit into the mould that public and critics felt should yield the typical actor of his day, he was damned by many of his contemporaries and subsequently passed over by the next generation of theatre historians. Posterity has been led to think of him as an interesting failure, taking Hazlitt's word for it that he was never an actor of genius. I am not so convinced. No star performer lasts as long in the public favour as Macready did unless he is gifted with something beyond the ordinary and the award of 'genius'—often so casually bestowed in the critics' honours list—can so easily depend on which night you happen to be there.

I find it hard to damn with such faint praise a man who did so much to enhance his profession. The plea cannot be entered that the evidence is too flimsy to form an opinion one way or the other. His journals, which in their original state ran to well over half a million words, tell us more about the workings of an actor's mind than we could hope to glean from a dozen more erudite works. They have fire and life in them, they are frank, they are written from a frequently troubled heart, and they could not have been written by anybody other than a great actor. When they first came to light they were accounted too frank for comfort by his friends and descendants: heavily expurgated soon after his death by one of those well-meaning people who are the bane of historians, the original manuscript was eventually destroyed by Macready's only child by his second marriage, General the Rt. Hon. Sir Nevil Macready, Bart., at the outbreak of the first world war. An edition had been published in 1912 but from that date until 1967 the Journals were out of print and virtually unobtainable. It was left to Macready's fervent champion and distinguished biographer, J. C. Trewin, to redress the balance. Mr Trewin annotated and abridged the voluminous materials and included for the first time some 67 pages that had somehow escaped the General's carnage.

If Macready were a fictional character we could believe that he had been created by a team of novelists, each one passing him over like the baton in a relay race. He was forbidding, he was loving; he was full of spite, he was full of compassion; he had a monstrous temper inherited from his Irish father, he was brave and humble: such an inconsistent character would infuriate the novel reader. Whatever image he allowed to be presented in public, it was the mirror he held up to himself, the self-portrait he so meticulously worked on in his nightly prose stint, that gives us the real man. 'I do not feel myself at all satisfied with myself; *I cannot reach in execution the standard of my own conception.*' The italics are his own. It was this double agonising that makes him so fascinating—a man who could write of his bitterness at the ties which bound him to his profession ('I curse the hour it was suggested to me') and yet spent most of his working life striving to reach perfection in the very art he affected to despise. Few actors can have had less conceit: if he flayed members of his companies for their inadequacies, he scourged himself without mercy. Time and time again he returned home from the theatre and judged himself wanting. 'Acted in a very mediocre manner.' 'In the soliloquy after Iago's exit I in some degree asserted myself, and though not up to my own expectations . . . carried the house with me. From that point I should say the performance averaged good, but was not in any, except in that one outbreak, great.' 'I have not freedom enough to satisfy myself.' Yet these are not the entries of a failed man. When I carefully checked the diary dates against contemporary accounts, more often than not I found that performances Macready so savagely criticised had been well received. Applause meant little to him if he fell below his own standards; he was never lulled into complacency by public acclaim, and he had had enough of that to satisfy the average actor. So why is his reputation such as to suggest nothing more than a workmanlike but uninspired performer? The expression 'doing a Macready' has come down through the years to denote an actor given to ponderous pauses, and within the profession many have accepted this catch-phrase as the all-purpose verdict of the man. He paused, therefore he was dull. He was dull, therefore he could not have been a great force in the theatre. He was not a great force, therefore he was of little account. It is a depressing and unjust piece of logic.

Without wishing to over-state my case in his defence, I find Macready an endearing character whereas Kean, I am sure, was a monster for most of the time. If we trace Macready's career we find that having been born into the profession he should, by all tradition, have succumbed to the lure without protest. His father was a spasmodically successful actor-manager, and his mother a competent actress. He was the fifth of their eight children and the eldest surviving son, being born on 3 March 1793. By the time he was five years old his father had wisely relinquished his serviceable obscurity as a 'walking gentleman' at Covent Garden (a polite way of describing a small part actor) and young William moved with his family to the Midlands. There his father managed a small circuit of theatres centred in Birmingham. His parents made no attempt to force him into the profession. Having finally gained a measure of respectability his father had aspirations for his eldest son to go to Rugby, with an eye for the Church or the Bar. William did not quarrel with the decision. He went to Rugby, but Macready Snr proved as poor a businessman as he had been an actor and by the time William was fifteen his father had been forced into hiding to avoid a debtor's fate in gaol. William's schooling was brought to an abrupt end; he returned home to try and save the situation. His mother had died five years previously and as the eldest son he shouldered the responsibility with that solemn application that characterised the rest of his life. When his father was apprehended and taken to Lancaster prison, William pawned his watch and took over the management of his father's company, then playing at Newcastle. The courage required for such an unasked-for and unenviable task does not suggest he was lacking in personality. He cleared his father's outstanding debts, kept the company afloat and took the decision to become an actor himself—not, I suspect, from any sudden sense of vocation but because it was the most obvious way of saving another salary. He gave himself fencing lessons and set about learning by heart a number of suitable juvenile roles. Whereupon his father, released from prison, assumed command again and moved the company back to Birmingham. It was here on June 7 1810 that the young Macready made his acting debut, appearing anonymously as Romeo. From all accounts he acquitted himself was some flair and the experience, while not turning his head, committed him for life.

Perhaps in accepting his fate, in swallowing the disappointment he undoubtedly felt at having his education terminated so suddenly, he sublimated too much of his true personality. Perhaps for the rest of his working life (and he retired without regret as soon as he judged himself financially secure) he could never come to terms with himself. As Richard Findlater puts it: 'he could not escape his nature',but at the same time he remained pathologically ashamed of being an actor. 'I would rather see one of my children dead than on the stage'—and this not the utterance of a failure, but from a man who was by then at the head of his profession. He began at the top, for nobody can quarrel with being given the role of Romeo for a debut—and he was a stranger to the poverty and deprivation such as Kean had to endure before his just recognition. With the example of his father's penury before him Macready made sure that he never found himself in the same position. If the decision to become an actor had been forced upon him, he wasted no time in self-pity, but immediately applied himself to becoming a star actor, an innovator not a copier, despite the fact that his father first insisted that he model himself on the style of Macklin. 'In after life', Macready wrote, 'I had the difficult task of unlearning much that was impressed on me in my boyish ways'.

He applied himself to the task with near-religious fervour, coming closer to the early saints rather than Macklin: we are told that he would immobilize himself with bandages while rehearsing the most violent speeches from Lear, Macbeth and Othello. He was soon leading his father's company, though often in passionate opposition to his parent. From the very beginning he drove himself hard and to the end of his days was a martinet at rehearsals, scathing in his distaste for the lazy habits of some of his fellow players. They called him 'Sergeant' Macready behind his back and we have many eye-witness accounts of this brooding, baffled figure lashing out at those who fell below his minimum standards of behaviour and performance. He often terrified his colleagues on stage: the sword fight with Macready's Macbeth was always a hazard for his opponent; Fanny Kemble trembled when she played Desdemona to his Othello—'I quail at the idea of his laying hold of me in those terrible passionate scenes.' Here was a man who constantly had to hold himself in check, admonishing himself in his diary entries whenever that inner rage bubbled to the surface. Infuriated beyond endurance by Alfred Bunn the manager of Drury Lane, he knocked him down, was sued and paid £150 in damages for his loss of control. A big enough man to make a public apology, he confided to his diary: 'I can never never during my life, forgive myself.'

'Study, study, study', was Mrs Siddons' advice to him when, as a mere youth, he played opposite her at Newcastle during her farewell tour. 'Keep your mind on your art and do not marry until you are thirty.' He followed her instructions to the letter, did not marry until he was thirty-one and to the end of his career never ceased in his efforts to uncover the true meanings of the classic scripts. Shakespeare was his god and he was relentless in his efforts to restore the original texts, purging them of the accretions of Cibber, Nahum Tate and others. He sought to impose his reforms on public and players alike, though both were mainly indifferent to such niceties and both resented him for his single-minded zeal. The tasks he set himself often tested him severely; he frequently became physically ill from sheer frustration at the lack of progress. He faced and converted audiences who would have been wholly content with the second rate, happier with slapstick than with perfection. Their tastes were coarse and they were more prepared to give their allegiance to a rake like Robert Elliston than to an idealist such as Macready.

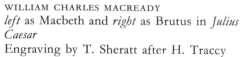

WILLIAM CHARLES MACREADY
left as Macbeth and *right* as Brutus in *Julius Caesar*
Engraving by T. Sheratt after H. Traccy

Perhaps it was Macready's misfortune to arrive on the scene in the most confused period
in our theatrical history with the drama starting the decline which was to last for three
decades. Managers such as Elliston and Bunn may have given the public what it
demanded but could hardly be described as restorers of dignity. Back-stage conditions
were still indescribable and much of the ground gained by Garrick had been lost.
Macready made no secret of his contempt for the majority of his colleagues, describing
them as 'Beasts of Hell'. He had his fair share of these 'miserable wretches' and until he
was able to impose his own disciplines on a resident company it was not unusual for him
to have to act with leading ladies too drunk to stand. In one sweeping fit of spleen he
lumped the whole profession together as 'either utter blackguards or most ignorant
empirics'.

Why then did he persist? He did not relish fame. He fought the 'beasts' back-stage and the 'brutes' in the pit, accepted his triumphs gravely and took his failures stoically. Studying his portraits he seems to have the face of a disillusioned politician, but he had no time for politics, nor did he curry favour in high places. He had few close friends in the profession and in his leisure hours sought the company of literary men such as Dickens, Thackeray (whom physically he somewhat resembled) and Bulwer Lytton. He was never a ladies' man in the traditional sense and certainly had none of Kean's open sensuality or Garrick's romanticism. That is not to say he was immune to the charms of the opposite sex—he made two happy marriages—but business and pleasure were cleanly separated and his first wife, an actress, retired from the stage immediately after their marriage. His many leading ladies may have respected his talents, though as with Fanny Kemble they often went in fear of him during a performance and their relationships ended at the stage door. 'Morosely', J. C. Trewin writes, 'he was the high master of his art; glumly he saved the theatre' and he took a jaundiced view of most things. 'My experience has taught me', he said, 'that whilst the law, the church, the army and navy give a man the rank of gentleman, on the stage that designation must be obtained in society (though the law and the Court decline to recognise it) by the individual bearing. In other callings the profession confers dignity on the initiated, on the stage the player must contribute respect to the exercise of his art. This truth, experienced too late, has given occasion to many moments of depression, many angry swellings of the heart, many painful convictions of the uncertainty of my position.'

A contradictory man, he aroused contradictions in others. Kean applauded his talents but was not too anxious to act with him. Queen Victoria went to many of his performances and was qualified in her praise, though we should not attach too much importance to her dramatic criticism since she reserved most of her accolades for circus performers, in particular a lion-tamer named Van Amburgh, whom she found 'quite beautiful to see, and makes me wish I could do the same'. As George Rowell remarks in his entertaining history *Queen Victoria Goes to the Theatre*: 'The notion of the Queen of England as a lady lion-tamer defies rational thought.' We know that Hazlitt denied Macready genius, Leigh Hunt felt that he seemed 'afraid of the poetry of some of his greatest parts' and the authority of these two literary giants was such that they silenced others who might have sung his praises. Yet G. H. Lewes had no hesitation in calling his Lear 'great' and Hunt and Hazlitt were generous in their opinion of his voice, calling it 'magnificent', 'the finest and most heroical on the stage'.

He became an actor to protect his father's honour; he stayed an actor to protect his own. Patently he did not suffer fools and made many enemies, but nobody denied that he had courage. Nowhere was this better demonstrated than during his American tour, when mobs organised in support of Edwin Forrest—an American star who felt that Macready had been responsible for his (Forrest's) poor reception in England—created a riot in front of the Astor Place Opera House in New York. There had been previous disturbances in Philadelphia, Baltimore and Richmond (where he played Hamlet with a macabre stage prop: 'They gave me the skull, for Yorick's, of a negro who was hung two years ago for cutting down his overseer'). In Cincinnati he again presented his Hamlet, but was dismayed by 'a most disgracefully imperfect Horatio, who had rehearsed on

Saturday and now knew nothing of words or business, one of those wretches who take to the stage as an escape from labour, and for whom the treadmill would be a fitting punishment. Acted . . . to a rather rickety audience, but I tried my utmost, and engaged the attention of at least the greater part of the auditory. In the scene after the play, with Rosencrantz and Guildenstern, an occurrence took place that, for disgusting brutality, indecent outrage, and malevolent barbarism, must be without parallel in the theatre of any civilised community. Whilst speaking to them about 'the pipe', a ruffian from the left side gallery threw into the middle of the stage the half of the raw carcase of a sheep!'

Having survived this outrage Macready next went on to New York to present his Macbeth. Forrest had been following him around the country, leasing theatres in the same towns and presenting identical productions in a deliberate campaign to discredit his rival. Forrest was already in New York at the Broadway Theatre when Macready arrived. He announced his Macbeth for the night of 7 May when Macready was billed to open in the same role at the Astor Place theatre. The pro-Forrest mob was out in force; rotten eggs were thrown at Macready and the tumult was such that he was forced to give most of the play in dumb show. He documented the riot with his usual care for detail: 'Copper cents were thrown, some struck me, four or five eggs, a great many apples, nearly—if not quite—a peck of potatoes, lemons, pieces of wood, a bottle of asafoetida* which splashed my own dress, smelling, of course, most horribly . . . The second act closed in exactly the same way. I dressed for the third and went on; the tumult was the same, the missiles growing thicker. At last a chair was thrown from the gallery on the stage, something heavy was thrown into the orchestra which made the remaining musicians move out.'

Not unreasonably Macready was disinclined to appear again, but a petition signed by forty-seven leading New York citizens, including Washington Irving and Herman Melville, persuaded him to change his mind and on May 10 he went down to the theatre to brave it out. He was relieved to see numbers of New York's finest in evidence both outside and within the theatre. Although his first entrance was greeted enthusiastically by those who had come to support him, the organised rabble soon gained the upper hand again. At the end of the fourth scene the police moved in and cleared the house of the anti-Macready faction. This enraged the far greater mob outside the theatre who began stoning the building.

'The second act passed, the noise and violence increasing, the contest within becoming feebler . . . The banquet scene was partially heard and applauded. I went down to change my dress, the battering at the building, doors and windows growing, like the fiends at the Old Woman of Berkeley's burial, louder and louder. Water was running down fast from the ceiling to the floor of my room . . . the stones hurled in had broken some of the pipes.'

Macready persisted in giving the entire play, refusing pleas from other members of the cast that he should bring it to a close. By the end of the fifth act the house 'was considerably thinned', as well it might have been! Changing in his dressing room, Macready heard a volley of musketry. Outside the Sheriff of New York, having read the Riot Act to the crowd estimated at twenty thousand strong, instructed the General in

* Resinous gum with strong smell of garlic

123

charge of the troops to take his own decision. With the situation out of control and having only seventy men at his disposal, General Hall gave the order for his men to fire over the heads of the crowd. The order was misheard and the soldiers fired straight at the crowd. When the streets were finally cleared there were thirty-one casualties, seventeen of them shot dead.

Macready was secreted out of the theatre and took refuge in a friend's house before leaving at dawn in a carriage to journey to Boston and eventually home to England. The whole incident had a profoundly depressing effect on him, but he displayed remarkable courage throughout, even to the extent of giving a reading in Boston as a token of his gratitude to those who had protected him. But it was the beginning of the end and two years later—on 26 February 1851—with 'not one feeling of regret' he gave his farewell performance at Drury Lane. Perhaps the memory of those fearful nights in New York was still uppermost in his mind, for he chose the role of Macbeth for his exit. We have his word for it that he said to himself, with profound relief: 'I shall never have to do this again'. The stage was behind him forever.

[11]

FROM PHELPS TO IRVING

A few months before Macready awarded himself premature retirement, a twelve year old boy with a pronounced stammer, the son of a travelling salesman, was paying his first visit to the theatre. He had been taken by his father to Sadler's Wells to see Samuel Phelps as Hamlet. Although two years previously he had undergone a religious conversion to the delight and comfort of his devout mother, that first glimpse of Elsinore was to change the course of his life, leading him away from the sacred to what many (first and foremost his mother) still thought of as the profane. The boy's name was John Henry Brodribb. He was later to change it to Henry Irving.

But before tracing the boy's progress it is necessary to pick up a few more threads, and accord Phelps due recognition. He is another somewhat neglected figure in our theatrical history, yet he is the one who bridges the story between Macready and Irving. He was an engaging character who started life as a printer and became, after the customary period of obscurity and poverty that is the characteristic of all but the few, 'an ornament to our calling, an upright man in every sense, both public and private'. My impression is that he had many similarities with Robert Atkins in this century—perhaps not a great actor, but a great fighter, a passionate believer in the theatre of intelligence, prepared to go to any lengths to prove his beliefs. He served his apprenticeship in a rough school and when eventually he made his mark in London Macready first encouraged him and then did his best to destroy him. He was engaged as a leading member of Macready's company at Covent Garden, but his mentor quickly decided he was too much competition—too popular with audiences and critics alike. Poor Phelps was one of those who suffered from Macready's violence on stage: playing Macduff to Macready's Macbeth in 1837, he was forced to defend himself with more realism than had been rehearsed. Macready apologised the following day and confessed that he had drunk too much wine. Phelps took no offence, but nevertheless endured further humiliations at Macready's hands; he was tied to an onerous contract which he could not break and with deliberate malice Macready made sure he was only cast in minor roles. The ploy failed when mounting debts compelled Macready to relinquish his lease of Covent Garden and move over—no longer his own master—to the Haymarket. Webster, the manager of the Haymarket, doubtless aware of the situation, ignored Macready's casting suggestions and employed Phelps as the chief supporting actor. For the opening season he alternated the two men in the roles of Othello and Iago: Phelps proved to be the more acclaimed in both, being

Left SAMUEL PHELPS as Wolsey from the painting by Johnston Forbes-Robertson
Reproduced by courtesy of the Garrick Club

Right Sadler's Wells Theatre, 1852

called the 'most natural' Othello since Edmund Kean by one critic. The experience
brought out the worst in Macready; he sulked and refused to perform either role again,
instead insisted on being allowed to play Shylock, while Phelps was relegated to the
minor role of Antonio. Once again Macready's plot to reassert his previous authority
came to grief. One critic went so far as to say that his Shylock was the worst piece of
acting he had ever seen. Phelps took his revenge in a self-defeating fashion, for we are
told that he walked through his entire performance 'undertaker fashion'. The episode
reflects no credit on either man and is an example of that silliness that sometimes infects
even the greatest of players when their ego is pricked.

I suspect that Macready had little stomach for continuing the feud and perhaps he
already had his eye on that country house in Sherborne to which he longed to go.
Exhausted by his own inner struggle and the long campaign he had waged, almost single-
handed, to bring a semblance of justice and common sense into the theatre, he was
intelligent enough to realise that such a petty squabble as he had engineered with Phelps
was beneath him. He took himself off into the provinces to recoup some lost pride and
make some money.

The tragedy of their relationship is that both of them wanted the same thing and had
they been in partnership rather than rivalry they would have been a formidable pair. The
inherited lunacies of the Bill of 1752 whereby the Lord Chamberlain was empowered to
suppress any challenge to the two patent theatres, Drury Lane and Covent Garden, meant
that the legitimate drama was in peril of collapsing altogether. Licences were only

granted on the strict understanding that the premises were used for pantomime, dancing or musical performances. Those who govern us have always been slow to realise that it is impossible to legislate against sex or the arts. Ways and means are always found to circumvent such ill-advised laws and in the case of the early 18th century theatre the law was quickly made an ass by the simple expedient of a single note struck on a piano at frequent intervals during performances of the classics. Thus the fringe theatres could contend that a Shakespearean tragedy qualified as a musical play or 'burletta' within the meaning of the Act. It was the theatrical equivalent of the massage parlour in sexual terms.

Denied legitimate room for expansion the drama had gone into a steep decline. Talfourd, Byron and Bulwer Lytton provided a few minor romantic works but real inspiration was absent from the scene. As Irving's grandson writes in his definitive biography of his ancestor, 'democracy was surging into the box office; a democracy, as yet boorish and ill-mannered, which demanded entertainment to its abysmally low taste'. I believe that this depressing situation was a further contributing factor to Macready's total disenchantment. He sought to reform the theatre from the inside out, believing that if he could impose his disciplines upon the actors the public would be swift to discern the change and react accordingly. It was a somewhat naive view of the audiences he sought to entertain. Yet he struggled on for many years, lending his considerable authority to Bulwer Lytton's petition for the law to be changed. Lytton was a member of Parliament as well as being a dramatist, and he eventually succeeded in drafting and presenting the Dramatic Performance Bill in 1833. This got through the Commons but was bitterly denounced by the Church and blocked in the Lords. It was another ten years before the Theatrical Regulations Act, removing most of the historical obstacles (though not censorship), became law. The fight continued into the middle of the twentieth century and even to this day legitimate theatrical enterprises can still be thwarted by that anachronism, The Lord's Day Observance Society.

Unfortunately, where the Arts are concerned, the passing of laws does not provide overnight solutions. The theatres now had a greater degree of freedom, but lacked the playwrights to fill them—and to a lesser extent the great star actors to perform there. It was a period of marking time. Many managers, anxious to test the waters, desperate for any novelty that would bring in the crowds, imported plays from France. The English versions were mostly hack translations—a clear example of the third rate being transformed into the fifth rate. Not surprisingly such expedient measures failed to provide any long-term answers.

So at the midway point of the nineteenth century, on the eve of Macready's retirement, and with no natural successor in view, the English theatre was at its lowest ebb for more than two centuries. It had failed to reflect the maelstrom produced by the Industrial Revolution; there seemed to be no dramatists capable of grasping the significance of the vast social changes, or take note of the shifts in population, despite the evidence of their own eyes and the popularity of Dickens' compassionate fiction. The theatre world was sealed off like some artistic ghetto, its occupants aimless and bemused.

It was left to Phelps to make the only positive attempt at a break out. With no great resources to back him, he took over the lease of the near-derelict Sadler's Wells theatre and over a period of eighteen years created an oasis of popular culture. He proved to have considerable business flair (of equal importance to artistic merit then as now) and, defying probability, brought to a poverty-stricken area of London a taste for real theatre that lingers to this day. He had to educate his audiences, wean them away from the knockabout entertainments they were accustomed to and give them a glimpse of another world. In this present century Lilian Baylis preached the same kind of down-to-earth evangelism at the Old Vic; she and Phelps both fought under the same tattered banner and both eventually raised it aloft in triumph. The only major difference between them was that Phelps was a working actor with a love and respect for Shakespeare's original texts, whereas Lilian Baylis knew little or nothing about actors (except their salaries!) and even less about Shakespeare. But their instincts were the same: they both saw the theatre as a form of religion and risked all to preach their gospels.

By the time the young Henry Irving-to-be paid his visit, Phelps was well established. His fame and his achievements were necessarily confined, but were nevertheless real. He had succeeded where others had not dared to tread. A far simpler man than Garrick or Macready, with no social pretensions, he lays claim to be recognised as one of the first real directors. He drilled his actors, but without Macready's overbearing attitude of personal superiority. A great believer in ensemble playing, a respecter of texts, he had the courage to nail his colours to the mast—for on the first handbills he issued he stated that his hope was that Sadler's Wells would become 'a place for justly representing the works of our great dramatic poets'. He has been eclipsed by such figures as Garrick, Kean and Irving, and yet in many ways—with the exception of Garrick—he did more to establish a tradition of acting than the majority of his more vaunted colleagues. During his tenure at Sadler's Wells he produced thirty-one out of Shakespeare's thirty-seven plays, a prodigious effort by any standards, and was responsible for restoring many of the original texts. Sadly, the lesson of his success was not taken to heart and after his death actors and managers once again lapsed into the old bad habits, but during the time when he occupied the Wells the English theatre had a humble home it could be justly proud of.

The only other figure of note contemporary with Phelps was Charles Kean, Edmund's son who, true to his father's promise, had been educated at Eton. It cannot be said that the experience enhanced his talents and in all probability, had it not been for the mixed blessing of his inherited name, his career would never have sparked. In fairness he had to overcome the double affliction of being his father's son and plagued with pronounced adenoids. Contrasted against his father, he threw a pale shadow and in the main failed to reconcile talent with ambition. He harboured dreams of grandeur and when with his wife, Ellen Tree, he ventured into management it was his announced intention to revive the greater glories of Garrick. He attempted most of his father's great tragic roles, though possibly he was motivated more from conceit than a desire to perpetuate his father's memory.

He was greatly favoured by the Queen and was made Director of the Windsor Theatricals, a position he occupied for nine years, but reading between the lines of Victoria's Journals I get the impression that she appointed him because she admired his wife's acting. Kean made a success of his office though his quest for further honours did not succeed. It was widely hinted that the Queen would reward him with a knighthood, and his efforts to attain that pinnacle of respectability in his profession cost him a great deal of money. Victoria was not as susceptible to such blatant exercises in self-advancement as some of the Prime Ministers of this century. During one season Kean recorded that he had lost nearly two thousand pounds for his pains and was further discomfited by an article in a weekly periodical describing him as 'Wet Nurse to the British Drama'. Another paper called him 'merely a noisy, yet most tricky commonplace'. The truth probably lies between the two: an ambitious man who could not totally suppress a basic vulgarity, far more interested in theatrical effects than in theatrical taste. We can however commend him for his perception in giving Kate Terry and her immortal sister, Ellen, their first professional engagements as child actors.

If we now return to Master John Henry Brodribb, we can begin to set the stage for the second half of the century—the Age of Irving. It has sometimes been a criticism of the English that we have too much tradition, and that we squander it. In coming this far in the story we have seen that where acting was concerned tradition was mostly a hit or miss affair. The central characters all wanted to be teachers rather than pupils, too concerned with their own day-to-day advancement to be bothered with establishing a code of conduct and professionalism that could be passed on to others. Just when things were on an even keel and it seemed reasonable to suppose that there would be a lull in the winds of change, then along would come another cyclone, a Mrs Siddons or a Kean, to scatter convention. Comparatively few actors could find permanent employment in London; most were condemned to the endless grind of the provincial circuit, poorly paid, under-rehearsed if rehearsed at all, seldom staying long enough in one place to establish credit let alone a reputation. To talk of an acting 'tradition' in such circumstances was laughable—the only tradition they knew or cared about was the tradition of surviving against the odds. If a Garrick, a Macready or a Phelps attempted to bring about a unified style, it quickly perished when they died or moved on. The managers, who might have shown the way, cared little for the overall quality of acting. They demanded stars, giant personalities who could tame and entice the unruly crowds, and if it was profitable to allow the stars to hog the stage to the detriment of the drama, they saw no reason to object. Nothing mattered as long as the house was filled. If there was some transient advantage to be gained by extracting the last ounce from a Master Betty, old feuds would be patched and rivals would share him. Once the public tired of the novelty, goodbye Master Betty and onto the next. What should it be? The freak casting of an American actress, Charlotte Cushman, playing Romeo to her sister's Juliet? Why not? That bloated has-been, Kean, wants to play Hamlet? Let him. There is always a public for fallen idols. The story of *King Lear* is not to your liking? Change it. Establish a permanent company, pay the resident actors a living wage, provide costumes and props—why should we? Out of work actors are plentiful, they have no standing in law or society, they deserve what they get—why should the world owe them a living? The pit doesn't want tradition, it wants blood, spectacle, a chance to boo, an opportunity for riot, excitement, that feeling of satisfaction when you have paid to see others fail.

Have I over-stated the case? I think not. We are still a long way from the gentility of the Edwardian theatre, a long way from Irving's knighthood, a long way from the drama of social conscience. The twelve-year-old Master Brodribb was to find his journey from Phelps' Elsinore to his eventual Camelot at the Lyceum a painful one. He had to forsake family and home, bring lasting sorrow to his mother, endure privation and a galling lack of recognition for nine years before London was given a chance to claim him.

He began his working life as a junior clerk with a firm of lawyers in Cheapside, later exchanging this drudgery for work of a similar nature with Thacker, Spink and Co., East India Merchants in Newgate Street. There, in more congenial surroundings, he sat at his ledgers for ten hours a day. Despite his inner determination, he had little reason to hope that he could ever realise his ambition to become an actor. His mother and father depended on him to advance himself in business to improve their lot, and his meagre salary was hardly sufficient to allow him any luxuries. He still had a pronounced stammer and was conscious that this was the first handicap he must overcome. With great singleness of mind he systematically set about preparing himself for the life he was convinced he would one day lead. He rightly decided that the first requisite for an actor was physical stamina, and before commencing work he swam in the Thames to strengthen his lungs. We are told that his diet consisted mainly of bread and butter, but that when hunger challenged ambition, ambition invariably won. Such few pence as he had to spend on himself he used to purchase books and playscripts or a ticket to the gallery at Sadler's Wells. He joined the City Elocution Class, run by a Mr and Mrs Henry Thomas to cater for the growing numbers of amateur actors from the new middle class who wished to sample the ecstasy but not the agony. Young Irving (and for the sake of clarity we will anticipate his change of name) worked hard to conquer his speech impediment and when given an opportunity to play Captain Absolute in a semi-public performance of *The Rivals* gained his first notice: the *Theatrical Journal* reported that he acted with 'intelligent tact and with great credit to Mr Thomas'. This early taste must have made him ever more anxious and with the persistence and cheek of the young he made himself known to a member of Phelps' company, a competent old actor called William Hoskins. Hoskins was obviously impressed because he consented to give Irving private lessons in elocution and mime, and it is nowhere recorded that he charged for this tuition. In addition, Irving found the time to learn the rudiments of fencing and sword fighting. In all these activities he had to endure the disapproval of his God-fearing mother. He was torn between filial duty and his growing conviction that he could only succeed by a complete break from the constrictions of family life. After other amateur appearances with Mr Thomas's group, he was offered the chance of accompanying Hoskins to Australia. When he declined Hoskins then introduced him to Phelps with a recommendation that Phelps engage him. The great man was not so easily persuaded of Irving's embryonic talents, and somewhat loftily advised him: 'Sir, do not go on the stage; it is an ill-requited profession.' When Hoskins made a further pleading, Phelps reconsidered and offered Irving a place in his company at the not ungenerous starting salary of two pounds a week. It was then that Irving surprised both men by declining: in his scheme of things the time was not advantageous. The only help he would accept was a letter of introduction from Hoskins to a well-known provincial theatre manager, E. D. Davis. Hoskins gave his word that when Irving decided the time was ripe the letter would have the desired effect. And with that he departed for Australia and out of Irving's life forever.

At this stage Irving's talents were not so obvious as perhaps he imagined, and he was fortunate that a few months after Hoskins had embarked his uncle Thomas Brodribb gave him a gift of a hundred pounds. This time he did not hesitate. His first act was to spend part of this unexpected windfall on the purchase of certain theatrical properties — the essential tools of his intended profession. He bought himself wigs, stage jewellery, buckles, lace and three swords. Thus equipped he presented himself at the Soho Theatre, one of a number of small houses where enterprising managers, always prepared to cash in on the latest fad, were prepared to put on plays in which, for a payment, amateurs could appear. First in the queue for an announced production of *Romeo and Juliet*, Irving plonked down three guineas and claimed the leading male role. It is at this point one realises he was a born actor, for it was now that he decided to change his name. The playbill for the Royal Soho Theatre, Oxford Street, boldly proclaims the 'First Appearance of Mr Irving as Romeo' for the night of Monday, August 11th 1856. Unlike Garrick, Irving did not conceal his new face behind a mask.

Three guineas did not buy immediate immortality, however. We are told that he was word perfect and acquitted himself reasonably well, although — denied proper rehearsals — he frequently lost his way in the unfamiliar scenery, mislaid his dagger during a vital moment in the drama, and at one point suffered the indignity of having his wig displaced. A Mrs Henderson played Juliet, but I have not been able to discover any accurate reports of her age or talents. A few admiring friends applauded his efforts and Irving's remaining doubts disappeared. He had survived the test he had set for himself.

He posted Hoskins' letter of introduction and back from Mr Davis came the offer of an engagement in his stock company at the Royal Lyceum Theatre, Sunderland for the new season beginning at the end of September. Irving then had to face telling his parents what he had done. To the end of her life his mother never forgave him and remained convinced that he was damned for all eternity. To his cousin and close confidante, Mrs Wilkins, he wrote:

'As regards the profession which I have chosen I consider it one of the, if not *the*, most intellectual there are.

'Actors are created like poets; you can never make one; of course I don't say everybody on the stage is really an actor, there are few. Too many enter it from idle motives and many mistake their calling, but the names of Shakespeare, Garrick, Kemble, Macready and many many others show that they were and are companions of the master spirits of the ages, and rank as gentlemen and scholars among Royalty and the aristocracy. A person may be as moral and good in that as in any other walk of life. There is much prejudice against it in our circle of society, and that is wearing off as the world grows wiser, but in the higher ones they are considered equals. I have a difficult task before me, and if I succeed it will be the most fortunate day of my life when I entered it . . .'

I find this letter touching—naive in parts, precocious in parts, the effort of a young man trying to justify himself, slightly scared, using adult arguments to convince himself as much as to convince his reader. He was soon to find out that not everybody who goes on the stage is immediately an actor, for his early experiences at Sunderland hardly lived up to his fevered expectations. He was given the role of Gaston, Duke of Orleans in Bulwer Lytton's *Richelieu* for his debut when the new theatre opened on September 29th. (The building had been burnt down the previous year, an often repeated fate, it would seem, for most theatres of the period.) His part had been heavily cut during rehearsals, reduced to a few odd lines and thus gave him little opportunity to shine as perhaps he had imagined he would shine. He played another minor role the following night in *The Lady of Lyons*, then on his third appearance as Cleomenes in *The Winter's Tale* disaster struck. He dried stone dead when his cue came and was unable to take advantage of the prompt. He finally ad-libbed to get himself off the stage and retreated to his dressing room to the sound of hissing from a disgruntled audience. Davis, the manager, acted with some charity, although one should not attribute too much generosity to him: Irving was not in receipt of a salary at this point, and although Davis forgave the lapse he might have been swayed by the fact that it was not costing him anything. What is true is that Irving was taken to one side by two of the veteran actors in the company, Sam Johnson and Tom Mead, and given sound advice and comfort. 'If ever I rise', he told them, with a passion that doubtless surprised, 'I shall not forget this'. He was as good as his word, and honoured the debt twenty years later.

But for all his brave words to the two old actors, he barely concealed his fears in another letter to a friend, written on November 24th 1856.

'. . . A young aspirant, therefore, has, or ought to have, a special independence of feeling for no-one knows what he may become. Speaking of them as a body, actors are intellectual, rollicking, good-natured independent, very polite, knowing, eccentric, short-haired, *today-care*, class of beings, with one great fault—jealousy. You meet with a few poor blighted looking creatures who, sadly unfit for the stage, have abandoned some good business for it and find their error too late—in fact the majority of them have mistaken their calling.

'The leading ladies are superior to the average standard of their sex—the minor ones inferior . . . I do everything in the bachelor style and enjoy myself alone . . .'

Was he really enjoying himself? One doubts it. A local critic had advised him to take the first steamer back to his comfortable home and abandon all hope of becoming an actor. His lifebelt was that he was in no hurry. We have already seen evidence of this in his declining to accompany Hoskins to Australia, and the otherwise astonishing decision not to accept Phelps' offer. More than any other actor I have studied he knew where he wanted to go, and how he wanted to get there, and he set his own pace. He had seen the 'poor blighted looking creatures' and he did not want to join their ranks. There were great obstacles to overcome, and he set about overcoming them. In later years he was to say: 'How strange it is that I should have made the reputation I have as an actor, with nothing to help me, with no equipment. My legs, my voice, everything has been against me. For an actor who can't walk, can't talk and has no face to speak of, I've done pretty well.' That was the older, venerated man speaking. The youth of eighteen had greater doubts, I suspect, but he concealed them well.

By the end of that first season he was in receipt of a salary—admittedly starvation wages of twenty-five shillings a week (exactly half what Phelps had offered)—but elected not to stay on. He wanted to put some distance between himself and those early humiliations. So from Sunderland he passed to the Theatre Royal, Edinburgh where he was engaged as a juvenile lead by the successful actor-manager R. H. Wyndham. There he gained first-hand experience of a star actor, for the company had secured the services of the Irish tragedian, Barry Sullivan, to play the title role in *Richelieu*. Irving was once again given the part of the Duke of Orleans and his salary increased to thirty shillings a week. He remained in Edinburgh for two and a half years, notching up the amazing total of 429 different roles in some 782 days, or to put it another way, a new role every two days! According to his early biographer, Austin Brereton, the record had never been equalled (in 1908) by any other great actor. It was a long apprenticeship and again emphasises that he was determined to pace himself, weaning the Edinburgh audiences, as Laurence Irving puts it, 'from active hostility to amused tolerance'. When he judged the time was ripe for a move, he gave notice, was granted a benefit and cast himself in the leading role of Claude Melnotte in the popular *The Lady of Lyons*. The gamble came off; he found the house packed for his farewell, made a gracious and frank speech from the stage and packed his bags for London.

His destination was the Princess's Theatre, long the home of Charles Kean and now managed by Augustus Harris.* As in Sunderland Irving was greeted by less than he had expected. Although engaged on a three year contract by Harris he was angered to be rewarded with an insultingly minor role and no billing. He had no option but to swallow his pride for a few weeks, but when cast as Osric to the Hamlet of an actor he considered inferior to most, and certainly inferior to himself, he asked for his contract to be terminated. It was a crushing setback, for he had wanted to return to London in triumph and thus go some way to convincing his mother that his choice of career had not been a mistake. With considerable courage he risked all on some solo readings and was fortunate to have two influential critics in his audience. Their verdict was complimentary and his London fiasco was salvaged. He received an offer to play in Dublin and replace an actor recently dismissed.

What he did not know was that he was replacing a popular favourite. Henry Webb, a comedian who managed the Queen's Theatre, Dublin, selected Irving more or less at random because he anticipated trouble and felt that he would be safer employing an actor ignorant of local politics. The unsuspecting Irving walked into a cauldron. George Vincent, the actor he had supplanted, was the darling of the gods and had no intention of allowing an outsider to replace him in the public's affection. While Irving was travelling from London to Dublin, Vincent spent his time and his money recruiting hooligans to his cause by the time-honoured method of standing treat in the less reputable ale houses. By the time Irving made his first appearance, playing Cassio to the Othello of T. C. King (a

* Father of the famous London manager of the same name, known as 'Druriolanus'.

leading man of the Barry Sullivan school), Vincent's scraggy army of fans was ready to do battle. They allowed Irving one night's grace and then embarked on a calculated and well-orchestrated campaign of disruption which lasted three weeks. In the end Webb was forced to call in the police and a pitched battle took place in the gallery before the rioters were finally overcome. There were no fatalities, as in Macready's case, but the experience was a hideous one for Irving. Considering his age and comparative lack of experience it says much for his courage that he continued to appear.

His next engagement was in Glasgow, where he joined Edmund Glover's mediocre company at the Theatre Royal. By the end of the summer of 1860 he had had enough and gave in his notice, despite the fact that he was almost penniless, and set out to try his luck in Manchester. Here he was more fortunate and within a few days had secured a position as 'a walking gentleman' in Manchester's Theatre Royal. This was then being run by a strange character called John Knowles. Knowles was an antique dealer, trading in marble and works of art, who treated the theatre as an extension of his main business. We are told that he was an arrogant Lancastrian who seldom spoke to the actors in his company, but had considerable business flair and ran what was then considered the most prosperous and efficient playhouse in the provinces.

Although he was once again in steady employment, Irving had not advanced his career and continued to receive the meagre salary of three pounds a week (only marginally more than he had earned in Edinburgh) and from this he religiously remitted seventeen and sixpence to his parents every Friday, for his pride was such that he had to convince them that he was still the master of his fate. What remained in his pay packet was scarcely enough to live on and he frequently had to borrow from his fellow actors before the end of the week.

He lacked all luxuries, but he gained the taste of real theatre for the first time in his life. Manchester audiences were more discriminating than any he had previously encountered, and he found himself in the company of fine actors, notably the American tragedian Edwin Booth. Despite the fact that he made no immediate impression on Knowles (indeed Knowles was prepared to fire him after the first few weeks) he was befriended and encouraged by the then stage manager and resident leading man of the theatre, Charles Calvert. It was entirely due to Calvert that his career prospered, and under Calvert's patronage he was gradually moved up in the company and entrusted with more important roles. The season he played with Booth was a turning point in his life, for this was the actor of his dreams, Booth was the first intellectual player he had been able to study at close range and the experience had a profound effect on Irving. He was thrust into a leading role one night when another visiting star, an old and frequently drunken tragedian G. V. Brooke (affectionately nicknamed The Great Gustavus) went missing at curtain time. Irving had rehearsed to play Cassio to Brooke's Othello, but when a panic-stricken stage management had failed to produce Brooke from any of the nearby taverns (he was later discovered dead drunk behind some scenery back stage) Irving was told he would have to go on as the Moor. Why Irving was selected for this dubious honour is not recorded, but in the best understudy tradition he did his duty and for the first time in his life took the centre of the stage in a great classical role. It would be pleasant to record that

GUSTAVUS BROOKE as Othello Olympic Theatre, 1848

he took the town by storm, but from all accounts the most that can be said about his performance is that he got through without any major disaster. The engaging Brooke eventually died a hero's death: refusing a place in the lifeboats, he stayed manning the pumps when the steamship *London* went down in the Bay of Biscay on her way to Australia.

Irving soldiered on, playing all manner of minor roles while his ambition smouldered but never caught fire. He acquitted himself well as Mercutio and earned some praise from the discerning Manchester critics; when his benefit came around he somewhat rashly chose to play Hamlet, but it was, we are told, a patchwork affair, borrowed from many sources and with little original invention. He fell in love with a talented young actress called Nellie Moore, but lacked the necessary resources to transform romance into marriage. From Manchester he went back to Edinburgh for a short season, then to Bury (where he again attempted Hamlet supported by a company of amateurs), and after that to Oxford and on to Birmingham, taking whatever was offered, since he was in no position to refuse any work. Thus, in 1866, after ten years as a professional actor, he came close to total despair, disillusioned, convinced that all his efforts had been for Hecuba. Nellie Moore had moved on and was now an established favourite in Buckstone's company at the Haymarket. His income for the previous year had been £75 — he was, as Laurence Irving puts it, 'almost on his knees'.

It cannot be said that Irving had greatness thrust upon him. Had his luck not turned there is little doubt that he would either have gone back to his clerk's desk or else spent the remainder of his days, like so many of his profession, in obscurity. But it was at this lowest point in his fortunes that he was recalled to Manchester and there he met the man who was to change everything. He was engaged to play a good role in a new play by Dion Boucicault.

We have seen how from the very beginning the English theatre had belonged to the actor. I think it is worth quoting W. A. Darlington—for many years the greatly respected theatre critic of the *Daily Telegraph*—in this context. In his volume of reminiscences *Six Thousand and One Nights* Darlington has a most perceptive and telling passage which is germane to this point in Irving's life.

Darlington wrote: '. . . at all material times, and in all places outside the playhouse, the actor was a person of no consequence whatever. If he had a rich patron his social status was about that of a footman . . . If he had no patron he was frowned on by the law and cold-shouldered by respectable people. His calling was not that of a gentleman, and except in a few rare cases, Garrick's being the most striking, no man of breeding was allowed to keep his place in society once he had turned actor; but if a gentleman wished to *write* for the theatre he could do so without the smallest loss of face. Yet century succeeded century, and no author showed any sign of grudging the actor his pre-eminence, or of having any desire, when he sat down to his desk, except to give the actor something to do. The reason for this was that until the nineteenth century hardly any writer regarded himself as a professional dramatist as that term is understood today, or worked in the theatre continuously enough to make his living out of it. Playwriting was not regarded as a branch of literature, nor was it all that well paid; and since it offered neither prestige nor money, it fell very largely into the hands of either poverty-stricken hacks or of lordly and condescending amateurs.

'It was perhaps a piece of poetic justice that it was an actor-author who at last brought an end to the dramatist's semi-amateur condition and gave him the chance to write for his living. This was Dion Boucicault, a prolific play-carpenter, who in the middle of the nineteenth century demanded to be paid by means of a royalty on the theatre's takings, instead of the variously calculated lump sums hitherto customary. As Boucicault was an actor's-theatre man *par excellence*, concerned above all to fit his plays to the actors' requirements it is curious to think that by making the dramatist financially independent he did more than Ibsen and almost as much as Shaw to bring the actor's theatre to an end.'

This, then, was the man who changed Irving's life by offering him the role of the villainous Rawdon Scudamore opposite young Kate Terry in *The Two Lives of Mary Leigh*. The play itself was no masterpiece, but in the role of Scudamore Irving found something ideally suited to his particular talents and he carried the production, sweeping it past the Manchester critics' condemnation to popular success. Two London managements bid for it and Boucicault opted for the offer from Miss Louisa Herbert who was then managing the St James's Theatre in London. He stipulated that whatever other changes she made in the cast, Irving was not to be replaced. It was a condition Miss Herbert was happy to accept and the road back to London was open to Irving at long last.

DION BOUCICAULT

Miss Herbert was that rare creature, an actress-manager, and had enjoyed a considerable success at the St James's (one of the loveliest theatres in London which, unhappily, was bulldozed in the late 1950s) for a long period. She often starred herself and was accounted a great beauty and no mean performer—her Lydia Languish was much admired. Rossetti used her as a model and she enjoyed the admiration of men as divers as Charles Reade and Ruskin. She was mistress of her own house and traded on her beauty and grace to get her own way in most things, as poor Irving was soon to discover.

She changed the title of Boucicault's play to *Hunted Down*, a more sophisticated and commercial title for the metropolis in her opinion. Irving was engaged for his original role, but also required to double-up as stage manager. He was in no position to argue about this, although I feel sure that it must have been somewhat of a blow, and he had a further disappointment when Miss Herbert decided that Boucicault's play could not be ready for the announced opening date of October 6th 1866. She quickly substituted a revival of *The Belle's Stratagem*, casting Irving in a role he had played in stock and to which he felt he was not well suited. He was very much the newcomer, though many of the established members of the company went out of their way to make him feel at home. There are times when the sentimental conventions of the theatre do come true, and this was one of them. Despite the fact that he considered the role of Doricourt inferior, he knuckled down to the rehearsals and on the first night found reserve supplies of that creative adrenalin necessary for any actor's survival. In his mad scene he electrified a hitherto indifferent first-night audience and they rose to him. The popular and indeed true description for his triumph is 'a show stopper' and Irving enjoyed an exit round for the remainder of the run.

Rehearsals for the delayed *Hunted Down* continued, and in addition he was required to supervise the stage-management of a new burlesque with the engaging title *Dulcamara, or A Little Duck with a Big Quack*. The author was a young barrister who also held a commission in a Highland Militia regiment. His name was W. S. Gilbert. He and Irving struck up an immediate friendship, doubtless because they both stood on the threshold of greatness and were not unaware of the common bond.

When *Hunted Down* eventually opened, Irving at last received the recognition he had courted for over a decade. George Eliot was amongst the distinguished first-night audience and legend has it that at the final curtain she turned to G. H. Lewes, then the editor of the influential *Fortnightly Review*, and asked his opinion of Miss Herbert's new star. ·

'In twenty years', Lewes said, 'he will be at the head of the English stage'.

George Eliot was not prepared to qualify her judgment. 'He is there, I think, already', she said.

More relevant to this account, the critics the following morning praised the novelty of Irving's acting style, for this was the first time they had been exposed to some of the mannerisms that were to become his trademark. In particular he had a curious way of moving on the stage which in later years was much commented upon and irritated his detractors.

From this point onwards my task is made easier by virtue of the fact that I have an abundance of reliable eye-witnesses to draw upon, some of whom survived into my own lifetime—notably, of course, the late James Agate. For so many years deservedly a law unto himself, Agate aroused the most violent reactions for and against his own style of dramatic criticism, but whatever anybody felt about his opinions, nobody denied that he was a man of the most passionate enthusiasms and had perceptions that many of his colleagues lacked. Self-opinionated (but, then, what critic isn't?), often arrogant, often showing off his cleverness in the manner of a precocious schoolboy, often infuriating when on a hobby horse, he was possessed of one great saving grace: dramatic criticism wasn't just a way of earning a living to him, it was a religion. He cajoled, he exaggerated, he blustered and at times threatened in order to convert the faithless. Many a Sunday his columns preached fire and brimstone sermons to those who doubted, and he kept after his flock, standing at the church door, as it were, to buttonhole them yet again. His famous series of autobiographies, with the take-it-or-leave-it running title *Ego*, were thinly disguised additions to the basic gospel. The enthusiasms poured over the brim of his personality like the vintage champagne he was devoted to. He blew verbal smoke rings around most of his rivals with the same hedonistic aplomb as he brandished his beloved Havanas. He was a thoroughbred who ran against the field with the same dash as the only other love of his life—his ponies. He was feared and he was fallible. There were gaps in his own personality which sometimes coloured his judgements, but once he had discovered a talent he was relentless in propagating his find. No student of our twentieth century theatre can afford to ignore him. He was a gossip as well as a critic, always digging for anecdotes, scavenging around for clues to the humanity of those he praised and condemned, because he wanted to give his readers and posterity the whole actor. In this he was unique. Although I never knew him personally, I often saw him at first nights and in the Ivy restaurant holding court. I did, however, have a long and intimate association with his protégé (and, many felt, rightful successor) the late Alan 'Jock' Dent, who as a young man arrived unannounced on Agate's doorstep and stayed to become his

Boswell as well as forging a separate and distinguished career as a dramatic critic in his own right. I knew Jock Dent to be an honest and intensely cultured man and my view of Agate is taken from him. If, as we approach closer to the present day, I quote from Agate more frequently than from others, it is because I believe that he had instincts about great acting that were superior to most. By his own admission he was often hasty or downright wrong about plays, but his judgments about the players could seldom be faulted. 'I don't consider myself particularly sound about plays', he once said to W. A. Darlington, 'but I don't just think, I *know* that I am the best judge of acting that there has been since Hazlitt.'

Obviously he had blind spots and favourites—despite certain indications to the contrary, critics are also human—but he did not hesitate to rap his favourites over the knuckles if he felt that they fell short of his rightful expectations of them. I find him consistently more readable than Shaw, whilst acknowledging that Shaw was a great critic and a great servant of the theatre. But Shaw always led a double life, using criticism as a stepping stone to other fames, and he is too much the self-appointed saint for my tastes, whereas Agate was an unabashed sinner. He believed that criticism 'is the knack of communicating to others the kind and amount of delight the critic has received from a work of art, or one of skilful and popular contrivance. The knack, too, of spotting and slaying the bogus and pretentious, even if all the world's pseudo-intellectuals are on their knees before it, high brow to low floor'.

He is particularly valuable where Irving is concerned. He saw Irving perform and thereafter never faltered in his belief that, pound for pound, Irving was the greatest actor ever to come within his sights. Although he returned to this verdict time and time again he had sufficient sense of humour to be mindful of a passage from Max Beerbohm's *Around Theatres* about 'that period when a man begins to bore young people by raving to them about the mimes whom they never saw'. It is a sharp lesson for all of us who attempt to describe past gods, and Agate commented: 'I have made it a rule never to talk about Irving unless some playgoing chit tells me that some nincompoop at Gunnersbury playing the lead in *The Donkey Has Two Tails* is a great actor. Then I let fly . . . For forty years I have felt about Henry Irving what Iago pretended to feel about Othello: "I am your own for ever." It has not been within the power of Time to weaken this.'

The Age of Irving does, of course, embrace the life of Ellen Terry, overlaps into the reign of Herbert Beerbohm Tree and eventually spills into the Age of Respectability. I hope to illustrate how Irving changed the whole standing of the profession, but rather than pile fact onto dead fact by laboriously tabulating each and every one of his numerous portrayals in one great indigestible wodge, I shall at this point take temporary leave of him. As far as Irving is concerned, London had been regained. The long years of obscurity were over, although he had some way to go before he reached his own summit, and we shall rejoin him at a later date.

For the moment we need to strike out beyond the mainstream and explore some of the tributaries. Eventually, we shall see how many of these currents converged to form the flood of talent that swept over the latter half of the Victorian era.

[12]

ENTER ELLEN TERRY

IRVING thought of Ellen Terry as 'the queen of every woman'; Oscar Wilde, at his most purple, called her 'our Lady of the Lyceum', and by the end of her career she had been canonised by the general public and was beyond criticism—the most widely admired, most persistently loved of any actress that has ever graced our stages. Shaw was enslaved by her although he did not see her until she was thirty. It is almost impossible to find any commentator of taste and note who disliked her: if they didn't totally admire her acting on occasions, they never faltered in their praise of her beauty and femininity. To read the verdicts of her contemporaries is to find nothing but a series of love letters, headed of course by the published and hotly debated correspondence that passed between her and Shaw. If Shaw's view of her was justifiably rose-tinted, then possibly it distorted his view of Irving. Whether he genuinely felt jealous of her relationship with Irving, or whether—given the perversity of his character—he engineered that jealousy to give his letters and reviews an added spice we shall never know. But if one contrasts Agate's opinion of Irving with Shaw's then one might imagine that two quite separate actors are being discussed.

Shaw was the social realist, Irving the romantic realist, and in between these two dominant and opposing male forces was the exquisite and beloved Ellen Terry. Despite the fact that she was born into one of the great theatrical families, Ellen was never stagestruck. With her elder sister Kate she served her acting apprenticeship in Charles Kean's company. Both girls were precociously talented but not in a brash way, for they shared a common and curious indifference to most of the trappings of fame. They were performers by force of circumstance rather any sense of vocation. Both led sheltered lives and although in later years Ellen's behaviour often ran contrary to accepted Victorian codes, she was never diminished by what, in other women, was more often than not considered outrageous conduct, and her reputation never suffered from it. By the age of nine she was a child actress; at sixteen she was a child-bride, married off to the sexually enigmatic George Frederick Watts. He was a fashionable and highly accomplished painter, some thirty years her senior, a man who had reached middle age surrounded by doting females of his own vintage and yet who felt the need to enter into marriage with an innocent adolescent girl. The various biographers of Ellen Terry and Watts have done their best to unravel the truth of this undoubtedly curious relationship. In her autobiography (which was certainly not ghosted and is one of the best written theatrical

ELLEN TERRY in *The Winter's Tale*
Left Aged 9, she made her debut as Mamillius
with Charles Kean, here seen as Leontes,
Princess's Theatre, London 1856

Right Aged 59, she played Hermione, with
Marion Melville as Mamillius, His Majesty's
Theatre, 1906

ELLEN TERRY
Portrait taken by Julia Margaret Cameron
at Tennyson's house in the Isle of Wight
Right ELLEN TERRY as Ophelia

memoirs ever published) Ellen Terry wrote: 'Many inaccurate stories have been told of my brief married life, and I have never contradicted them—they were so manifestly absurd. Those who can imagine the surroundings into which I, a raw girl, undeveloped in all except my training as an actress, was thrown, can imagine the situation.'

The truth is that few *could* imagine the situation, hence the subsequent conjecture, which continues to this day. On the face of it her marriage to Watts suggests the melodrama of a famous artist intent on becoming the seducer of adolescent beauty: it is not an unfamiliar plot in the late Victorian era with its pronounced double-standards of morality. But Watts was by no means a stock character. There is considerable evidence that he was sexually impotent and that the marriage was never consummated, though perhaps it would be more realistic to think that it was not consummated in any conventional sense. I find it hard to believe that a man of Watts' maturity, accustomed to a sybaritic way of living, would embark upon marriage to a sixteen year old girl in a state of mind that excluded any form of physical attraction. We have Ellen's word for it that she went willingly to the altar ('I was in Heaven', she wrote, 'for I knew I was to live with those pictures') and she was encouraged by both family and friends; to them it seemed a suitable, indeed propitious, match for the daughter of a moderately successful actor.

She became the proxy mistress of a large household, but was denied any real authority. Watts had apparently no intention of altering his previous way of life to accommodate his latest acquisition. She found herself suddenly mixing with such luminaries as Gladstone, Disraeli, Tennyson, Browning and Holman Hunt and it is not without significance that none of these august characters appeared to think it in the least odd that their friend should have taken a teenager as his wife. At the time of her marriage she was so innocent that she believed Watts' first kiss had made her pregnant, and confessed as much to her mother. (She later repeated this in a letter to Shaw, and the passage was suppressed when their correspondence was first published.)

I suspect that Watts was something of a hypocrite. He was at some pains to convince others that his motives were pure, that he felt compelled to marry this child in order to save her from a life of debauchery. This we know is totally at variance with Ellen's upbringing and family background—there can hardly have been a child less exposed to the seamier side of her profession—and Watts was careful not to publish his justification for general consumption, but confined himself to writing to members of his intimate circle. The person he really needed to convince was himself. He told his friends that the proposed marriage was a moral necessity and that it would involve him in considerable sacrifice. Such honourable intentions can always be satisfied outside marriage, but after circulating this humbug he married her.

No doubt to the child it was a great adventure, a new excitement with fairy-tale undertones and it again illustrates that she had no qualms at quitting her blossoming stage career. She revealed as much in her memoirs: 'Of one thing I am certain—while I was with Signor, the name by which Mr Watts was known among his friends, I never had one single pang of regret for the theatre. This may do me no credit, but it is *true*. I wondered at the new life, and worshipped it because of its beauty. When it suddenly came to an end, I was thunderstruck; and refused at first to consent to the separation, which

was arranged for me in much the same way as my marriage had been.'

Perhaps in her innocence she looked upon the marriage as just another piece of play-acting in a different setting. Perhaps, to be fair to Watts, his impotence (if indeed the marriage was never consummated) was brought about by guilt, a common enough clinical reason. Certainly he craved her forgiveness in later years; eventually, albeit curtly, she bestowed it and apparently bore him no lasting grudge. Her daughter Edith Craig adds an interesting footnote to the episode in the American edition of her mother's autobiography. 'Ellen Terry, writing of her marrige to Watts in after years, says that in many ways it was a happy one. This was a generous exaggeration, very natural in a woman who on her own confession was always "incapable of sustaining a resentment". Mrs Watts, aged sixteen, may have been too young and flighty to be trusted with the usual prerogatives of a wife, but she was kept in a state of tutelage at Little Holland House, for which neither her youth nor her temperament prove an excuse. "The Signor" was surrounded by a little court of married women of his own age, presided over by "Beauty" (Mrs Prinsep), who seem to have made it their business to keep his child-wife in order. She was subjected to a humiliating surveillance and had strict injunctions not to open her mouth in the presence of distinguished guests.'

With the marriage at an end, Ellen returned home to her parents in a very disturbed state. 'I hated my life, hated everyone and everything in the world more than at any time before or since.' Her parents' behaviour throughout seems almost as strange as Watts'. They adored her, they were not insensitive to her plight, yet it must be assumed that they had a blank spot, as so many parents do, when the chance of a 'suitable' marriage came along: how else can one explain their initial behaviour? As a family they had always been close knit. After the Keans had departed for America, Kate and Ellen had toured England under their father's management, presenting 'A Drawing Room Entertainment'—the two young sisters frequently acting all the roles, male and female, in a series of short plays interspersed with piano recitals. They did not endure the hardship and deprivation that characterised Edmund Kean and his brood before he gained fame in

London. 'I tasted the joys of the strolling player's existence without its miseries', Ellen wrote.

By the time she had been banished from Watts' 'court' her sister Kate had become an established leading actress in London. Ellen had no desire to taste again those 'joys' and had to be driven back to the stage by her parents. To be charitable, perhaps they believed this was the right therapy for her, but the experiment failed within a year. Yet it was during this year—1867—that she acted with Irving for the first time. They came together in a revival of Garrick's boiled-down version of *The Taming of the Shrew*. She was then twenty and Irving twenty-nine and they were strangers to each other. 'Henry Irving was nothing to me and I nothing to him. I never consciously thought that he would become a great actor. He had no high opinion of *my* acting! . . . He played badly, nearly as badly as I did; and how much more to blame I was, for I was at this time much more easy and skilful from a purely technical point of view.' There was little awareness from either public or critics that history was in the making on this occasion. Irving was a failure as Petruchio— Ellen Terry speaks of the 'trouncing' he received. When the production closed they parted and were not reunited for a further eleven years.

Soon after this occasion she disappeared—literally, giving rise to a macabre coincidence, for shortly after she left home without explanation the body of a young girl, assumed to be a suicide, was taken from the Thames and the physical similarities were sufficient for her father to identify the corpse as Ellen. On the contrary, Ellen was very much alive. She had decamped to a life of rustic simplicity in a small cottage in Hertfordshire with a gifted architect named Edward Godwin, a friend of the family whom she had previously met in Bristol. Her deception of her family and subsequent flight could possibly have been her way of getting back at them for their part in the Watts marriage. Equally, she was still legally married to Watts and in receipt of an annual amount of conscience money from him, and was therefore living in sin with Godwin. A hundred years ago this was a step few women were brave enough to take in open defiance of society. The £300 that Watts allowed her each year carried with it a condition that the money was forthcoming only 'so long as she shall lead a chaste life'. So one can easily understand why Ellen felt the need to deceive those closest to her.

Only by the purest and most fortunate of chances was the tragic misunderstanding resolved. Learning of her father's grief Ellen rushed back to London to console him. She found the family in mourning for her—surely an incident that Dickens would have savoured!

Edward Godwin was a widower. A handsome and gifted man, he had none of Watts' sexual inhibitions, and for a time the idyll brought great happiness to them both. Ellen bore him two maverick children: Edith Craig and Edward Gordon Craig, the latter inheriting some of the genius of his mother and father which he used to blaze his own, often misunderstood, frequently ignored, trail through the theatre. The children did not take Godwin's name; when the liaison withered after six years and Ellen eventually married a second time they assumed her second husband's name for a period. This marriage, destined to be as unfortunate as her first, was to a soldier-cum-actor called Charles Wardell who went under the stage name of Charles Kelly. The final name Craig was chosen by Ellen

EDWARD GODWIN at the time of his association with Ellen Terry   *Right* CHARLES READE

in arbitrary fashion simply because she thought it had a good theatrical ring to it.

Thus we have a glimpse of Ellen Terry's formative years, plots sufficient for half a dozen melodramas, each one of which contrasts starkly with the straightforward rags-to-riches story of Irving's early life. Even her second return to the stage is not without its measure of dramatic improbability, for it involves a famous novelist, Charles Reade, leaping back into her life over a country hedge—'like some ludicrous Mephistopheles' in Gordon Craig's phrase—to tempt her back to the theatre.

Ellen had known Reade as one of the frequent visitors to Little Holland House. Although mostly remembered as the author of *The Cloister and the Hearth*, Reade began his literary career as a dramatist and had many successes, the most notable being *Masks and Faces* produced at the Haymarket in 1853. When he made his startling reappearance in her life things were not going well between her and Godwin. They had moved from Hertfordshire and were living in a cottage designed by Godwin in Harpenden. The Arcadian bliss had recently been disturbed by the bailiffs, so that when Reade called her a fool and urged her to come back to the stage she was more receptive to the idea than at any time since her romantic retirement. Reade offered a leading role in his latest play *The Wandering Heir*, suggesting that she take over from Mrs John Wood in the part of Philippa Chester.

By her own account, Ellen answered him by saying: 'Well, perhaps I would think of it if some one would give me forty pounds a week.'

145

Reade struck the bargain there and then. 'Done!' he said. 'I'll give you that and more.' He was to confide to his notebooks that she was as 'hard as a nail in money matters, but velvet on the surface'.

Reade gives us a more detailed glimpse of the Ellen Terry of this period. Like countless others he was not immune to her charms, but found her egotistical, 'always wanting something "dreadful bad" today, which she does not want tomorrow, especially if you are weak enough to give it her, or get it her. Hysterical, sentimental . . . A creature born to please and to deceive. *Enfant gâtée, et enfant terrible* . . . Downright fascinating . . . In good hands a very amiable creature but dangerous to the young. Even I, who look coldly on from senile heights, am delighted by her.'

He also wrote a detailed physical description of her which was much quoted at the time. 'Her eyes are pale, her nose rather long, her mouth nothing particular. Complexion a delicate brick-dust, her hair rather like tow.'* Yet somehow she is *beautiful*. Her expression *kills* any pretty face you see beside her. Her figure is lean and bony; her hands masculine in size and form. Yet she is a pattern of fawn-like grace. Whether in movement or repose, grace pervades the hussy.'

She accepted his offer of forty pounds and began rehearsals for *The Wandering Heir*, a play suggested by the famous Tichborne trial, a nineteenth century *cause célèbre* which continues to fascinate even to this day. Reade was no fool. He knew he had a commercial trump card in Ellen's return to the stage and played it accordingly. She was not billed prior to the first night, but he fathered the rumours and allowed it to be known that the new Philippa was to be played by an actress reappearing 'after a long period of retirement'. When the card was turned face up, surprise was accompanied by delight and triumph. She was welcomed back by critics, public and friends 'as if it were six minutes instead of six years since I had dropped out of their ken.'

There are so many clues, interlocking like the most intricate of *Times* crossword puzzles, which surround the young Ellen Terry's life. Was she perchance George du Maurier's inspiration for *Trilby*? Certainly du Maurier had frequently observed her at Little Holland House, a little girl 'thin as paper and white as a ghost, with drowned eyes . . . she brushed past me like a broken-winged bird' in the words of another contemporary. Reade—'Daddy' Reade as she called him—became a sort of Svengali, although not as sinister as du Maurier's celebrated creation. He bombarded her with notes about the details of her performance 'telling me what I had done ill and what well . . . Dear, kind, unjust, generous, cautious, impulsive, passionate, gentle Charles Reade . . . He seemed guileless, and yet had moments of suspicion and craftiness worthy of the wisdom of the serpent. One moment he would call me "dearest child"; the next, with indignant emphasis, "*Madam!*" ' Did these two separate ingredients ferment in du Maurier's subconscious eventually to produce his vintage theatrical potion?

She seemed to inspire a peculiar kind of love in a variety of men, most of them much older than herself. In her childhood Lewis Carroll, with his now well-documented penchant for little girls, had been greatly attracted to her. When she returned to the stage in Reade's play he was still a fervent admirer, though the Rev. Charles Dodgson ousted

* Coarse and broken part of flax or hemp.

Carroll when he confided to his diary that although he still found her 'simply wonderful' he could not bring himself to hold any conversation with her or her family because she had 'so entirely sacrificed her social position that I had no desire but to drop the acquaintance'.

Had he but known, it was a view shared by her parents, for she was still ostracized by her family. When she made the decision to resume her stage career she moved herself and her children to a small house in Taviton Street, off Gordon Square. Godwin came with them and it is surprising that there was no public scandal or press gossip attendant upon her newfound theatrical success. But domestically the relationship between them had been stood on its head. She was no longer the infatuated, junior partner, docilely awaiting her lover's return. It was Godwin who remained at home and as her total love for him began to wane, so he began to whine, adopting a conciliatory attitude towards her in glaring contrast to his previous cavalier behaviour.

The Wandering Heir ran for one hundred and thirty nights before being replaced by another of Reade's pot-boilers, an adaptation of his best-selling novel *It's Never Too Late To Mend*. Ellen once again took the leading role, but despite the apposite title, even her admired talents could not sustain such mediocre material. In an effort to recoup his losses, Reade took the entire London cast of *The Wandering Heir* out on the road. Godwin stayed at Taviton Street with the children.

The tour was not a financial success and Ellen's salary, although always paid promptly, was reduced to £25 a week. She and Reade quarrelled frequently, though it seems transparently clear from her own account of this period that she often engineered their spats because 'when we made it up he was sure to give me some "treat"—a luncheon, a present, or a drive.' She knew how to manipulate him and it is impossible to exclude an element of eroticism from the relationship of this sixty year old man with the young 'hussy' of twenty-six. Reade enjoyed playing games of blind-man's-buff with her—surely the ploy of a man too old to risk buying the goods, but not too old to want to touch them? She learnt much from him, and he never stopped wanting to teach and improve her. He realised that her technique had not yet caught up with her inherent talents. She had a good voice, but it was rusty—she needed his help to know how to breathe properly. He remonstrated with her for being 'limp': 'No great quality of an actress is absent from your performance. Very often you have *vigour*. But in other places where it is as much required, or even more, you turn *limp*. You have limp lines, limp business, and in Act III limp exits instead of ardent exits.' He taught her the first rule of playing comedy: pace. It is impossible to turn an actor into a comedian unless he is born with an inner ear which senses the ridiculous, but granted that such a sense does exist, then variations of pace can be implanted. (I can think of no better example in this century than Rex Harrison's masterly Professor Higgins in *My Fair Lady*. He crammed more variation of comedy pace into that one performance than some actors achieve in a lifetime.)

It was during this tour that Ellen first makes mention of her second husband, Charles Kelly. He had the role of a farm labourer in *Rachael the Reaper*, a one-act curtain-raiser that preceded *The Wandering Heir*. In his quest for total realism Reade insisted upon having real livestock on stage—pigs, sheep, a goat and a dog. The pigs happily took flight before the first performance, but poor Kelly still had to contend with the remaining animals. Ellen recalled that 'on the first night, the real dog bit Kelly's real ankles, and in real anger he kicked the real animal by a real mistake into the orchestra's real drum!' There was nothing wrong with her ear for comedy in that passage.

At the end of the tour she returned to Taviton Street to find that Godwin had become a convert to a new feminine cause in support of women being allowed to enter the closed profession of architects. Practising what he was about to preach he had taken on as his pupil a young lady named Beatrice Phillips. He was to marry her in less than two years.

In addition to this new development Ellen was also greeted by some old familiars: the brokers' men. There was little of value to be taken, but what little there was, was taken. Godwin, either indifferent or else too battered by now to stir himself, was content to rely on Ellen as the breadwinner. Once again luck came to her rescue in the guise of an unexpected offer from the actor-manager Squire Bancroft to play Portia in a production of *The Merchant*. The luck also extended to Godwin, for out of the blue Mrs Bancroft invited him to be the 'archaeological adviser'. Godwin's first designs for the theatre were ahead of their time, just as his son's subsequent innovations were ahead of his.

I find it curious to note how many times *The Merchant of Venice* has been the vehicle for change in our theatrical history. We have read how Kean made his first impact in London by playing the Jew contrary to tradition, and now we have Godwin confusing the Victorian audiences with his scenic inventions. 'It all looked so unlike a theatre, and so much more like old Italian pictures than anything that had been previously shown upon the stage', was Squire Bancroft's own explanation for the failure of the production. 'It may be that it all came a little before the proper time, and that we saw things too far in advance . . . I count it a failure to be proud of.' Then he went and spoilt it all by adding: 'nor should it be forgotten that the absence of Mrs Bancroft was another serious drawback to the attraction, for Miss Terry had still, in those days, to earn the brilliant position she now owns, and of which her acting in this production was, without doubt, the foundation stone.' The good Squire—whose name was later to be perpetuated in the Bancroft Gold Medal, the highest prize awarded by the Royal Academy of Dramatic Art—was too loyal to his wife, Marie Wilton. Although very talented, she would have made a hopeless Portia, being better suited to burlesque and principal boy roles. We are told that with her pert little face and Gibson girl figure she provoked laughter 'as soon as she stepped out of the shadow of the wings'. The truth is that the Shylock of Charles Coghlan was accounted an abysmal failure. Poor Coghlan was a much respected leading man, but on this particular occasion he floundered miserably and the play fell apart.

We have a graphic account of his agony from Ellen Terry's own pen. 'Coghlan's Shylock was not even bad. It was *nothing*. You could hardly hear a word he said. He spoke as though he had a sponge in his mouth, and moved as if paralysed. The perspiration poured down his face; yet what he was doing no one could guess. It was a case of moral cowardice rather than incompetency. At rehearsals no one had entirely believed in him, and this, instead of stinging him into a resolution to triumph, had made him take fright and run away. People felt they were witnessing a great play with a great part cut out.'

Ellen Terry, on the other hand, with 'her front hair in massive curls, carried down in

148

smaller curls to the ears', made an immediate impact. For her first entrance she wore a china-blue and white brocade dress which she described as 'like almond blossom'. There was a single red rose at her breast and as she stood there in Godwin's elaborate setting (which he had based on Veronese's *Marriage in Cana*) the whole house burst into spontaneous applause. 'I was very thin', she wrote, 'but Portia and all the ideal *young* heroines of Shakespeare ought to be thin. I moved and spoke slowly. The clothes seemed to demand it, and the setting of the play developed the Italian feeling in it, and let the Elizabethan element take care of itself'.

The production ran only three weeks, but in that short space of time the mould of her legend was cast. Oscar Wilde wrote a sonnet for her, Whistler, Swinburne, and other leading members of the aesthetic movement made her the living embodiment of their creed. Somewhat surprisingly Henry James stood aloof from the general acclaim. He was in the minority, for 'every one seemed to be in love with me', Ellen wrote with an engaging lack of modesty. 'I had sweethearts by the dozen, known and unknown. Most of the letters written to me I destroyed . . . but the feeling of sweetness and light with which some of them filled me can never be destroyed . . . Elation, triumph, being lifted on high by a single stroke of the mighty wing of glory—call it by any name, think of it as you like—it was as Portia that I had my first and last sense of it.'

Here was a different aspect of the tradition we are searching to pinpoint. As I try to pull all the threads together and the final pattern starts to become visible, I am more and more conscious that it will be a coat of many colours. It could well be that, like Dame Edith Evans, Ellen Terry was fortunate in coming to stardom swiftly, without having to serve a long, and possibly bad-habit-forming apprenticeship in the provincial stock companies. The curious episode of her marriage to Watts removed her from the theatre at that tender age when precocious talents are at their most vulnerable; the six year retirement in the country with Godwin brought her to maturity as a woman and at the same time spared her the conflicting emotions of a young mother who is also trying to have a career. On the surface these may seem mundane observations to apply to analysis of a great actress's career, but I believe them to be valid. By his own admission 'Daddy' Reade did not 'pretend to be as good a writer of plays as you are an actress, but I do pretend to be a great judge of acting in general'. With a keener sense of timing than he brought to the majority of his plays, he jumped back into her life at exactly the right emotional moment; whatever his motives he knew gold from counterfeit. He carefully shaped her and she was still pliable enough to be shaped. Instead of spending her formative years being influenced by older actresses, as would have been the normal fate of somebody in her position, she spent them almost exclusively in the company of older men. When finally she emerged luck favoured her twice in quick succession: she first had a showy role in an indifferent play, then a great classical role opposite a leading actor who was not equal to the occasion; both instances increased the odds for her personal triumphs. That is not to take away from her achievements, for in addition to the luck factor, she brought to the stage a new naturalness of manner at a time when those rivals she was soon to vanquish were still clinging to the old, pedantic rhetoric.

What Ellen Terry lost on the emotional roundabouts—and it must be said that she was not lucky in love—she recovered on the theatrical swings. When the affair with Godwin finally ended she suffered great hurt. But an artist seldom fails to make use of private grief, and actors use the raw clay of experience as the basis for those emotions they allow the public to see. 'You have to be desperately unhappy', Dame Edith Evans used to say, 'before you can play comedy, so that nothing can frighten you'. Ellen was a superb comedian.

When Watts finally consented to divorce her for adultery, her subsequent marriage to Charles Kelly floundered on the rocks of conflicting careers and was short-lived. He tried the traditional solace of the bottle, and when he died Ellen admitted to herself that she was not the marrying kind. She had no shortage of admirers and would-be lovers, and a vast public to worship her, and it was to her public that she gave herself.

There was always the element of the unexpected in her career: witness the fact that Irving chose her to be his consort at the Lyceum without ever having seen her act beyond the brief excursion they had shared in the sham *The Taming of the Shrew*. The greatest and most sustained partnership in the English theatre brought together two people as different in character and background as it is possible to imagine. Irving had so many disadvantages to overcome. Ellen had only one—her own lack of personal ambition. Modesty is so frequently a pose in the theatre, but Ellen Terry never pretended to an emotion she did not feel. Irving on the other hand was often forced to invent a personality to fit his ambitions.

Sir John Gielgud has this to say about them both:

'I always think that the tradition of Shakespeare changes with the leading actors. Irving created one tradition of acting which suited his companies. He changed the people round him to play with him, and what makes his theatre so interesting to us now is that he and Ellen Terry had completely opposite methods. She was very swift and natural, but with certain pictorial pauses in her acting which made her very effectively the heroine of the play, and he was the strange magnetic opposite. The company round them must have been a mixture of the tradition of the actors before Charles Kean's time.'

A mixture. I am sure that Sir John with his unerring instincts and keen eyes and ears for theatrical truth has used the right word. With the start of the Irving-Ellen Terry reign at the Lyceum the mixture was to be stirred again.

『 13 』

THE BELLS RING OUT

T HE second half of the nineteenth century saw far-reaching artistic and physical changes come about in the theatre, as revolutionary in their way as anything Burbage accomplished

When we look about us today and total the number of theatres that have either been destroyed or converted to other uses, it is difficult to imagine that by 1900 Britain had thousands of theatres up and down the country, many of them supreme examples of this highly specialized architectural form, the culmination of a frenzied building boom and matched only by the classical Greek and Continental Baroque periods. It is only in this century that squalid indifference to our heritage, aided in some cases by German bombs, has reduced many of the finest examples to rubble. In addition, many of those still standing are a disgrace to those who operate them, the exteriors filthy beyond belief and in those interior sections where the public seldom ventures, little better than slums.

Theatre architecture is more often linked to the social climate of any given period than to the actual drama then in favour. The great surge of building activity which took place during the second half of the nineteenth century owed more to the inventions and affluence of the Industrial Revolution than it did to the demands of the dramatists and actors who were to occupy the new theatres.

The first major change was of course the introduction of gaslighting during the decade 1825–35. This in turn subtly influenced costume and set design and the way in which the actors applied their make-up. It also forced the authorities to take better precautions against fire hazards, hitherto, as we have seen, a neglected aspect of theatre design. (Wyatt's fourth Drury Lane, for example, made much use of cast and wrought iron and included a primitive form of water sprinklers throughout the house.) Although the major building boom dates from about 1858, the existing London theatres were constantly being altered and redecorated from the beginning of the century; many of the ideas were pirated from abroad and adapted to local taste and needs.

'Taste' was a key Victorian word, and spread outwards from the throne. The lead in theatregoing was given by the Queen when she revived the custom of receiving performers at her Christmas 'theatricals' at Windsor Castle. Whatever amused the monarch sycophantically delighted the emerging upper middle classes, and her approbation brought about a revised opinion of the theatre and its inhabitants. In following her example and noting that members of the royal family frequently attended the London theatres, the new and less riotous audiences in turn forced the managements to provide more creature comforts. Carpets were laid, programmes were printed with more care and detail, more stall seats provided as respectability eased out the rowdiness of the pit, but progress in other directions was less visible. The new patrons were still subjected to the old style of acting in endless revivals of mediocre plays.

Again we have the spectre of Shakespeare's genius still inhibiting the emergence of new dramatists. How else does one explain the fact that in a period which saw the publication of some of the greatest novels in English literature, the majority of new plays were so puerile? The challenge was there but it was not met until the end of the century, and even then it came from beyond these shores.

The only dramatist who can be said to have attempted to come to terms with the challenge of the age was the prolific Tom Robertson. He made it his short life's work to introduce a measure of realism into the theatre and provided the Bancrofts with many of their most successful offerings at the old Prince of Wales theatre in Charlotte Street. Taking practical advantage of the new theatre architecture, he used his considerable knowledge of stage management and design to persuade the Bancrofts to let him experiment. Rejecting the *trompe l'oeil* of most sets, he devised practical doors with handles which opened them and stage rooms that looked as though people lived in them. He became the apostle of realism, and then found that there were no new plays capable of being performed within his proposed revolutionary settings. That being so he began to write plays himself, bringing commendable invention to his plots and what was considered daring colloquialism to his dialogue. Nowadays if we read such of his plays as *Caste, Society* or *Ours* they sound strangely stilted to our ears, but in their own time they were as startling as the debut of Pinter. (Even so, when *Caste* is performed today it remains an acceptable dramatic offering and in construction is infinitely superior to many of the banal modern plays that, inexplicably, monopolise a single theatre for years to the overall detriment of my profession.)

It was a tragedy for the English theatre that Robertson died before he could fully realise his many ambitious plans. W. S. Gilbert was a would-be convert to his philosophy, though he encountered considerable opposition when he attempted to put Robertson's ideas into practice. Without the support and understanding of the Bancrofts it is probable that Robertson would have died a disappointed man at forty-two, but Squire Bancroft, an endearing eccentric—in appearance more like a member of the landed gentry than a leading actor—gave him his head and through him made a large personal fortune. Bancroft allowed Robertson to become the nearest equivalent of a modern producer; allowed artistic control of his own material, he and Bancroft demonstrated that the drama of realism could profitably challenge the old order. Given the rapacious mentality of most theatrical managements, never slow to jump on the latest commercial bandwagon, it may seem surprising that Bancroft did not have more immediate imitators, but the truth of the matter is that Robertson stood more or less alone and was totally faithful to his mentor.

Unable to emulate Bancroft's success, many of his rivals derided Robertson's achievements, labelling him as the chief exponent of the 'cup-and-saucer' drama. This

152

was a view not shared by the more intelligent actors, who were more than anxious to embrace the new style demanded of them by Robertson's texts. Gradually there was a move away from the traditional method whereby leading actors came on and 'made points'. The plays that Robertson created demanded a tighter discipline and although there was no real comparison, we find that there was a shift towards the ensemble playing that Garrick had once tried to impose on his company. As W. A. Darlington pointed out, 'it was only by comparison with the stage rant churned out by contemporary scribes that it [Robertson's dialogue] seemed restful and easy' and the actors fortunate enough to work under the Bancroft aegis were proud to be part of the experiment. The main problem was that after Robertson's premature death he had no natural successor. The rest of the London theatres continued to present either Shakespearean revivals or turgid, second-rate pieces, often hacked from Parisian originals. The Bancrofts stood alone in attempting to foster any alternative to the old system.

Despite the fact that he was a friend and admirer of Robertson, W. S. Gilbert still found it easier and more lucrative to produce a series of flatulent dramatic works, as lacking in humour as they were in inspiration. For reasons I have always failed to comprehend, the writer of comedies is never accorded the same measure of respect given to the writer of tragedies. It is almost as if the critics secretly despise themselves for being made to laugh, and it is this curious attitude which has driven many a gifted writer of comedy to abandon his true role and embark on serious works in the mistaken belief that humour is an inferior medium. Gilbert needed the inspiration of D'Oyly Carte to be persuaded to team with Sullivan and even though their long and brilliant collaboration brought nothing but lasting glory to themselves and the theatre, to the end of his days he longed to be taken seriously. That his colloquial dialogue for the Savoy operas owes a debt to Robertson's pioneering efforts is easily discernible, and thus in two different schools we have a shift of emphasis stemming from the same source.

All these factors—the changing architecture of the period, the introduction of gaslight, the emergence of the upper middle-class anxious to ape the attitude and tastes of a monarch they came to sanctify, the brave encouragement by the Bancrofts of Robertson's theories—all combined, fortuitously, to give the theatre a decade of affluence, during which time a new audience was recruited. It was a theatre still dominated by the actors, and it was not until the 1890's that the dramatists brought about the next revolution. With the exception of Gilbert and Sullivan's devotees, most audiences still went to see a particular actor or actress rather than the play, and it was not until Arthur Pinero's *The Profligate* was produced in 1889 that the dramatist started to become the focus of interest. A one-time small-part member of Irving's company at the Lyceum, Pinero was determined to improve the status of the dramatist. Of course the irony is that the better the play the more likely it is to strengthen the status of the star performer. Such was the case with Pinero's *The Second Mrs Tanqueray* which established the legend of Mrs Patrick Campbell.

In addition to Pinero the last decade of the century also consolidated the reputations of many other distinguished playwrights, headed by Wilde and including Henry Arthur Jones, Haddon Chambers, Stephen Phillips, Paul Potter (who adapted du Maurier's

Trilby) and of course the writer destined to be the most dominant influence of them all, Bernard Shaw, who started slowly and was handicapped by his initial determination to preach rather than entertain.

Wilde, by contrast, came to the craft of playwrighting fully armed. He was almost too gifted, too brilliant for his own good; provoking envy by the ease of his success, making enemies with his flamboyant disregard of conventions and eventually ensuring his own tragic downfall by his inability to curb his conceit. The theatrical profession behaved with singular lack of compassion towards Wilde when his star burnt itself out; in the last years of his life there were few amongst his previous admirers (many of whom had made large sums of money from his talents) who had the courage to acknowledge their debt or his genius. It is a squalid episode from any angle and there are few documents more poignant than the catalogue for the auction of his possessions, issued 'by order of the Sheriff' for Wednesday April 24th 1895. After the press campaign had unleashed 'an orgy of Philistine rancour', in Frank Harris' words, his creditors lost no time in claiming their extra pound of flesh. Even his children's toys came under the hammer and years later his son, Vyvian Holland, described the sale as 'a scandalous piece of barefaced robbery'. I have examined a rare copy of that catalogue (possibly the only one still in existence) and it makes sad reading. From margin notes scribbled by a Brompton Road dealer we learn that many of his beautiful books, the majority of them signed first editions, went for a few shillings. The descriptions in the catalogue, a few of which I select at random, speak for themselves: *128 A proof Etching, a portrait of Ellen Terry, and an engraving, La Cigale; 154 A large quantity of photographs of Celebrities; 163 A Japanese embroidered silk gown; 197 India matting, as laid; 227 Cans, pails, etc in housemaid's closet; 237 a very large quantity of toys.* Most of his manuscripts were stolen, a portrait of Whistler went for six pounds and the house at 16, Tite Street, Chelsea was ransacked. As a final footnote to this shameful event they did not even print his name on the catalogue for fear, presumably, that his crime might contaminate those upright citizens who handled it.*

But perhaps Wilde did have the last laugh. From the long list of dramatists who made their mark during this remarkable period, he remains the most durable—his humour dateless, his sense of theatre capable of bridging the years and entertaining countless generations of theatregoers. He elevated drawing room comedy to an art form, and with *The Importance of Being Earnest* gave us the best-written farce in the English language.

Irving played no great part in encouraging new dramatists. With a writer's venom Shaw dismissed him as having 'no brains', but Shaw was dishonest where Irving was concerned and in later life had the grace to admit as much. He confessed that many of the articles he had written in the *Saturday Review* in which again and again he attacked Irving, because of his 'extraordinary insensibility to literature', were prompted as much by a desire for self-advancement as for soberly assessing Irving's qualities. I am inclined to agree with Darlington's verdict that Shaw, 'like many other dynamic characters who are quite sure they are right, was always totalitarian at heart'. As indicated earlier, Shaw's attitude towards Irving was rendered suspect because of his feelings for Ellen Terry,

* Even before Wilde was condemned George Alexander erased his name from the advertisements, while still profiting by keeping his play on the stage.

NELLY MOORE (with whom Irving was in love) in *Brother Sam*, Haymarket Theatre, 1865. Beside her under the tree is Edward A. Sothern, the star of the production

FLORENCE O'CALLAGHAN
Irving's wife

though I sympathise with him to the extent that he was the victim of his own curious sexuality. He never suffered for love as far as we can tell and although he once wrote that the sexual experience was vital to an artist's progress 'because of its power of producing a celestial flood of emotion and exaltation' his late marriage to Charlotte Payne-Townshend could hardly be described as a passionate relationship.

Irving, on the other hand, did suffer. The first, and probably the most important, love of his life was the young actress Nellie Moore. His extreme poverty precluded marriage at the time when they first met; their careers separated and for a while Nellie outdistanced him, becoming a valuable member of Buckstone's company at the Haymarket. When eventually he triumphed in London he renewed his wooing of her, but both were ambitious and prey to the usual ill-informed back-stage gossip. They drifted apart and Irving met the woman who was eventually to become his wife, Florence O'Callaghan. They were first introduced at the time when Irving was still smarting from the failure of his affair with Nellie Moore, and he was particularly susceptible to the charms of a beautiful and intelligent woman who made no secret of his attraction for her. There was parental disapproval from afar—Florence's father was a Surgeon-General in the Indian Medical Service—which in time-honoured fashion only served to fan the flames. The plot took a further twist when Irving and Nellie were once again brought together in a production of *Oliver Twist*, with Irving cast as Bill Sykes and Nellie playing Nancy. They enjoyed a mutual triumph during the run of three months, and were later re-engaged for H. J. Byron's new play *The Lancashire Lass*, a tawdry little melodrama of no lasting merit. During the run of this play Nellie Moore was struck down with scarlet fever, and died from it. In the opinion of his principal biographers this tragedy indirectly overshadowed his whole life. Eventually overcoming his grief and the Surgeon-General's disapproval he married Florence O'Callaghan, only to find that he had married a shrew who was wholly incompatible with his way of life.

His career was stagnating at the time of his marriage and he was in danger of being type cast as a villain, and though his instincts revolted at the succession of trashy roles offered to him, he was in greater need, with his new responsibilities, of a regular salary. He achieved renewed success in another of H. J. Byron's pieces, with the less than engaging title *Uncle Dick's Darling*, and it did at least lift him out of the rut of melodrama. It was then that he was introduced to three young men known collectively as the Jew, the Gent and the Gentile. This trio—David James, H. J. Montague and Thomas Thorne—were in business together and had taken a lease of the Vaudeville Theatre. They offered Irving a position in the company at a salary of ten pounds a week and he immediately went into rehearsal for their opening production of *For Love or Money*. Work often begets work and during the run of *For Love or Money* he was approached, somewhat mysteriously, by a budding young dramatist who asked him to read the manuscript of his latest play *Two Roses*. The reason for the air of mystery was soon explained to Irving. James Albery, the author of *Two Roses*, had written it on a commission from Irving's three employers. He believed that the character of Digby Grant was made for Irving to play, but was worried in case David James claimed the role for himself. In the event the subterfuge proved unnecessary, the role went to Irving and it proved to be a major landmark in his career. Written with Dickensian gusto, it was played by Irving with relish and this was the role which led him to his destiny at the Lyceum.

Towards the end of the ten-month run of *Two Roses* he was granted a benefit, and gave his fans added value for their loyalty by making a surprise appearance to recite Thomas Hood's celebrated poem *The Dream of Eugene Aram*—a full-blooded, macabre piece about a conscience-stricken schoolmaster-murderer. Irving pulled out all the stops, giving in the words of the *Observer* report: 'acting as is now seldom seen and the thought must have struck many in the theatre whether, with our little plays and pretty sketches, our dainty realization of every day life, our clever sarcasms, our elegances and sensation drama, we are not losing sight of those great passions, that tragedy of human life, which it belongs to the actor to interpret.'

One of those his performances struck was an American impresario with the resounding name of Hezekiah Bateman, who styled himself 'Colonel' Bateman. He was in London for the express purpose of launching his third daughter, Isabel, on a stage career and to that end had recently taken a long lease on the more or less derelict Lyceum Theatre. (This was the third Lyceum, the second of those built by Samuel Arnold, and subsequently restored and enlarged by Fechter. It had ruined several lessees and was considered an unlucky house.)

'Colonel' Bateman was something of a male Mrs Worthington with unlimited ambitions for his offspring. He had already made valiant efforts with two more of his daughters, Virginia and Kate, steering them with more skill and success than Noël Coward's celebrated stage-mother, notably Kate who was already respected and famous on both sides of the Atlantic. There was a fourth daughter, Ellen, who had disappointed him by marrying at the age of fifteen. All his efforts were now centred on Isabel, a

COLONEL HEZEKIAH BATEMAN   ISABEL BATEMAN

reluctant but obedient young lady of considerable beauty who had deep aspirations to become a nun rather than the actress of her father's dreams. From all accounts the 'Colonel' was something of a charlatan, but an engaging one. A failed actor himself who had played juvenile roles with Charles Kean's company, he had assumed the rank of colonel, married the daughter of an expatriate English comedian, and forged a career as a theatrical impresario in order to satisfy his own thwarted longings through his children—an improbable character indeed to turn up out of the blue and change the course of Irving's life.

In a sense Irving and Bateman were birds of a feather: both recognised that ambition often demands that we embrace the most unlikely bedfellows. Bateman wanted something from Irving and was prepared to pay generously; Irving wanted something from Bateman—matching his own shrewdness against the 'Colonel's' fanatical ambitions for his daughter, he agreed to go to the Lyceum as leading man on condition that his new employer would agree to the production of a play in which Irving had great faith. The deal was struck. Irving was engaged for three years at a starting salary of £15 a week, rising by £2 increments, to £19 in the third year. For his part, Bateman agreed to Irving's solitary demand. The play Irving named was *The Bells*.

This was in April 1871. The Lyceum season was to open in September with *La Petite Fadette*, based on a short story by George Sand and laboriously reworked by Mrs Bateman to provide a suitable star vehicle for her daughter. Irving, miscast as a lovesick peasant, had a much inferior role and inevitably disappointed the critics who by now were expecting great things from him every time he appeared.

Alas, good intentions are seldom enough to ensure success in the theatre. The unfortunate Miss Isabel Bateman had been saddled with an impossible task. Her father was all but blind to her deficiencies as an actress, yet even he had to admit defeat after a few nights. James Albery was hastily summoned and cobbled together a version of *Pickwick* to replace the failure of *La Petite Fadette*. Despite the fact that he hardly did justice to Dickens' masterpiece, he was sufficiently a craftsman to construct a marvellous role— Jingle—for Irving. When the play opened Irving, by general consent, was the only redeeming feature. Poor Isabel had been 'rested' by her father, and it was common knowledge that he was rapidly running out of funds. The Bateman family was nothing if not united, and Kate Bateman came to the rescue, baling out her father to the tune of several hundred pounds a week from the profits of her own provincial tour. The 'Colonel' accepted gratefully but even he knew that such an arrangement could not continue forever. It was at this moment that Irving reminded him of his promise regarding *The Bells*.

The Bells was not a brand new play. It had been around for some time and in fact at the very moment that Irving chose to extract his half of the bargain another production was being prepared for the Alfred Theatre, Marylebone. (Both were adaptations from the French of *Le Juif Polonais* by Erckmann-Chatrian. Irving's version was by Leopold Lewis.) The 'Colonel' hesitated in the face of this competition, but Irving insisted that the rival version was inferior and remained vehement that he could meet all challengers and triumph in the central role of Mathias. Bateman bowed to his leading man's passionate conviction and rehearsals commenced.

The Lyceum production was beaten to the post by twelve days, but in the rival version at the Alfred the role of Mathias was played for burlesque and dismissed as a fiasco by critics. Even so the omens were not good. There was no great enthusiasm on anybody's part to repeat the punishment at the Lyceum on November 25th 1871. The first night house was sparse, filling those back-stage with a deep and well-founded gloom.

Irving, as Mathias, had to wait fifteen minutes into the opening act before making his first entrance. One never knows what goes through any individual actor's mind on a particular first night. Some, like the late Robert Donat, are made physically sick with nerves; others enter the theatre hours before curtain rise and then are incapable of starting to apply their make-up until the quarter has been called; others still rely on superstitions and talismans; yet more cannot bear to be spoken to (Edith Evans always took a vow of silence before an opening night); a few take to drink; others like Edmund Kean need the catharsis of sex (on the war-time opening night of Rattigan's *Flare Path*, that brilliant but flawed actor Martin Walker locked himself in his dressing room with a Berwick Street tart); and the majority merely sit staring at the dressing room mirror wondering why on earth they ever joined the profession. Thus it would be a foolish historian who attempted to describe Irving's thoughts as he stood at the back of the seat awaiting his cue, but we can be certain that he was conscious of the enormity of his gamble. The stage 'snow' machine went into action and he flung open the door. He was all but engulfed in a fur cap and a large, snow-spattered coat, and for added effect carried a whip which he waved in greeting. He had not been given a memorable entrance line: it bordered on the anti-climactic, given the circumstances. Had luck not been with him that

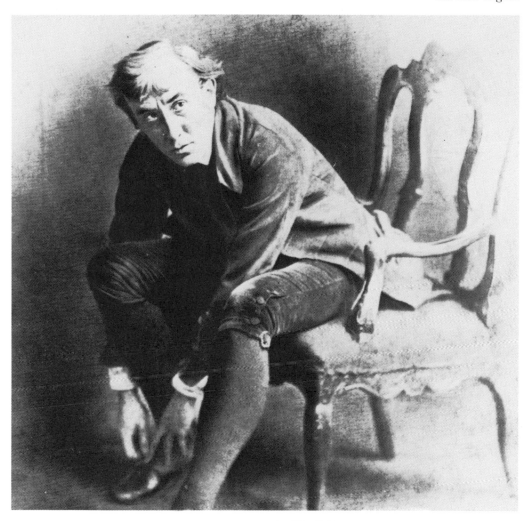

HENRY IRVING in *The Bells*

night it would only have needed one wit in the gallery to have shouted some suitable rejoinder and the mood and Irving's performance would have been shattered: careers have been blighted by such incidents. But whatever his fears, and he must have had many, Irving surmounted those opening seconds. We are told that he delivered the line 'Tis I' as 'Tz I' and then strode downstage, sat in a chair and started to remove his gaiters.

He stepped out of the snow into the setting of a small inn in Alsace and into a pre-Hammer film plot. It is Christmas Eve, melodrama's favourite date on the calendar. Mathias, the prosperous innkeeper and burgomaster, is preparing for his daughter's marriage to the local chief of police. His affluence and standing in the community stem from an undetected murder he committed fifteen years before. At the time of the crime he was facing ruin and saw the opportunity of restoring his fortunes by murdering a rich

Jewish traveller. By dramatic coincidence he had dispatched the traveller on another Christmas Eve. He had waited until the Jew left the inn, pursued him across the fields, intercepted his guest's sledge and killed him. The body had been thrown into a pit of lime and the disappearance of the Jew remained an unsolved and eventually forgotten mystery. Now fifteen years later he has become increasingly haunted by his memory of the sound of the sleigh bells on his victim's sledge. He believes that his only hope of salvation is his daughter's marriage to the chief of police.

The plot is further complicated by the fact that he visits a mesmerist in a local fair. It is an early variation of the truth drug ploy. Mathias is terrified that the mesmerist's powers will make him reveal his dread secret. On the eve of the wedding he dreams that he is in court on trial for the murder—the judge sends for the mesmerist to elicit the truth by putting the accused into a trance. In his dream the device works, he is found guilty and condemned to be hanged. The following morning when his family come to rouse him for the wedding, Mathias is still in the grip of the nightmare. Staggering from his bed, clawing the imaginary hangman's rope around his neck, he dies in their arms.

It is a play that needs an actor of genius to hold it back from the brink of absurdity. It needs an actor who totally sublimates and conceals the bare bones of the plot and who suspends the audience's inclination to disbelief by the very power of his own convictions. And he must accomplish this from his very first lines.

While Mathias bends to remove his gaiters the assembled inmates of the inn are discussing the mesmerist who has the gift to send people to sleep. 'What is more', one of the characters remarks, 'when they are asleep they tell him everything that weighs upon their conscience'. When the key word 'conscience' was spoken, Irving became motionless. Gordon Craig, who saw Irving perform *The Bells* at least thirty times, has described what followed. 'Irving was always in the centre—he had no inferiority complex. . . . By the time the speaker has got this slowly out—and it was dragged purposely—Irving was buckling his second shoe, seated, and leaning over it with his two long hands stretched down over the buckles. We suddenly saw these fingers stop their work; the crown of the head suddenly seemed to glitter and become frozen—and then, at the pace of the slowest and most terrified snail, the two hands, still motionless and dead, were seen to be coming up the side of the leg . . . the whole torso of the man, also seeming frozen, was gradually, and by an almost imperceptible movement, seen to be drawing up and back, as it would straighten a little, and to lean a little against the back of the chair. . . . Once in that position—motionless—eyes fixed ahead of him and fixed on us all—there he sat for the space of ten to twelve seconds, which, I can assure you, seemed to us all like a lifetime, and then said—and said in a voice deep and overwhelmingly beautiful: "Oh, you were talking of that—were you?" And as the last syllable was uttered, there came afar off the regular throbbing sound of sledge-bells.

'There he sat looking at us, and there sat the others, smoking and musing and comfortably motionless, except for the smoke from their pipes—and on and on went the sound of these bells, on and on and on—nothing else. Again, I assure you, that time seemed out of joint, and moved as it moves to us who suffer, when we wish it would move on and it does not stir.'

This was the first of those extraordinary moments that Irving brought to his performance, making the first night 'almost hideously painful' in the words of an eyewitness, and as with Mrs Siddons in years gone by, producing an effect that was powerful enough to make members of the audience faint. I cannot believe that nineteenth-century spectators were necessarily more sensitive than their modern counterparts, and since I have been unable to discover any dissenting voices, we must unquestioningly accept that Irving's personality was overwhelming in this role. From this quiet and economical beginning he built his characterisation—carefully applying layer upon layer of horror until the tension was unbearable. The final climax terrified all who saw it, for he appeared to carry out a public execution on himself: his whole being transformed by the force of his actor's imagination, he projected an image of man-made horror across the footlights and there and then consecrated himself as the greatest theatrical personality of his time. It was a performance he was to repeat over eight hundred times in the next thirty years, and to people like Ellen Terry, Beerbohm Tree, Gordon Craig and Agate the memory of that performance was never erased.

As though to impress upon critics and public the extent of his new-found authority, he was not content to leave it at that. The first-night audience had no sooner recovered their breath when the curtain went up again to reveal Irving in a different guise: a black beaver hat tipped over one eye, a mocking gait, and a style of speech that bore no resemblance to Mathias' croaking delivery, he gave a shortened version of *Pickwick*. His characterisation of Mr Alfred Jingle, shorn of previous rough edges, was now perfection. 'One would have thought', said an observer, 'that Dickens must have seen him first and then put him into *Pickwick Papers*'. It was a daring piece of bravado, and due credit must be given to Bateman for allowing Irving such freedom. In the course of a single evening Irving demonstrated that he was the only and rightful successor to the crown. The Lyceum and Bateman were saved. Henceforth nobody would ever name the theatre without, in the same breath, speaking of it as Irving's personal property.

To celebrate his total victory he enjoyed a modest supper party with a few intimate friends, but the occasion was soured by his wife's behaviour. She sat apart from the joyous gathering, though Irving gallantly gave the impression that he was unaware of her boorish behaviour. On their journey home in a cab he consciously stole Edmund Kean's remark and promised Florence, 'We, too, shall soon have our own carriage and pair.' Her reply must surely go down as the definitive bucket of cold water. 'Are you going on making a fool of yourself like this all your life?' she asked him. It says much for Irving that he did not strangle her on the spot. Instead he stopped the cab—they were crossing Hyde Park Corner—and instructed the driver to continue the journey without him. He never returned home and he never spoke to his wife again. In the whole history of the English theatre there can scarcely have been a more curious postscript to total triumph.

[[14]]

THE LYCEUM: GRANDEUR AND MEMORIES

I THINK one of the main reasons that both Ellen Terry and Irving were revered both by the public and their colleagues is that they were both basically kind people, totally different in personality and outlook, but yet both determined to raise the status of their profession. It would be poetically satisfying to state that their long professional association spilt over into their private lives—to be able to round off their glorious story by the revelation that they were also lovers, that Shaw's jealousy was well-founded. They were close enough to be lovers, but all that has come down to us is that they shared everything but their beds.

When Irving first called on Ellen Terry to offer her a position in his Lyceum company, he took his dog with him. This domestic touch had predictable results, for Irving's inherent shyness seems to have communicated itself to his pet, who 'misbehaved' on Ellen's carpet. By now he had taken over the management of the Lyceum, borrowing the money in order to become his own master at last. He had come a long way since their previous meeting eleven years before.

The story of how he had acquired the lease of the Lyceum again illustrates his humanity and the love and respect he inspired in others. 'Colonel' Bateman had proved a stalwart friend and an astute business partner, supporting Irving at every stage, and bringing to the Lyceum his brash, but effective style of American know-how and publicity. Together they had succeeded in placing the Lyceum firmly on the map to the point where it challenged the centuries-old supremacy of Drury Lane and Covent Garden. During the four years of their partnership there had been none of the petty squabbles and chicanery so characteristic of the relationships that Garrick, Kean and Macready often endured with their various landlords. Following the spectacular success of *The Bells* Bateman had allowed Irving to broaden his experience by tackling a great classical role and together they presented what was for many years considered the definitive *Hamlet*.

Expectations of failure ran high amongst those who are always on hand to pre-judge the abilities of those they cannot approach in talent. But Irving was prepared for them, and was determined to give a performance that was, as far as he could judge, utterly true to Shakespeare's conception. His artistic innovation was to discard the flamboyance of his exalted predecessors and present the play as a domestic tragedy with Hamlet as a young man forced to act in a manner foreign and abhorrent to his basic nature. Since theatregoers of this century have seen many interpretations of the role that stem from the same psychological approach it is difficult to imagine the effect that Irving's new portrayal had on his first night audience. They were slow to give their approval and we are told that until he came to the great scene with Ophelia actor and audience remained out of touch with each other: they did not condemn him nor did they applaud him, the atmosphere was one of respectful lack of comprehension as to his purpose. Irving had been saving his big guns, and in the scene with Ophelia he stupefied his audience, unleashing a broadside of vituperation. Nobody described this better than the French critic, Augustus Filon, who said that this moment was 'Irving's Marengo'. Another spectator wrote 'a hurricane of applause shook the benches, and everyone felt that the tall, seemingly nervous actor, who, with ruthless nonchalance had thrown overboard the conventional, pathetically puffed-up prince, to make of him an unconstrained gentleman with a tingle of melancholy upon him—that this actor was the new Hamlet, the Hamlet of the future'.

Ellen Terry who was present on that first night spoke of Irving making the audience 'come to him'. Her other comments regarding his performance are equally illuminating and the more valuable for coming from a fellow actor with inside knowledge. When in later years she played Ophelia to his Prince of Denmark she told that at rehearsals he would constantly remind the company that 'we must make this play a living thing' and that his concentration was such that 'he worked until the skin grew tight over his face, until he became livid with fatigue'. As a member of the audience on that opening night in 1874 she describes his make-up as 'very pale' but added 'this made his face beautiful when one was close to him, but at a distance it gave him a haggard look. Some said he looked twice his age'. She was particularly perceptive about his playing of the advice to the players scene. As Irving gave the famous speech 'it was not advice. He did not speak it as an actor. Nearly all Hamlets in that scene give away the fact that they are actors, and not dilettanti of royal blood. Irving defined the way he would have the players speak as an *order*, an instruction of the merit of which he was regally sure.' It was her verdict that having seen many Hamlets—among them those of Fechter, Charles Kean, Rossi, Frederick Haas and Forbes-Robertson (and not forgetting her own son, Gordon Craig, to absolve her of obvious bias) 'they were not in the same hemisphere'.

Despite the overwhelmingly favourable reception of his performance and the fact that the Lyceum production ran for two hundred nights—an unprecedented total for a Shakespearean play—there were some violently dissenting voices. James Spedding, accounted a reliable critic in his day, found Irving 'simply hideous . . . a monster!' Another body of opinion described him as a grotesque comedian whom Bateman, with trans-Atlantic sorcery had passed off as a tragic actor. Shaw, as we know, was affronted that Irving ever attempted Shakespeare. 'I sometimes wonder', he wrote, 'where Mr Irving will go when he dies—whether he will dare to claim, as a master artist, to walk where he may any day meet Shakespeare whom he has mutilated'. Shaw's main criticism of Irving was that he was always Irving, an observation made with wittier insolence by Agate who wrote that every character Irving played 'only just missed being Mr Gladstone'. Now to deny critics an opinion would be to deny them an existence, but it seems to me that what really offended Shaw was that Irving had more success at playing himself than Shaw did at writing himself. Agate, on the other hand, was merely unable to resist the joke even though it seems strangely at variance with his consistent eulogies.

Poor Bateman died before he could enjoy the full fruits of their joint triumph. He died of a heart attack following an altercation with the proprietor of a restaurant, the scene of a celebration dinner to mark the hundredth performance of *Hamlet*. His widow, ever a resourceful woman, carried on in his place. She was anxiously maternal where Irving was concerned and he, for his part, assumed the position of surrogate father to the three unmarried daughters. But he missed the day to day guidance that the 'Colonel' had provided. Emboldened, no doubt, by the tremendous commercial success of his *Hamlet* he next turned to *Macbeth*. Mrs Bateman encouraged this new venture since it would allow her to cast Kate Bateman as Lady Macbeth. Once again Irving was determined to present a novel interpretation and perhaps in his new-found authority he misjudged the extent to which he was physically suited to certain of the great classical roles. His *Macbeth* did not live up to anybody's expectations, not even his own. He was to confide to a friend that he had 'fallen below his ideal'. His detractors (and like most successful men on the way up he was accumulating his fair share) were delighted. They included Henry James, recently arrived in London from Paris convinced of the superiority of French culture. When a certain breed of Americans discover Paris, France, then even to this day they behave as though they alone have been granted sight of the Holy Grail. Lifting his literary skirts like a lady engaged upon charity work who is obliged to cross to the wrong side of the tracks, he described Irving's acting as that 'of a very superior amateur' having prefaced his evaluation of *Macbeth* by stating 'there is a want of delicacy in speaking of the first theatre in the world one day and of the London stage the next . . . if you talk about one you forfeit the right to talk about the other'.

In addition to facing James and other critics Irving was also concerned with the wider issues that affected his entire profession. He was feeling his way towards the summit and with the instincts of a born leader he did not shirk responsibilities. His own success had opened doors for him, but the majority of his colleagues were still regarded as pariahs by many sections of society. In particular the Church was still denouncing the stage from its pulpits: those clergymen who felt compelled to venture into the Devil's territory often went incognito. Irving decided to answer them in kind and gave a spirited defence of his profession at the conference of the Church of England Temperance Society. It was the first shot in a campaign he fought for most of his life.

Set against this public crusade he was also having to contend with personal problems back-stage. Mrs Bateman had inherited her late husband's well-meaning but misguided ambitions for Isabel, and almost before the controversy surrounding *Macbeth* had died down she announced that Irving would next appear as Othello, with Isabel as Desdemona and Kate Bateman as Emilia. The timing was hardly propitious. The great Italian tragedian, Salvini, had recently appeared in the role at Drury Lane and his performance in his native tongue had been proclaimed the work of genius. Irving could not have been unaware of impending comparisons and with his usual thoroughness looked for ways and means of varying the conventional conception of the Moor. He commissioned Sir John Tenniel to design his costumes in the style of a serving Venetian general, and instead of 'blacking-up' gave himself a bronzed look. From letters he wrote at the time he sensed that he was pushing too hard at the doors of tradition: the public are not always receptive to change and he had now challenged old ways three times in succession, forcing the pace too early in the game. Even so his growing reputation was such that *Othello* survived for forty-nine performances, again constituting a record.

Resting himself from Shakespeare, his next appearance was as Philip II in Tennyson's *Queen Mary*, the third play in a trilogy depicting the making of England. It was lifeless drama, more the product of a Poet Laureate than a man of the theatre (it is curious how often the honour of becoming Poet Laureate effectively dehydrates talent). Irving's role was a small one yet it proved to be one of his most effective. Once again Ellen Terry was there to give us her evaluation. She found his study in cruelty 'spellbinding' and was also generous in her praise of Kate Bateman ('*very* good'). What is fascinating is that she considered Irving never did anything better to the day of his death, and although she wrote this at a much later date, long after their reign at the Lyceum had ended, she saw no reason to change her original opinion. If she was right then Irving is confirmed as a genius in my opinion, for it would take genius to bring Tennyson's play to life.

Irving toured after this, taking the Lyceum company to the provinces with *Hamlet*, *Charles I* and *The Bells*. When he returned to London for the winter season of 1877 he was preparing *Richard III* and he was the first leading actor to throw out all Cibber's embroideries and return to the unblemished text. In view of the thin enthusiasm that had greeted his innovations for *Macbeth* and *Othello* it was a courageous decision, and courage was rewarded. Here was the historical Richard, not the grotesque, shapeless cripple so beloved by his brother actors in the past. He brought a malignant humour to the role, emphasising the Plantagenet king rather than the stock villain with *Punch* hump. In a graciously symbolic gesture old Chippendale, who had acted with Edmund Kean, presented Irving with the sword Kean had used in the role.

His next great success was when he took Charles Reade's adaptation of *Le Courier de Lyon* (which Reade had originally fashioned for Charles Kean) and persuaded Reade to rewrite it under his guidance. He retitled it *The Lyons Mail* and played the dual role of Lesurques and Dubosc. This exercise in versatility proved one of his most enduring popular successes, and his characterisations—the former a hero falsely accused and the latter an unmitigated villain—were finely judged. With the Lyceum as his base, and with a growing repertoire of proved worth, he was able to widen his appeal and embarked on regular tours of the provinces. He still had to contend with many scurrilous critics and was forced to resort to law on two occasions in order to prevent the circulation of libellous pamphlets. His work-load was enormous and he became more and more conscious that his most pressing need was a permanent leading lady who could give him stronger support.

Matters were brought to a head when it became obvious that Isabel Bateman had fallen hopelessly in love with him. At twenty-four she was a tragic victim of circumstances. Urged into a profession for which she had little enthusiasm, the original devotion she had given to her father was now transferred to Irving. Irving had the added attraction of being a great romantic figure and her infatuation is wholly understandable. This

IRVING as Macbeth
From a drawing by Sir Bernard Partridge

IRVING as Philip of Spain, in Tennyson's
Queen Mary, Lyceum, 1874
From the painting by J. M. Whistler

development caused Irving a great deal of embarrassment, since there was no escaping from it and he found himself incapable of returning her love. The poor girl was unable to conceal or control her passion, and the situation rapidly got out of hand. It became obvious to Irving that he had to act quickly and decisively to avoid disaster. He needed an artistic partner free from any emotional involvement, and this was the decision he communicated to Mrs Bateman in a delicately worded letter.

From all accounts Mrs Bateman must have been a remarkable woman. Although she never wavered in defence of her daughter and had already intimated that she would have no objection to Isabel living with Irving until such time as his divorce became absolute, once she was convinced of his true feelings in the matter, she behaved with commendable common sense and generosity. Rather than let the situation drift into rancour that would reflect no credit on anybody, she immediately proposed that she should allow Irving the opportunity to take over the lease of the Lyceum as soon as possible. He was quite properly astounded by her attitude and must have applauded her wisdom. Lacking the necessary resources to purchase the lease himself, he had to borrow the money. For the second time he had reason to be thankful to a woman. An elderly lady, Mrs Hannah Brown, the companion to Baroness Burdett Coutts, the granddaughter of banker Thomas Coutts, who had befriended him a few years previously, provided the necessary £1500. The sum of money was not large and was a further indication of Mrs Bateman's generosity towards him; there is no doubt that had she offered to sell the lease on the open market she could have raised a great deal more. Irving accepted the loan and the matter was speedily resolved.

With considerable fortitude Mrs Bateman announced that she had purchased the lease of Sadler's Wells and intended to refurbish it and make it a going concern. Her lease was for thirty-four years, but she died within three years, the theatre heavily in debt. It was inevitable that many of their mutual friends blamed Irving for her sorry end, but perhaps they did not realise the extent to which an impossible human problem had determined his original decision. Kate Bateman never forgave him; the hapless Isabel eventually took the step she had for so long contemplated and entered holy orders, but before retiring from the world she continued to act until such time as she had paid off her mother's debts. It was a sad end to what had once been a happy and creative association.

Free at last to take his own decisions, Irving lost no time in contacting Ellen Terry and their reunion took place during the third week in July 1878. Her immediate impression was that he had lost 'much of the stiff, ugly self-consciousness which had encased him as the shell encases the lobster,' though 'his manner was very quiet and gentle'. A salary of forty pounds a week was agreed, plus 'a half clear benefit'. It was the start of what was to prove to be the most enduring and brilliant partnership in the English theatre.

There is a revealing passage in Ellen Terry's memoirs written twenty-eight years later. In giving her opinion of Irving she confessed 'I, of all people, can perhaps appreciate him least justly, although I was his associate on the stage for a quarter of a century, and was on the terms of closest friendship with him for almost as long a time. *He had precisely the qualities that I never find likeable.*'*

She went on to state that Irving was an egoist—'an egoist of the great type, *never* "a mean egoist" as he was once slanderously described—and all his faults sprang from egotism, which is in one sense, after all, only another name for greatness. . . . Perhaps it is not true, but, as I believe it to be true, I may as well state it: *It was never any pleasure to him to see the acting of other actors and actresses*** . . . What I have written so far I have written merely to indicate the qualities in Henry Irving's nature which were unintelligible to me, perhaps because I have always been more woman than artist. He always put the theatre first. He lived in it, he died in it. He possessed none of what I may call my homely qualities—the love of children, the love of a home, the dislike of solitude. I have always thought it hard to find my inferiors. He was sure of his high place. He was far simpler than I in some ways. He would talk, for instance, in such an ingenuous way to painters and musicians that I blushed for him.'

* The italics are mine.
** This time the italics are Ellen Terry's.

By her own words, let alone the evidence of others, it was from the beginning an inspired but curious relationship between them. It is my belief that it was their very differences of personality and outlook that cemented the partnership, and if from afar outsiders took the simplistic view, bracketing them as Beauty and the Beast, then they probably enjoyed the joke and the resulting interest at the box office.

Gordon Craig agreed with part of his mother's description of Irving's character. Craig felt that Irving had 'inherited some strange demon or other which put a kind of terror into people'. He belonged to that breed of actors who always feel more secure when they are disguised. This is Sir John Gielgud's view as well as my own. Sir John told me that he felt Irving 'couldn't really bring himself to give that distinction which he bore as a man unless he was disguised in robes and crowns. Although Shaw tried to persuade him to play Barrie's *Professor's Love Story* and Ibsen's *The Pretenders*, he could not bring himself to change what was, I suppose, his intrinsic style. The only modern play he ever did, *The Medicine Man*, was a ghastly failure.'

If we return to Ellen Terry's comment that Irving never derived pleasure from seeing other actors perform, against this we have to set his ability to pick talent. He chose such fine young actors as Frank Benson, William Terriss and John Martin Harvey to join his Lyceum company. Terriss was to meet with a tragic end. He was murdered outside the door of the Adelphi Theatre. When the news was brought to Irving he remarked bitterly: 'They won't execute his murderer—Terriss was an actor.' During research for the BBC programmes which were the genesis of this book, my producer, John Knight, came across a recording made by John Henderson, who was the ten-year-old call boy at the Lyceum at the time of Terriss' murder. Henderson recalled that he knew the man who murdered Terriss: 'His name was Prince. He was simply a hanger-on at the theatres and in all the bars in the Strand. If he saw anybody he knew he'd get a cheap drink. Well, *Secret Service* was going on, a big success at the Adelphi and there was a private door, a stage door William Terriss used to get away from the autograph hunters. He got his key in the door this night at 7 o'clock and he got a knife in his back and he dropped. His leading lady came along a few minutes afterwards, Miss Millward, and he died in her lap.'

Terriss had been Jessie Millward's lover and Irving's behaviour towards her after his murder tells us much about the man. Jessie's position in society was such that she was not expected to attend the funeral. But on the morning of the burial, Irving went to her flat carrying a bunch of violets and a message of condolence from the Prince of Wales. He insisted on escorting her to the funeral, an 'act prompted by his own tenderness of heart, by his loyalty to his dead friend and by his unerring divination of the public mind', in Laurence Irving's words.

It is also worth recording that this was not an isolated act. When Oscar Wilde was being shunned by everybody, Irving was one of the few who extended a gesture of sympathy. He again sent a bunch of violets, with the sure instinct that a floral remembrance would comfort a man who had always lived in the admiration of beauty.

Can Irving and Ellen Terry be said to have established a 'tradition' of acting? In the purest sense the answer must be no, because there is no direct line from their joint reign at the Lyceum, no 'Irving School' of acting that has been passed on to succeeding generations. What they did establish was a new standard of excellence, a fresh dignity to the theatre. When Gladstone offered Irving the first theatrical knighthood, Irving initially refused and then, at the second time of asking, took the honour as the cloak of respectability on behalf of his much maligned profession. Ellen Terry was also eventually honoured with the female equivalent and made a Dame of the British Empire, though her accolade came late—thirty years after it had been conferred on Irving and only three years before her death. There were many who argued that Irving's eventual acceptance was pure self-advancement, and he was keenly aware of the debate that would follow his knighthood. He made his point of view public in an address given to the Royal Institution of Great Britain. 'Official recognition of anything worthy is a good or at least useful thing. It is a part, an important part, of the economy of the State; if it is not, of what use are titles and distinctions, names, ribbons, badges, offices, in fact the titular and sumptuary ways of distinction? Systems and courts, titles and offices, have all their part in a complex and organised civilisation, and no man and no calling is particularly pleased at being compelled to remain outside a closed door . . . Acting may be evanescent, it may work in the media of common nature, it may be mimetic like other arts, it may not create, any more than does the astronomer and the naturalist, but it can live and can add to the sum of human knowledge in the ever varying study of man's nature and by man and its work can, like six out of the seven wonders of the world, exist as a great memory.'

I find this a profound passage and it seems to me that Irving's description of acting as 'a great memory' is as close to the truth as we shall ever get. Acting is to the majority of us remembered pleasure, and the recollection of great performances in great plays is one of the most elusive things to pass on to others. The very first great performance that we witness in the flesh is likely to colour our reactions to everything that comes after it, for so often our opinions are conditioned not so much by the excellence of an individual player, as by our mood at the moment we witnessed it. Emotions are governed by so many external factors. Whether we admit it or not we are greatly influenced by our physical reaction to any particular player. To cite a trite example it could well be that more people would emphatically prefer the excellence of, say, Gary Cooper, to the excellence of, say, Sir Donald Wolfit. But it would be impossible to bracket these two outstanding personalities together and describe them both as 'great actors'. One developed a screen personality and a technique for acting to the camera to a high degree of excellence, and the other was an actor cast in the classical mould who in certain roles elevated the art of acting to the peaks. Therefore comparative arguments as to the superiority of one of these players to the other are useless, even though to the layman they were both 'great actors'. One cannot criticise Gary Cooper's legions of fans for preferring him, since the majority of them would never have had an opportunity of seeing Sir Donald Wolfit. And this criterion can be applied across the whole spectrum of acting. All memories are valid to the person who retains them.

It would be foolish, therefore, to compare Irving's greatness with those who came before him or came after. Like any other leading player he can only be judged in the isolation of his own time. The best we can do is to assemble as much evidence as we consider reliable, some of it for and some of it against, whilst all the time remembering that each generation demands that the actor holds up a different mirror to society.

Irving's greatest contribution was not that he established a tradition but that he broke with one. Henry James at his most waspish deplored this fact and even resented Irving achieving any success: 'That an actor so handicapped . . . by nature and culture should have enjoyed so much prosperity is striking proof of the absence of a standard, of the chaotic condition of taste.' What he was really saying was that he hated anything that did not conform to his definition of taste, and he was churlish in not giving Irving any credit for surmounting those 'handicaps'. Irving himself was not self-deceived; he anticipated some of his critics and was always conscious of his physical deficiencies and his mannered way of speaking. But he made these work *for* him; there was nothing accidental about those eccentricities that so annoyed James, Archer and Shaw. He was nothing if not a realist and nobody can deny him the fact that he was, supremely, a man of the theatre. He did not despise his calling like Macready, he did not use the stage as a means of self-advancement socially, like Garrick in his later days, he was not a talented dilettante, he was always committed to the theatre and the theatre alone. Max Beerbohm, in his obituary, described him as 'intransformable' but 'multi-radiant'.

There has always been an anti-Irving camp, with Shaw as the founder member, and they judge him by externals only, giving little credit for his less-public achievements. He did not die a rich man although during the course of his long career he probably made as much money as any other leading actor before or since. From the profits of his numerous provincial and American tours he ensured that the high standards of excellence at the Lyceum were maintained. In other words he put back as much as he took and the devotion of his companies to the 'Guv'nor' (as he was always called) speaks for itself. Loyalty in the theatre is never taken for granted and has to be earned.

It is not difficult to understand why Shaw attacked him so consistently. Irving was the figurehead of the actors' theatre, and personified the reactionary forces as far as Shaw was concerned. He had rejected Ibsen (and indeed Shaw) and was therefore an ignoramus. It never seems to have occurred to Shaw that Irving knew his own limitations; that because he was a romantic realist he instinctively shied away from attempting the new drama of ideas. He did not feel he could do it justice, nor did he think that his public would accept him in such plays, and he can hardly be blamed for not wishing to empty his theatre. I also have the suspicion that Irving was more than a match for Shaw and that this further rankled. There was an occasion (following a revival of *Richard III* towards the end of Irving's career) when Shaw wrote in condescending terms to explain a misunderstanding about his review. Irving's reply was masterly.

'. . . You are absolutely wrong in your polite insinuation of the cat out of the bag—as I had not the privilege of reading your criticism—as you call it—of Richard. I never read a criticism of yours in my life. I have read lots of your droll, amusing, irrelevant and sometimes impertinent pages, but criticism containing judgement and sympathy I have never seen by your pen.'

This exchange took place during the protracted deliberations concerning Shaw's *The Man of Destiny* which at one time Irving was said (so Ellen Terry reported) to have liked. In Laurence Irving's memorably amusing description Shaw was 'like a middle-aged

170

IRVING as Becket
From the photograph by Julia Margaret Cameron

spinster preoccupied with preserving a virginity upon which nobody had designs.' He had no sooner offered the play to Irving (for obvious commercial reasons) than he was worried lest Irving's acceptance of it would signal that Irving was attempting to corrupt him. They eventually met to discuss the matter face to face on Irving's terms (not ungenerous in view of Shaw's inexperience) and on Irving's territory. Ellen Terry wanted to be present at the meeting, anticipating the need of a peace-maker, but funked it at the last moment. The two men were incapable of understanding each other and the meeting was a failure. It is doubtful whether Shaw could ever have accepted the real reason for Irving's eventual rejection of the play, which was, bluntly, that he didn't think it was good enough. One can sympathise with any author who is rejected, but Shaw's demands were too arrogant and his attacks on the Lyceum too consistent for Irving, and in the end even Shaw recognised this. He was 'reconciled' by the sincerity of Irving's final postscript to the episode. 'His reply', wrote Shaw, . . . 'amounted to "For God's sake let me alone".' The Guv'nor was tired and the end was near, for despite the many glories of his long career the closing years were marred with personal and professional tragedies. His health, which had never been in doubt, suddenly failed him; the irreplaceable store of Lyceum scenery was destroyed by fire, and burdened by debts he was forced to relinquish control of the theatre to a syndicate of businessmen. By 1902 it was all over. The Lyceum was dark.

Irving toured the provinces in the years remaining to him looking, as Ellen Terry remarked, 'like some beautiful grey tree', and he died a long way from his beloved Lyceum, in Bradford, struggling 'to keep the date' as we say in the theatre. He played Shylock on the Monday night, Becket on the Tuesday. The following night he gave *The Bells* for the last time, then Becket again on the Friday. Athene Seyler, that consummate comedienne, was present at that performance as a child of sixteen and later recalled her impressions of him. 'I remember so vividly his coming across the stage for his final entrance. I remember that he trailed one foot a little and this most significant and most moving appearance greatly affected me. When he came to his death scene I actually fainted in my seat.'

After the performance Irving collapsed. Curiously he had changed the last line in the play that evening from 'God's will be done' to 'God is my judge'. He rallied slightly and was taken back to his hotel where he rested on a chair in the foyer. Losing consciousness, he fell from the chair to the floor. A local country doctor happened to be having a drink in the manager's office and hearing somebody call for medical aid, went to give assistance. As Laurence Irving describes it: 'An old gentleman whom he did not recognise, lay unconscious on the floor; his head was supported by a frail little fellow who was quietly weeping.' The sad irony is that the doctor had to ask whom he was attending.

And so he died, and was brought back to London to lie in state, as befitted a prince of the theatre, in the ground floor of the Baroness Burdett-Coutts' house at the corner of Stratton Street and Piccadilly. There, all through the day before his burial in Westminster Abbey, his friends filed past his laurel-shrouded coffin. He died in harness and he died penniless, aged sixty-seven, unreconciled to his wife who survived him.

Irving was a sentimentalist, steeped in the romance of the theatre, and he never strayed from his chosen path. Those he often infuriated berated him for not aiming higher, but he aimed as high as he could in those things he did to perfection. As he said to the young Russell Thorndike, 'there are only two ways of portraying a character on the stage. Either you can try to turn yourself into that person—which is impossible—or, and this is the way to act, you can take that person and turn him into yourself. That is how I do it!' He did it supremely well and many, like Agate, surrendered to him. In a rare moment of total candour, writing to Jock Dent, Agate confessed that, as a critic, he was not in the running with Hazlitt. 'In the spectrum of dramacology (*sic*) I approximate to mauve, and you remember Whistler's "Mauve is only pink trying to be purple". Compared with Hazlitt my purplest passages are a sickly puce. And then I haven't Shaw's knowledge, Max's wit, Walkley's urbanity, Montague's style. Besides, I don't particularly want the stuff to live. I might have wanted if there had been an Irving to write about, but there hasn't. I tell you, Jock, that I would give the whole of Olivier, Richardson, Wolfit and Gielgud for the smile the Old Man gave the little serving maid at his first entrance in *The Bells*!'

From the critic to the son of the woman most closely associated with Irving—Gordon Craig: 'People tried to delude the world into believing that he was a great artist, a great personality, a great anything you like, but they would never admit the great actor. They said the same of Ellen Terry: that she was not a great actress, she was a great woman, a great dear and she had a great heart. To me it seems quite simple that if anybody could play the fourth act of *Hamlet*, that scene which is called Ophelia's mad scene, as Ellen Terry did then that person is undoubtedly a very great actress. I can recall scenes from *Much Ado About Nothing* played by Ellen Terry, and from *The Merchant of Venice*, too. Both of which I have seen performed in Europe by all sorts of people who are considered skilled actresses, but who had not even begun to know what it meant to act Shakespeare. Ellen Terry was very much a daughter of Shakespeare and when she spoke his prose it was as though she was only repeating something she had heard him say to her in the next room, and would then come straight onto the stage and say it. It seemed the easiest thing in the world to do when you saw her do it, and the unskilful part of the world supposed that it was as easy as it seemed and that, being easy, it could not be acting. And another unskilful section of the same public finding Irving forcing his soul said, 'Oh, that's so unnatural it can't be acting.' The unskilful thought Ellen Terry no actress because she was so natural, and Irving no actor because he was so unreal. Never were these critics able to explain how it was that the huge audiences were so hushed to listen, so still and watching, so careful to watch, nor why when the curtain fell there came from this undemonstrative and British public, chiefly in the pit, a roar of uncontrollable joy and enthusiasm, a torrent of applause, a waving of handkerchiefs and hats and cries of 'Bravo, bravo!'

〖 15 〗

AN ACTOR'S ACTOR—
BEERBOHM TREE

I N the entire history of the English stage it would be difficult to find a more engaging character than Sir Herbert Beerbohm Tree—that Cyrano without the nose who brought such panache to his public and private lives and never pined for unrequited love. It was part of the lifelong joke that he was only half English; his ancestors came from Lithuania and through the years they had married into the fringe of the German aristocracy establishing themselves as members of the ruling class in the triangle of the three Baltic States. Lithuania was the country of Teutonic legend where knights were bold and often hideously unlikeable, so presumably Tree's sense of humour was mostly provided by his English mother. Julius Beerbohm, his father, was the youngest of a brood of twelve—a long way down the line in the pecking order for inheritances—and wisely decided to seek his fortune abroad. He went to Paris and thence to London where he became a corn trader and married an English girl, Constantia Draper. She gave him three sons and a daughter and then died. Julius promptly switched his affections to her sister, Eliza, who seems to have been one of those cheerful, useful spinsters—so thick on the ground in Victorian times—who were always around to help out with domestic chores. Julius, who was something of a dandy, extremely well educated and with a Germanic contempt for most of the Puritan conventions of Victorian England, saw no reason why he should not marry Eliza. English law forbade such a liaison, so he took her to Switzerland, married her there quite legally, then returned to London to set about starting a new family. As with his son, Herbert, he believed that man was born to reproduce himself, and Eliza dutifully provided him with a further five children of whom Sir Max Beerbohm was the youngest, separated from Herbert by almost a generation.

Some of his father's utter disregard for convention rubbed off on Herbert and although he bowed to parental wishes and attempted a career in the City, his heart was never in it and he had a passion for indulging in mimicry and amateur theatricals from an early age. There were some who said he remained an inspired amateur for the rest of his days, but this is a harsh and spiteful verdict. The truth is that he took few things in life wholly seriously and developed his famous 'vagueness' to a fine art, finding it a useful shield against bores, an escape from the dangerous word 'yes'. Although extremely capable when he set his mind to it, he preferred to exhibit himself as unworldly, cultivating an alter ego that in the end became his most brilliant, sustained performance. Behind the public mask there lurked the perennial adolescent, but bearing no

TREE as Hamlet
Haymarket, 1892

TREE as Fagin in *Oliver Twist*
His Majesty's, 1905

resemblance to the Peter Pan of Barrie's arrested imagination: Tree did not fly *out* of bedroom windows. With an energy one can only admire he managed to lead a full and complicated double life, for he found it difficult to resist a pretty face, and although he was outwardly a pillar of establishment respectability and rewarded with a knighthood, he managed to organise his career and love affairs in such a way that both flourished. He wrote himself a complicated plot and performed it in style, borrowing incidents and dialogue from Oscar Wilde's pen and anticipating the inventions of Frederick Lonsdale. On one side of his stage he presented his legal wife, Maud Holt, playing a drawing room comedy, and on the other side, less well illuminated, he gave second billing to Beatrice May Pinney, appearing under the deed-poll name of Reed in a domestic and human drama. He provided these two ladies with a reasonably large cast: Maud gave him three daughters and May topped her with five sons and a daughter, and with one or two minor mishaps a good time appears to have been had by all. Had he not chosen to have been an actor he might have achieved lasting fame as a tight-rope walker.

For a period after his death it was fashionable to depict him as something of a buffoon, unfavourably comparing his cavalier approach to the theatre and life in general with Irving's single-minded dedication. But Tree was anything but a fool; he took the measure of the age he lived in and acted accordingly, exploiting its eccentricities and turning them to his own advantage. Hesketh Pearson sub-titled his biography of Tree *His Life and Laughter* and twenty years later Madeleine Bingham called hers *The Great Lover* with the sub-title 'His Life and Art'. The composite picture which comes down to me through the years is divided fairly equally between the two: there was much art and a great deal of laughter. He played the central role of Herbert Beerbohm Tree with sustained brilliance and seldom, if ever, stepped out of character: in the year of his death, at the age of sixty-four, he became a father for the tenth time and possibly died regretting he had not achieved the round dozen. This last child, a son named Paul who is still alive, was the result of a love affair with an actress and dancer, Muriel Ridley. Both families continued the artistic line. The three Tree daughters, Viola, Felicity and Iris, all made their mark in society, and one of May Pinney-Reed's sons was Sir Carol Reed. A contemporary descendant is film actor, Oliver Reed, who seems happily determined to keep the flame of eccentricity alight.

Tree was undoubtedly possessed of enormous charm and said of himself, 'I cannot help being exceptional'. This wasn't a typical actor's conceit, and although a certain arrogance swelled his personality as it does any leading actor, Tree, like Sir Ralph Richardson, derived genuine pleasure from being enchantingly different—what used to be called a 'character'. One of the most revealing stories about him was told by his half-brother Max, who recalled an incident when Tree was accosted in the street by a friend. ' "How are you, Tree?" the friend enquired. Tree adopted his dreamy look, gazed around the street and replied: "I? Oh, I'm radiant." ' Max Beerbohm commented: 'He looked radiant, it was obvious that he felt radiant, and he told the simple truth in saying that he *was* radiant . . . When he was managing His Majesty's Theatre the gigantic risks he often took never caused him to turn a hair. He was glad if things were going well; if they weren't he had a plan for making them do so within a few weeks. He could look Ruin in the face and say, "Oh, I'm radiant"; whereat Ruin always slunk away . . . foiled again.'

The theatre was never a matter of life and death to him, as it was with Irving. He admired Irving, was on friendly terms with Irving, frequently rivalled Irving, but he was not blinkered to life's other pleasures as Irving was. Because of this his contribution has been down-graded by those who take it upon themselves to dole out History's Honours List. There has always been a snobbish vein running through most dramatic criticism; one failure in a classical role is frequently accounted game, set and match, the memory of the player's so-called shame never forgotten, but brandished time and time again. Now there is nothing basically dishonourable in failing as Hamlet, yet over the years this particular role has become the yardstick by which entire careers are either extolled or dismissed. I have never understood this bigoted school of thought, and whereas other equally spectacular failures are conveniently (and indeed rightly) cast into a cupboard, if an actor does not measure up to a hypothetical scale of excellence as the Prince of Denmark he is never allowed to forget it. This may make for easy copy, but it is very poor justice.

Tree did not succeed as Hamlet. He failed on a grand scale and his performance gave rise to some of the most quoted witticisms in theatrical folklore, headed by W. S.

Gilbert's 'His Hamlet was funny without being in the least bit vulgar' and Wilde's 'My dear Herbert, *good* is not the word'. Splendid stuff and well worth preserving, but as Max Beerbohm and others have pointed out, Tree was not crushed by them; his sense of humour extended to himself—always the acid test of a humorous man—and when a colleague professed that, in keeping with the critics, he hadn't thought much of Tree's moody Dane, Tree said 'No, but it's a good part, isn't it?' We also have the word of other friends that he was 'a magnificent fellow in failure'. Philip Carr gave us one example of his good-natured resilience: 'It was at the end of the first night of a new play that had not been a success. The gallery was loud in its disapproval—louder than it would be today, at least in the case of an established management. It called persistently for the author, and it left no mistakes possible as to the reception it meant to give him. Tree himself stepped out in front of the curtain. "The author is not in the house," he said, "but I am always here, ready to receive your hoots".'

In keeping with his half-German monarch, Tree epitomised the flamboyance of the Edwardian age. It was a world of 'understated immorality and overstated decoration' in Madeleine Bingham's phrase, where Art was allowed to approach but not mirror real life, and Tree latched on to this at an early age. His rise through the ranks was steady if not spectacular and four years after he turned professional he was leasing and managing his own theatre, the Haymarket. At the time of their first meeting his wife had been a stage-struck bluestocking who came from bourgeois stock. It has been suggested that she was only attracted to Tree because she believed he could help advance her career, but I feel that this is uncharitable. She loved him despite initial parental opposition (they did not want her marrying a man with frayed cuffs—a classic example of inverted snobbery) and she continued to love him throughout their married life even though his infidelities stretched her patience to near-breaking point on numerous occasions. They were alike in resolution but opposites in temperament, a combination that ensures friction in any partnership but which, in the theatre, is a guarantee of fireworks. Their path might have been smoother had she been his equal in talent. She excelled in certain roles, but her range was limited, a fact of life she was reluctant to admit; when Tree became a successful actor-manager her determination to share his star billing was the main cause of their domestic discontent. Yet he was faithful to her in his fashion and conducted his affairs as discreetly as his personality allowed ('adultery with all home comforts' in Frank Harris' words). Maud Tree had far greater social ambitions than her husband and there was an element of guile in her acceptance of the Pinney-Reed love nest in Putney: she had a mind to end her days as Lady Tree. It would be a mistake, however, to dismiss her as the pale shadow of the partnership. She had a powerful and pungent wit and amongst the surviving members of her family she is still remembered with affection. Of her husband's peccadillos she said: "Herbert's affairs start with a compliment and end with a confinement". Yes, she was jealous, but then she had plenty to be jealous about and things did not improve with the passing of years, for as Madeleine Bingham remarks, 'all ages were dangerous for Herbert'.

If, in the end, Tree does not merit his portrait in the classical hall of fame, he occupies a place of prominence in the entrance to the gallery of our most distinguished players. In an age that bored easily, he revitalised the theatre, taking over from but not slavishly imitating Irving. He made a token bow in the direction of Ibsen, thus earning Shaw's gratitude, and was more adventurous than Irving in the encouragement of new playwrights. Despite his half-brother Max's lukewarm appraisal of du Maurier's novel *Trilby*, he was quick to see its basic theatricality and how it could provide him with a startling characterisation. He was an 'actors' actor' and to this day his exploits, on and off stage, are recounted in green rooms and theatrical pubs whenever 'in' jokes are swopped. The British public are always quick to respond to a streak of humanity in their public figures and once they have given their affection they remain steadfastly loyal. Tree inspired such loyalty in his audiences and the actors who surrounded him and they feasted on his eccentricities. He brought life and vitality to his work; lavish in all things, he liked nothing better than to carry theatrical spectacle to extravagant extremes. Despite his lack of success with *Hamlet* and *Macbeth*, he produced no fewer than seventeen Shakespearean plays, a record that still stands comparison with most commercial West End managements. We should also record that he produced and performed Wilde's *A Woman of No Importance* ('A charming fellow', Wilde remarked, 'and so clever: he models himself on me.') and although Shaw may have delivered himself of the opinion that he was 'the despair of all authors' he did entrust him with the first production of the best play he ever wrote—*Pygmalion*. The legends which surround this landmark in the London theatre are enough to fill a book, and those who delight in such accounts should make a point of searching out Richard Huggett's highly diverting *The Truth About Pygmalion*.* Mr Huggett's reconstruction is masterly and gives a blow by blow account of how three of the most entertaining egotists the theatre has ever produced—Shaw, Mrs Patrick Campbell and Tree—slugged it out.

(My favourite anecdote of this episode took place at the end of two long months of rehearsal, with Mrs Pat being particularly trying throughout. Shaw had all but exhausted his own charm in an effort to get his own way with two such individual stars, and stomped off to his home in the Adelphi to put his *Final Orders* on paper. The letter he wrote to Tree apparently consisted of eight closely written pages of good natured abuse—I say 'apparently' because, alas, it was never preserved amongst Tree's papers. Perhaps Tree deliberately destroyed it in order to give added weight to his reply: 'I'm not saying that insulting letters of eight pages are always written by madmen, but it is a most extraordinary coincidence that madmen always write insulting letters of eight pages.' Whatever the content of Shaw's original one I can't help thinking that Tree had the last word. Huggett's concise dictionary of *Pygmalion* contains a hundred such gems and gives us a fascinating glimpse of a theatrical Centre Court Mixed Final with Shaw as the umpire whose rulings were constantly being challenged.)

He raised the money (by today's standards the remarkably low figure of £200,000) and built His Majesty's Theatre, always referring to it as 'my beautiful, beautiful theatre' and, according to Richard Huggett, managing to make four syllables out of 'beautiful'. 'On the morning of the day it was due to open with a spectacular Royal Gala premiere of a play called *The Seats of the Mighty*, Tree was standing at the bottom of the Haymarket

* Wm. Heinemann, 1969

MRS PATRICK CAMPBELL
in A. W. Pinero's *The Second
Mrs Tanqueray* St James's
Theatre, 1893

gazing in ecstasy at his creation. There were the banners and posters proclaiming Mr Beerbohm Tree's Company and huge blown up photographs of him in his most famous roles. The whole facade of the theatre was covered with 'Mr Beerbohm Tree this' and 'Mr Beerbohm Tree that'. Then along sauntered Irving, enjoying the morning sunlight, and as he passed Tree preening himself, he said: 'Morning, Tree. Working?'

If Tree was often the butt of other people's jokes, he gave us good as he got. Most stage humour has a cruel streak in it for it feasts on the unsuccessful. Ben Travers tells one such story of a 'rather down and out, passée actress, out of work and very hard up and wanted a job. She had been of old in Tree's company and so she appealed to him and said: "Please, Mr Tree, give me something. You know what I can do. I can do anything. I can be anything from Lady Macbeth to the cloakroom woman." And he replied: "My dear lady, we already have a Lady Macbeth and she *is* the cloakroom woman." ' In more serious vein, Travers also recalled that Tree took the utmost pains to ensure that his own productions were designed for maximum effect. 'In *A Midsummer's Night's Dream* he introduced live rabbits and I saw *Nero* with Tree making his triumphal entry into Rome in a real chariot with real horses. In *Julius Caesar* there was an actor called Charles Fulton who played Caesar and Tree made him wear a bladder of ox blood under his toga so that when he was stabbed he bled profusely. When motion pictures first started—flicks, the early flicks—Tree took advantage of this to have in *Twelfth Night* live waves breaking on the back-cloth.'

When he produced *Macbeth* his stage management recruited 50 real guardsmen as 'supers' and rehearsed them for the battle scene. They entered into the spirit of the occasion, knocked each other out, and in an excess of enthusiasm for their new-found occupation, chopped great lumps out of the scenery. One soldier swung his sword with such force that it cut a huge hole in the backcloth. 'Stop!' cried Tree. 'Never hit a backcloth when it's down.'

Clifford Mollison as a small boy was in the audience for one of the performances of Tree's *Macbeth*. 'He was ludicrous as Macbeth, and indeed as Othello. The fight between Macbeth and Macduff in the last act—Arthur Bourchier played Macduff and he was equally bad—well they had these claymores which they drew and brandished at each other. Then they obviously thought: 'Oh, blimey, this is a bit hot, a bit dangerous', so they threw the swords away and got the daggers out. They locked wrists with the daggers. Then they thought: 'Well these are a bit pointed' and they threw those away, and took up their shields and sort of leaned up against one another. And then eventually Macbeth seemed to die of heart failure. It was the funniest thing I've ever seen. I can remember my father and me crying with laughter in the stalls.'

For his production of Stephen Phillips' *Ulysses* Tree staged the prologue, which introduced various classical characters, with Prometheus chained to his rock having his vitals devoured by the eagle. At the dress rehearsal for this scene the young actor cast for the role of Prometheus appealed to Tree for advice: 'Guv'nor, what notice am I supposed to take of the bird?' Tree replied: 'The bird? If you get the bird by all means hoot back!'

It is curious that this joker in the pack should also have been the founder of an acting school. It opened in Gower Street and it eventually became the Royal Academy of Dramatic Art. Tree knocked together two old houses and opened the doors with George Bancroft as administrator. It was a strange venture for a man who had consistently denied that acting could ever be taught, and one is tempted to believe that it was another of his elaborate practical jokes that people took too seriously and from which he could not retreat. He made sure that his eldest daughter, Viola, was one of the earliest pupils, and then his enthusiasm for the project disappeared. He supported it with benefits at His Majesty's for two years and then handed it over to a Council of elders, amongst them Squire Bancroft, George Alexander, J. M. Barrie and Cyril Maude. Robert Atkins, destined to become a Falstaffian character of great influence in the theatre, was one of those who applied for admission. He recited a test piece for Squire Bancroft afterwards being required to sit for an 'exam' before being allowed to pay his six guineas tuition fee. At a later date Atkins joined Tree's company and was with him in *Hamlet* the last time he played it. 'His daughter Viola was Ophelia and I was walking on. At the end of the play about eight of us in the cast had to gather behind the back curtain and sing a solemn hymn while Tree played his death scene. I don't know what happened, but something went wrong and we were all over the place. Miss Tree was watching her father die, realised we were all at sea, rushed round the back, plunged in amongst us, punching right and left while all the time shouting, "You've ruined my father's death, you've ruined my father's death".'

Another young walk-on who progressed to a distinguished career, William Armstrong, described how he played a sailor in Henry Arthur Jones' *The Dancing Girl*, one of Tree's biggest successes. 'In those days I was very keen about make-up and often used to go into the theatre an hour or two before the curtain and try all kinds of facial experiments. One night I felt I'd got a wonderful effect of a rather emaciated sailor. I found myself standing next to Tree as I waited to go on. He looked at me and said, "Come here, my boy. Come here." So I shuffled closer and he said: "It's a wonderful make-up, wonderful! No, no, don't be nervous, I'm interested in make-up. Just explain what's the meaning of those very curious lines under your eyes." So I said, "Well, Mr Tree, you see they sink the eye and accentuate the cheek bone." "Marvellous, marvellous," he murmured, "but you've got a curious line on one cheek and nothing on the other. What's the meaning of that?" I replied, "Well, sir, it throws out this cheek and sinks the other." "Wonderful, wonderful," Tree said, then added, "But, of course, you can't go on like that".'

It seems to me that Tree, a man as easily bored by his own performances as by anybody else's, comes closer to the popular view of an actor than most of his contemporaries. In a sense he was a throwback to the old days, not a despicable strolling player, because he liked good living and enjoyed the perks of fame, but possessed of the old cavalier attitude that characterised the earliest players. Naturally he adapted himself to the Edwardian era, but there was something of the vagabond about him which belonged to a bygone age— he was an Elizabethan wolf in Edwardian sheep's clothing. He infuriated a lot of people by his studied carelessness but he gave value for money on and off stage and for that was ultimately forgiven for most of his sins. His memory was so uncertain on first nights that he would have a whole army of call-boys stationed at various points, some of them actually on stage, hidden behind pieces of scenery. Richard Huggett describes how on the first night of *Pygmalion* they were concealed behind the pillars in the Covent Garden scene, in the fireplace in Higgins' study and behind the ottoman in the Wimpole Street set. 'Not that it made much difference, because one gathers that his fluffing and mumbling were distressingly evident. Shaw used to say, 'You've got to learn your lines, Sir Herbert.' And Tree would reply, 'But I do know my lines. I do. I do. I swear to God I *do* know my lines.' To which Shaw responded: 'Oh, I don't dispute that for a moment, Sir Herbert. I willingly concede that you do know your lines. But you certainly don't know mine.'

Even so the House Full boards were out every night. Shaw at the age of fifty-seven suddenly had a major commercial success on his hands and—with a bow in the direction of a single word 'bloody'—was on his way to becoming a legend. Tree on the other hand did his best to turn the play on its head, playing Higgins as a romantic in love with Eliza (much to Shaw's fury, although when the film was eventually made with Leslie Howard, he apparently relented and allowed a hint or two of romance to creep in. When *My Fair Lady* reached the stage after Shaw's death and made him a posthumous millionaire there was no mistaking the fact that Higgins and Eliza were due to exchange more than carpet slippers as the final curtain came down.) It was typical of Tree to find the enormous acclaim for the play, Mrs Pat and himself irksome. 'This horrible, relentless success is killing me', he remarked. 'Oh, damnation to Art!' Was it a pose, a *bon mot* to go the rounds of the clubs and further enhance his reputation for eccentricity? I think not entirely. I believe that by this time he was no longer aware that he was a character in most people's eyes. I have often observed how certain actors, sometimes from conceit but more often in self-defence, gradually shed all traces of their own personality and assume one that gives a false impression of their true nature. It is perhaps more noticeable in great comedians, possibly because the effort of living up to their stage image is so wearying that they begin to play Hamlet in real life in order to survive. Either that or they go mad. W. S. Penley, the original Charley's Aunt, finally became so at one with the character he played that in the end he walked out of the theatre still wearing the 'aunt's' clothes; Dan Leno was another who had manic schemes for escaping his comic destiny, and closer to our own times, the late and great Tony Hancock took his unique talents and systematically set about shredding them.

Tree never cracked as did so many of his fellows, but there is other evidence to suggest that there were times when the pressures, both professional and domestic, bore down heavily. Perhaps his escape valve was to make mock of success, to challenge destiny and dare it to destroy him. He must have been an immensely strong character, but such men are often the first to break, and his salvation, which he worked out for himself, was never to take anything too seriously. In addition I think he realised that, as himself, he was always in danger of being dull; that is why he relied so heavily on disguises, making himself unrecognizable, using funny voices, funny accents, employing every character trick he could think of. Nor were his talents confined to the theatre: he was an accomplished writer of short stories and his literary efforts were another way of escaping from fame and from himself. He went to Marienbad every single year, leaving Maud, the theatre and all other pressures behind. Revealingly, in one of his short stories he describes a character who desperately needed to get right away, to 'switch himself off'. There were minor flirtations to be had in Marienbad, for he never plunged himself into complete darkness: there was always a single bulb burning.

He went to Marienbad during the last year of peace. On his return to London, one of his famous leading ladies, Constance Collier, was acting in Maeterlinck's anti-war play *Monna Vanna*. She described her feelings and a fateful chance meeting with Tree the day war was declared. 'None of us had grasped the significance of the leading articles in the papers, or the whispers of war. It all seemed grossly exaggerated, and so the night of the declaration came as a complete surprise to most people. We did not realise what it meant. After the performance I went with several members of the company to the gates of Buckingham Palace in the hope that the King and Queen would come out on the balcony. It was the gayest scene, crowds round the Palace and boys riding about, cheering and shouting on the tops of taxi-cabs, and everybody in the streets singing and buying little flags and sticking them all over themselves.

'I walked back up the Mall and down the Haymarket arm in arm with three friends, and by then we were cheering and singing. In the darkness, leaning against the railings, we came upon Herbert Tree. His face was ashen. He seemed stricken. His whole manner was a shock to me. It was my first realisation of the seriousness of it all. I never forgot the expression in his eyes. They were filled with the horror of the tragedy that was upon the world. He stopped me and said "You won't be singing those songs long, my dear." Then

CONSTANCE COLLIER
as Portia in *Julius Caesar*
His Majesty's, 1905

he passed on without another word. He looked a broken man.'

This hardly suggests a man of no sensitivity and supports my belief that the personality Tree presented to the world at large and which in countless anecdotes has come down to us as that of a man who played at being an actor as he played at life, is a false one. It would be an exaggeration to place him alongside Garrick or Kean, but that is not to say he did not enrich the theatre as surely as they did. He applied his talents in erratic fashion, not always doing himself justice, but the theatre is constantly in need of personalities such as Tree to foster the very necessary public belief that actors are illusionists, makers of magic, larger than life, and always unpredictable.

Unlike Irving he did not die in harness. He kept a love-nest, a small cottage in Birchington on the Kent coast. Beyond the garden with its few windblown roses, hollyhocks and sunflowers he had a view over the sea to the Goodwin Sands. It was one of his favourite retreats and he spent the long summer days of June 1917 working on the script of his next production—a play by three Americans for which he had high hopes called *The Great Lover*. As was his habit he had brought with him hampers of delicacies from Fortnum and Mason's. It was a tranquil existence but shattered one morning when the daily help arrived to find him in a heap at the bottom of the staircase. 'I think I've broken my leg', he said. When the doctor arrived he diagnosed a ruptured tendon above the kneecap. Tree was taken back to London to Sir Alfred Fripp's nursing home in Henrietta Street, Covent Garden. There he underwent an operation which was a complete success, and he was soon back to his usual form. Two weeks later on July 2nd, sitting up in bed peeling a peach for his after-dinner dessert, he fell forwards, dead. The enforced rest, insisted upon by Sir Alfred in accordance with the then standard post-operative practice but now considered dangerous, had caused a blood clot to form, and this killed him. He was sixty-four years old.

Had he been forewarned he might have left us one last witticism about such a fitting end. For to die peacefully while eating a peach and in the belief that your return to public life will be in the role of a great lover is a fate that any actor would savour, and perhaps none more so than that complete actor named Herbert Beerbohm Tree.

[[16]]

THE GREAT ACTOR-MANAGERS

IF one accepts that Beerbohm Tree was Irving's main rival, then from the evidence Johnston Forbes-Robertson should have been Irving's legitimate successor. However, as we have seen many times before, the pattern is often broken by the personalities of those involved. In Forbes-Robertson's case we have the paradox of the finest romantic actor of his day who did not relish being an actor. It would be convenient to dismiss this as a pose, a pre-Garbo shunning of the limelight, a public attitude which does not always ring true. But it seems that he was genuine in his dislike of the publicity and notoriety that his looks and talents brought him. Unlike Irving, Tree, Alexander, Martin-Harvey and some of his other exalted colleagues he was not, by nature, a true man of the theatre. He did not court nor derive customary pleasures from applause; the excitement of his calling was not something he cherished and at the end of his career he had been knighted for services to a profession he insisted he had never enjoyed, and he stated that it had always run contrary to his basic temperament.

He was born of a love-match, the son of cultivated and intelligent parents, the first member of his family to take to the stage, and he started life with more material advantages than the average actor of his day. If one traces his ancestors there is a link, albeit remote with Duncan I, the same Duncan who was murdered by Macbeth. By a telling coincidence Macbeth was the first role he ever played, at a Christmas party in 1866 as a boy of thirteen. His career spanned three reigns, and he derived the title of his autobiography from this fact.* He was strikingly good-looking—'wonderful to behold' in Ellen Terry's words, and Rossetti used him as the model for the head of Eros in his painting of *Dante's Dream*. Today those good looks would probably work to his disadvantage, for we are passing through the era of the anti-hero and our leading men and public idols are not required to have the Byronic, or Rupert Brooke-like beauty so admired by earlier generations. Currently the young admire the bizarre, a cult which has produced, by a series of artistic mutations, the grotesque punk look with its accompanying lack of talent. One hopes it will prove only a passing fad and before the end of this violent, confused century there will be a great romantic revival. The type of male beauty that Forbes-Robertson possessed meant that he had to work that much harder to convince people he was an actor who demanded to be taken seriously. Beauty in a woman has never been a theatrical drawback, and has often excused minuscule talents,

* *A Player Under Three Reigns*—Fisher Unwin 1925

184

but in a man, although he may attract a great number of faithful fans, it usually means he has to demonstrate greater abilities than his feminine counterparts if he is to have critical success over a long period.

Forbes-Robertson was never called upon to serve a back-breaking apprenticeship and like so many of the characters in this continuing story his career overlapped into the lives of others already familiar to us. For his second professional engagement he was chosen by Charles Reade to play in *The Wandering Heir*, the play which marked Ellen Terry's triumphant return to the stage. Her verdict at that time was double-edged. She found him 'a dreamy, poetic-looking creature ... full of aspirations and ideals'. One of his aspirations was to be deserving of her love, for the moment he met her he was immediately attracted to her. She was kind to him and he became friendly with the Godwin-Terry family, but his emotional cause was a lost one. What impressed Ellen Terry most was his talent as a painter and in fact she advised him to give up the stage in favour of a career as an artist. In view of his subsequent feelings about the theatre it is somewhat surprising that he did not act on her advice. He had considerable gifts as a painter, and accepted commissions from Irving and others (his portrait of Phelps as Cardinal Wolsey, reproduced on page 126, hangs in the Garrick Club).

His greatest success was as Hamlet. There are many who believe that he was the perfect Hamlet, approached only by Gielgud in this century. He played it for the first time in 1897 when he was forty-four and after twenty-three years on the stage, and yet those who saw him thought of him as a youth giving 'the most humanly natural of any impersonation known on the contemporary English stage'. Irving generously made the Lyceum available to him, lending the standing set and props, and was so stunned by the performance that he never again attempted the role himself. On the morning after the tumultuous opening night, Irving met him at the theatre and greeted him with the words: 'Well, you've done it ... and now you must go and play Hamlet all over the world.' If we remember Ellen Terry's statement that Irving could not bear to watch other actors, then his unstinted praise takes on added warmth. Ellen Terry had played her part in guiding a reluctant Forbes-Robertson to greatness, because even after Irving had offered him the Lyceum he still had doubts. Hamlet had been played to death, he argued with her; people were sick of it. She countered this by asking him whether musicians should stop playing Beethoven merely because other musicians had played him in the past? He could find no answer to that and allowed himself to be persuaded.

Mrs Patrick Campbell was an 'original and unconventional' Ophelia to his Hamlet and some of that unconventional originality can be judged from an episode that took place on the night that Ellen Terry was in front. On a whim, and because she 'felt naughty' she played half of the performance wearing a fair wig and half with her own hair, apparently in the hope that Ellen Terry would express a preference. Miss Terry, wisely one would think, declined to pass judgement and later admitted to Shaw that 'I cannot like her Ophelia'.

Sir Ralph Richardson, on the other hand, thought Mrs Pat 'the finest actress I ever saw in my life. I've never seen anything to approach her since and she was wonderful at conveying terror—terror, which plays such a huge part of the drama: fear, horror, very

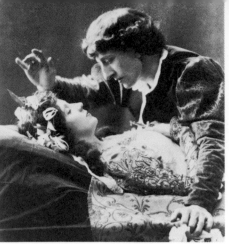

FORBES-ROBERTSON as Hamlet

FORBES-ROBERTSON and MRS PATRICK CAMPBELL in *Romeo and Juliet*, Lyceum, 1895

very difficult to act. It's far easier to act a good man than to act the Devil. Mrs Pat as Hedda Gabler frightened the life out of one. A terrible appearance: large black eyes, huge mane of black hair—she walked across the stage, revolver in hand with all the terror of the movement of a puma which you see when you go to the zoo, when you think, "My goodness, I'm glad those bars are pretty thick." A baleful glance, sinewy step, incredible cruelty! Never will I forget the effect when she took the letters, Lövborg's letters, and flung open the studio stove. She opened it with a poker, the lid fell back with a clang, and she took the letters in her hands, looked at them and said, "My child and Lövborg's. I'll singe your baby locks." Then threw them into the flames. It was like looking straight into hell.'

We are told that even as an old woman, fat and ugly and trundling through *Hedda Gabler* with inadequate supporting actors, she could still rivet the attention by a sudden piece of business. Richard Huggett describes her as somebody 'who had no predecessor and no successors. She was a unique phenomenon, like a comet passing through, lighting up with a kind of splendid dark brilliance the world around her, and then vanishing'.

So many anecdotes concerning her eccentric behaviour and biting wit have come down to us. Sir John Gielgud somehow survived playing opposite her in Ibsen's *Ghosts* at the beginning of his career when her advice to him was the daunting: 'Keep still. Gaze at me. Speak in a Channel steamer voice . . . speak as if you were going to be sick.' In her private life she was just as outrageous and left us with the observation: 'Marriage is the deep, deep peace of the double-bed after the hurly-burly of the chaise-longue.' But perhaps the most amusing of all is concerned with the twilight of her years when, as a deaf and somewhat pale shadow of her former self, she was persuaded to witness a performance of Dame Sybil Thorndike as Medea. Given a prominent seat in one of the stage boxes she promptly fell asleep before the play began and was still asleep when Dame Sybil made one of her celebrated wailing entrances. Mrs Pat woke with a start and in clarion tones shouted: 'There's somebody in the room!'

Forbes-Robertson endured the pains and pleasures of an intimate relationship with the ever-audacious and unpredictable Mrs Pat, both on and off stage. They shared the management of several theatres, though he confessed that he had always found the 'speculative and gambling nature of theatrical management . . . distasteful to me; and I knew that my own personal efforts as an actor would be considerably handicapped by all the extra labour and anxiety which management entails'. True to character he often chose plays which allowed Mrs Pat and his other favourite leading lady, Gertrude Elliott, to outshine him. He later married Miss Elliott, a move which did not totally endear him to Mrs Pat. As Richard Findlater says, 'Forbes-Robertson seemed to lack the appetite for supreme power which had marked most great actors' and despite his great popularity as a romantic idol he never gave himself a permanent base, but merely leased theatres on an ad hoc basis, thus robbing himself of a consistent policy.

Authors liked him because he was faithful to their texts and seldom interfered like Tree. Shaw wrote *Caesar and Cleopatra* for him and of course he scored one of his greatest successes in Jerome K. Jerome's curious play *The Passing of the Third Floor Back*, sometimes rudely called 'Jesus in Digs' which still crops up in repertory companies as an enduring museum piece. 'Vilely stupid', was Max Beerbohm's verdict when it first appeared, but the public thought otherwise and Forbes-Robertson found himself saddled with a play which he came to despise, but which the public never tired of. Perhaps all lasting favourites have to have a streak of 'twaddle and vulgarity' in them for while there is always a certain, but limited audience for the theatre of ideas, the taste for non-demanding basic entertainment remains remarkably consistent through the centuries and frequently is the only fare that keeps the theatre afloat. Students of the drama may deplore this fact, but students of human nature will tolerantly understand it. Satire, we know, is something that closes on Saturday night and any management bold enough to present nothing but the most high-minded repertoire of plays is usually forced to admit defeat and return to a more mixed bag.

So what do we make of a man who, knighted for distinguished services to his profession, confessed that 'never at any time have I gone on the stage without longing for the moment when the curtain would come down on the last act. Rarely, very rarely have I enjoyed myself in acting. This cannot be the proper mental attitude for an actor, and I am persuaded . . . that I am not temperamentally suited to my calling. For years I have fought hard against this "ego", but seldom would I reach that impersonal exaltation, so to speak, which it seems to me an actor should be able to attain'.

There is a link here—the same relief at the end of the journey—with Macready, and when he finally retired he remained faithful to his resolve until his death twenty years later. If the present generation thinks of him as a leading Edwardian, it is worth noting that he did not die until just before the outbreak of the second World War, having taken his leave of the stage in 1916 and then not in England, but at Harvard. There he gave his last performance as Hamlet. He had played the role many hundreds of times over a period of nineteen years, 'beginning at the mature age of forty-four, and ending in my sixty-fourth year. . . . Yet I stripped myself of Hamlet's garb with no sort of regret, but rather with a great sense of relief. . . . On looking back, it seems to me that I was far more nervous on the last performance of Hamlet than on the first. It is said that nervousness is a necessary attribute for the actor, and that he who does not suffer from it is rarely of much

187

account in his art. It may be so, but all I can say is that as far as I personally am concerned, it has been nought but a shackling handicap'.

Perhaps therein lies the clue to his whole personality, though I am always dubious about the cut and dried dogma that surrounds human behaviour. Most of us have encountered gross and boorish behaviour at social gatherings, only to be told that the offender is 'basically very shy and that is why he becomes so aggressive'. Yes and no and then again maybe. Where actors are concerned their temperamental make-up is far more complex, and even on the evidence of his own words it would be too glib to explain away Forbes-Robertson's summing up as merely a chronic case of the first-night nerves. Had he been a failure as an actor and made no impression on the public one might be tempted to say he regretted not having chosen a different career. But being an actor did not prevent him from being an occasional painter and he had twenty years retirement in which to resurrect those talents.

Conjecture as to any public man's motives is always an interesting party game, but seldom leads us to the truth. There is a connection between politicians, actors and the clergy, all of whom share the common need to convince the public of their sincerity if they are to prosper. Some are driven by conviction, some by arrogance and a lust for power, others are mere opportunists who cloak their real motives by borrowing other people's ideals, but all, presumably, can only continue in the firm belief that there is an audience for their particular talents: it is only on very rare occasions that we come across a public figure who lives in splendid isolation, uncorrupted by fame, genuinely humble, a reluctant hero. Perhaps Forbes-Robertson belonged to this minority, for all who knew him intimately spoke of him as a man of near-saintly character, devoid of conceit and deserving of Shaw's last words on the subject. Shaw wrote to him that, in his career, he had proved 'that to reach the highest rank it is not necessary to be an egotist or a monster'.

While Forbes-Robertson was doing a far, far better thing in private, his contemporary Sir John Martin-Harvey was doing it rather more flamboyantly at the Lyceum. As the old century ended he took the town in a sentimentalised dramatization of Dickens' *A Tale of Two Cities*, achieving the same sort of fame as Ronald Colman when he played Sydney Carton in the film version. It is perhaps worth remarking what an enormous influence Dickens has exerted over the drama. He did of course create characters that actors could get their teeth into and he believed in good old fashioned plots; the combination has proved irresistible to dramatists for over a century and as I write this Lionel Bart's *Oliver!* is enjoying a splendid revival in the West End while on television a serial of *Hard Times* is being given a repeat. One is hard put to think of another novelist who can equal Dickens' record as a source of plays, films, musicals, one-man shows. Roles like Fagin have attracted actors as widely separated as Tree and Sir Alec Guinness, and at regular intervals we find that a new generation of playwrights and film-makers rediscover the old favourites. Dickens may not be so widely read as he was a century ago, but through the medium of the drama his genius is constantly being paraded.

Martin-Harvey's version, entitled *The Only Way*, was suggested by his leading lady of many years standing, Angelita Helena de Silva, whom he eventually married in the year

SARAH SIDDONS and JOHN PHILIP KEMBLE in *Macbeth,* 1738
From the oil painting by Thomas Beach, Garrick Club

EDMUND KEAN as Sir Giles Overreach in Massinger's *A New Way to Pay Old Debts,* 1816
From a painting by George Clint, British Theatre Museum

J. MARTIN-HARVEY in *The
Only Way*, 1899

GORDON CRAIG in *The Dead
Heart*, Lyceum, 1889

of his greatest triumph, 1899. But too great a success in one particular role sometimes has
the effect of blighting a career, and although he was a commendable Hamlet, and also
gave a good account of himself as Richard III, his many journeys in the tumbril led to a
guillotining of what might have been a more varied and distinguished classical career. He
was in the same line as the other great actor-managers, carrying on the tradition of a star
personality surrounded by lesser lights, yet he never achieved the prestige accorded to
Irving. His name rings out, for it sounds as an actor's name should sound, and he was
responsible for major scenic innovations in his Shakespearean productions. He came
under the influence of Max Reinhardt before the First World War, and then
enthusiastically embraced Gordon Craig's revolutionary ideas. The *Hamlet* he took to
Stratford in 1910 dispensed with the realistic settings so beloved by Irving and Tree.
Instead, using immense triangular pillars and cunningly arranged drapes set against a
concave white backcloth, he created a setting where 'everything was suggested, nothing
was declared'—a conception which allowed the actors to perform without distraction. It
was a bold concept and did not meet with general approval. Craig's designs were, of
course, of heroic proportions and many of them were incapable of being transferred from
the drawing board to the stage—either by reasons of cost or size. As often happens,
compromises had to be made and these sometimes reduced Craig's original ideas from the
sublime to the ordinary. Craig needed a permanent home with facilities that could
accommodate his whole vision and a management prepared to risk vast sums of money.
So many of his ideas and designs were decades ahead of their time, and the theatre lacked
producers and directors who were on his intellectual level. Of course his influence
worked through in the end and is still felt today, even by those who scarcely remember
his name; modern stage design can hardly be said to have surpassed Craig's inventions of

seventy years ago. We are either given indifferent neo-realistic settings or else no settings at all, something I find a matter for regret. Our most promising young designer, Sean Kenny, who exhibited such flair and theatrical originality (who will forget his set for *Oliver*?) and who seemed to me the natural successor to Craig, died before he could fully realise his enormous talents. It is odd that in an age when the theatre has a life and death struggle to survive against television and the cinema, managements seem content to ignore the impact of imaginative settings on audiences. There seems to be a conscious fear of theatricality; time and time again one goes to the theatre to be faced with a bare stage, the play beginning without even the rise of a curtain and the illusions constantly destroyed by the actors moving their own props and furniture and the stage-staff going about their chores in full view of the audience. Why this should be considered superior to an imaginative decor is, I confess, beyond me, and I do not think I am being reactionary. If the theatre ceases to intrigue then it is in danger of becoming an artistic dodo. We cannot expect our audiences to do all the work for us, because if the day comes when we can no longer distinguish between a stage and a parking lot then why should audiences bother to attend? There is a vast artistic difference between the *suggestion of reality* which enables each individual member of the audience to create his own world as he watches the unfolding of the drama, and *the reality of the obvious* which leaves nothing to the imagination and which must, by its starkness, its drab, ordinary sameness prove a distraction. If children see the hands working Punch and Judy they rightly feel cheated. I cling to my belief that the theatre is something more than a platform and an actor with all his nerve ends exposed. In the same way, to make the drama the subject of formal study, to treat acting as a theory rather than the product of instinct must make us lose touch with its essential spirit. W. A. Darlington stated that 'plays are meant to be acted . . . not read at a desk . . . a truth which the academic mind assimilates with difficulty'. To sit for an examination paper based on a play of Shakespeare's, to make an appreciation of our greatest playwright a duty rather than a pleasure, is one of the grosser idiocies of our education system, the more so when one considers that the average schoolteacher of today has little or no opportunity of witnessing Shakespeare being well acted, yet is compelled to compound his or her ignorance by passing it on to the younger generation.

Martin-Harvey made a valiant attempt to build a bridge between tradition and progress. His close attention to detail was a byword in the theatre, and nobody was in a better position to observe this than his dresser, Machugh, who bequeathed us this first-hand account. 'Harvey was very particular about his stage. Some of the stage-hands we used were market porters and the like, and they used to come on with great big thick heavy boots. They would come clomping over the stage during one of his speeches and of course it upset him. He said, "We'll have to stop that, you know, we'll have to get these men to change their boots and put on plimsoles." And then he noticed a lot of marks on one of the sets. Finger marks, dirty hands all over his Chamber scene. "How has this happened?" he said. And somebody told him, "Oh, it's the stage hands." "Well, they must all wear gloves," he said. So they all had to wear white gloves. He wouldn't have the curtain rung up until he came down from his dressing room and had gone on the stage to look at everything. He'd move a chair here, a table there and say, "Ah, this light's too strong, let's have a blue . . . turn it down a bit, and this amber, bring that up a bit more".'

Then we have Sir Harold Hobson's memory of his early theatregoing days. 'My principal memory of the theatre is going to see Martin-Harvey and Martin-Harvey again and after that Martin-Harvey again, and always in *The Only Way*, which immensely moved me. It was a play that Irving asked Harvey not to do. He used to go up the steps of the scaffold, holding the hand of Mimi the seamstress, played by his wife. He said, "Hold my hand." They went up together, and as he got to the very top of the stage there was an enormous roar from the crowd. A roar of hatred. Then it seems to me that, instantly, the whole scene was changed and there in the middle of the stage, not at the side, was the scaffold with the guillotine knife. Martin-Harvey stood on it, saying, "It's a far far better thing that I do than I have ever done." I expected this to be produced in stentorian tones of enormous courage and defiance. But it wasn't. He had a very quavering voice. I came away wondering if I'd seen a proper performance, if he hadn't suddenly been overcome with nerves. But I saw him over and over again and it was always the same and I realised that was a very closely calculated effect.'

That great farceur Robertson Hare was another young man who came under Martin-Harvey's spell. 'I can't describe how electric his production of *Oedipus Rex* was. Well, he nearly broke my arm on the first night. I happened to be playing one of the torch-bearers, just after the terrible thing of his eyes being put out. He had clots of blood all over him. It looked dreadful. He gripped my arm—I never forgot it—and then he went down on his knees before his big speech and I thought, I must bear it, I won't squeal. And as he went down, he tripped—oh, it was cleverly done, the whole thing was pure theatre. He caught his foot in his robe and fell and stayed down. He *had* to stay down, because the house was in an awful uproar. I saw them fainting. If one woman fainted every night, then we had twenty, and I thought: why do people pay money to come along and see this terrible tragedy? But of course they came to see Harvey, it was a tribute to him. And at the end, we were left on the stage, but he went through the auditorium, straight to the back, and as he went the lights dimmed. It was a wonderful, wonderful production, I wouldn't have missed it for anything.'

I warm to the phrase 'pure theatre', especially when it comes straight from the heart, as in Robertson Hare's case. And when the lights dimmed on the great heydays of the Victorian actor-managers, it was the passing of an era, but other torch-bearers were waiting in the wings. Some we have already met, and some like William Poel and Harley Granville-Barker were waiting to be called: the theatre of ideas was about to replace the theatre of spectacle.

THE PLAY OF IDEAS:
SHAW AND GRANVILLE-BARKER

GRADUALLY, almost imperceptibly, there was a shift away from the actor's theatre. Irving died in 1905, Tree in 1917, and although there were lesser giants carrying on the traditions of the actor-manager the great heydays were numbered. There were new forces at work, anxious to bring about changes, but there was no cohesive revolution. One faction, led by Granville-Barker and Shaw, wanted to push the English theatre into the twentieth century, while that lonely innovator, William Poel wanted a return to the purity of the Elizabethan era.

The late Sir Lewis Casson, for so long a pillar of our theatrical society, knew Poel intimately and felt that it 'was largely his hatred of Irving's productions that moved him towards the Elizabethan theatre. One of his main principles was that you must carry out the dramatist's intentions. He considered that Irving twisted Shakespeare's plays to suit his own view of what he thought the part ought to be, and anything that distracted the audience's attention from the words like elaborate scenery and so on was a hindrance not a help.'

I am not sure that there isn't a basic flaw in Poel's argument. Like most revolutionaries, whether they wish to move us backwards or forwards, Poel was arrogant in his conviction that he was right and everybody else was wrong. It cannot be safely assumed that Shakespeare would have been totally opposed to his plays being performed in elaborate settings: he might have been flattered, entranced; given the facilities he might have written on a grander scale than he did in order to take advantage of Irving's conceptions. There is a great deal of evidence to suggest that he wrote to order and was not particularly manic about his words being altered. As we have seen he was a working actor turned dramatist and he wrote for what existed. Given his undoubted genius, I see no reason why he would not have changed his approach with equal expertise had the circumstances been different.

This central obsession probably cost Poel the recognition that was rightfully his, and today his name is only known to scholars and a few of the faithful who are still alive. He soldiered on for fifty-two yeras, and was responsible for at least a hundred productions between 1880 and 1932. Many critics dismissed him as a crank, for prophets usually disconcert the majority of us. Darlington felt that he 'carried his holy zeal to lengths which, to any but the elect, must have seemed absurd' and there is little doubt that he was often irritating and pedantic, roaring down on anybody who did not embrace his gospel

WILLIAM POEL
as Father Keegan in Shaw's *John Bull's Other Island*, from the painting by H. Tonks

GEORGE BERNARD SHAW
in the 'nineties

without question. Sir Lewis Casson delivered a softened verdict. 'I wouldn't say he was actually a crank, but he was very near it. He was fanatical about what he did believe in and that always leads to difficulties. His driving force in the theatre was really a religious one. He was a very religious man in the cause of humanity—a rationalist who hated dogmatic religion, and he found that the theatre suited him best in teaching humanity, and that the Elizabethan theatre of Shakespeare answered his requirements better than any other. Because of his religious views he would not have anything to do with the commercial theatre or the well-known actors who were working in it. He felt they were tainted with the money-making philosophy, Thus all the time he was doing his main work he was dealing with fairly inexperienced actors, sometimes totally unskilled actors, and therefore he had to work out every detail of the text, making as it were an orchestral score out of it, so that he knew and could tell an actor exactly how to speak every single word in the play. He would cast the play as far as possible orchestrally, with certain parts representing the bass, some the tenors and the baritones, some the light soprano and some the contralto. I remember rehearsing hard for a fortnight on the Duke in *Measure for Measure* and at the end of two weeks he told me—very sadly, because we were great friends—I couldn't play the Duke because the quality of my voice was not what he wanted. Eventually I played the Provost instead.'

Poel's determination to work with actors who were outside the commercial theatre led him to the young and inexperienced Edith Evans. I have dealt at great length with Edith's career in my authorised biography of her, *Ned's Girl*, and I do not propose to plagiarise myself in detail, but I cannot omit repeating that Poel was responsible for Edith's debut. She had acted in amateur theatricals under the tuition of a gifted woman called Miss Massey who ran a company called The Streatham Shakespeareans, and Poel happened to witness a performance of *Much Ado About Nothing* in which Edith appeared as Beatrice. As a result he took her under his wing and guided her towards a career that was to last for sixty-four years and which may well rank her as the most distinguished actress of this century when future historians pronounce their verdict. When Poel discovered her she had no inkling that her destiny was to be a professional actress. She was a young milliner, born and bred a Cockney despite her Welsh surname, and had no theatrical background or formal training for the stage. She was to say in later life 'God was very good to me, he never let me go on tour' and to the end of her days she remembered Poel with affection and gratitude. Her comments about him echo those of Lewis Casson. When she played in *Troilus and Cressida* for him at Stratford-upon-Avon she was paid three guineas (most of Poel's apostles performed for love rather than money) and she recalled that he said to her 'Ah, she ran away with all my tunes'. To Edith he was 'a nice old man', the man who had given her the escape route from making hats. 'He thought he'd got a gold mine in tunes when he found me. Course he was noted for giving people tunes, which is the way we all talk really. Most people talk up and down, but I suppose I had a lot of *natural* tunes.' When she confided this to me she was in her seventies and well aware that through the years she had become the impersonators' favourite target, her extraordinary voice—'Some people like it, some people don't' she said—imitated with varying degrees of accuracy at every theatrical gathering. It *was* an extraordinary instrument, needing no microphone to fill a theatre, for she belonged to the old school that scorned such aids, and because she had never been exposed to the grind of touring or forced to grapple with a variety of roles to which she was ill suited, her technique was entirely her own. Many imitated her, none approached her, and although often the aunt-sally for cruel parodies (often given by homosexuals who were curiously attracted to her unique qualities) she could electrify an audience with some of her effects, and she guarded the secrets that Poel had implanted in her at a tender and impressionable age.

By pure accident Edith arrived on the theatrical scene at the precise moment of change. I can best liken it to a railway junction where the main line suddenly branches in half a dozen directions. Tree and Irving had never moved far from the terminal, but now people were shunting out in all directions, and Edith, standing on the platform with little or no inherited luggage, could take her pick. She explored several branch lines before settling on her ultimate destination, which was to be the Old Vic, with the indomitable Lilian Baylis both stoking and driving the engine.

But before we get to Miss Baylis we must take note of a quasi-disciple of Poel's, Harley Granville-Barker, whose reign at the small and unfashionable Court Theatre in Sloane Square under the management of J. E. Vedrenne transformed the London theatrical scene. In three years Vedrenne and Barker were responsible for presenting thirty-two new plays, including eleven by Shaw, Galsworthy's first attempt at the drama, *The Silver Box*, and representative offerings from Yeats, Housman, Masefield, Maeterlinck and Schnitzler. By any standards, at any time, it was a dazzling achievement, the more so because they were always swimming against the tide. Barker was not 'stiffened by fanaticism' like Poel, though he shared Poel's passion for the authentic Shakespearean texts, and today his convictions live on in his famous *Prefaces* while most of his less academic triumphs are all but forgotten. With Shaw and Poel he shared this passion for the words—the words came first. Turning again to Lewis Casson we learn that he had 'an extraordinary knowledge of speech. His mother had been a Victorian reciter at private

HARLEY GRANVILLE-BARKER,
1901

homes and places, and when he was quite a schoolboy he used to share the recitals with her. I was overwhelmed by his personality. He took Poel's method of analysing the text and interpreting it through definite, stylised music and used that method to translate *all* emotion and *all* thought into actual music of speech: the whole outline of the thing was fixed, and any delicate shading of acting was really a harmonic on that framework.'

This may be difficult for the layman to follow, but perhaps I can simplify it by saying that Sir Lewis always learnt his lines to musical tunes. He heard the tunes in his head and this gave him the rhythm of his speech, so that in a sense he did orchestrate his performances. (I am reliably informed that when towards the end of his career his memory drifted he would sometimes dry stone dead. When that happened he would hum to himself and the elusive words would return.)

Barker was undoubtedly a man of vision but the great promise of his early years was never to be fully realised. In collaboration with William Archer he worked out a detailed plan for a National Theatre, including fictitious names for the whole company, the first year's repertory and the casting of those fictitious names for all the different roles. He was twenty-five when he embarked on this project and he had already laid out the plan of his life, intending it to culminate in his managing the long-awaited English National Theatre. But it never happened. The outbreak of the 1914 war wrecked all his hopes and he never recovered from the disappointment. Dame Sybil Thorndike felt that 'waste' was a good description of his life, and by coincidence this was the title of one of his best-known plays. He was a man 'spoilt by something', she thought. 'His influence was not as big as it should have been, and he was a tragic figure. He had the power to make something of the English theatre which would have swept the world.' She felt that the theatre had become 'sunk into realism. A man like Barker could have taken up something like Picasso, taken the ordinary things and made them universal instead of particular. We make things particular in the theatre, and a particular thing is not what is wanting from great art. It is the particular taken into the universal'.

It is also interesting to note that Lewis Casson felt that Shaw and Barker didn't really agree. 'They were both fascinated with interpreting the text to make the emotion and thought of every sentence clear, but Shaw's methods were much broader—more theatrical I suppose one must say—he really gloried in clap-trap. Shaw didn't really depend on the face, he depended entirely on the voice, whereas Barker with modern lighting was able to do a great deal more with the face. Shaw drew his lines very strongly, where Barker would have delicate curves.'

As one sifts the evidence, not circumstantial but the testimony of actors who worked with and alongside Barker and Shaw, we can see that it was a revolution with too many leaders, and the cause they were trying to serve finally fragmented. Shaw was a marvellous actor who never had to earn his living as one and could therefore afford to have theories. The public, all demanding, were never interested in causes but in effects, and no matter how much energy and invention and dramatic expertise is applied behind the scenes, audiences in the final analysis come to be entertained, thrilled, shocked, fascinated by the actors. Once the curtain is up the actor is the prime target, the only interpreter. He can be fired the moment he comes off stage, or else be given pages of notes to modify his next performance, but for those minutes or hours when he stands before the footlights he controls everything. The average audience is not fanatically concerned with off-stage revolutions, or obsessively aware of trends: the contact is with the actor, the shock of one personality on many, the ability of the human face and the human voice to convey emotion, making, as Dame Sybil said, the particular into the universal. This was the lure of the great actors, and Shaw, blinkered like most authors, found the dominance of the actors hard to stomach. Barker, no mean actor himself, thought differently and although they joined forces and were collectively responsible for bringing about major changes in the structure of the English theatre of that period, their differences ultimately ensured that the revolution petered out. Shaw remonstrated that 'the art of acting is half strangled by the fashionable tailor' and one can understand his rage and frustration. He had a gospel he wanted to preach, and I think it irked him that he had to employ actors to preach it. They were a necessary evil, unreliable, egotistical, conceited, too conscious of their own importance: but necessary. In moving towards respectability they had lost sight of what Shaw felt was their true function. He wanted his players to be walking arguments selling his wares, and this is against the actor's basic nature, because the actor wants to sell himself.

Although Shaw went on to become the venerable legend and Barker faded to a classroom relic, it was Barker who made the most lasting impression on the theatrical scene, shattering many preconceived notions of how Shakespeare should be presented with his famous 1912 season at the Savoy. There he opened with *The Winter's Tale*, following this two months later with *Twelfth Night* and in February 1914 with *A Midsummer Night's Dream*. All three provoked controversy, yet only one achieved real success with the public—this was *Twelfth Night* which ran for 187 performance, and was the only one to be favourably reviewed by most of the critics. The other two had all kinds of abuse hurled at them. His plans for *Macbeth* and *Antony and Cleopatra* were shelved when war broke out, and he never staged another of Shakespeare's plays. Even so his influence remained and continues to the present day. He took the best of Poel and gave his Shakespearean productions some of the pace and vehemence he felt had been characteristic of Burbage's theatre. Darlington describes Henry Ainley's performance as Leontes in *The Winter's Tale* as 'my first experience of really passionate acting, and it convinced me once and for all that the theatre's first concern was with emotion'. Trusting Darlington's judgement we can see another reason why Shaw and Barker drifted apart, and Darlington went on to say that when the new method was contrasted with Forbes-Robertson's Hamlet he felt that with Forbes-Robertson he was attending a service in a great cathedral, conducted by a pious and eloquent bishop. In view of the great changes that Barker instigated, it is sad to record that he died a disappointed and somewhat bitter man and there is irony in the fact that his final legacy to succeeding generations should be a series of *Prefaces* which, although shot through with masterly scholarship, seem by their very erudition to mock the urgency he brought to the living theatre.

Despite his ultimate failure Barker was always at the upper end of the market. There were others like Sir Frank Benson who were still barnstorming across the country with the old style Shakespearean presentations. Benson was very much of the old school and, according to Sir Tyrone Guthrie, 'the productions were battered and tattered; the dresses fusty and dowdy; the company no more than so so, and Sir Frank himself was getting pretty old. He'd been a very handsome man and proud of his fine physique. It was sad to see this rouged, gaunt ruin of masculine beauty pretending to be Hamlet. But it would be ungenerous to dwell only on the shortcomings of him and his company. It was from their performances that I, like thousands of others of my generation, first began to see why the plays of Shakespeare are considered masterpieces—to realise what great elaborate pieces of construction they are: dramatic cathedrals. I came to see that not only were they interesting as narratives, but how, over and above and through the narrative are implied meanings, like the echo in a cathedral. I began to feel what richness of character was there, to hear what melody was in the lines.'

Here again we are given the musical simile, Guthrie detecting the hidden melodies even while he was critical of Benson's tattered productions. Benson was another actor who had been a member of Irving's company at the Lyceum. Irving once said to him: 'You're too modest, Benson, too modest, you know. . . . Or at least, you pretend to be.' It was a sign of the times that although Benson never had the glamour of Irving or Tree and was much closer to the old actor-laddie image so beloved of caricaturists, he too was honoured with a knighthood; and in fact he was the only actor ever to be knighted in an actual theatre. Before Irving there had been no theatrical knights, and now there were half a dozen: the walls of respectability had truly been scaled.

Yet another great character from this period was Sir Philip Ben Greet whose career was so closely linked with Lilian Baylis at the Old Vic. And as we move further into the twentieth century we find closer links between the many distinguished players who, with the powers of endurance that seem to characterise their generation, survived almost to the present day. Sybil Thorndike trained at Ben Greet's Academy of Acting in Bedford

F. R. BENSON as Romeo   LILIAN BAYLIS, 1933

Street when a young girl and later joined his company as an understudy for one of his American tours. 'This is going to be hard work', he told her, 'so you'd better learn everyone's part, because they are sure to be ill. You don't get ill, do you?' 'Never', she told him, since this is an answer required of any young understudy. 'Well, you needn't boast', Greet replied. 'This was typical of him', Dame Sybil wrote many years later in an introduction to Winifred Isaac's biography of Greet. 'Any sign of being pleased with oneself, either in parts, or physical health and he'd knock one flat off one's perch.'

It is Greet's association with the Old Vic, at a time when life in that amazing building separated the men from the boys, which claims our detailed attention. Today theatregoers are conditioned to seeing our leading Shakespearean players in the concrete stillness of the National Theatre, with its subdued lighting, plush bars and general air of tranquillity, but the atmosphere of the Royal Victoria Hall in the Waterloo Road—once described as a 'licensed pit of darkness'—was vastly different. Ben Greet first went there during the first World War when it had no box office (bookings were taken in the stage box), no dressing rooms, no wardrobes and no scene dock. The only water supply for the artists was a single tap on the prompt side of the stage, and dressers brought water round in basins. Lilian Baylis, eccentric in all things, used to cook sausages and mash on a gas ring in the wings between shows, and sometimes during the show. It was with good cause that Greet described the enterprise as a 'Family Theatre' for audiences could enjoy a Shakespearean performance with the aroma of bacon and eggs wafting across the pit. A sense of patriotism brought Greet to join forces with Lilian Baylis and together they survived the German air raids and existed in working conditions which today would bring about a General Strike. Even as late as 1929 things were still more or less the same. Guthrie described a visit he made as 'an eye-opener'. He had gone to witness Gielgud in *The Merchant of Venice* and although he found the production 'immensely elegant' with the comedy scenes 'played lightly, wittily, without the ham-fisted vaudeville knock-about which was then the way too many actors treated it' he was still amazed by the atmosphere in the theatre itself. 'The old house was shabby, even grubby. Rather rude and angry crones shoved a programme into your hands; the attendants at the doors wore

frightfully ill-fitting uniforms over their own grey flannel bags and had a tendency to grip their noses between grubby finger and grubby thumb and blow hard onto the grubby carpet. But the house was packed, and the enthusiasm of the unspoilt, intelligent audience was infectious. It was a very different audience from the much richer, smarter, blasé audience who went to the Cochran revues, or the bearded, cheery, leery mob at the Palladium. The Old Vic audience, one felt, was composed of people who you could die to please, who wanted to have their horizons enlarged, who would come out to meet new ideas and new challenges, whose imaginations were limber and supple, like an athlete's muscles. . . . For the first time in my life I saw new social possibilities in the theatre.'

This Old Vic audience had not been gathered together by chance. If we are to believe Lilian Baylis, God played an important part in calling the faithful to the Waterloo Road. She was, by any standards, defiantly unique, a 'first-class Cockney from South Africa' (in Hugh Walpole's description) and had a contest ever been run to discover 'The Woman Least Likely to Run A Theatre', would have won hands down, and probably on her knees. She inherited the burden of the Royal Victoria Hall from her equally astonishing aunt, Emma Cons, and with a missionary zeal more usually associated with the African Bush, set about what was to become her life-long crusade. She was 'under educated', thirty-nine years old, a devout, if unorthodox, Christian and a spinster. Her only tenuous connection with the world of entertainment was that she had been a child violinist. If she thought about art at all, she thought it 'a kind of medicine dispensed to the poor and needy', a description which fitted most of the inhabitants in the area adjacent to the theatre. From Aunt Emma she inherited the passion but not the wherewithal and from the very first day her main preoccupation was money.

Sybil Thorndike first met her in 1914, two years after she had taken command of the leaking ship. 'I was astonished at her extraordinary old-fashioned slang. She was talking to a carpenter in the most extraordinary way. I thought, what a darling she sounds. And then she came up to me and said, "You're a church girl, aren't you? Good. Father's a parson? Good. I'd like you here." She didn't care tuppence whether I could act or anything. She was very deeply religious and she liked people who felt something the way she did. She told us that she went to church . . . "and I said, Lord God, please send me a good actor. But send him cheap." She did everything on prayer. Whatever came to her in Mass—she was an Anglican—she would act on in the day, and if we all argued with her and said it was wrong and that she oughtn't to do it, she said: "No, that's what came to me this morning in church and I'm going to do it." And it generally proved right. I don't think she knew much about Shakespeare. I don't think she'd ever seen one of his plays right through. I remember when I first had to play Lady Macbeth, I found it very difficult. It's a terrible, terrible part to play. Lilian said, "Don't talk nonsense. It's quite easy. You want everything for your husband. Lady Macbeth wanted everything for *her* husband. What's wrong in that, and what's difficult?" And, do you know, it's quite true, it made sense. It was a very good comment.

'I remember that when I was playing St Joan they asked me if I knew anybody who was like her . . . and I said the only person I knew was Lilian Baylis.'

Stories about her abound and it would seem that few of them are apocryphal. Robert Atkins once recalled that he used to hear 'the rows between Miss Baylis and Mr Greet. I was playing in Macbeth, with Dame Sybil Thorndike as Lady Macbeth. I was in the wings, waiting to make my entrance, Lady Macbeth was on stage. Mr Greet was in the prompt corner, dressed ready to play a small role, that of the Doctor. Miss Baylis came down to him and they started having a row. He moved out of the corner, I went on and began my scene. They moved round behind the backcloth, shouting at one another. Before our scene was over they had worked round to the other side of the stage and I could see them both. He'd taken off everything but his shirt and there she was keeping his shirt from following the rest.'

Whether by luck, with God's help, or a combination of the two, when she picked her actors she generally picked quality. Almost all actors of note in the second half of this century served under Lilian Baylis. Ernest Milton caught the attention of Ben Greet as a young man and Lilian promptly wrote to him: 'Ben Greet has told me that I have found me' (*sic*) 'leading man'. Milton went to see her. 'She was very straight. She said, "Would you like to help us, dear?" And I said, with great courage and aplomb, "Yes, if I can play Hamlet." Whereupon she said, "You have the face for it, dear, and we're looking for a Hamlet".'

So if we talk about an 'Old Vic tradition' we have to acknowledge that it came about because of this indomitable little woman who had no theories about acting, who was not familiar with any of the great actors of the past and who worked entirely from religious inspiration allied to her own instincts. No novelist would dare to invent her, she is too improbable and her success story too banal. But there she was, cooking her steaks and bacon and eggs in the wings during the last acts of the matinees, regarding her actors as if they were naughty children in the nursery, paying them as little as she could get away with, yet inspiring in them lifelong devotion. Lacking any knowledge of the classics herself she hired producers with the same unerring judgement that she applied to the choice of actors. After Ben Greet (who was also High Church), came Russell Thorndike, Robert Atkins, Andrew Leigh, Harcourt Williams and Tyrone Guthrie, an unbroken line of talent. Greet and Atkins fought tooth and nail with her, though no lasting offence was

ERNEST MILTON as Hamlet, Old Vic, 1921

taken or given; Leigh and Williams enjoyed a calmer relationship; all four brought their own individual stamp of authority to the Waterloo Road. Although the surroundings changed but little in nearly two decades, the plays produced within the crumbling walls and the actors who performed them established new standards of excellence. If on the surface everything seemed haphazard and hand-to-mouth, then this was a false impression of what was really taking place. Lilian Baylis was no fool. She had a sure eye for any publicity that would do her beloved theatre some good. It was said that she was a professional beggar and that rich people used to run at the sight of her—only they were seldom able to move fast enough. The very fact that she was no respecter of persons, however exalted, gave her an edge, disconcerting friends and enemies alike. Harcourt Williams recalled that when Queen Mary visited the Old Vic, Lilian proudly pointed out a portrait of her aunt hanging alongside a much smaller portrait of George V. 'The reason it's not quite so large as Aunt Emma's', she told the Queen, 'is because your dear husband hasn't done as much for the Old Vic'. She couldn't be bothered with artistic temperament and had little use for the usual conceits that actors are heir to. I particularly like the story told of two young people in her company who fell in love and wished to get married. Since they seldom had any time off it was difficult for them to plan the actual day. They finally plucked up courage and went to Lilian and explained the situation. 'Haven't got time for gossip, dear', she said. And that was that.

She created a world apart from the mainstream of the West End theatre and from her tiny office she exerted an influence that was as profound in its own way as anything since the age of Garrick. She probably wouldn't have understood or employed Garrick, he would probably have been too grand, and certainly too expensive for her. As she told Sir John Gielgud when he was negotiating his own contract to join Harcourt Williams' first season in 1929, 'we'd love to have you here, but of course we can't afford stars'. In Agate's phrase she had 'some at least of the characteristics of the Rock of Ages'. During the early years her enterprise was mostly ignored by the critics and she returned the compliment. She knew that the hard core of her audience didn't read them, nor did they care overmuch for West End reputations. It was a people's theatre and 'her' people came to enjoy themselves vociferously; she took note of their reactions and supplied their needs according to her means. She spent £15 on a set and resented it, £20 a week on a leading actor and reviled herself for giving way to such extortion.

There is little evidence to suggest that Lilian ever wandered far from her own stronghold. She lived in glorious isolation, an obsessed, lonely but contented woman. When the stars she made deserted her for richer pickings in the West End, she forgot about them. If they asked to be taken back, as sometimes happened, they came back on her terms or not at all, and she remained stoically unimpressed by the fame they had achieved away from her theatre. Even film stars like Charles Laughton received the same treatment. It was their privilege to do Lilian's and God's work at the Old Vic and as the reputation of the theatre grew, enticing more and more fashionable playgoers to make the pilgrimage, and the first-string critics were stirred to record what was taking place, the number of established players who were prepared to accept her terms grew to an impressive list.

The journey from the West End to the Waterloo Road was a short one and yet when stray visitors came upon the Old Vic they found a different artistic language being spoken. Both Andrew Leigh and later Harcourt Williams, influenced by Poel and Granville-Barker, developed more pace in their Shakespearean productions. Within the limitations of the budgets set by Lilian they moved away from Poel's total austerity, but they did embrace his conviction that the words be given their full value and that the text was inviolate. It was not to everybody's liking and during Williams' first productions his actors were accused of gabbling. It was all in strange contrast to the post-war drama occupying the stages of the West End where the acting had become quieter and more naturalistic (with many leading men attempting to ape the 'dangerous ease' of Gerald du Maurier with varying degrees of success). Only Shaw, returning to his old address in Sloane Square and breaking his war-time silence with his first full length play since *Pygmalion*, kept the flag of revolution flying. The play was *Heartbreak House* and there were many who felt the flag was at half mast. His comedy in the Chekhovian manner was dubbed 'Jawbreak House' by some of the critics who felt, like Maugham, that Shaw was a great wit 'but he talks too much and too long. He cannot tolerate being interrupted while conversing'. Little did they know at that time, 1921, that he was busy writing an even longer play, the pentateuch *Back to Methuselah*, which made *Heartbreak House* seem like a curtain raiser by comparison, since the five parts of *Methuselah* took four nights to perform in its entirety when eventually produced by Barry Jackson at the Birmingham Repertory. But for all his radical ideas, Shaw was still writing about the old moralities, while Barrie, Galsworthy, Henry Arthur Jones and others of the old Edwardian guard shuffled on to the parade ground for a last inspection. Again, turning to Maugham, we learn that it was now that the young Noël Coward knocked at the door with impatient knuckles . . . 'then he rattled the handle, and then he burst in. After a moment's stupor the older playwrights welcomed him affably enough and retired with what dignity they could muster to the shelf which with a sprightly gesture he indicated to them as their proper place'. Coward was the new breed, brittle, too brittle in the opinion of his detractors, but the post-war generation was longing for a spokesman who spoke their

NOËL COWARD as the page-boy, with CHARLES HAWTREY and
LYDIA BILBROKE in *The Great Name*, Prince of Wales Theatre,
1911

GERALD DU MAURIER

NOËL COWARD and LILIAN BRAITHWAITE in *The Vortex*, Everyman, 1924

language and who could give dramatic shape to the new morality. He had given the theatre some amusing light comedies, before startling his elders with *The Vortex* at the Everyman, a small try-out theatre in Hampstead. Prolific during this period as few playwrights before or since, Coward's primary reason for becoming a dramatist was to provide himself with roles that would advance his career as an actor. *The Vortex* was the turning point, establishing him as a dramatist and all-round performer who could never again be dismissed or ignored. The production became a *cause célèbre* and after twelve performances at the Everyman transferred to the Royalty in the West End where it ran for 224 performances and survived a further two transfers. In its day it had the same divisive impact as Osborne's *Look Back in Anger* three decades later when once again we had a post-war generation anxious to overturn the old order. (Gielgud felt that 'when *The Vortex* came on there was such a battery of establishment actor-managers who were so powerful, and there was such a strong feeling in the theatre—so many of the men had come back from the First War, you know, very strong virile characters—and all this was considered decadent and effeminate. Whereas, now, decadence and effeminacy is kind of mixed up with virility. The 1956 John Osborne *Look back in Anger* was rather different. That was a much more surly, basic kind of rebellion. It wasn't so fancy. Perhaps it's become much fancier again in the last ten years.')

Coward was the complete man of the theatre, yet with that spite that is reserved exclusively for those who achieve success early in their careers, throughout his life he was often the target of ill-informed and unfair criticism. The legend grew up that he was facile and therefore uncaring, the very reverse of the truth. He had enormous artistic courage and placed total emphasis on professionalism in all things. It would be difficult to over-estimate his contribution to the British theatre of the twentieth century. He achieved success in so many fields: in his music, much of which became indispensable to the popular repertoire the moment it was written; in his plays, his own performances, his productions, his revue sketches, his novels, short stories, his films and one-man night-club shows, he exhibited a diversity of talent that few can ever approach. In addition he was a mentor to many young actors and actresses, giving of his time and advice with a generosity that was never publicly exploited. In time and with justification he became known as Master, always exerting an influence on his colleagues, inevitably suffering the fate of all *enfants terribles* and becoming a venerated sage—though never in his own eyes. He made a point of honour to try and keep up with changing modes and could trade punches with most of the younger set, coming out of his corner again at the very moment they thought the white towel was about to be thrown. A criticism often levelled at him was that he relied too heavily on sentimentality, and when it became unfashionable to even mention the two words British Empire his themes were condemned as jingoism. But he outlived, out-distanced, out-shot and in the end won over the majority of his critics because he demonstrated that he had staying power and because in most cases they simply weren't in his league. Yes, he was a sentimentalist and a patriot during periods when both were considered passé, but he never renounced his beliefs for the sake of currying transient favour. His over-riding love was the theatre. He was a product of the theatre, he served the theatre and he served his public. He made no attempt to become a

ELLEN TERRY as Lady Macbeth
From a photograph by Window and Grove
Mander and Mitchenson Theatre Collection

EDITH EVANS
as the Countess in the film of *The Queen of Spades*
Photo BBC Hulton Picture Library

RALPH RICHARDSON and JOHN GIELGUD in Harold Pinter's *No Man's Land,*
Old Vic and National Theatres, 1975
Photo Reg Wilson

great classical actor; he was a social observer of limited range, but within that range he was unsurpassed. He gave to our drama at least half a dozen plays that stand comparison with the best light comedies ever written in the English language, and as an interpreter of his own works he was without a peer.

Like so many of our great performers he sprang from nowhere, in his case the lower middle-classes which most social commentators in our enlightened age classify as no-man's land. His mother took in lodgers and he was acting by age eleven, making his debut as Prince Mussel in a children's play called *The Goldfish*. Then he auditioned for Charles Hawtrey for a minor role of a pageboy in the last act of *The Great Name*. 'I came on and electrified Hawtrey. . . . I gave a sort of full-out, grand performance, forgetting I was supposed to be a little pageboy. I heard him say to his stage manager, after I'd walked off, "Tarver, never let me see that boy again."' Hawtrey later relented, engaged young Master Coward, was worn down by this enthusiasm and taught him the rudiments of comedy. It was a debt Coward always acknowledged. 'Practically everything I know about comedy I learnt from him.'

Hawtrey, like Gerald du Maurier, belonged to that select band of comedians who perfected their art to the point where many people felt that they had ceased to act and were merely projecting their own personalities. It was a school of acting, much admired by the public and other actors, exemplified by such players as Seymour Hicks, Cyril Maude, A. E. Matthews and, closer to our own times, Ronald Squire, Cecil Parker, Michael Wilding, Roland Culver and Rex Harrison. Olivier, for instance, thought that du Maurier 'brilliant actor that he was, had the most disastrous influence on my generation, because we really thought, looking at him, that it was easy; and for the first ten years of our lives in the theatre, nobody could hear a word we said. We thought he was being really natural; of course, he was a genius of a technician giving that appearance, that's all.'

Gielgud had similar early memories: 'I always thought that acting meant panting and crying and laughing and being very impressive, fighting duels and jumping up with enormous impressiveness . . . and yet when du Maurier came on in the last act of *Dear Brutus* . . . his face when they told him that the child was a dream was so extraordinary and yet he appeared to do absolutely nothing. I remember thinking what a pity it was that he never played in Chekhov or Ibsen. He was such a great actor, but in those days leading men like du Maurier had such vehicles provided for them, and they were themselves such an enormous draw with the public that anything they bothered to put on was always a success, and so they had no urge and no particular temptation to go into the classical field.'

Lilian Baylis had put Shakespeare back on the map but in the eyes of many the Vic remained a tatty little company of unknowns and incompetents. The post-war generation demanded less-demanding entertainments, bright spurts of cynicism such as Maugham provided, or else the urbane comedies of Frederick Lonsdale and others. Shaw was a law unto himself, removed from all other schools and although, in the twenties, he struck out for posterity with *Methuselah* and then, most notably, with *Saint Joan*, he remained an isolated figure that nobody could pigeon-hole. We must not forget that the country was moving towards the General Strike of 1926, and in the sullen aftermath of war, although those with leisure and money were able to set trends, the vast majority of the population, under successive weak governments, had not the energy or the will to follow such trends, which in any event were mostly confined to London and a particular section of London at that. There was some good new drama—Clemence Dane's *A Bill of Divorcement*, the steady output from Maugham, the core of comedies from Lonsdale, some solid plays from St John Ervine and, of course, Sherriff's *Journey's End*, the most famous of a spate of plays and novels that attempted to record the horror of the trenches. But for the most part people felt compelled to turn away from the nightmare of those four terrible years, to wipe their emotional slate clean, and many of them could not bear to look back into the abyss. Du Maurier's adored brother Guy was one of those who had not come back, and the news had been broken to Gerald by telegram during an evening performance of *Raffles*. From that moment onwards, according to his daughter, Angela, 'before a first night he always sent up a prayer to his dead brother'. Another daughter, Daphne, the distinguished novelist, felt that her father was 'a great amateur, but also a terrific professional. He combined these two things exquisitely. An amateur by birth, a professional by intuition and experience. He certainly ended his days a complete professional, having started his career as an amateur without training'.

Sir Felix Aylmer felt that 'Gerald had the same attitude to the theatre as Irving, in the sense that he believed the theatre is the place where actors *act*. He said, "I am a professional actor, not an interpreter of great dramatists or anything like that. What I have to do is to have material to act. I've got to collaborate and put in my part of it." And that's what Irving felt and did.'

So if one takes a historical bird's eye view of the Twenties, one looks down on a quadrille being performed, the dancers endlessly changing partners, coming together, separating, trying to keep in step with each other. They weave in and out in intricate patterns so that at times the whole scene becomes a blur.

We have Edith Evans, like du Maurier, starting her career as a gifted amateur. Poel found her, Poel influenced Granville-Barker who in turn teamed up with Vedrenne who employed Edith. Then there is Coward forcing his acting talents on Hawtrey and afterwards writing his own words and music, his career criss-crossing that of the young John Gielgud. And although Gielgud came from the Terry family he seemed curiously unprepared for his eventual role in the theatre. He understudied and eventually went on for Coward in two plays, *The Vortex* and *The Constant Nymph*; he was helped early in his career by Nigel Playfair, and it was Playfair who gave Edith the role of Millamant in *The Way of the World* a few years later. Gielgud confessed that he had always thought of Irving as a god, although he had never seen Irving act, but only read about him. He was two years younger than Ralph Richardson, and three years older than Olivier. Richardson, who termed himself an 'undisciplined, tangled, muddled, disaster of a chap', blundered into an acting career after flirting with a variety of possible alternatives— painter, journalist, chemist—and finally bought his way into a semi-amateur troupe with what remained from a small legacy. Olivier, educated at a high Anglican church school where the priests favoured theatricals, played Brutus at the age of ten and was seen and complimented by Ellen Terry, whom he confessed he had never heard of. Breaking out from an atmosphere of genteel poverty ('probably the most fertile ground for ambition there can be') he survived a stint with a troupe called the Lena Ashwell players, who performed mostly in public swimming baths, the group being known, affectionately, as The Lavatory Players, before having the good fortune to meet and he befriended by Sybil Thorndike and Lewis Casson. He next joined Sir Barry Jackson's Birmingham theatre which was also an early home for Ralph Richardson; both played the same role of Richard Coaker in tours of *The Farmer's Wife*.

Eventually all these different careers, all this talent, seemed to come to flower at roughly the same time. The year 1924 is an auspicious one, for in that year Sybil Thorndike played *Saint Joan*, Coward starred in *The Vortex*, Edith Evans made her own history in *The Way of the World* and Gielgud first attempted Romeo. With the exception of Coward, all of them gravitated towards the Old Vic, all possessed iron self-disciplines and all were fortunate in that, at the start of their careers, the theatre was still the most potent form of entertainment, as yet not seriously challenged by the cinema. It was inevitable that, eventually, the cinema would seduce some of them away for varying periods, but they never completely deserted the legitimate theatre. (Although Edith Evans appeared in a silent film in 1915, five years after her amateur debut, she did not respond to the siren call of the movies for another three decades.)

One cannot say that there was concerted action to bring about a classical reformation in the theatre, but it so happened that because of their varied experiences at the Old Vic and the satisfaction they felt as individuals in suddenly grasping what Shakespeare was all about, a reformation did take place. It was Gielgud who brought Shakespeare back to the West End and proved him commercially viable. His early attempts at the classics had not been judged a success. He felt that his Romeo opposite Gwen Ffrangcon-Davies had been 'a frightful mess. . . . I just wasn't ready. I didn't know how to select what I wanted to do, or put over emotion. I just enjoyed indulging in my own emotions, and imagined that that was acting. When I was on the stage I felt it was my duty to do something, give something, and be something. And through imagination, intense imagination, and tremendous emotional desire, I did create a certain effect, but it was always very tense. I think people found me affectedly artificial and over-strung. . . , I exhausted myself most terribly, I used to be absolutely whacked playing the big classical parts and trying to live every moment of them; it didn't occur to me that there are places where you really must do nothing'.

Reading this frank admission conjured up a different Gielgud from the one we know today who, with his other knighted colleagues, personifies the second great age of English acting. It was not by chance that when, in 1967, the BBC launched a series of programmes under the title *Great Acting*, the eight principals taking part were, in no order of preference, Olivier, Sybil Thorndike, Ralph Richardson, Peggy Ashcroft, Michael Redgrave, Edith Evans, Gielgud and Coward. Dame Peggy and Sir Michael Redgrave were slightly later starters than the other six, and although the list is not a complete one— for there are other names to be gathered into this account—if we take these eight names we are looking at a remarkable assembly of talent. It is difficult to believe that their collective worth was ever simultaneously equalled in past centuries.

In his erudite Preface to the published transcripts of these valuable television programmes Hal Burton, the producer of the series, confirmed my own belief that 'without the existence of the Old Vic, it is doubtful if all of them would have reached their full stature. This unique theatre, under the management of Lilian Baylis, was able to offer all of them in turn the right parts at the precise stage in their development when they needed the big Shakespearean roles to stretch their latent powers to the uttermost limits'.

How were they stretched? Well, in her first season at the Vic Edith Evans played thirteen different roles within the space of seven months. In their joint season of 1930–31 Gielgud and Richardson played twenty roles between them. Olivier was learning comedy and how not to giggle on stage from Coward in *Private Lives* during that same year 1930 and it was not until 1935 that he teamed with Gielgud to alternate Romeo and Mercutio in Gielgud's own production. Gielgud had already given a memorable Hamlet, and achieved enormous success in Gordon Daviot's *Richard of Bordeaux*. It seems crass to talk of rivalry in such company, but the fillip was there, the theatre was alive with challenge. Richardson in his studied, courtly way, has revealed that when he and Gielgud first acted together at the Vic he 'didn't really like him at all'. He was playing Caliban to Gielgud's Prospero and at one point in the rehearsals Gielgud stopped everything to explain where he felt Richardson was going wrong. Such incidents do not always lead to happy endings in the theatre, but on this occasion Richardson took the advice. 'The scales fell off my eyes. I thought, "This chap I don't like is a very great craftsman, he's a wonderful fellow, he knows an awful lot about his job". And from admiration for him, as a professional, came friendship and admiration for him as a man, because he's a wonderful chap and a great director.' In exactly the same manner but away from the Old Vic and in the West End, Coward was putting Olivier through his paces, and we have Olivier admitting, 'I think Noël was probably the first man who took hold of me and made me think, he made me use my silly little brain. He taxed me with his sharpness and shrewdness and his brilliance, he used to point out when I was talking nonsense, which nobody else had ever done before. He gave me a sense of balance of right and wrong. . . . Thrilling, very inspiriting . . . a tremendous influence.'

It could loosely be described as a school of acting—but a scattered school, with no formal curriculum, merely a number of star pupils exchanging exam papers and marking each other accordingly. They went from the commercial West End to the Old Vic, or to Birmingham and Liverpool, and back—the former subsidising the latter. There was a feeling of purpose in the Waterloo Road, a resumption of serious studies, as it were, after the hols. On the face of it they were a most unlikely group to be tumbled together; widely differing in personality and approach, but all fortunate to be emerging at a time when the theatre was once again finding greatness.

I have mentioned Peggy Ashcroft and Michael Redgrave, who enrolled slightly later than the others, but the list of talent anxious to take the entrance exams was an impressive one. If one looks down the roll of honour at the names of those who brought such distinction to our stages from the Thirties onwards one finds an abundance of great personalities. Sir Alec Guinness, of course, Donald Wolfit, Francis Lister, Leon Quartermaine, Robert Donat, Jack Hawkins, Herbert Lomas, Emlyn Williams, Sir John

Clements, Wilfrid Lawson, André Morell, Eric Portman, Roger Livesey, Marius Goring, Sir Godfrey Tearle—to take almost a random selection of the men who were complemented by an equal number of the ladies. In addition to the brilliant and tragic Meggie Albanesi, the incomplete list must include Dame Lilian Braithwaite, Dame Flora Robson, Jessica Tandy, Martita Hunt, Beatrix Lehmann, Constance Cummings, Diana Wynyard, Cathleen Nesbitt, Sonia Dresdel, Athene Seyler and Mary Clare.

In retrospect it seems, and in comparison with today was, a golden age, for the talents on stage were surrounded by great designers, directors and impresarios. We had the Motleys, Gladys Calthrop, Basil Dean, C. B. Cochran, Guthrie—naturally—Miles Malleson, Murray Macdonald, Esme Church, Irene Hentschel (a neglected figure who was far in advance of Women's Lib), Maurice Browne, Harold Clayton and George Devine. The most forceful of theatrical managements, H. M. Tennent, under the tasteful dictatorship of Hugh 'Binkie' Beaumont was in the ascendant and would, during the Forties and Fifties, become all powerful. There were new dramatists to serve the changing needs and as Hal Burton has pointed out, it was also a period when the masterpieces of Chekhov became the perfect antidote to the Shakespeare canon. During the Thirties there were two memorable productions: Komisarjevsky's *Seagull* in 1936, and Michel Saint-Denis's *Three Sisters* in 1938, both still remembered for their exquisite ensemble playing.

Acting in the grand manner gradually assumed its old supremacy, but it was great acting adapted to the mood of the time, devoid of bombast and rhetoric, more physical than in Irving's day, most robust than that favoured by Forbes-Robertson, and with a better balance between the spoken word and the sense behind it. Alongside this we had a vital musical comedy theatre with stars equal to the challenges; we had the Aldwych farces, the Cochran revues, A. P. Herbert, the multi-talents of Ivor Novello, a thriving repertory system and a host of small, outer London theatres able and anxious to experiment with new dramatists, casts and directors. Now it all seems too good to be true, for although the cinema challenged the total supremacy of the legitimate theatre during this period, it never succeeded in destroying it. The Odeons and Gaumonts proliferated up and down the country, but there was still a regular and enthusiastic audience in every major city for the living theatre. Television was still an amazing toy that few believed would ever catch the popular imagination or be afforded by the popular purse (after all radio was amazing enough!) and the spectre of Bingo had not yet walked the battlements of derelict theatres. Every West End success was followed by at least two companies touring the provinces, critics had space in the popular newspapers, and going to the theatre was, for most, a glamorous occasion. There were sixty-two theatres in London alone, and they were seldom dark for more than a few weeks at a time. What price glory!

[[18]]

GIELGUD

I T is Sir John Gielgud's contention that all acting is unreal, that 'although truth is the most important thing in acting, the way it is presented has to be in some patterned or selected form, presented in a way that is *not* true; just as a painter with paint cannot produce a real tree, so an actor even with words cannot produce a performance without knowing where the modulations come, how the speeches balance with the speeches of other performers, how the pace, rhythm and colour must be controlled. I think it is extraordinary that for so many years the theatre survived without directors. We've been brought up in the directors' theatre in my time, and we can hardly believe that it was possible that in the old days the star just ordered the other actors about to suit himself. He just gave a kind of coloratura soprano performance, as I suppose a great opera singer still does today. Yet style must obviously be evolved more by the director than by the actors. The director is there to put the style into or onto the play. Very often I don't think it altogether helps the actors to know what the director is trying to create. In fact, one of the great thrills of my life was working with Komisarjevsky when suddenly, at the dress rehearsal when the scenery and the lights and the costumes appeared, we all suddenly saw what we'd been working on for weeks.'

This shift of emphasis towards the director during the Twenties and Thirties is worth examining in more detail, for it brought about fundamental changes. Since I am a director myself, but was an actor, I will attempt to give the case for both plaintiff and defendant. According to Kenneth Tynan the English 'have never really warmed to theatrical directors'. He wrote this in 1954, and perhaps his judgement would be different today, because at the time he was bemoaning the fact that the English did not respond to despotism in the theatre. I think there are subtler shades to the argument: the best directors (not necessarily the most successful) are not despots in my experience, but benevolent dictators, capable of listening as well as signing death warrants. Most actors have been exposed to what is known, facetiously, as the early-Otto Preminger school of directing, and there are many examples in the theatre of students who have graduated with honours. Basil Dean, for example, although a dedicated and gifted man of the theatre, gained a reputation for conducting his rehearsals with an iron fist concealed in an iron glove, and in the end the bigger names avoided him.

Gielgud's talents matured during the transition period of this century when the monopoly of the star actor was gradually eroded, and although the star still commanded

l to r JOHN GIELGUD as Hamlet, New Theatre, 1934; as Richard II, Old Vic, 1930; Queen's, 1938

his rightful position in the theatre, he lost his total authority and began to share the honours with a growing band of 'star' directors. In Gielgud's case he was fortunate, as he gratefully admits, to work with men of the calibre of Harcourt Williams and Theodore Komisarjevsky. Of the two, Komisarjevsky was the dominating influence and Gielgud met him at a crucial point in his development. Komisarjevsky first came to England at the invitation of Sir Thomas Beecham to produce opera; he arrived armed with a formidable reputation, having been director of the Imperial and State theatres in Moscow. He was a man for all seasons: an architect, costume designer, musical arranger, a rebel with a cause, and undoubtedly a near-genius. There was, however, a self-destructive element in him which manifested itself in eventual cynicism towards any country that afforded him a temporary home. Gielgud worked with him for the best part of a decade and during this time not only consolidated his position as an actor of classic stature, but assimilated and later put into practice many of the ideas that Komisarjevsky had introduced. In particular the partnership of the two men brought about a minor revolution in the production and playing of Chekhov in this country.

Gielgud had played Chekhov before—first for J. B. Fagan's company in Oxford (Trofimov in *The Cherry Orchard*) a production which later transferred under Nigel Playfair's management to the Lyric, Hammersmith. This venture produced mixed reactions, sharply divisive, from both critics and public. Agate told his radio audience it was 'the best play in London' while some of his colleagues thumbed it down as the worst. It was sufficiently a success to encourage another manager, Philip Ridgeway, to go into rehearsal with *The Seagull* at the Little Theatre in the Adelphi. On this occasion Gielgud was cast as Konstantin, with a young Valerie Taylor as Nina. Komisarjevsky found it 'very funny', a verdict that was not intended to be complimentary. Obviously he did not view the production with an open mind—his sister, Vera Komisarjevskaia, a star of the Moscow Arts Theatre, had created the role of Nina for Stanislavsky—and he persuaded Ridgeway that if Chekhov was to be produced for the further education of the English, he could only be entrusted to an expert. Ridgeway, to his credit, agreed and Komisarjevsky was engaged to direct *Three Sisters, Ivanov, Uncle Vanya* and a more authentic version of *The Cherry Orchard* in the tiny theatre across the river at Barnes Bridge. Gielgud along with Margaret Swallow was chosen to join the new venture; the rest of the Lyric cast were rejected by Komisarjevsky.

Interestingly enough, Komisarjevsky's devotion to Chekhov as a master dramatist did not prevent him from making copious, and some thought curious, cuts and alterations in the text. If purists find such behaviour offensive and a variation on the previous habits of the star actors, who seldom hesitated to mutilate any author if it suited their purpose, they should turn to Hugh Hunt's defence. Putting the case for the director-turned-dramatist, he poses the question: 'Can we have a work of theatrical art which is at the same time a distortion of the author's intention?' Mr Hunt then answers himself with an emphatic yes, justifying it by comparing it to a fine portrait which bears no resemblance to the sitter. I am not so sure. In the first place a portrait which bears no resemblance to the sitter may be a damn fine painting but to my mind is in no way a portrait. Equally it would seem that the first and final obligation of a director is to be faithful to an author's *intention*. He may so direct his actors so that they travel by divers routes, but unless they arrive at the author's avowed destination then surely their journey has been in vain? We have seen how, in the past, *King Lear* was sometimes given a happy ending. Presumably Mr Hunt would have found this a damn good portrait of a 'happy mad king'? We could take it further and have penicillin administered to la Dame aux Camélias in the last act, have the Winslow Boy found guilty, or, the ultimate absurdity, allow Romeo and Juliet life-restoring heart transplants.

These desperate quests for innovation at any cost are traps that can snare the experienced director as easily as the newcomer. They stem, I believe, from those periodic fits of madness that affect all creative people: we convince ourselves that the best we have done in the past would now be considered *déjà vu* and that, therefore, we must spring ourselves like jack-in-the-boxes to produce startling surprises. Any attempt to anticipate public taste is a fool's game. The artist must always work from self-conviction, though the commercial theatre inhibits when it does not actually strangle true originality and the wonder of it is that anything worthwhile ever sees the light of day. There is a cynical saying in the entertainment world—too often acted upon, alas—that we are all only as good as the last thing we did. Thus if the last thing was a failure, we are immediately scrap-heap fodder. I prefer the dictum put forward by the American director Billy Wilder. When he heard somebody denigrating the work of a colleague who had suffered three flops in a row and was subsequently being avoided by the establishment as a plague carrier, Wilder remonstrated: 'No, you are wrong. We are all as good as the *best* thing we ever did.'

We have seen how the theatre existed for many centuries without embracing the talents

Richard of Bordeaux, by Gordon Daviot (*l to r*) JOHN GIELGUD, GWEN FFRANGCON-DAVIES and FRANCIS LISTER, New Theatre, 1933

The Importance of Being Earnest (l to r) GEORGE HOWE as Canon Chasuble, JOHN GIELGUD as John Worthing, MARGARET RUTHERFORD as Miss Prism, Globe, 1939

of directors; a hit and miss existence, dominated by the star actor or actor-manager intent on consolidating his own position at the expense of others. All too frequently the dramatist was the acquiescing whipping boy, a collaborator at his own emasculation, poorly paid, seldom consulted once he had delivered the pages, eventually corrupted to the point where he betrayed his colleagues, rewriting others just as he had been rewritten. When the function of the director came to be recognised the dramatists hoped that their status would at last be improved, but once again they found they had merely exchanged task-masters, for the directors wanted to be stars. Not until the establishment of the Dramatists' Guild in America was there any concerted attempt to give the writer his proper place in the theatre, though it must be pointed out that flagrant abuses still take place, perhaps less so in the theatre than in films, and the written word is always the first thing to be sacrificed in any contest between actor, director and dramatist. It is a very curious fact of theatrical and film life that nearly everyone in a position to offer employment is a noted improver of scripts. It is a rare event to meet anybody who does not know how a play or a film script should be written. With few exceptions producers conduct their affairs in such a way as to infer that the true Utopia would be a society in which the writer did not exist.

It is often confusing for the layman to differentiate between the function of the producer and the function of the director. In simplistic terms, the producer is the one responsible for raising the finance and bringing together the various creative elements, and the director is the one who physically melds those elements into the finished products. Very often they overlap, but for the purposes of this chronicle the reader should assume that when I use the expression 'director' I am referring to those who orchestrate the actors.

As a race they can be sub-divided into a number of categories. There are those who are content to plot the moves of an entire play before coming to the first read-through and are then incapable of any deviation from their blueprint. They are seldom true interpreters of a dramatist's work, nor are they really of any assistance to the actors: they are policemen on traffic duty. Of equal hindrance to the betterment of the drama is the director who comes to the first rehearsal with a completely open mind, trusting to luck that the actors will provide inspiration as the days go by. This is an animal that most actors have encountered at some point in their careers, and he frightens them to death. The majority of actors are timid creatures during the rehearsal period, desperate for the odd word of encouragement that will stifle their ever-present sense of inadequacy. The best directors of actors can always detect the reflection of the firing squad in their eyes and hand them the metaphorical cigarette of hope. The best director of all, in my opinion, is he who can illuminate the dramatist's intentions and release the actors into giving something beyond their normal range while at the same time so shaping the stage as to delight the beholder's eye. As with all great art it is the technique of concealing technique that deserves our highest admiration, for once an audience is made aware of the wheels going round then that audience is distracted from the true purpose and its enjoyment is disturbed, either consciously or unconsciously. If the right balance is not struck—if, for example, the settings are so striking that they dwarf the action and the spoken word—then the whole becomes fragmented. The placing of actors in such a way that the effect they are trying to create is visible to the entire house should be a primary concern of the director, yet time and time again we find this elementary rule ignored and whole sections of the audience are denied what they have paid to see. It is my belief that the function of the theatre is to make illusion a reality, and to achieve this the director must employ a number of artifices; he must ensure that his actors are lit in such a way that their dramatic efforts are complemented by the lighting and not destroyed by it; he must create visual emphasis by the way in which he places his actors on the stage. In the cinema the audience has no choice where to look and the degree of enlargement on the screen is such that emphasis can be made with the minimum of effort. But in the theatre an audience can make its own choice and the width of the proscenium arch allows for easy distractions. Most people have heard of the expression 'up-staging' which is a device employed by the selfish actor to ensure that he has a monopoly of attention. Likewise it is common practice for some actors to indulge in distracting bits of 'business' while another actor is talking: some plump cushions, or ostentatiously wave a handkerchief at a crucial moment in their colleague's big speech. And when the audience's eyes flick to this the dialogue is lost and the unsuspecting actor (who probably has his back to what is going on) wonders why he did not get the laugh he had been expecting. In the theatre we all make our own 'close-ups', selecting that part of the stage action that interests us most. A good director should be aware of this and so arrange his groupings that all attention is focused in a certain spot for the climaxes.

All this is by way of explaining the function of the director as opposed to the function of somebody who merely stage-manages the action, as was the case in previous centuries. I have already described how Gielgud came under the influence of Komisarjevsky at a crucial point in his career, and when eventually he formed his own companies and began to find himself as a director, he applied many of the lessons he had acquired through his long and rewarding association with Komisarjevsky. As a director, he is more fluid than was his original mentor, apt to change his mind frequently when plotting the movements of his actors, but bringing his own quality of mercy to his casts, since he knows full well what tortures they endure. There is a school of thought which maintains that working actors do not make good directors, but it is not a theory I go along with, and in the case of Gielgud and Olivier, it is patently untrue. It can only be an advantage for a director to have a complete understanding of the actor's mentality, for that is the clay he has to mould: the dramatist supplies the shape, but the actors have to fill out that shape. Gielgud's great strength as a director is that he has consummate taste. This was perhaps best demonstrated during the war and immediate post-war years when he was responsible for a series of most elegant productions. Because of his immense authority and standing in the profession he attracted quite extraordinary casts, and because he is held in such high respect by his fellows they trusted him far more than their individual personalities usually allowed. And if an actor has this trust in his director he inevitably blossoms. Gielgud has had his share of success and failure, both as actor and as director, but any play directed by him is distinguished by an elegance that few can emulate—a fusing together of the many separate elements that go to form a complete dramatic whole, and a refusal, when he is acting in a play that he has directed, to hog the limelight at the expense of others. In this respect he has always been the most generous of performers, placing great reliance on teamwork. He is at his superb best when handling high comedies such as *The Importance of Being Earnest* and *Love For Love* and indeed in this area he has no peers.

Yet he remains the most difficult of all our current great actors to pin down. The mercury in his emotional barometer is never still, it fluctuates with as many subtle variations as his voice is capable of, responding to ever-changing moods. It would be false, for example, to think of him as merely a classical actor, yet this is the pigeon-hole that many critics have placed him in. He is a constant experimenter, a man who has said of himself 'the theatre has given me everything I ever asked for, but too soon'. Perhaps this is why, in his seventies, having paid little attention to a parallel film career in his middle years, he is now embarked upon a whole series of screen performances in roles that are often totally the reverse of the image he has hitherto nurtured.

From his Terry ancestors (his mother was the niece of Ellen, the daughter of Kate) he inherited 'a certain facility', as he modestly put it, but his early upbringing, although obviously he was conscious of his exalted stage connections, was conventional. He was educated at prep and public school in the best middle-class tradition and destined for a career as an architect, but while still at Westminster steered himself away from a further university education and announced his intention of becoming an actor. His parents gave him qualified approval, putting aside their ambitions for him on the understanding that if he had not succeeded as an actor by the time he was twenty-five, he would return to architecture.

At the age of seventeen he was awarded a scholarship at Lady Benson's acting academy in Kensington where, as in most such establishments, there was a preponderance of girls to boy students. Apparently not over-impressed with his Terry background, Lady Benson is said to have told him that he walked 'exactly like a cat with rickets'. With that candour that has inspired a thousand theatrical anecdotes, he later admitted he was 'handicapped by a strange way of standing and a still stranger way of walking' and although understandably humiliated by Sir Frank's wife, he did nothing to correct this characteristic, while remaining acutely self-conscious about it. Honesty about himself, and what amounts to a compulsion to be candid about everybody and everything, has been one of his most disarming traits throughout his life. He writes almost as well as he acts, bringing to the written word the same casual elegance, and his early volume of autobiography is rightfully a collector's item. In it he revealed that he obtained his first professional job 'entirely through influence', but felt he needed more formal training and after three months as an understudy and general factotum, applied for and again won a scholarship at the Royal Academy of Dramatic Art. While a student there he attracted the attention of Nigel Playfair and was briefly employed by him. From the R.A.D.A. he went to join J. B. Fagan's weekly repertory theatre in Oxford. (Fagan was a disciple of Granville-Barker and it is another example of the cross-pollinisation of ideas and talents, a kind of incestuous inter-breeding so characteristic of our theatre during the first thirty years of this century.) As Richard Findlater has pointed out, Gielgud was unusual in that he received *formal* training for the stage which, albeit brief, was more than any of his predecessors. Perhaps he sensed that he was too gifted in one direction—'the imaginative part of my playing came too easily'—but sorely in need of technical instruction. Lady Benson's crass remark could hardly be said to have relaxed him. He knew that he had the mental equipment to tackle the great classical roles, but for a long period he felt inhibited when called upon to perform anything physical.

Despite the inadequacies of the weekly repertory system, he learnt a great deal from Fagan and it was in Oxford that he got his first taste of Chekhov, playing Trofimov in *The Cherry Orchard*. ('We were all absolutely bewildered by the play' he has said, and one can imagine that particular week in Oxford with Fagan's cast struggling to master the intricacies of Chekhov during the day while playing something else at night.) Gielgud has never enjoyed disguises as much as, say, Olivier and when we study some of the early photographs his make-ups are, frankly, bizarre. For Trofimov he modelled himself on his brother Val, who was later to bring such distinction to the production of radio drama. Whether his brother appreciated the comparison is nowhere recorded.

Between seasons at Oxford he was brought to London by Barry Jackson and given his first major Shakespearean role—Romeo to the Juliet of Gwen Ffrangcon-Davies. In the best, if slightly farcical tradition of theatrical folklore, he owed this engagement to one of the old breed of agents, Akerman May. More flamboyant than many of his clients, Mr May sported what was then considered the correct attire for gentlemen of his calling—a fur-coat—and the letter of introduction he sent to Gielgud is a masterly example of agents' hyperbole.

April 1924
Dear Mr Gielgud,
If you would like to play the finest lead among the plays by the late William Shakespeare, will you please call upon Mr Peacock and Mr Ayliff at the Regent Theatre on Friday at 2.30 p.m. Here is

an opportunity to become a London Star in a night. Please confirm.

Yours very truly,
AKERMAN MAY

Such a letter has to be worth 10% of anybody's salary!

Life, however, was not quite as simple as Mr Akerman May suggested. Gielgud had to give three auditions before the role was his and although the opportunity was undoubtedly there, he did not become a London Star in a night. During rehearsal he had been helped and encouraged by his Juliet—'Gwen told me not to be frightened of our clinches'—and had survived a dress rehearsal conducted by Ayliff with the iron fire curtain down. Since we are told that Ayliff invariably wore a toupee with a straight fringe, the sight of him only a few yards away taking notes could hardly have inspired too much passion in Verona. In addition Gielgud had been told to wear a fright-wig himself, coal black and parted in the middle which gave him the appearance of one of the Bronte sisters. When the play finally opened he was accused of most of the crimes that juveniles are heir to; the usually gentle Ivor Brown publicly shouted what Lady Benson had only whispered within the privacy of her own walls. 'From the waist downwards Mr Gielgud means absolutely nothing. He has the most meaningless legs imaginable', wrote Mr Brown in a review that would have driven most young actors to put their head in the nearest gas oven. At least four other critics complained of effeminacy in his performance. Basically it was the fault of inexperience and the strain of continuing to appear in the face of such devastating criticism finally took its toll: he collapsed in the middle of the balcony scene one matinee, the reason being diagnosed as pneumonia, but there is little doubt that there were other contributing factors.

When he went back to Oxford he first played Marchbanks in Shaw's *Candida* and to his credit it was this performance that caused the young Harold Hobson to discern something beyond the previous evidence. Sir Harold has since written that he felt himself 'instantly in the presence of a great actor'. Then, as we have seen, Gielgud went back to London, first understudying and then taking over from Noel Coward in *The Vortex* and *The Constant Nymph*, the latter play giving him his first long run. Like Edith Evans he was fortunate in that he escaped serving a long apprenticeship in the treadmill of repertory; fortunate again in working with a director of the calibre of Komisarjevsky who encouraged him to tackle roles that were beyond the conventional juvenile leads; and finally fortunate that Harcourt Williams had the perception to invite him to join the Old Vic and sink his teeth into some of the major Shakespearean parts. At the time Williams made his suggestion Gielgud was acting in *The Lady with a Lamp*, having once again taken over a role, on this occasion from Leslie Banks. The star of Reginald Berkeley's play, centred around the life of Florence Nightingale, was Edith Evans, and it was Edith who convinced him that he should take up Williams' offer. She had been the first 'star' West End actress to cross the Waterloo Bridge and she urged her young stage lover who nightly died in her arms 'covered liberally in fuller's earth' not to hesitate. It was more intelligent advice than Gielgud had been offered by a previous leading lady, the ever-formidable Mrs Patrick Campbell. Had Mrs Pat, Lady Benson and Ivor Brown ever combined forces it is doubtful whether the young Gielgud would have matured into the distinguished Sir John, but like so many of his breed he had remarkable powers of recovery without which no actor can continue, for the strictures they must endure are too cruel.

He stayed at the Vic for two seasons, from 1929 to 1930 and during that period played a series of contrasting roles, including Romeo (again), Richard II, Oberon, Mark Antony, Orlando, Macbeth, Hotspur, Prospero, Malvolio, Benedick, Lear and Hamlet, as well as giving his first John Worthing in *The Importance*, Sergius in *Arms and the Man*, Cleante in *The Imaginary Invalid* and The Emperor in *Androcles and the Lion*. He was not perfect casting for all these roles, but under Harcourt Williams' fatherly tuition he was encouraged to dare more, and before the end of the first season Williams had persuaded him to take a hand in the direction of some of the plays. The rest of the company were all destined to make their own names in due course and included Adele Dixon, Leslie French and Donald Wolfit. Coupled with his experiences in Oxford, where he had worked alongside Guthrie, Flora Robson, Veronica Turleigh and James Whale, plus the fact that, as second choice, he had taken over three major roles in the West End, he was not only steadily building a reputation, but was conscious that the competition was fierce. The burden of being a leading actor and, in Gielgud's particular case, being thrust into the great classic roles at a very early age with limited experience, is something that both layman and critic do not always appreciate. He had to face and conquer many challenges, some public, some private, and who is to say which is the greatest? The actor in a theatrical company co-existing through a long season, constantly rehearsing new plays, performing in the evenings, attending costume fittings, perhaps covering more than one role at a time within the same play (since understudies for every separate role are too expensive an item), is prey to every human foible. They are constantly in each other's company for up to sixteen hours a day, six days a week, and in addition to coping with all the ordinary human emotions they must also come to terms with professional emotions. Just to confine a conventional bunch of people to one building for months on end would be asking for trouble, and the Old Vic company of 1929 was hardly conventional except that, like most families, it suffered from a chronic shortage of money. The top salary was £10 a week.

Gielgud did not give 'the definitive Hamlet of his generation' until 1934, and the production of 1929 although distinguished was merely the negative from which the 1934 was eventually printed. The most notable aspect of the early production was Gielgud's comparative youth. At twenty-five he was nineteen years younger than Forbes-Robertson and twelve years younger than Irving had been when they first played the part. Nowadays theatregoers are familiar with youthful Hamlets; it is the mode and many people considered it odd for anybody over the age of thirty-five to attempt the role. We are living in the age of the Youth Cult and all that that implies, but in 1929 Gielgud's youthful appearance and the quicksilver quality of his remarkable voice were something of a revelation. Ivor Brown, perhaps regretting his earlier and all-too-personal dismissal, announced that 'this performance puts him beyond the range of the arriving actors; he is in the first rank'. Apparently he saw something to admire below the waist on this occasion.

But taking the two seasons at the Vic it was Gielgud's performance as Richard II that proved the turning point in his career. He has described his own attitude to the character: 'Richard is, after all, a very affected and elaborately romantic, attitudinizing part. . . . When I first went to see Lilian Baylis—she was a canny old lady, sort of landladyish—she said, "Oh, well, there are a few parts going. We might give you Hamlet but, you see, we've got Gyles Isham* in the Company, and two or three other good actors. We can't promise anything." So I rather jumped at the parts she *had* offered, and Richard II was one of them, which really decided me to go. The extraordinary thing, looking back, is to think how quickly one gobbled up those plays. We did eight or nine plays a season. . . . I learnt them, rehearsed them, and played them, with about three weeks rehearsal; then we gave about nine or twelve performances only. It was a marvellous bosh-shot, you know, at all these great parts; and in certain moments of Macbeth and Lear and Hamlet and Richard II, I know I played them better then than I ever played them afterwards, when I had time to study them and really rehearse them properly. Because you sort of played it like charades, you got an idea of the character and you just buzzed on and had to do it.'

He felt that when he played Shakespeare's Richard II his performance was the result 'of an old kind of acting that I inherited from the Terrys and what I call the *panache* actors I admired so much in my youth: a certain gift of projection and an unreal kind of romantic acting, which I did with so much conviction for myself that I did manage to convince the audience.' The actual character of Richard II has a particular significance in Gielgud's career, for in 1932 he directed himself in his first West End play—Gordon Daviot's *Richard of Bordeaux*, a highly effective piece of theatre which, when it first appeared, was considered by many to be the finest historical play since Shaw's *Saint Joan*. It is historically more accurate than Shakespeare's version of the same reign and concentrates in more explicit scenes on how Richard came to be corrupted by events. There are certain roles which certain actors can be said to have been 'born to play'—though one must add that sometimes they are denied the opportunity, or for a variety of reasons never get around to (witness the fact that Olivier never gave us a Cyrano). *Richard of Bordeaux* was tailor-made for Gielgud, a rare marriage of dramatist and actor that bestows distinction on both. To this day older theatregoers speak of the 1932 production with misty awe, for in many it provokes a nostalgic remembrance of fabled days. The surprising thing is that while many lesser works are treated to periodic revivals Daviot's supreme achievement is continually overlooked. Gielgud directed the first production with consummate, romantic tenderness against the pastel settings by Motley. He was reunited with his first Juliet, Gwen Ffrangcon-Davies, who played Anne of Bohemia, and the rest of the cast was handpicked from a bran-tub of excellence. That fine, and now sadly almost forgotten actor, Francis Lister, complemented Gielgud with his sardonic portrayal of the king's friend, Robert de Vere. And there were others, too; Wolfit, Frederick Lloyd, Henry Mollison, Walter Hudd, H. R. Hignett, George Howe, Richard Ainley and the actor-novelist Reyner Barton; here was the lesson of team-work, not just one jewel, but a

*As an undergraduate, Isham had enjoyed considerable success as Hamlet in the 1924 O.U.D.S. production.

whole crown in a field of gold. It would be pleasant to record that the ensemble playing presented to the public eye, the appearance of total unanimity amongst the cast was repeated back-stage, but this was not so. During rehearsals Gielgud had several times clashed with Wolfit and Mollison over the interpretation of their roles and at times the feelings between them were acrimonious. In Wolfit's case the animosity was never repaired and he remained critical of Gielgud to the end of his days. I cannot help thinking that this unhealed sore affected Wolfit's whole career and I shall have more to say on the subject in a later chapter.

Gielgud's career was assuming a zig-zag course at this time. Prior to *Richard of Bordeaux* he had achieved a qualified success in Priestley's *The Good Companions*, taking the role of Inigo Jollifant, a performance he later repeated in one of his rare screen appearances of this period. He followed this with a remarkable study in a remarkable play, *Musical Chairs* by the young playwright Ronald Mackenzie. Mackenzie would undoubtedly have developed into a major dramatist, but was killed at a tragically early age in a car crash. He wrote 'foreign' plays in the sense that he was out of the mainstream of British drama, heavily influenced by Chekhov, but able to shape those influences to his own view of life. His dialogue was more cynical than Chekhov, he had a gift for exploring the darker corners of human personality and his characters were immediately believable. Gielgud was to act in his only other play *The Maitlands*, which again is worthy of closer study than we can give it here. In addition to Gielgud the cast included Stephen Haggard, a young actor who bore some resemblance facially and in talent to Montgomery Clift, and like Clift was never to enjoy a long life or realise his full potential. In *The Maitlands* Gielgud played a seedy, Graham Greene-ish schoolmaster and this performance, immediately following his elegant Richard of Bordeaux, shocked some of his new-found admirers, for in general audiences are conservative and once they have given their favours to a new idol are often disconcerted if that idol immediately changes direction. There is no logic to this, but it has been observed many times over and in certain cases has temporarily blighted careers.

We now reach 1934 when Gielgud revived his Hamlet at the New Theatre in his own production, the one that was destined to revolutionise West End taste towards the classics, dragging Shakespeare back across the Waterloo Bridge and encouraging a whole new audience to realise that great acting was not necessarily dull because it was set in the framework of a schoolroom set-play. Again he chose 'Motley' to fashion the overall design of his production. He surrounded himself with a notable cast: Frank Vosper as the King, George Howe as Polonius, Jack Hawkins as Horatio, Laura Cowie as the Queen and Jessica Tandy as Ophelia. Alec Guinness, then at the start of his career, played Osric. The result proved to be a landmark for Gielgud and for Shakespeare in the twentieth century. The production achieved a run of 155 performances, a total only approached at that date by Irving's 200 at the Lyceum in 1874. Gielgud has said that Hamlet 'is a part one has to play too often . . . ideal in a repertoire, but I only did that once in 1944. Then it was wartime, of course, and we used to give two performances of three and a half hours on the same day, which was really a marathon and I used to dread it. I used to think, 'This is the last time I'll play this wonderful part, and I really know about it now and I think I *could* play it, but I can't do it twice today!' And then one begins to devise ways to save oneself, or one plays one scene well and another badly. You become frightfully over-critical and can't give yourself to the part in a spontaneous way. I think perhaps the best performances I ever gave were at the rehearsals in New York, when I was on my mettle to show what I could do to the American company. But it was fearfully hot weather and the director, who liked me very much and admired my performance, was very ruthless. In order to help the company he used to make me go through scenes again and again and again: I remember doing the nunnery scene six times over running, when I knew it by heart and knew what I wanted to do with it. This exhausted me before we ever opened in New York and then I had a six month run there. So I've always felt with Hamlet that I could play it, but I mustn't have to do it quite so often. I've had fifteen years of it and over that period I've played in six different productions, two or three I'd done myself. I had an enormous knowledge of the part, but when I directed it for Burton in America I felt I had no more to give to the play. It was stale to me, I didn't feel I contributed much except to try and make it as effective for him as I could. It's very important that you study your Hamlet first, see what he wants to give in the part, then try and build the production around him. It seems to me it's that kind of play.'

Gielgud followed *Hamlet* with *Romeo and Juliet* as his next Shakespearean production, sandwiching Obey's *Noah* in between. Despite the fact that there was a mixture of styles—French director, Michel Saint-Denis, American translator, Arthur Wilmurt—and the fact that the play is worthy rather than inspired, he gave a good account of himself as the aged Noah, hiding his thirty-one years behind a mass of false hair, and blacking out his teeth. It is worth repeating the eye-witness account by E. A. Baughan: 'For the first time since he has become a star, John Gielgud made an appearance without any applause. Who was the old man working on the Ark while he sang "Life on the ocean wave"? His red face (strangely suggestive of the rubicund W. C. Fields) peered out of a mass of grey hair. That could not be John Gielgud. But it was.'

Curiously enough the production of *Romeo and Juliet* came as an afterthought. Gielgud had planned to present a new version of *A Tale of Two Cities* written in collaboration with Terence Rattigan, and in fact they progressed the project to the point where Sir Bronson Albery was enthused enough to give the go ahead for the autumn of 1935. The Motleys commenced work on the settings and preliminary casting took place. Gielgud intended to double the roles of Sydney Carton and the Marquis de St Evremonde, and hoped to secure Fay Compton, Martita Hunt and Mary Clare for the leading female characters. But according to his reliable biographer Ronald Hayman, a ghost from the past scotched the whole idea: '. . . a letter arrived from Sir John Martin-Harvey, who was now almost seventy, demanding that the project be abandoned. He was planning, he said, to play Sydney Carton again himself in another farewell tour of his version of the novel. . . . Surely John could not want to take the bread out of an old man's mouth? After consulting Agate and several other drama critics who, surprisingly, all took the view that Martin-Harvey was in the right, John and Albery reluctantly abandoned the whole scheme.'

There is perhaps some irony in the spectacle of eminent drama critics proving to be such reactionaries, squashing what might have been a fascinating venture, one that could well have changed the course of Rattigan's career, moving him towards his serious plays at a very early age. It is also shining proof that actors do take heed of what critics say.

It was only now that Gielgud was forced to think of a suitable alternative and decided upon *Romeo and Juliet*. By happy coincidence both Edith Evans and Peggy Ashcroft were, as we say, 'available' to repeat their performances as the Nurse and Juliet they had given for Gielgud in his 1932 production for the O.U.D.S. (On that occasion Christopher Hassall, still an undergraduate, had played Romeo and Terence Rattigan gave his all as a musician with one line.) It was Gielgud's original intention to alternate the roles of Romeo and Mercutio with Robert Donat, but Donat declined the experiment and the second choice was Olivier, who accepted. As with *Hamlet* this production met with commercial as well as critical success, and broke all existing records for the play with a run which extended to 186 performances and afterwards toured the provinces.

He had the taste for direction by now and was much in demand, bringing his now surer touch to two plays by Rodney Ackland—*Strange Orchestra* and the memorable *The Old Ladies*, in which Edith Evans gave a *tour de force* study in malevolence as she terrorised Jean Cadell and Mary Jerrold. By 1936 he had also directed Maugham's *Sheppey, Spring 1600* by Emlyn Williams, Gordon Daviot's *Queen of Scots* and *The Merchant of Venice* for the Old Vic. Then came the exquisite revival of *The Seagull*, with Gielgud playing Trigorin and surrounded by one of the most perfect casts ever assembled. In addition to Peggy Ashcroft as Nina and Edith Evans as a superb Madame Arcadina, Komisarjevsky had secured Stephen Haggard, Frederick Lloyd, George Devine, Clare Harris, Martita Hunt, Leon Quartermaine, and Ivor Barnard. To round it off, the 'workman' was played by Alec Guinness. In the contemporary photographs Gielgud, mercifully renouncing any further echoes of W. C. Fields, looks like a young Diaghilev.

He next took his Hamlet to Toronto and New York. His Ophelia on this occasion was Lilian Gish and his Queen, Judith Anderson. Again he was hailed as 'the greatest Prince of Denmark of this generation', praise indeed from the land of John Barrymore; and with that characteristic use of the possessive adjective whereby Americans claim any visiting artist as their own, he was described as 'one of the abiding glories of our stage'.

He returned home flushed with success but was soon brought down to earth, for his next venture was a failure. This was a romantic piece especially written for him by Emlyn Williams and had, to our permissive-age ears, a somewhat curious title, *He Was Born Gay*. Gielgud was cast as the 'lost' Dauphin, Louis XVII, son of Marie Antoinette, and although the play did well on its pre-London tour, it survived for only twelve performances at the Queen's Theatre.

In talking of this period in his career, Gielgud has said that he felt he had 'exploited to the full the pangs of hysterical youth' and felt the compulsion to back his own judgement and go into management for a trial year with four classic revivals.

But before embarking on the venture he wrote to Granville-Barker, a genuinely humble solicitation to somebody he revered. Barker acted on the compliment with a reply that is worth quoting at length:

June 1937

'I am only afraid that any counsel—such as it would be—might increase and not lessen your distraction. For distracted—if I guess right—you must be; between two aims; the one, which is really forced on you, a personal career; the other, the establishing of a *theatre*, without which your career will not be, I think you rightly feel, all that you proudly wish it to be. It was Irving's dilemma; he clung on to one horn of it for a number of glorious years; then he was impaled on the other, and it killed him. It was Tree's, and he would have died bankrupt but for *Chu Chin Chow*. George Alexander, thrifty Scotsman, replied to me when I congratulated him on the twenty-fifth anniversary of his management: Well, I've not done much for the drama (though in a carefully limited fashion he had) but I've paid salaries every Friday night without fail, and *that's* to my credit. And it was. I won't say that there too was my dilemma; because I never had such a career in prospect, I should suppose. But I pinned my faith to the *theatre* solution; and finding it—with a war and a 'peace' on—no go, I got out. It must be your dilemma, I think; for you have rather the Irving than the Alexander conception of your job. . . . The question is, have times changed? Can you yet hope to establish a theatre. If not the blessed 'National' Theatre (but names mean nothing) such a one as Stanislavsky's or even Reinhardt's of thirty years back? For that you'll gladly sacrifice as much of your personal career as need be—this I see; but naturally you don't want to make the sacrifice in vain. Is a compromise practicable? I don't know. Everyone English will be for compromise, just because they are English. And even the work has to be done in England. Perhaps one must accept there the fruits of the national virtue and failing combined. It makes for good politics but bad art. And so it is you see, that the question (for me) opens up; no longer for me a practical question, therefore I can still say *Theatre or nothing* and not suffer. For you a devilishly practical one; so, who am I to counsel you? Only I'd say: do not expect to pick more than a few grapes from thistles and don't expect them always to be of the best quality!'

Barker could hardly conceal his own heartbreak between the lines, yet the letter is masterly in posing the basic question that a Gielgud or an Olivier and those who have come after must answer. Any actor caught in the same dilemma must choose between the personal career and the establishment of a permanent theatre. Barker asked: have times changed? This was in 1937, and they did not change until 1961 when Olivier finally grasped the nettle, first at Chichester as a dress rehearsal for his ultimate decision, then the acceptance of the first directorship of the long-awaited National Theatre. Both Gielgud and Olivier had flirted with management in the intervening period and each had his champions when Who Should Run the National? was being endlessly debated. In the best of all possible worlds a partnership between the two men, the acknowledged leaders of their profession, would certainly have been remarkable, but by the time the opportunity arrived, their personalities were too fixed, and perhaps in truth, by then, too opposite. The post went to Olivier and he honoured it to the extent that it ruined his health. And all those years before Barker had predicted the outcome. 'Everyone English will be for compromise', he had written, 'just because they are English', and in that he was proved right. Not that the choice of Olivier was a compromise, or that he compromised in any artistic judgements, but the situation itself was the compromise, brought about by forces outside the theatre. Any artistic endeavour that is dependent upon government subsidies will be subject to repeated changes of government policy expressed by government-appointed watchdogs. Few politicans have any great regard for the Arts, for the Arts are low in the pecking order of vote-catchers; favours are bestowed grudgingly and always on an elastic band. And to be fair, few actors are actively interested in politics or politicians, so there is seldom any real interchange of positive ideas. Firstly Olivier, and subsequently Sir Peter Hall, was called upon to achieve the impossible: to run an enterprise entirely dependent on the public whim, but whereas people have a choice when it comes to buying a car, there can only be one National Theatre. It is therefore inevitable that any responsible director of the National will try and provide a variety of entertainment within the confines of a single building and in so doing ensure that the enterprise consistently makes a loss, for actors, like politicians, cannot please all of the people all of the time. And since, as a nation, inspired from below, we have been schooled to the belief that industry, trade unionism and exports are the Father, Son and Holy Ghost and that a penalty goal scored in the dying minutes of a World Cup Final is worth more than all 37 of Shakespeare's plays, it is small wonder that our National Theatre begrudgingly bestowed is now begrudgingly supported.

When Barker wrote to Gielgud he was writing as an expatriate beyond the battle; his concise advice, forged from bitter experience, went to the heart of the matter. Gielgud was the born actor, but not the born administrator. The fact does not diminish his other great talents, but it perhaps helps to explain why he hesitated then and why, in subsequent years, although periodically drawn to the image of himself as actor-manager, he only indulged this ambition at spaced intervals. It is a matter for real regret that he was not involved in the Old Vic seasons of 1944–1949. They were halcyon years for the British theatre and brought together Olivier and Richardson in triumphant form; had the trio been completed with Gielgud we would have had the quintessence of all that is finest in our varied acting tradition under one roof, and the result could not have failed to have been an even greater milestone.

So when he did take the plunge, following Barker's advice to the hesitating player, he set himself high standards and high tasks, choosing as his four presentations, *Richard II*, in which he wisely re-established his authority by repeating his earlier triumph; *The School for Scandal* (Joseph Surface), *Three Sisters* (Vershinin) and Shylock in *The Merchant*. Separately and as a whole the venture proved commercially successful—he was able to pay the wages every Friday—and as always he relied on *ensemble* playing from a distinguished company that included many familiars and a few new faces—Dennis Price, Michael Redgrave, Harry Andrews, Dorothy Green, Angela Baddeley. Motley again designed all the scenery and costumes for the opening production, and Michel Saint-Denis was brought in to direct Chekhov. Gielgud's reputation had never been higher, but the concentrated and prolonged effort had exhausted him. He confessed that he was 'anxious for once to appear in modern clothes' and when Hugh Beaumont, the newly created managing director of H. M. Tennent, offered him a large salary to act in Dodie

Smith's endearing family comedy *Dear Octopus*, he accepted at once—though with his usual candour pronounced the role 'not a very interesting one'. His leading lady was Marie Tempest and the combination proved irresistible to audiences. Although the opening night coincided with the Munich crisis, the play was an immediate and lasting success. Perhaps without knowing it, he chose wisely, not only for himself but for the theatre in general. It was a time when the old values hovered on the brink; Munich granted us all a brief stay of execution and Dodie Smith had written her play at the perfect moment. She is, in my opinion, a most underrated playwright and it was with particular pleasure that I welcomed the 1967 revival with Cicely Courtneidge, which again proved that time had not withered any of Dodie Smith's old skills.

Like Edith Evans, Gielgud has never been too enamoured of long runs and he welcomed a legitimate reason for leaving the cast of *Dear Octopus* after ten months. He was invited to repeat his Hamlet, first at the Lyceum, then at Elsinore itself. The choice of the Lyceum was a poignant one: the theatre was scheduled for demolition. In 1939 with the prospect of war before them conservation was not uppermost in most people's minds, yet somehow the building was reprieved. It lingers on to this day, the six Corinthian columns at the front of house now supporting a peeling and battered pediment. Irving's temple has, to some minds been defiled. One can say: other times—other fashions, but true theatregoers must regret that a neon sign has replaced the playbills of yesterday, and that the neon now reads MECCA BALLROOM, a palace of delights where the faithful are encouraged to enter with promises of 'an after-shave sample for every boy' or 'a free holiday for two in exotic Majorca'. The pavement at the rear of the building, where Irving and Ellen Terry used to enter, was festooned with a mass of uncollected garbage when last I visited, and alongside was a derelict car park with warning notices for non-existent guard dogs and the inevitable graffiti: GOD IS NOT DEAD—HE'S BEEN BUSTED was scrawled above the dustbins where a solitary meths drinker sorted out his evening menu. Yes, the Lyceum has been saved for posterity!

Forty years ago, in June 1939, Gielgud brought to a close the theatrical history of this great playhouse. Fay Compton was his Ophelia (she also played the role for John Barrymore) and this time Jack Hawkins played the King opposite Laura Cowie. By happy chance Granville-Barker was paying a visit to London during the rehearsal period and at Gielgud's invitation attended one of the run-throughs. He must have shared the general sadness at the closing of such a theatre, but at least the last curtain came down on a great actor playing a role that is synonymous with our native acting tradition.

When the war eventually came the following year Gielgud was busy rehearsing the role of Maxim de Winter in *Rebecca*, but in a panic move prompted by expectations of mass air raids, all the London theatres closed after the declaration of war, and *Rebecca* was shelved (the role of Maxim de Winter being eventually played by Owen Nares). Suddenly jobless, Gielgud hastily got together a revival of *The Importance of Being Earnest*—something he had presented in a series of charity matinees a few months earlier, revealing to the world not only his own delightful John Worthing but also unveiling Edith Evans' definitive Lady Bracknell. Edith's 'great essay in dragonhood' has passed into theatrical legend and the echoes of her delivery live on to daunt any contemporary actress brave enough to follow her. In later years she grew to loathe even the name Lady Bracknell ('I've played her everywhere except on ice and under water', she once boomed at me, and even as she said it I heard the swish of a handbag.) When she died few commentators could resist giving her Lady Bracknell undue prominence in their obituaries. Of course it had to be included; it was a great landmark performance, but she felt it dominated and at times obscured better things. She was not proud of her performance in the way that she was proud of her Nurse in *Romeo and Juliet*, her Daphne Laureola or her Mrs St Maugham in Enid Bagnold's *The Chalk Garden*. 'Lady Bracknell was one of my easy ones', she told me. 'I don't know why everybody went on about her so much.' The secret was, I think that Edith never consciously thought of her Bracknell as a comic character. She confided that she had modelled her performance on titled women she had come in contact with as a young milliner; *they* hadn't been funny, deference to them had been obligatory, for to cross them meant dismissal. I often witnessed icicles forming whenever, towards the end of her life, strangers would begin every conversation with a reference to *The Importance*; on one occasion a very foolhardy gentleman actually gave his rendering of the 'handbag' line in her presence and without a gesture or a word she laser-beamed him to ashes. At one period there were whole armies of Edith-Bracknell impersonators doing their party pieces at every theatrical gathering, such was the force of her performance on a whole generation. What was eventually committed to celluloid in Anthony Asquith's 1951 filmed version had little of the impact of Edith in the flesh, but at least it serves to remind us of true greatness. To Edith it became like a love affair that had gone wrong; she did not want to be reminded of it and she was right to resent the assumption that she and Lady Bracknell were indivisible.

The Times gave its verdict: 'If the past theatrical decade had to be represented by a single production, this is the one that many good judges would choose.' I was caught by Agate's description of Gielgud's John Worthing; Agate felt that he had adopted the pose, abstracted air and elevated chin of somebody about to sneeze; the comparison with John Philip Kemble was there for all to see, since Agate had filched Hazlitt's description of Kemble as Coriolanus. Ronald Hayman felt that Gielgud 'gave a subtle parody of his own seriousness in a tragic role, fully exploiting the comedy in putting on a display of unfelt grief'. He was, as Agate summed up, irresistible, and having seen the performance myself I would only add that I have never seen such perfection in artificial comedy.

Gielgud volunteered for active service the moment war broke out, in company with many other leading actors of the day. Informed by the authorities that he would not be enlisted for several months he directed Michael Redgrave in *The Beggar's Opera*, and in fact played and sang Macheath when Redgrave was temporarily indisposed. When the theatres reopened again and England settled down to the phoney war that existed until the fall of France, to Gielgud came the honour and the task of reopening the Old Vic, with Guthrie as his partner. It was their joint decision to invite Granville-Barker to return and direct the first of the two plays they had selected, *King Lear*. True to character Barker laid down certain ground rules: his name must not appear on the programme and he would only spend ten days on the rehearsals. Guthrie and Gielgud accepted his terms, but although the final outcome was a fine production there were certain delicate moments along the way. After the read-through Barker told Gielgud he had spoken only two lines correctly. Gielgud took this on the chin and if we contrast his behaviour with the way in which Kean dealt with his stage-manager's comments, placid as they were by comparison, we can see how the status of the director had avanced in the twentieth century. True to his word, Barker departed back to France leaving Guthrie to rehearse the players with his (Barker's) Preface to *King Lear* as the working bible. Lewis Casson, who was another member of the company, also took a hand and conducted some of the rehearsals before Barker returned once again to take control. In Gielgud's words 'he inspired and dominated everyone like a master-craftsman . . . not using any notes, but sitting on the stage with his back to the footlights, a copy of the play in his hand, tortoise-shell spectacles well forward on his nose, dressed in a black business suit, his bushy red eyebrows jutting forward, quiet voiced, seldom moving, coldly humorous, shrewdly observant, infinitely persevering and patient.'

In this 'the first genuine theatrical occasion of the war' Gielgud evoked something in his audiences that some of the critics failed to discern: he was acting a role that demanded he rise to the spirit of the times, and this he did with 'brilliant exactness', tracing Lear's progress from worldly to spiritual authority. Perhaps more gratifying to him than his reviews, good though they were on the whole, was an extraordinary letter from Edith Evans; she wrote from the heart and he never forgot her generosity. 'I wanted to come up', she concluded, 'and share your mood and sorrow, I wanted to be *in it* with you, not as an actress but as a woman'.

It was Barker's final glimpse of what *his* National Theatre might have been. Invited to direct the second production of the short season, *The Tempest* with scenery and costumes by the young Oliver Messel, Barker declined, saying he had nothing to contribute, and in his place George Devine and Marius Goring co-directed. Gielgud's Prospero was compared to a character painted by El Greco, set against the shimmering gauzes of Messel's designs, as though the play was taking place in the Escorial where the strong light ripples through the dry air. The play opened on May 29, 1940 and closed the night that France capitulated, June 22. It was the last performance to be given in the theatre as Lilian Baylis had known it; she had died three years previously and thus was spared witnessing the destruction of her home when it was bombed in 1941. It was fitting that one of her 'boys' should speak the final incantation, for Gielgud's Prospero encapsulated the tragedy that was taking place in the outside world, and to those who were there on the last night it seemed that once again the lights of reason were being extinguished all over Europe.

[[19]]

OLIVIER

OLIVIER once said that if he had not been an actor he would have 'gone mad'. That being so he turned his face against madness at the tender age of ten and was resolved on no other course. The son of a High Anglican clergyman, born into a family that had served the church for five generations, he was by his own admission destined to be nothing else but an actor, the natural progression from his father's own thwarted ambition. As a child he trod the same Pimlico pavements as the young Noël Coward and Edith Evans and was befriended by Sybil Thorndike and Lewis Casson who, witnesses to his schoolboy performance as Brutus, confirmed his own verdict: they, too, thought he was born to it. In appearance more like his mother ('something of the gypsy') he had an austere upbringing; his father was a remote figure who in company with most clergymen lived a life of genteel poverty. When he was thirteen his mother died and forty years later he was not ashamed to say he had been looking for her ever since. Educated at a small choir school belonging to the church of All Saints in Margaret Street near Cavendish Square, and lacking any formal stage ancestry—if one ignores the fact that five generations of clergymen denotes a passion for pulpit oratory—he was fortunate to be taught by a remarkable priest, Father Heald. Dame Sybil described Heald as 'a brilliant man with a great knowledge of the theatre . . . way ahead of his time. His productions were more advanced than anything else in the theatre at that period. He was using the whole of the auditorium—the aisle as well as the stage'. Father Heald's enthusiasms were transmitted to the young schoolboy with the broken front teeth, and it was Father Heald who cast him as Brutus. He also played Katharine in *The Taming of the Shrew* in another school production and was, according to Dame Sybil, 'wonderful . . . a bad-tempered little bitch, and he looked just like his mother in the part'.

Olivier's father made no protest when his son decided upon a professional career, and he passed from Father Heald to the equally remarkable Elsie Fogerty, for so many years the teacher and mentor of scores of our leading players, who was the Principal of the Central School of Music and Drama, then located at the Albert Hall. Olivier met the challenge of his father's one condition—that he win a scholarship- and at the age of seventeen enrolled for a year's tuition. A fellow student was the young Peggy Ashcroft. This was the summer of 1924 when Gielgud was attempting his first shaky Romeo, Edith Evans grave her transcendent Millamant and Sybil Thorndike her Saint Joan. Had Ivor Brown been in the same mood to criticise Olivier's appearance as he had Gielgud's he would have found 'a weed . . . I was a miserably thin creature well into my acting career. My arms hung like wires from my shoulders'. In truth the drama-student was near starvation most of the time, unable to exist on the £50 bursary that went with his scholarship. He was forced to accept an allowance of £12 a year from his recently-remarried father, and supplemented this by taking a job as an assistant stage manager between terms. Through the good offices of one of his teachers, the actor and producer Henry Oscar, he obtained a walk-on towards the end of 1924, his first professional engagement on a London stage. These occasional forays into the world of real theatre supplemented his meagre income but cannot be said to have advanced his career in one spectacular leap, as is favoured by most novels dealing with stages heroes. He was a star pupil at Miss Fogerty's Academy, sharing the end of term honours with Peggy Ashcroft, but life in drama schools bears little or no resemblance to the rat race that faces anybody embarked on a professional life in the theatre.

There are some echoes of Garrick in Olivier's early experiences, but none of Kean or Irving. I have already touched upon the sterile practice of measuring theatrical greatness. In John Cottrell's scholarly biography of Olivier published in 1975, he has a quote from Olivier on this very subject. 'You can't say what is best in this business', Olivier maintained. 'It's not like a runner in a race and he does a hundred yards in nine seconds. He is the fastest, so he is the best.' In agreeing with this contention, I have tried throughout this book to suggest not the cut and thrust of outright competition but the threads of evidence that connect one great actor to another. The moment that any young actor or actress takes the first and, where talent is concerned, usually irrevocable step, then consciously or unconsciously they become, with the passing of time, imbued with the *spirit* of previous generations of actors. For one thing we are the most insular of groups, we feast upon our own legends and are never more content than when elaborating upon our own insularity. Olivier had no precedents, he did not come from a famous theatrical family, but he was immediately plunged amongst the near great, and there is no keener spur to ambition in a beginner than to see others perform to perfection that which he longs to perform even adequately.

Because Olivier is what he is, and I am thinking more of his accumulated and memorable achievements than of the fact that he is the first actor ever to be elevated to the peerage, it is inevitable that whenever his life is being discussed or written about the question of comparative greatness is raised. An American actor, William Redfield, the author of a much-quoted book called *Letters from an Actor*, chauvinistically nominates Marlon Brando as the supreme actor of our time. I have no quarrel with his chauvinism — why not? — though his verdict seems a trifle emphatic when, patently, Mr Redfield is not of an age when he could have seen the sum total of Olivier's work. Perhaps aware of this, he later qualified the absolute by adding: 'Ironically enough, Laurence Olivier is less gifted than Marlon Brando. He is even less gifted than Richard Burton, Paul Scofield, Ralph Richardson and John Gielgud. But he is still the definitive actor of the twentieth century. Why? Because he wanted to be. His achievements are due to dedication, scholarship, practice, determination and courage. He is the bravest actor of our time.'

I would go further. Olivier is one of the most complex actors of our time, somebody

LAURENCE OLIVIER aged 15, as Katherine in a school production of *The Taming of the Shrew*

In *Richard III*, New Theatre, 1944 LAURENCE OLIVIER as Richard, JOYCE REDMAN as Lady Anne

In *Romeo and Juliet*, New Theatre, 1935 (*l to r*) LAURENCE OLIVIER as Romeo, EDITH EVANS as the Nurse, JOHN GIELGUD as Mercutio

who has consistently tried to solve 'the most difficult equation . . . the union of the two things that are absolutely necessary to an actor. One is confidence, absolute confidence, and the other an equal amount of humility towards the work. That's a very hard equation'.

When starting out to solve the equation, Olivier left drama school clutching his Dawson Milward Cup awarded to the best male student of his year, and proceeded to put his worst foot forward. Fired from an early engagement for fooling around, he earned a quick familiarity with the actor's most consistent role—that of an out-of-work. Generosity and luck came his way through the intervention of the Cassons, who gave him a walk-on at £3 a week in their production of Shakespeare's *Henry VIII*, in which he partnered the young Carol Reed (then an aspiring actor) in carrying Dame Sybil's train. The contract was extended to a second play, a revival of Shelley's *The Cenci*. In an interview she gave many years later Dame Sybil recalled that 'we just knew he was going to be a very fine actor. But we weren't career minded then. . . . We didn't care whether we were in London or Timbuctoo as long as we were acting. There wasn't nearly so much emphasis on stardom and publicity'.

It was an unprepossessing start to a great career, and in the months following this short engagement he was once again no stranger to poverty. Straitened circumstances for an actor are more self-destructive than for others. Failure, like terminal illness, embarrasses some people and no matter how desperate an actor may be, he must constantly conceal the fact—appearances are frequently everything: questions of talent often take second place. In Olivier's case he had many strikes against him: 'teeth that were set too far apart and eyebrows that grew too thickly and without shape across his nose. He had a thatch of unmanageable hair that came far forward in a kind of widow's peak, and his nose was a broad one. He wore very unbecoming suits, much too old-looking for a young man. He told me in later years that they were cast-offs from an uncle, altered to fit him.' This description is taken from the autobiography of the late Denys Blakelock, who Olivier once said was 'the first human being in my life that I could really think of to myself as "my friend"'. They first came together as understudies in Sir Barry Jackson's company during the 1926 London season. Jackson's name is forever associated with his Birmingham Repertory theatre which, together with the Liverpool Repertory, constituted the two finest training grounds for young actors outside London. Liverpool produced Robert Donat, Diana Wynyard and Rex Harrison, Birmingham gave us Cedric Hardwicke, Ralph Richardson and Olivier, amongst others. The latter trio made each other's acquaintance in a farce called *The Barber and the Cow*. Hardwicke was the established star of the company, with Richardson the rising talent and Olivier very much the new boy. This first meeting between two men who were later to dovetail their talents with such memorable results was inauspicious, and when the tour of *The Barber and the Cow* finished they went their separate ways. Olivier stayed on with Jackson's company and was cast as one of the juveniles in Eden Phillpotts' endurable comedy, *The Farmer's Wife*. He toured with this for a further six months before going back to Birmingham to make his debut there in another Phillpotts comedy, a one-act curtain raiser called *Something to Talk About*. In view of the fact that he now had a measure of the security he craved, it is revealing that he still could not resist putting that security at risk. He enraged the director, W. G. Fay, by rewriting his part—'gagging' is the stage euphemism—and was only saved from being fired by Jackson's intervention. Surviving this episode, typical of his cavalier attitude at this period, he played a wide variety of roles as the resident juvenile lead and his versatility blossomed. In real life he was an incurable romantic, given to frequent infatuations, including one for Ralph Richardson's first wife, which further confirmed Richardson's initial reaction to him as a brash young man. He was reunited with Peggy Ashcroft in the Birmingham production of Drinkwater's country comedy *Bird in Hand* (in which that extraordinarily gifted actor Herbert Lomas scored a notable success) and later joined the London production at the Royalty. Peggy Ashcroft's role was now being played by Jill Esmond and this time the would-be philanderer was snared; Miss Esmond was later to become his first wife. The stability of a West End success plus thoughts of marriage prompted him to undertake a metamorphosis. To some of his friends he became, almost overnight 'a ravishing-looking young man' and once again we can turn to Denys Blakelock as the Boswell of his formative years.

'He had somehow got his hair to part at last; he had had the gaps between his teeth filled in, his eyebrows trimmed and straightened and he was beautifully and rather gaily dressed. He had stopped short at his nose, though he has made up for this since by remodelling it with nose clay into one shape after another in almost every part he has played in the last twenty-five years!'

The transformation later included a painted-on Ronald Colman moustache, a dressing-room experiment which was part of his determined effort to secure the leading role in *Beau Geste* which Basil Dean was preparing. Dean had seen his performance in *Bird in Hand* but was not overly impressed, and although a real moustache had now replaced the grease-paint it became increasingly obvious that Dean would require something more before he was convinced of Olivier's suitability. The opportunity came in a Sunday performance by the Stage Society of a first play by an unknown playwright named R. C. Sherriff. Olivier had no great opinion of the play's chances, but accepted the leading role because it would give Dean a further opportunity to judge his talents. The play was, of course, *Journey's End* and the role that of Stanhope. 'Not even the excellent notices he got', wrote W. A. Darlington, 'made him think of *Journey's End* as anything but a stalking-horse for the greater prize. And the prize was his. On the strength of his playing of Stanhope, Basil Dean offered him the part of Beau Geste . . . and Olivier accepted without the least suspicion that he was throwing away the substance and grasping at a shadow'.

Journey's End became legend, while *Beau Geste*, despite a spectacular production by Dean, complete with real Maxim gun firing blanks, lasted only four weeks. As final irony, Agate awarded the acting honours to Jack Hawkins, aged eighteen. Was it a fatal choice on Olivier's part? In the short term the answer has to be yes, because his career was blighted for the next year and a half. Colin Clive on the other hand, who took over the role of Stanhope in Sherriff's play, went from obscurity to fame overnight, was offered a Hollywood contract and a life style to go with it. These same rewards would certainly have been Olivier's, although ultimately they were of no lasting comfort to Colin Clive.

Blazing, instant fame is not always what it at first appears. So many actors in the past few decades have become household names in television series, only to find they have lost all personal identity, becoming so closely associated with the character they have created that they can never live it down. (One notable exception is the American actor, Richard Chamberlain, who endured many years of hard labour as the young Dr Kildare. This, combined with his extraordinary good looks, persuaded most critics to write him off but he came to England, went into a provincial repertory and set about persuading them to take him seriously, giving a most creditable account of himself as Hamlet.) Colin Clive never achieved such a peak again; he made a number of films in Hollywood but failed to capture the mass popular audience and died in 1937 with Stanhope as his one lasting memorial. Olivier may have cursed his luck as the notice went up on *Beau Geste*, but disappointment is not only a recurring event in an actor's life, it is also a spur to ambition. In Olivier's case it compelled him into a number of other failures while all the time *Journey's End* was still playing to packed houses. Yet the paradox is that to play a number of leading roles in short runs ensures that an actor is frequently parading his versatility in front of the public and critics. This is what happened to Olivier. As compensation for the fiasco of *Beau Geste*, Dean cast him in *The Circle of Chalk*. It proved a failure. The same fate awaited *Paris Bound, The Stranger Within* and *Murder on the Second Floor* which marked his first visit to New York.

It can be seen that his early experiences hardly anticipated the great classical career that lay ahead. Persuaded by Noel Coward that failure could become an addiction, he took the somewhat dull, second-string role of Victor Prynne (a typical Coward name for a dull second-string charcter) in *Private Lives*, and enjoyed his first taste of full houses plus the not unwelcome regular salary of £50 a week. He was still sporting his Ronald Colman moustache and appeared to have no burning desire to emulate Gielgud and Richardson who that same year, 1930, were both at the Old Vic. Olivier married Jill Esmond during the run of *Private Lives* and when Coward took the production to New York, the new Mrs Olivier took over the role originally played by Adrianne Allen. Luck continued to favour them; while in New York they were both signed to lucrative Hollywood contracts and Olivier was lost to the stage for the best part of three years.

The Hollywood they found found in 1930 was a city in transition, the atmosphere of which was best exemplified in that engaging musical *Singing in the Rain*. The silents were out, the talkies were in, the only trouble was that few of the old silent stars could actually put two words together. The businessmen who ran the studio could, on occasion, put three words together with an effort, and the most popular three of the period were 'Get me talkers'. For a decade or more that blessed plot of Californian soil became forever England, since most of the new recruits were British to the core. They even had a flourishing cricket team that could field such players as C. Aubrey Smith, Ronald Colman, Boris Karloff, Anthony Bushell, Herbert Marshall, Clive Brook, Nigel Bruce and Basil Rathbone. The British actors were favoured because their voices recorded well on the primitive sound equipment, and since the Americans have always had an inferiority complex about a British accent, our native leading men ousted the home-grown competition for a time. The Oliviers were signed to the RKO studios, though in

In *The Entertainer* by John Osborne LAURENCE OLIVIER and JOAN
PLOWRIGHT, Palace Theatre, 1957

the best traditions of the flesh market, Miss Esmond was immediately loaned out to
Paramount. (During the great hey-days of the studio system, when every major company
had whole armies of actors under contract, it was standard practice to keep them working
like battery hens. A contract player would get a basic weekly salary fifty-two weeks a year,
and the studio that owned them would then hire them out at a profit to a rival studio, pay
the basic salary and pocket the rest. If the actor refused to be so treated he was put 'on
suspension'. It was the most refined form of luxury torture, and contract artists were
encouraged to live beyond their means, borrow in advance of their salaries and thus place
themselves at the studio's mercy. If they elected to go on suspension a very unsubtle form
of arm-twisting took place. Precluded by law from acting elsewhere, they either starved
or admitted defeat. And since to most of them the pleasures of that lotus land were all too
seductive, most rebellions were short-lived.)

His name constantly pronounced Oliver, forced to wear baseball gear for the statutory
publicity photographs, Olivier was pushed into a programme-filler: a sixty-six minute
melodrama called *Friends and Lovers*, in which he played a Lieutenant in the Indian Army.
Life in the Khyber held a peculiar fascination for the Hollywood of the Thirties and if we
view some of these old epics today they suggest a sketch by the Monty Python team or

some inspired parody by Peter Cook and Dudley Moore. The dialogue was invariably of the 'I-don't-like-it, Hugh, I-don't-like-it-one-bit' variety and the heroines were given to arriving on the scene of battle on gun carriages dressed as for the Royal enclosure at Ascot. *Friends and Lovers* had in addition to Olivier, Erich von Stroheim, Adolphe Menjou and a lady named Lili Damita in the cast, but even the combined talents of this cosmopolitan group were not sufficient to transform the basic dross. Olivier's contribution was ignored by the majority of the critics.

After a long arid stretch, during which time the weekly salary cheque assuaged his material needs, it was Olivier's turn to be loaned out. He went to the Fox studios to make another melodrama, this one set in old St Petersburg (there never was a young St Petersburg in Hollywood's book) called, variously, *The Yellow Ticket* or *The Yellow Passport*. He was co-starred opposite Elissa Landi, Lionel Barrymore, Mischa Auer and Boris Karloff and a sinister time was had by all. Fortunately on this occasion he was in the hands of an experienced and stylish director, the inimitable Raoul Walsh—a man more colourful than most of the characters he helped to create. Then came *Westward Passage* and increasing disenchantment with his lot. He was cocooned in luxury, he had many friends, he enjoyed the climate, but all the while ambition was curling like cherry-tree leaves afflicted with blight. It was 1932 and America was in the grip of the Depression. RKO studios, under the control of the young David O. Selznick who, with his agent-brother Myron, was to scythe through the ranks of the old guard, weathered the storm better than most, and the Oliviers' contracts were maintained. Jill Esmond was happier there than her husband; he felt there must be more to his life than to be paid to be unemployed, since he had a keen appreciation that, in the last analysis, all an artist has to sell is time. He fretted to be away and when the chance came to return to England to star opposite Gloria Swanson in *The Perfect Understanding*, he grasped at it intending that this would be his film swan song before resuming his theatre career. Alas for good intentions, Swanson's attempted come-back proved a fiasco and nobody connected with the film emerged with any glory.

Even so the aura of Hollywood bestowed some gloss and he was quickly got a secondary role in Keith Winter's *The Rats of Norway* which, despite its title, was concerned with goings on in a boys' school. Acting alongside Gladys Cooper and Raymond Massey, he found himself in a hit, and received gratifying personal reviews considering the size of his role. Just as he was settling down to enjoy a long run he was invited back to Hollywood by MGM with the surprising offer of starring opposite Garbo in *Queen Christina*. I say 'surprising' because Garbo, who had final approval of all her leading men, could hardly have placed this young and inexperienced British actor at the top of her shopping list. The director Rouben Mamoulian later claimed that the idea was his, he having rejected the somewhat ravaged John Barrymore. However, Mamoulian's memory seems slightly at fault, for he was under the impression that Olivier was on the MGM lot at the time, whereas he was still playing in *The Rats of Norway*. The whole episode from beginning to end is shrouded in a certain mystery, though the passing of time appears to have softened the edges of what proved to be a distressing experience for Olivier.

It took him a month to negotiate his release from the Keith Winter play, then he and Jill Esmond sailed back to America with accompanying fanfares, since the mere mention of the name Garbo was enough to make the average journalist reach for the high notes. They sailed with understandably happy expectations, but offers from film companies, then as now, are seldom all that they appear at first glance. When they arrived in Hollywood Olivier found that he was required to make a test with Garbo before the contract was confirmed. It wasn't put like that, of course; it never is, but that was the fine print. At that moment in suspended time Garbo had almost as much power as the Swedish Queen she was about to portray. The test piece selected by MGM required Olivier to plunge in at the deep end and play a highly sensitive love scene with the most highly sensitive screen actress that a combination of the publicity machine and the lady herself has ever devised. At the best of times screen tests impose intolerable burdens on those unfortunate enough to be taking part, and this one proved to be the worst of times. There was no rapport between Olivier and Garbo, or rather Garbo resolutely declined to thaw: Olivier had to make screen love to a block of Swedish ice. Perhaps I am not alone in finding certain aspects of Garbo's calculated aloofness a tiresome bore, and her lack of generosity towards a young actor who had come 7,000 miles for the privilege of embracing a statue seems to me a prime example of unforgivable behaviour towards a fellow artist. The result was a foregone conclusion. With commendable generosity Olivier now refers to the episode without rancour, but at the time it must have been a bitter and humiliating experience. He was fired and the role went to the previous era's Great Lover, John Gilbert, a prematurely aged, confirmed drunkard. When eventually the film was released and Garbo sailed her profile towards the distant horizon of legend, poor Gilbert sank behind her without trace and four years later he was dead. It is even possible, I suppose, that, unintentionally, Garbo did Olivier a favour by dismissing him. The actual shooting of the film was beset with temperament and long delays, witnessed at close hand by Sam Behrman who was constantly rewriting the screenplay. In Behrman's opinion Olivier would have been ideal, but had Olivier been cast and succeeded as Garbo's leading man he might well have joined the ranks of the permanent British colony and enjoyed a lucrative, but ultimately dead-end career; certainly the whole course of his life would have been changed for the second time. His rejection of *Journey's End* had fortunately proved only a temporary set-back, and now Garbo's rejection of him again halted his progress. Refusing to be mollified by MGM's offer of another test, this time for Romeo in Walter Wanger's projected screen version, he went back to the stage to appear in the New York production of Mordaunt Shairp's *The Green Bay Tree*. Compared to the current nightly fare on television Shairp's mild exploration of a homosexual theme would nowadays hardly raise an eyebrow, but in 1933 it was considered highly contentious. Jed Harris, who directed, felt it would be amusing to have two very masculine actors in the leading roles. He cast another Englishman, James Dale, opposite Olivier and throughout the prolonged rehearsals encouraged them to camp it up, just as in later years Stanley Donen felt it would be good box office to have Richard Burton and Rex Harrison perform the homosexual couple in the screen version of *Staircase*. Harris, a man of immense verve and influence in the American theatre, noted for his acid and often cruel wit, conducted a lifelong romance with himself. Olivier and Dale loathed his tyrannical methods, but this personal antipathy towards Harris ultimately worked for the actors in performance rather than against them. Depressed by Harris, detesting the role of the effeminate Julian Dulcimer, Olivier used the adrenalin that Harris induced as fuel for an electrifying study in the disintegration of a character. He and Dale scored considerable personal successes and much to his dismay—for once again he was anxious to be home— the play was a hit and ran until March 1934.

Then it was London again and an offer from his early mentor, Coward, who had chosen Sam Behrman's *Biography* as his first experiment in management. Ina Claire was imported to repeat her American triumph, but this time it was Coward's turn to add to Olivier's quota of failures. He followed this by taking over from Ralph Richardson in Gordon Daviot's *Queen of Scots* which Gielgud directed (and thus we have another coincidental interchange between the three). Given only eight days rehearsal before the opening night, Olivier's performance as Bothwell was maliciously described as 'more Hollywood than Holyrood' by one critic, and the play did not take.

Coward invited him to give a second blood transfusion to *Theatre Royal*, a satire on the Barrymore family by Edna Ferber and George F. Kaufman. He was asked to keep the play alive during a three week pre-London tour until Brian Aherne could arrive from Hollywood to take over his role. It was hardly the most flattering of offers and Olivier's first reaction was to cold shoulder it, but having read the part he decided that he would be Machiavellian. He was resolved to make himself indispensable. Rehearsals commenced with the aged Marie Tempest—never one to give an inch when she could take a yard —Aherne was delayed and by the time he arrived in England the play had opened. Miss Tempest was not in a mood to contemplate another round of rehearsals while continuing to play at night, and in any event Aherne, having witnessed Olivier's performance (a carefully studied and athletic take-off of John Barrymore) had second and third thoughts. The dilemma was resolved by Miss Tempest. She was not going to rehearse and that was that. Aherne departed to play Romeo to the Juliet of Katharine Cornell; Olivier congratulated himself that the ploy had worked with a happy ending for all concerned. Alas, the euphoria did not last long. In an excess of physical enthusiasm he misjudged one of his Barrymore leaps from a balcony and broke an ankle. His occasional triumphs seemed destined to be short-lived, and although he could take advantage of his real-life injury in his next appearance—that of a crippled hotel-keeper in Keith Winter's *Ringmaster*—once more the personal acclaim he received for a bravura performance failed to attract an audience; the play closed after only eight nights.

Perhaps weary of trying to conduct his life to accommodate the whims of others, he launched into management with a light-weight comedy, *Golden Arrow*. 'Laurence Olivier Presents' was, in later years, to signify a standard of overall excellence, but at this first attempt he judged wrongly. Agate, at his most scathing, pronounced that 'thoughout the evening Mr Olivier had not one single word to say that was worth speaking or hearing'— surely one of the most damning notices that any actor-manager could receive. *Golden Arrow* is remembered for one thing only: it introduced Greer Garson to the London stage, and in this Olivier was more perceptive than Agate.

Throughout this period in his life Olivier failed to notice there was a classical actor screaming to be released from the smart West End, tailor-made suits he now sported. Gielgud, Richardson and Peggy Ashcroft had all had their baptisms of fire by now; they had not flirted with a movie career or taken Hollywood's fools' gold and in many aspects they had outdistanced him, certainly in critical acclaim. When one views the sum total of Olivier's extraordinary achievements, it is difficult to reconcile the middle and later years with the first decade. In an effort to establish himself as a romantic leading man he had lost valuable ground without finding valuable experience. On the surface he had an air of success; he was handsome, well liked, married to an attractive and talented partner, and appeared to be in the swim; but he was intelligent enough to realise that his career lacked a positive sense of direction. After Hollywood came Denham—a contract from the engaging, volatile Alexander Korda now seeking to challenge the American screen monopoly with a rival British film industry. It would be too simplistic to raise Freudian reasons for Olivier's apparent need for financial security, but perhaps there were remaining undertones—he had after all been required to share his father's bathwater in the general economies of his childhood. Equally, one cannot discount the flattering guile of Korda, noted for his ability to charm birds and money out of the trees (sometimes, as in the case of the Prudential Assurance Company, out of whole forests). It was not easy to resist Korda's blandishments for, following the international success of his *Private Life of Henry VIII*, he exuded an air of total confidence. He was signing the cream of British talent; Denham was to become the local equivalent of Culver City, headed not by a blubbing despot such as Louis B. Mayer, but a cultured impresario. Olivier joined Laughton, Raymond Massey, Merle Oberon, Leslie Banks and Richardson in Korda's impressive roster of stars. Life was pleasant; he and Jill Esmond had a fine studio house in Cheyne Walk; they presented an idyllic picture of two successful young people who were going places. Only Olivier knew that although he was travelling hopefully he had no planned destination in mind.

It was now, in the latter half of 1935, his future was decided for him by two other actors. Gielgud was planning his new production of *Romeo and Juliet* and intended to alternate the roles of Romeo and Mercutio. When Donat declined to share the honours, the offer passed to Olivier. In many ways it was a curious decision on Gielgud's part, for he and Olivier had little in common and their styles of acting were poles apart. There was always a danger of conflict during the rehearsal period, because both men held very positive views. In Gielgud's case he was vastly more experienced in playing Shakespeare, and although it was felt that there were commercial advantages in presenting such a dramatic duel, there was also an ever-present risk that the experiment would unbalance the production.

Olivier said: 'I was fighting a cause. Understand, I've admired John Gielgud all my life, with complete devotion, but I've never thought of myself as quite the same actor as he is. I've always thought we were the reverse of the same coin, perhaps. If you have a coin, I've seen the top half John—all spiritual, all spirituality, all beauty, all abstract things; and myself all earth, blood, everything to do with earth, humanity if you like— the baser part of humanity. I suppose I must have sensed a possible sort of rivalry between us which might last all of our lives, because whatever it was that he had made me go for the other. When I was playing Romeo I was carrying a torch. I was trying to sell realism in Shakespeare. I believed in it with my whole soul, and I also believed that Johnny was not doing that enough. I thought he was paying attention to the exclusion of the earth, to all music, all lyricism, and I was for the other side of the coin.'

Gielgud said: 'When Olivier and I alternated the part of Romeo I was so angry because I thought I spoke it more skilfully that he did. But when it came to the physical movement and the impulse of the part, he beat me hollow. And I remember Ralph Richardson saying to me, "When he stands under the balcony, you know the whole character of Romeo in a moment, because the pose he takes is so natural, so light, so animally correct, that you just feel the whole quality of Italy—the character of Romeo and Shakespeare's pulse." I thought that an extraordinarily true criticism of his performance which was absolutely wonderful in that way. And everything he does is based on that assumption. It gives him an enormous power to be able to make his body obey him so well that he can almost characterise straight away.'

If Olivier's personality bent him towards reality, the need to present Romeo 'as a mere boy almost incoherent in the grip of his first adult passion', then Gielgud's first concern was for the poetry with passion taking second place. Both went their own way, though not without some spirited argument during the rehearsals, and predictably Olivier's reading of Shakespeare's lines offended the purists. The first round went to Gielgud, with honourable mentions to Edith Evans' matchless Nurse and the tender Juliet of Peggy Ashcroft. The fact that his theories had been rejected made Olivier lose confidence, despite the compensation that the controversy was good box office. But he swept all before him with his sardonic, fatalistic Mercutio, a role to which he could bring all his physical talents. It was ideally suited to his temperament and the reality that, to some, had offended in his portrayal of Romeo, now appeared as a revelation. The contrast between the two men proved a perfect balance and the production in this version became a triumph. (W. A. Darlington points out that, interestingly enough, Olivier had written to Richardson for advice on the interpretation of Mercutio. Richardson was then playing the same role in New York.)

With another of those curious twists of fortune characteristic of his professional career, he was next called upon to play Shakespeare on film. Paul Czinner was to direct his wife, Elisabeth Bergner, in *As You Like It*, Miss Bergner having played Rosalind with considerable success on the stage. A salary of £600 a week was dangled in front of Olivier, difficult to refuse despite his new resolutions. He could excuse himself on two grounds: Shakespeare and the reputation of his co-star. 'It's a big chance for me to play with Miss Bergner. No one can play with Bergner without learning something from her.' Alas for gentlemanly expectations, the experience proved that you can only learn from somebody if they are actually present. Miss Bergner, indulged by her husband, established a routine whereby she did not start work until the afternoons. This resulted in Olivier as Orlando addressing an absent Rosalind to the left or right of camera, with a continuity girl or assistant giving him the cues. Miss Bergner was not alone in such practices; throughout the history of the cinema certain stars have declined to speak off-screen lines when it comes to somebody else's close-ups. Naturally when the two complementary pieces of film are edited together audiences are unaware of the true facts, but it is a most disconcerting experience at the time and hardly conducive to integrated performances. First Garbo and now Bergner; Olivier must have despaired of finding a leading lady who didn't want to be alone.

Reactions to his finished screen role were mixed, but no doubt he stored away his grievances and hoarded his own ideas for the presentation of Shakespeare on film, allowing them to germinate until he embarked upon his war-time classic film of *Henry V*. As with a writer, all experience is ultimately of creative value to an actor.

It was now that he joined forces with Richardson and together they presented Priestley's *Bees on the Boat-Deck*, an engaging comedy that sadly did not find any general approval. Once again Olivier felt the icicle of Agate's disapproval. The critic thought that his portrayal of a second officer 'is no officer at all, but a young gentleman from behind the counter of a bank or stores'. But perhaps this was 'Captain' James E. Agate writing with a touch of inverted snobbery, for this is the way he styled himself in his early published works.

Olivier changed uniforms but remained in the navy for his next venture—a Korda epic derived from A. E. W. Mason's *Fire Over England*—in which Olivier at his most athletic helped save England from the threat of the Spanish Armada. He joined Flora Robson (as Good Queen Bess), Raymond Massey, Leslie Banks, his old drama teacher Henry Oscar and that gifted but flawed actor Robert Newton. Also in the cast, playing a maid of honour to Elizabeth I, was Vivien Leigh. This most British of subjects was characteristically directed by an American, William K. Howard, for Korda wanted the Hollywood touch as he set out to conquer the international market. The result confirmed most people's opinion that, in Korda, the native film industry had finally found a saviour, and with typical British indifference to detail conveniently ignored the fact that he was Hungarian. The film met with general acclaim, proved a personal triumph for Flora Robson and was even admired by Hitler. It was also the film that first brought Olivier and Vivien together as screen lovers, and set the seal on their tempestuous relationship.

With the release of the finished film Olivier stood at the crossroads of his professional and personal lives. He was twenty-nine, had been tipped as the natural successor to John Barrymore as the screen's leading romantic actor, he was in love with and loved by one of the great beauties of the age, and could now command a handsome salary from either the West End theatre or Korda's empire. He had chosen unwisely in the past and had lived to regret it. It was now, at Tyrone Guthrie's suggestion, he took a sober judgement, turning his back on Shaftesbury Avenue and Denham and electing to cross the Waterloo Bridge—that symbolic thoroughfare for so many of this century's leading players—signing on to join Lilian Baylis' Salvation Army at the collecting-box-salary of £20 a week.

[[20]]

RICHARDSON : REDGRAVE

I
T is wholly typical of Sir Ralph Richardson that he should describe his early life as 'a complete disaster, a most frightful muddle' for in his golden years he has carefully cultivated an engaging and eccentric image—Beerbohm Tree as an Isle of Man TT competitor—which belies a keen intelligence and cloaks his unique and very special talents as an actor. The sight of him arriving at the stage door of the National on his powerful motorbike, complete with crash helmet and leather jacket, is one of the greater glories of our theatre, for to combine the outward appearance of a tearaway with the inner talents of an Irving at the age of seventy-eight is a feat that few could bring off with dignity.

The origins of such endearing eccentricities can be traced back to his childhood when 'as a little boy of nine or ten', as he told us, 'I used to practise deaths. I used to fall off groynes into the shingle and lie asprawl, pierced with assegais, or shot with arrows, torn to pieces by wild Indians. I enjoyed this very much. It was a great consolation to me in my very lonely youth. This dressing up period was rather stronger, in me, than it is in most children, and it lasted a long time. Perhaps, after all, acting is something to do with dressing up. I often think that actors are the only people who have preserved, in some way, this childish nonsense of liking to put on some tremendous helmet or something. They'll do it still, it's awful, but it's part of the business of acting.'

His many admirers will hear his voice as they read the above confession of faith; the lilting, slightly apologetic tone as Sir Ralph reads from his book of revelations. They will detect sacred and profane fragments not of Barrie's Peter Pan, but of a tougher boy lurking within the mature man, the perennial juvenile masquerading behind the mask of the distinguished theatrical knight—an actor through and through who has enjoyed the rewards he merits yet has never been corrupted by them; retaining a sense of proportion, never courting idolatry, but receiving it gracefully as his right; a courtly man, deriving as much simple pleasure from his collection of Tompion clocks as he does from less enduring articles; above all a man of humour and integrity.

We have seen how Richardson's career became inextricably bound up with the careers of his two companions in excellence, Olivier and Gielgud: a professional bond forged in friendship and mutual respect. Now, in his still roaring seventies, it is difficult to reconcile the urbane leader of his profession with the 'undisciplined, tangled, muddled, disaster of a chap' who became a small-part London actor at the age of twenty-three after flirting with a variety of bizarre alternatives. Discipline—not of the martial order, but

242

discipline of the spirit—is something that Richardson has always felt is vital to the development of any actor. He refers to it as 'the sinews', that necessary resolve an actor requires when 'night after night, whether you feel like it, whether it's sunny, whether you want to get out and play cricket, whether you want to go to the cinema, of having to give a performance of the same part'. He received his first taste of this when he joined Barry Jackson's company for *Yellow Sands* and unlike some old boys does not scorn the grounding that early schooling gave him. He has acknowledged that he, more than most, needed such discipline and that it has stood him in good stead ever since.

Again it is interesting to note how often the same names crop up when we trace the careers of our great contemporaries. Harcourt Williams, that rumpled, vegetarian mentor of so many fine actors, was responsible for inviting Richardson to join his Old Vic company in 1930–31. The idea was that Richardson should join Gielgud for his last season and, after Gielgud's departure, take over as leading man. He played Prince Hal to Gielgud's Hotspur, Caliban to Gielgud's Prospero, Enobarbus to Gielgud's Antony, always encouraged and guided by Harcourt Williams. 'He never bullied, he never worried you, he found out what you could do best and brought the two bests together. He himself was a terrible bundle of nerves. He was always eating Bemax in the stalls and rushing up and down and pulling his hair; but he made us calm, he took all the calmness out of himself. A very unselfish and delightful fellow.'

It was during this first season at the Vic that Richardson met Bernard Shaw. They were doing *Arms and The Man*, with Gielgud as Sergius and Richardson as Bluntschli (a role he was to repeat thirteen years later opposite Olivier during their great partnership at the New Theatre). Shaw attended many of the rehearsals; he was always the frustrated actor but, according to Richardson, 'wonderfully courteous, wonderfully polite . . . I think perhaps the most polite man I've ever met in my life, especially sensitive to actors'. Behind the courtesy and the politeness was a determination to have his plays performed exactly the way he intended; he told Richardson that although he was going to be a very fine Bluntschli, there was one basic flaw in his interpretation. 'When you come in', he said, 'you show that you're very upset, you spend a long time with your gasps and your pauses and your lack of breath and your dizziness and your tiredness; it's very well done, it's very well done indeed, but it doesn't suit my play. It's no good for me, it's no good for Bernard Shaw. You've got to go from line to line, quickly and swiftly, never stop the flow of the lines, never stop. It's one joke after another, it's a firecracker. Always reserve the acting for underneath the spoken word. It's a musical play, a knockabout musical comedy.'

If we extract from this advice the phrase 'always reserve the acting for underneath the spoken word' it would appear that he took Shaw's dictum to heart for it gives us a general view of Richardson's style. He always seems at his best when portraying characters baffled by the human comedy. I have witnessed so many performances by Sir Ralph that linger in the memory simply because of this very quality. To snatch at a few at random, I recall his Uncle Vanya, his Inspector Goole in Priestley's *An Inspector Calls*, and most notably his Dr Sloper in *The Heiress*. We can bracket these with a score of screen performances that lay witness to his versatility—passion held in reserve, a gift, as Richard

The Heiress, Haymarket, 1949 (*l to r*) RALPH RICHARDSON, PEGGY ASHCROFT and JAMES DONALD

Far left RALPH RICHARDSON as Bottom in *A Midsummer Night's Dream* Old Vic, 1937–38

Left RALPH RICHARDSON as Peer Gynt and SYBIL THORNDIKE as Aase, New Theatre, 1944

Right RALPH RICHARDSON as Falstaff in *Henry IV*, Parts 1 and 2, New Theatre, 1945

Findlater puts it, 'for suggesting a deep-rooted kindness and tenderness behind a stolid ultra-English reserve'. And again, associating myself with Findlater's evaluation, he has made his portrayals of failures whether by concidence or intent, something of a speciality. I would not wish to suggest that he has deliberately type-cast himself, for this would be inaccurate as well as offensive; but it is a fact that he has been called upon many times to bring his own, unique gifts to the portrayal of human flotsam. Better than any actor I have ever seen, he has the power to move his audiences with the minimum of effect. He keeps bathos firmly at arm's length, and this was never shown to greater advantage than in his memorable Peer Gynt of 1944 –a baffled, vulnerable Everyman who seemed to those of us who went to the New Theatre after five years of war, a symbol of man's invincibility.

It was this quality in Richardson that obviously inspired Priestley to write expressly for him and their partnership, extending to half a dozen plays, was a happy marriage between dramatist and interpreter. In particular Priestley's *Johnson over Jordan*, produced just before the outbreak of war, gave Richardson a role ideally suited to his talents and stage personality. There is a lightness of touch about his finest performances that few of his contemporaries have ever equalled: he seems to ignite the fuse of a comedy line and then stand back to share the enjoyment with his audiences. Again, he has always suggested the schoolboy prankster hiding within the grown man and seemingly it spills over into his private life, for we have the evidence of his passion for motorbikes and his love, sometimes ill-placed, of homemade fireworks. Like Edith Evans he has been much imitated, for his intonations, his droll delivery and his love of the prolonged, but controlled, pause lends itself to parody; however, his impersonators lack the divine spark of the original. There is an actual texture to his comedy playing; as Tynan said of his magnificent Falstaff, it 'was not a *comic* performance: it was too rich and many-sided to be crammed into a single word . . . deliciously and subtly funny'. As Falstaff he at all turns suggested that in the midst of laughter there are tears, for when Sir John was so coldly rejected by his new king, Richardson gave us 'the emptiness of complete collapse'—the blubber became dead flesh before our wet eyes, the whale was stranded without hope of rescue.

This innate comic sense is Richardson's greatest asset, on and off stage; both here and in America devotees of late-night television talk shows have frequently been treated to an effortless flow of inconsequential reminiscences, frequently monologues of self-mockery that have, at their centre, a hard kernel of truth. He has said of himself: 'I think I could come on and say, "I'm from the Gas Works, I've come to read the meter," and I think that people would believe me. But it's strange that John Gielgud, whose acting I admire extravagantly (I think he is one of the greatest actors living) could not come on and say, "I'm from the Gas Works, I've come to read the meter." People would not believe that he came from the Gas Works. Then the other curious thing is that at the end of *The Tempest*, John has come on and said, "I am the Duke of Milan" and you believe it. He *is* the Duke of Milan, absolutely splendid. Now, I have played in *The Tempest* and I have said, "I am the Duke of Milan," and no one has believed me for one moment.'

This self-honesty extends throughout his career and is rare enough in a great actor to be commented upon, yet is a characteristic shared by Olivier and Gielgud. While stating that his Iago was 'not too bad' Richardson had no hesitation in admitting that his Othello and Macbeth were disasters. 'They are parts that I would wish to play more than any other. And in the bathroom I'm rather good. I don't know what it is. I found, when I came to play Macbeth's "Is this a dagger that I see before me?" . . . I just damn well *didn't* see the dagger and neither did anybody else. Perhaps I haven't the necessary emotional imagination. An actor's got to believe that he's all right in himself, otherwise he can't convince others; and I never believed that I was right myself in those parts. They attract me more than anything. I'd give half my life to be able to play Othello perfectly.'

This streak of total honesty about his own shortcomings (sometimes real and sometimes exaggerated) reveals as much of the actor as it does of the man himself. There is so much critical brouhaha written and talked about the theory of the actor's craft that it is refreshing to be allowed an insight into the workings of a real actor's mind. Richardson has described his art as 'a waking dream. It's not real, is it? But it has to have for you the reality that a dream has. This can't be sustained all the time throughout a whole performance; some of it is mechanical. The dream comes and goes. You may get a successful dream in the First Act, and the Second Act may just be mechanical and you think, "Oh, dear, this is no good." Curiously enough you may, as it were, fall asleep again in the Third Act and it all seems to have the reality of a dream for you once again. . . . Therefore three or four layers of consciousness are at work during the time an actor is giving a performance.'

Time, fame and the deserved knighthood have bestowed a kind of saintliness upon

Ralph Richardson and possibly because his private life has been less turbulent than some, and his public image therefore less exploited, the respect accorded to him has not always been equal to his achievements. It is my view that the contribution he has made with such steadfast integrity for the past fifty or more years is, in its totality, equal to any of his contemporaries. He seems to me to epitomise the English acting tradition, for he has not borrowed, he has invented: he is a true original. He does not remind us of others, others sometimes remind us of him, and therein lies his secret. Despite his failures in some of the great classical Shakespearean roles he is in the direct line of descent from Burbage and Garrick: a bit of a swashbuckler, with a basic love of 'dressing up', a love of *acting* in other words; a bit of a 'card', a character who, by the sheer force of his personality, compels others to pay him the compliment of imitation; and above all somebody who has advanced the status of his profession. He has never possessed Gielgud's fluency with verse, but remains Gielgud's superior in the speaking of prose and can bring to a straightforward piece of drama something akin to genius, if not genius itself. To quote once again from Richard Findlater, Richardson's acting 'seems to soar far beyond the needs of naturalism, towards the Alps of great art'.

*   *   *   *

If Sir Ralph can be said to have made a speciality of affable failures, then Sir Michael Redgrave has, on occasions, claimed a monopoly of intellectual failures in the characters he has played. In many ways his career, after a false start, has been more straightforward than some of his rival contemporaries. Although he came from a long line of actor ancestors, he was discouraged from following historical precedent by his mother, the actress Margaret Scudamore. Mrs Redgrave may have given birth to her son in theatrical lodgings, but she was determined that his destiny should be different from her own. She had married an actor, George Ellsworthy ('Roy') Redgrave, who had a successful if not spectacular career, mostly in the provinces and subsequently in tours of Africa and Australia. Margaret Scudamore followed her husband to Australia (Michael was baptised in Melbourne) but the marriage did not survive the journey; she was to return to England with her three-year-old child and later divorce Roy Redgrave. Neither of them ever saw him again. This domestic tragedy was to have a profound effect on them both, and no doubt influenced Margaret Scudamore in the choice of career for her son. She remarried, and we are told that 'new material comfort was accompanied by emotional insecurity' as far as Michael was concerned. He did not rebel against his mother's decision, perhaps because he had witnessed the seamy side of theatrical life at an early age and felt a sense of alienation towards the father who had caused his mother so much hardship. His new step-father had no such theatrical connections; he was a wealthy planter and happy to provide a superior education for his step-son on condition that his wife's wishes were respected. The young Michael Redgrave seemed content to turn his back on his pedigree and fall in with his mother's and stepfather's plans. He was sent first to Clifton College, where he assiduously cultivated his complementary talent as a poet and author of short stories and was also accounted a remarkable Lady Macbeth in the school dramatic society. Such early and heady success as an actor did not alter his resolve, however, and when he left Clifton he had set his sights on a journalistic career. His mother's advice—'too many people go into the theatre for what they can get out of it, and not enough for what they can put into it'—was something he had taken to heart, for at that time he felt he had very little to give. In addition, and doubtless from personal experience of tall actors, Margaret Scudamore felt that his height (he is six feet three inches) would be a distinct disadvantage to an acting career. He had enjoyed his amateur 'star' status in the school productions, and a brief professional walk-on at the Apollo Theatre in 1926, aged sixteen, but he had an acknowledged literary bent and this claimed all his affections. He might have gone straight to Fleet Street upon leaving school; an introduction of his mother's produced an immediate offer to join the staff of the *Western Farmer's Journal*, but he was deflected by another chance encounter with the publisher Ivor Nicholson who persuaded him that travel and some experience of life were more valuable to a serious writer than the humdrum security of a farming paper. So in the best tradition of the romantic student he went to pre-Nazi Heidelberg, spending the best part of an enjoyable year there. Germany not only gave him a chance to broaden his literary horizons; it also introduced him to the world of opera, satisfying both his love of music and the theatrical. When he returned to England his whole outlook towards the drama had changed. He had not yet resolved his own destiny, but he had glimpsed another side of the theatre, far removed from the provincial memories of his childhood, and the seed had been planted. In addition he had tasted university life by occasionally attending lectures at Heidelberg, and he took the decision to try for Cambridge. He was accepted by Magdalene in the winter of 1927 and quickly gained a reputation as a poet. Having contributed to *The Granta* and edited *The Cambridge Review* for a term he joined forces with Anthony Blunt and Romilly Fedden to produce a new magazine called, appropriately, *The Venture*. It survived for six issues, acquiring much kudos for its contents and a fair-sized debt which Redgrave had to meet out of his own pocket.

While working towards an honours degree in modern languages and English literature, he indulged his undoubted talents as an actor with the A.D.C. Theatre and, most notably, the Marlowe Society. The latter company was noted for its verse speaking, under the inspired guidance of George Rylands, and Redgrave received plaudits not only from the locals but also from visiting London critics for his Edgar in *King Lear* and Prince Hal in *Henry IV, Part I*. Very much the daring and much-sought-after young man on the university trapeze, he became a recognised Cambridge character for whom great things were predicted: a triple-threat man—poet, player and editor. Yet when he left Cambridge in 1931 at the age of twenty-three, the predictions of friends and tutors proved false. The country was in the middle of the slump, the choice of employment was severely limited and in the end he opted to become a schoolmaster, so often the first refuge of those with frustrated artistic ambitions. Even then life might have gone in a different direction, but once again the fact that he was above average height for an actor decided against him. Because of his reputation for verse speaking he had been invited to take part in a BBC poetry programme with Robert Loraine and Fay Compton. Loraine was about to tour America and during the course of conversation someone suggested that he might offer

MICHAEL REDGRAVE and EDITH EVANS in
As You Like It, Old Vic, 1936

MICHAEL REDGRAVE in *Uncle Harry* Garrick
Theatre, 1944

Redgrave a place in the cast. Loraine reacted with a candour that was probably not intentionally wounding but which made 'a devastating impression' on Redgrave. 'He couldn't go on the stage with *me*', Loraine said. 'Much too tall.' This clarion echo of his mother's words squashed all further thoughts of a professional acting career for a further three years, during which time he obtained a teaching post at Cranleigh. It was to prove a blessing in disguise for, as at Cambridge, he was able to develop as an actor within the leisurely routine of an academic life, gaining invaluable experience without the pressures of the commercial theatre. During his years at Cranleigh he was given every facility to experiment and as director, designer and star actor of the Cranleigh productions he provided what *The Times* described as 'an exhilarating break in the tradition of school dramatics'.

Thus we have another variation: one of our most distinguished leading actors being encouraged, in the first instance, to turn his back on tradition, then reversing history and forging a new tradition of his own. His artistic ventures at Cranleigh allowed him to explore his talents as a director, though he had no hesitation, once he had the taste, of casting himself as Hamlet, Prospero, Lear and Samson Agonistes. Highly impressed by a visit to Michel Saint-Denis' Compagnie des Quinze, he confessed: 'I suddenly became fired with what it means to be a director and to have an ensemble company that really does express a point of view. And I dreamed that I could do something of the sort.'

This dream, allied to his success as an amateur actor at Cranleigh, drove him to make the break. Like so many of those we have already discussed, his first thought was to try for the Old Vic and he duly gave an audition to Lilian Baylis. She made some vague promise that he would hear in due course. 'Well, I didn't hear, the summer term started, and I thought "I shan't hear anything. I must spread my nets a little wider." So I went up

249

to Liverpool over the Whitsun weekend holiday, and on the very day I was going to see William Armstrong who ran the Rep., a contract arrived from the Old Vic for three pounds a week. So I thought, "Well, if the worst comes to the worst, I can go back to that." It wasn't the worst, because I should have been very glad to go to the Vic. But William Armstrong was so impressed that I had a contract for London and that I wanted to come to a theatre in the provinces that he said, "How much is your contract for?" and I said, like a fool, "Three pounds a week," and he said, "I'll give you four." I've always thought, ever since, that if I'd said eight, he would have said nine.'

There speaks the born actor.

He was, by his own confession, 'still very, very conceited'—a common fault amongst gifted amateurs (Redgrave's true status at that time), for they can indulge their conceits without much fear that they will meet their peers. With his four pounds a week he could now call himself a professional and he knuckled down, under Armstrong's kindly administration, to learning what the real theatre was all about. Liverpool Repertory, although enjoying a high reputation and playing to packed houses nearly every night, was not slanted towards the classics. Armstrong mostly relied upon reproducing proven West End successes, only tipping his hat towards Shakespeare once a year. He was a great discoverer of young talent and once under his wing many of his discoveries flourished and went on to greater things. Fortunately the population of Liverpool was big enough to sustain a three-week run, so Redgrave was never forced to find the short cuts that actors in weekly repertory are condemned to.

What he did find was a kindred spirit in a young actress named Rachel Kempson, who came to Liverpool after a stunning debut at Stratford as Juliet. They were cast opposite each other in John van Druten's *Flowers of the Forest*, and before the season had ended they had announced their engagement. The marriage survives to this day and in addition to producing three remarkable children—Vanessa, Corin and Lynn—Rachel Kempson, though frequently overshadowed by her more famous husband, has never been obliterated by him. Now at an age when most people in other professions are thinking of retirement it has fallen to her to become the main breadwinner, and her own career flourishes. Michael Redgrave has been beset with illness in recent years, yet again he has not succumbed under the burden, but fought it. He has adapted himself to unhappy circumstances and produced a notable evening's entertainment that has toured the world.

In those far off halcyon days at Liverpool, the young couple were swiftly married and enjoyed a partnership that flourished both on and off stage. With rare luck they were both noted by Tyrone Guthrie when he visited the theatre, and offered the juvenile leads at the next season at the Vic. Olivier and Edith Evans had already been engaged as the stars, but having profited from his first negotiations, Redgrave held out for a seventeen pound advance on the original three pounds offered by Lilian Baylis. Somewhat to his amazement Miss Baylis agreed, and he had a contract that equalled the salary paid to Olivier and Edith.

The Old Vic season of 1936 was notable on many counts, but undoubtedly the highlight was the Rosalind of Edith Evans, her exquisite swan-song in a role she had already made her own. She was then forty-eight, yet in the opinion of those who saw her in the Watteau-like forest of Arden of Esme Church's production, she drew and painted 'a Meredithean lady rich in mind' and incredibly youthful in appearance. She said of herself: 'I was about thirty years too old for it. But there was a Rosalind in me somewhere. I got myself very slim, so that I didn't look ridiculous, and it was the first time I had ever had my hair cut short, and it was a battle that I won. As Shaw says, Rosalind is at the loveliest time of any woman's life, when she's just falling in love and she knows that she's welcome.' Without knowing it at the time, Shaw was a true prophet in that Edith fell victim to her 'five-minute love', as she later, wistfully referred to it. Redgrave, twenty years her junior, played Orlando to her Rosalind in real life as in the play. And when in his eulogistic review Alan Dent wrote that 'in the end the audience is made one with Orlando' he little realised that, like Shaw, he had stumbled upon a hidden truth. It fell to me as her biographer to reveal the true nature of that brief encounter between Edith and Michael Redgrave, for with an honesty and generosity that is rare enough in any walk of life, Sir Michael and Lady Redgrave readily consented that I should make public that hidden truth. It is mentioned again here not for any spurious effect, but because the relationship between the young actor and the acknowledged great actress had a profound influence on Redgrave's career. There was no hint of scandal, then or in future years; Edith was a very moral woman, strong enough for both of them at the time, and Lady Redgrave wise enough and feminine enough to forgive. To the end of her days Edith revered her Orlando, and he retained her respect and returned her lasting affection. At her memorial service in St Paul's, Covent Garden, he read one of her favourite sonnets, Wordsworth's *Upon Westminster Bridge*, a farewell sharing of their mutual love of poetry. He has always acknowledged the debt he owes her, both as a man and as an actor, readily admitting that he was more influenced by her than any other performer. Echoing the lessons she taught him, he has described the basic difference between a great artist and other mortals as a question of morality. 'Without moral values', he said, 'nothing is achieved and nothing is created'.

Redgrave came to acting fully equipped intellectually and then taught himself to approach it emotionally, which is not the normal order of things. Again it was Edith who posed the all important question: 'What sort of actor do you want to be?' His reply that he would like to play all manner of parts did not satisfy her. She said, 'No, no, I don't mean that. I mean do you want to be like John, or Larry, or do you want to be like Peggy Ashcroft, or me? What sort of standards are you aiming at?' The challenge in her question made him take stock of himself. He came to the realisation that he would have to have a certain goal, that until now he had been toying with a romantic ideal, seeing himself as the director of a fine ensemble company, but neglecting to think it through. Of all our leading actors of this century he has been at some pains to attain absolute mastery of the vocal line; yet at the same time he has compelled himself to flatten the poetry that always threatens to surface when he speaks prose. (Terence Rattigan was one of the few playwrights to sense this conflict in Redgrave and create a role that allowed him to display both facets. I am referring to his famous screen role in *The Way to the Stars* in which Redgrave played a RAF officer. On the surface he was the complete, taciturn bomber pilot; beneath the mask he concealed the emotions of a poet. John Pudney's celebrated poem, with its matter-of-fact pathos, which was used in the film, made his reputation soar, but it was the image of Redgrave's under-stated performance that lingered in the memory, despite the fact that he had one of the smallest roles.)

I have always sensed this inner struggle with Redgrave. At one time he carried Stanislavsky's *An Actor Prepares* like the one true gospel, but later confessed that 'I misused what I read in much the same way as the later disciples of what is now called The Method have misused it; that is to say, I thought it permitted me to do anything that came into my head, regardless of whether it was right for the play.' In some performances audiences were made too aware of the wheels going round; he had studied the role he was playing so deeply that all spontaneity was gone from it. He struggled to remove this over-emphasis, coming to the conviction, first suggested to him by Saint-Denis, that 'anything that is underlined is bad art'. He is at his most compelling, his most affecting when portraying ineffectual people. He seems to have a natural sympathy with them and in a long list of memorable performances given over thirty years, his Tusenbach, Uncle Vanya and Uncle Harry stand out in stark relief.

I have particular cause to remember his clumsy, bespectacled murderer in Thomas Job's *Uncle Harry*; I saw it while I was still a callow student at the Royal Academy of Dramatic Art and the performance burnt into my consciousness: this, I thought, is what great acting is all about and I strove to model myself on Redgrave's style. I remember my absolute fury when James Agate dared to disagree with my verdict, writing that 'here and now I take the responsibility of advising Michael Redgrave to give up the intellectual drama and devote himself to the profession. (The secret of intellectual acting is that anybody can do it.)' This was Agate at his most pedantic, I felt, and my loyalty towards Redgrave increased in like proportion to Agate's scorn. What struck me then in my formative years was Redgrave's amazing versatility. I hardly missed any of his major performances and still recall with undiluted pleasure the panache he brought to Patrick Hamilton's *The Duke in Darkness*, and the contrast between his doomed aristocrat in that play and his connubial lover in Becque's neglected *Parisienne*.

Another difference between Redgrave's career and that of his most celebrated contemporaries is that he had no sooner established himself as a leading actor in the West End than he entered upon an equally successful film career. Unlike Olivier he stepped straight into a film destined to become a classic in its genre—Hitchcock's comedy-thriller *The Lady Vanishes*, scripted by Launder and Gilliatt. He was also luckier than Olivier in another respect: he did not run foul of silent or absent leading ladies, but was cast opposite the down-to-earth young Margaret Lockwood. At the time he was not passionate about the medium and avowedly took the role simply because he wanted to earn more money to support his growing family. He had only recently appeared (under Gielgud's management) in the much acclaimed season at the Queen's Theatre, and there were some who felt his rapid ascent to leading man status had outstripped his talents. Such criticism was immediately silenced by a powerful Bolingbroke to Gielgud's Richard II, but in Guthrie's production of *The School For Scandal* which followed he was unhappily cast and the mocking voices were heard again. He defended himself by stating, quite truthfully, that he had characterised his Charles Surface in obedience to his

INGRID BERGMAN and MICHAEL REDGRAVE in *A Month in the Country*, 1965

director's wishes. The scales were tipped again, this time heavily in his favour, with this third appearance, as Baron Tusenbach in *The Three Sisters*. There are aspects of his own character that might have come from Chekhov's pen and he has been able to turn these to great advantage whenever he has played Chekhov. He was in superb company on this occasion and he rose to the collective heights. Saint-Denis' production was described as 'a miracle of co-ordination' and one comment from Rupert Hart-Davis must have given particular satisfaction to Redgrave. Hart-Davis wrote that 'One cannot help feeling that they approach the much-described harmony of Stanislavsky's actors'.

His decision, therefore, to ask for a release from Gielgud (he had already been cast as Bassanio in *The Merchant*) in order to take up a five-year film contract seemed inexplicable to the purists. The greater financial rewards had proved too tempting, though in later years he admitted his defection from the legitimate theatre at that point in his career was 'a big mistake, and I count it against myself'. In all probability his conscience worried him and that was the reason for his admitted indifference to screen acting. He has confessed that he did not try to give of his best to Hitchcock's film until one of his co-stars, Paul Lukas, who admired him extravagantly, remonstrated with him about his obvious lack of effort. The gentle but valid criticism went home; from that moment onwards he set about proving that he could act as well for the camera as he could for a live audience.

Climbing High, a Jessie Matthews musical rewritten into an inferior celluloid farce, followed *The Lady Vanishes*. At this time Redgrave had not been seen in the finished Hitchcock film, but the studios felt they had, in Wardour Street jargon, 'a hot property' on their hands and were anxious to exploit their acquisition by trundling him into one film after another in quick succession. *Climbing High* failed to live up to its title, but it did introduce Redgrave to Sir Carol Reed, then at the start of his illustrious career as a film director. Reed had decided that he was never going to succeed as an actor and had switched to films. While still making *Climbing High* Redgrave was cast opposite Elisabeth Bergner in *Stolen Life*, and like Olivier before him had to accommodate the Czinner-Bergner method, a far remove from his beloved Stanislavsky. For his third starring role he had been farmed out to Paramount Pictures at an inflated salary from which he did not benefit. The Hollywood publicity juggernaut went into action, flattening his objections as it conditioned the public to accept a star they had yet to see. It was a technique Hollywood had perfected and in the end he was swept along by it, manufactured against his better judgement into a romantic figure that filmgoers would buy sight unseen.

Redgrave was too intelligent not to realise the long-term dangers in such a campaign of induced hysteria. With commendable foresight he had insisted that his film contract allowed him leave of absence for six months in any year in order to pursue his career in the theatre. Having established this pattern to his life, he has adhered to it throughout his career. There are some who say that by splitting his career into two separate halves he has denied the status of a great classical actor, but I do not subscribe to this. Redgrave is a superb actor in either medium and it is absurd pedantry to seek so to restrict any actor working in the latter half of the twentieth century. Redgrave himself has gone on record in saying that he has seen screen performances 'that are as great—to use a word I don't really like using—as any that I've seen on the stage.' Outsider observers might well include some of his own, notably his classic essay in horror in the ventriloquist segment of *Dead of Night* directed by Cavalcanti. Film exists as an art, and television drama often gives the home viewer better value for money than either the West End theatre or the cinema. It would therefore be an act of folly for any actor totally to cut himself off from these alternative showplaces and the height of artistic snobbery to condemn any actor who so rings the changes. The pity of it is that not more examples of our acting tradition have been captured on film or video tape for the benefit of future generations. There is a crying need for a national archive of such material, for how else are we to preserve that part of our heritage?

Redgrave's next theatrical venture during his first foray into films was Rodney Ackland's adaptation of a Russian play *The Days of the Turbins* by Leo Bulgakov, which appeared under the English title *The White Guard*. The plot, set in the days of the Russian

Revolution of 1918, had Chekhovian undertones and provided two fine roles for Redgrave and Peggy Ashcroft. It was the first offering of a new venture launched by Saint-Denis and the strong company also included Glen Byam Shaw, Marius Goring and George Devine. *The White Guard* proved to be an admirable choice and was enthusiastically received, but like so many other enterprises of that period fell victim to the Munich crisis, which as older readers will remember produced a nation-wide paralysis: audiences simply stayed at home, fearful of losing contact with the radio bulletins. In an attempt to retrieve the situation Saint-Denis pushed forward with a star-encrusted production of *Twelfth Night*. He had hoped to secure Edith Evans as Maria with Richardson as Sir Toby and Olivier as Malvolio to complement Ashcroft, Redgrave and Goring, but for various reasons the pieces did not come together. Saint-Denis' 'great design' collapsed from a combination of West End economics and the international crisis. *Twelfth Night*, as finally produced, gave Redgrave an opportunity to create a brilliantly unorthodox Aguecheek that, contrary to tradition, dominated the play, and was much admired. But there was no yearning for comedy even of this high order in those sombre days and Saint-Denis had to admit defeat.

Between the demise of this valiant attempt by Saint-Denis to establish a permanent company and the outbreak of war, Redgrave again experimented with a new dramatic form: T. S. Eliot's cold and demanding attempt to dress Greek tragedy in bank clerks' clothes, writing verbal algebraic equations rather than poetic drama, the product of a man who was always more interested in form than in content. The play was *The Family Reunion* and in accepting the difficult role of Lord Monchensey Redgrave found himself faced with (in the words of the play's director, Ashley Dukes) 'perhaps the hardest task that any young actor has set himself in our generation'. After the event Mr Dukes added a defensive postscript: 'If he' (Redgrave) 'has weaknesses in *The Family Reunion*, they arise from his own honesty of purpose: there are things in the play that he does not understand and will never understand, and therefore cannot interpret'. This rather begs the question that, as the director of the piece, Mr Dukes did not understand it either, and was therefore unable to answer Redgrave's many queries. Succeeding revivals of the play have also singularly failed to decipher Mr Eliot's true purpose. *The Family Reunion* is an acknowledged landmark in twentieth century drama but, like the statues on Easter Island, nobody has been able fully to explain just how it got there.

Shortly after the run of Eliot's play finished war was finally declared, and in October 1939 Redgrave was touring in Benn Levy's *Springtime for Henry*; doubtless he was in need of light relief after wrestling with the mysteries of Lord Monchensey, and deliberately gave himself a change of pace. So, using the outbreak of war as a convenient staging point, I shall take temporary leave of our quartet of leading actors and travel back to pick up the ladies.

⟦ 21 ⟧

THE GREAT DAYS RETURN

LET us begin, fittingly, with Dame Peggy Ashcroft's evaluation of Edith Evans, for she is Edith's rightful successor as the first lady of the English stage, possessing, as Edith did, that chameleon quality of being able to assume an ageless beauty.

In her opinion Edith was 'a totally intuitive artist who had, as well, an extraordinary wisdom. She *felt* rather than thought. I remember asking her about a line she said as the Nurse in *Romeo and Juliet*, "Edith, how did you find your way to say that line in such a way that it is an unforgettable line?" and she said, "Do you know, I used to pray about that line—how to say it—and it came to me." I first saw her when I was a student, then when she played Millamant at the Lyric, Hammersmith I had a one-line part and was her secondary understudy. Five years after that we played together for the first time, Juliet and the Nurse in Gielgud's production for the O.U.D.S., something we repeated four years later at the New. She could tell you so much and teach you so much and was a marvellous influence on me.

'There were two sides of her. She was very boisterous and gay, and at the same time very shy and withdrawn, a rather lonely person. Her greatest quality was her search always for the truth. Nothing satisfied her if she didn't feel that it was really the truth about a character. She didn't like playing unsympathetic parts and wouldn't have dreamed of playing Lady Macbeth. If she did play a role that was rather unsympathetic, like Madame Arcadina in *The Seagull*, she had the ability to be like that—that was part of her genius, I think.'

As Edith did, and possibly equally influenced in her off-stage behaviour by Edith's example, Peggy Ashcroft has always kept her audiences at a distance. Whenever she has violated this self-imposed rule it has not been to advance her own career, but to champion some libertarian cause. Passionate about her political views, though less strident than Vanessa Redgrave in attempting to convert others to her beliefs, she has throughout her career worked to improve the status and conditions of her colleagues while at the same time zealously guarding her artistic integrity. In this she is closer to Dame Sybil Thorndike than Edith, for despite the fact that Edith also worked hard to establish the formation of Equity, she was not a political animal in any active sense.

The pattern of her early life was conventional. She was born in 1907 to middle-class parents and although her mother had been an amateur actress who studied under Elsie Fogerty, this was an isolated incident in an otherwise untheatrical background. Her father was an estate agent who died in the first World War. Mrs Ashcroft gave qualified approval to her daughter's ambitions to become a professional actress; she was allowed to enter the Central School of Speech Training on the condition that her studies prepared her for a teaching career. Her mother died before she had completed the course and it was Elsie Fogerty, who could always detect the difference between real talent and mere aptitude, who guided the adolescent orphan towards her real love.

The young Miss Ashcroft made her London debut in a fringe theatre and then had the good fortune to attract the attention of Nigel Playfair, a man with an enviable record for spotting winners. This led to her employment in his Lyric, Hammersmith company where, as she has related, she understudied Edith. Her progress through the ranks was steady, if unspectacular. 'At first', she said, 'there was the excitement of going from part to part and trying to get one job after another. Whatever I was asked to do, whether I liked the play or not, I had to do it—you must do it. Sometimes I longed to walk out because I thought it was nonsense, or rubbish, or I couldn't do it, or something like that; but fortunately I never did. And then gradually, I think, I did have this feeling that it was a disordered profession; I wasn't slowly building from one thing to another. . . . I think the point is that you can be awfully bored and fed up with your own acting, the business of having to do it all the time . . . but the thing that you don't get bored and fed up with is the theatre . . . [Acting] is sometimes an escape from life or it can be an enlargement of life. I think, too, many people say you have to live in order to be able to act, and that what you put into your performance is what you've learned from life. But I have a theory that you can learn about life from acting, because an author's creations of character can teach you a great deal about psychology.'

Her first real success came from an association with an actor-manager of the old school, Matheson Lang. She appeared in his 1929 production of *Jew Süss* adapted from Feuchtwanger's famous novel. Years later Sir Harold Hobson was to write that her performance as Naomi gave him the instinctive feeling that he was 'in the presence of greatness'. She had one quality that was lacking in most of the leading ladies she was shortly to challenge; quite apart from her youth she had sex appeal, not the animal appeal of Mrs Pat in her prime, nor the pre-Raphaelite attractions of Ellen Terry, but the appeal of a modern, emancipated woman. Her beauty was not conventional, but on stage she moved in such a way as to draw all eyes to her. Such a quality, allied to good bone structure in the face, is worth more than the chocolate-box prettiness, of transient duration, that takes some young actresses further than their talent merits. In this respect she reminds one of Gertrude Lawrence, who also had the ability to make her audiences fall in love with her, yet who had a face that did not photograph well. It is hard to describe such actresses without falling back on clichés—'star quality' for instance or 'glamorous appearance', and indeed one I have already used, 'sex appeal'. In Peggy Ashcroft's case she was unique in that she directed herself towards the classics and the serious modern dramatists, challenging people to forget her beauty and concentrate on her acting. It is always harder for a really beautiful actress to be taken seriously, for there is a perverseness about certain critics who seem to resent beauty and talent going hand in hand. It is permissible, it seems, in musical comedy or lightweight drama, but to introduce sex into the classics often makes them uneasy, almost as though an element of sexuality is against the rules. This attitude is especially noticeable when, in contrast, some average ingenue with ample bust measurements is granted a critical latitude sternly withheld from flatter, plainer Janes. Since the dawn of Tynan's scatological revolution, full frontal nudity bestows an immediate amnesty, the sight of pubic hair, nipples and navels often being considered more worthy than the Bancroft Gold Medal. Life for many aspiring young actresses today must be very irksome, and with the old parrot cry of the pimp shouting 'give the public what it wants', standards, as well as trousers, drop ever lower.

All this is mercifully a long way from the young Peggy Ashcroft, who throughout her career has used her artistry to suggest a latent sexuality. Two of her most notable performances—Catherine Sloper in *The Heiress* and Hester in Rattigan's *The Deep Blue Sea*—gave us poignant studies of a woman physically in love beyond her means. (As a side note to Rattigan's best straight play, first produced in 1952, it is worth noting that Dame Peggy might never have played the leading role. Rattigan wrote an early draft, which I read, in which Hester Collyer was a male role, the whole plot being built around a burnt-out homosexual relationship. Because of prevailing attitudes Rattigan was persuaded by Hugh Beaumont to rewrite completely, switching all the roles to conform to the then moral climate. The fact that the result was a resounding triumph does not suppress the thought that Rattigan's change of heart was a tragedy for his progress as a leading playwright. He was often reviled for being too competent, too facile, for making it all seem too easy; unfair criticism, in my opinion, towards a man who prided himself on his craftsmanship. He had the talent and the technical skill to break through ahead of the times he lived in, to give us a homosexual play that was concerned with aspects of love rather than aspects of salacious scandal, but it was not to be. There is a savage irony in this: he was hurt by and longed to escape from the *French Without Tears* image that dogged him throughout his career. In *The Deep Blue Sea* he produced his most mature writing, yet was still chastised in some quarters while knowing in his heart that he had once written the play that his detractors maintained was beyond him, and had then suppressed it. A decade or so later, with censorship removed from the theatre at last and in the changed moral climate, he would almost certainly have insisted on sticking to his original conception. But the moment had passed and he was never able to regain the lost ground for by then the younger generation of playwrights had swum with the tide; he was stuck with his own Aunt Edna label, a commendable defence, but inevitably turned against him. He wrote many fine plays, plays that deserve to live, but the one great play, that was always well within his reach, he allowed to slip away.)

The depth of experience that Peggy Ashcroft brought to *The Deep Blue Sea* stemmed from over twenty years' dedication to the refinement of her art. A renowned classical actress, she was in a modern play giving a completely modern performance, surprising even her most ardent admirers. Her scenes with Roland Culver and Kenneth More were played in a totally colloquial manner, that reminded me of the best French films, and she invested them with an inner intensity of feeling that few, if any, could emulate. It was on every level a remarkable portrayal and when set against her bitter virgin in the Henry James adaptation, *The Heiress*, or her enigmatic murderess in Enid Bagnold's *The Chalk*

PEGGY ASHCROFT as Desdemona with
PAUL ROBESON in *Othello*, Savoy, 1930

PEGGY ASHCROFT and EDITH EVANS as
Juliet and the Nurse, New Theatre, 1935

Garden it illustrated that she is an actress who can move from the classical to realism without compromise to either style.

Her first professional performance in a Shakespearean production took place in 1930, when she was cast as Desdemona opposite the Othello of Paul Robeson. The innovation of Robeson in the role should, in theory, have given us the best Othello on record. In appearance Robeson was ideal: he had the physique and a magnificent voice. The preliminary announcement of Maurice Browne's presentation aroused the highest expectations, but sadly the fascinating experiment did not live up to the prior word of mouth. Robeson evoked immediate sympathy and was impressive during the early scenes, but then appeared to have little or no comprehension of Shakespeare's motives. He was also handicapped by his inability to master the verse: the great singing voice proved a lack-lustre instrument in the famous set speeches. Peggy Ashcroft, on the other hand, gave notice that she was an actress to be watched. Writing of her first entrance in the play, Gielgud wrote 'it was as if all the lights in the theatre had suddenly gone up.' While the unfortunate Robeson stumbled with the words she was unanimously praised for the quality of her elocution.

Her career was subsequently influenced by Komisarjevsky; she was briefly married to him, but although the personal relationship did not long survive, the ideas he implanted in her, and the individual way in which she interpreted those ideas to suit her own personality and talents were to prove an enduring legacy. Her association with Gielgud followed as a natural course, and as noted she was the Juliet for his first O.U.D.S. production of *Romeo and Juliet*. Later she joined Gielgud at the Old Vic for Harcourt Williams' last season there. Like Edith Evans before her she embraced a wide variety of

Left In Terence Rattigan's *The Deep Blue Sea*, PEGGY ASHCROFT with RAYMOND FRANCIS (*left*) and KENNETH MORE, Duchess Theatre, 1952 *Right* PEGGY ASHCROFT as Queen Margaret in *The Wars of the Roses* (Stratford-on-Avon and Aldwych, London, 1963–64)

roles, including Imogen in *Cymbeline*, Portia in *The Merchant* and Lady Teazle in *The School for Scandal*—in all she played ten parts in as many months. In later years she referred to that season as 'a killing venture, quite beyond my scope at the time, and I knew it.' The Vic had been a gruelling testing ground for so many of our leading players; it built character as well as reputations and in view of the salaries paid it was certainly a case of 'Art for Art's sake'. In a sense it must have had some similarities with an exclusive public school; it bestowed a certain mystique upon its successful graduates, and one has to add that, as with real public schools, it aroused certain resentments; not every commercial West End management was impressed by Lilian Baylis' old school tie. When her first term at the Vic ended in 1933 Peggy Ashcroft found it difficult to adjust; she appeared to lose confidence in herself and since it was during this period that her marriage to Komisarjevsky ended in divorce the domestic tragedy helped to throw her off course. It was not until two years later that an offer from Gielgud (ever the artistic Good Samaritan) brought her back into the mainstream of theatrical life. She joined him in his season at the New to repeat her passionate Juliet, with Gielgud and Olivier alternating as Romeo. She was hailed as 'the finest as well as the sweetest Juliet of our time' giving a performance that 'technically . . . is perfection'. To Gielgud acting with her made it impossible for him 'to use a false note or play in an artificial or declamatory manner'. Only Agate, grumpy as ever where the young Miss Ashcroft was concerned, withheld his blessing; for a long time he had a blind spot about her and if he was compelled to praise the parts he never praised the whole. To Agate she was immature—'a nice little girl in a wood' had been his dismissal of her Old Vic Rosalind—and he often wrote like a chair-bound old bachelor who resents that the young can enjoy themselves. What is revealing, and what Agate did not sense, is that she had little self-confidence. The constant struggle to find the right role and the right company and atmosphere in which to play that role was something she found hard to come to terms with. She knew what she wanted, the problem was to find others who felt the same way. The ordinary commercial theatre with its pressures and compromises did not satisfy her. She had as her ideal a company of like enthusiasts who could enjoy the rewards of ensemble playing; where casts would not be hastily assembled and thrown into frenzied rehearsal merely to accommodate the purely financial needs of a theatre owner whose prime consideration was that his building should not remain dark for longer than three weeks. She was not alone, nor was she the first to think in this way. It had been Shaw's ideal and Granville-Barker's; likewise Gielgud had long harboured the same dream, and with his greater experience and reputation once again he was the instrument that brought her closer to her ideal. In association with Michel Saint-Denis it was his intention to establish a permanent company, and Peggy Ashcroft was invited to join them for the first season. We have seen how the nine-month repertoire of plays— *Richard II, The School for Scandal, The Three Sisters* and *The Merchant of Venice*—achieved what was then thought to be impossible: the classics as an economic proposition in the heart of the West End. Only Gielgud's disenchantment with the humdrum day-to-day demands of management brought the venture to an abrupt end. A small nucleus from the original company remained with Saint-Denis and attempted to revive the experiment elsewhere. This was the venture that ran foul of the Munich crisis, but did give Miss Ashcroft and Michael Redgrave a limited and much applauded run in *The White Guard*.

A subsequent marriage to a leading Q.C., Jeremy Hutchinson, and the arrival of a son and a daughter by this marriage resulted in periodically long absences from the stage, revealing another side to her single-mindedness. This contrasts with the picture often presented of leading actresses which suggests that they always sacrifice family and friends to their careers. Just after the outbreak of war she added her lustre to the legendary Gielgud production of *The Importance of Being Earnest*, playing Cecily Cardew as to the manner born, and Cecily Cardew is not the easiest of roles, for juveniles that have to carry plot seldom are. During the war she gave few major performances and it wasn't until 1944 that she gave Agate another opportunity to be peevish about her when she played the title role in Webster's *The Duchess of Malfi*, though there were many others who disagreed with him. During all this time she was still searching for her ideal and it wasn't until she found a home with the reconstituted Royal Shakespeare Company that she enriched our stages with her accumulated experience of life and the theatre and seemed to have reached her Xanadu.

Throughout her career she has been at pains to give as much as she takes from the enjoyment of her craft and that she is not always given the credit due to her stems from the fact that she is, like the actress she most admired, Dame Edith, a very 'private' person. She has never had any time for the vulgarities of theatrical publicity and because we live in an age where the medium is the message, reticence is often interpreted as dullness to those who set themselves up as the arbiters of public taste. A little knowledge is a dangerous thing in the hands of the gossip columnists and no knowledge at all disturbs the poor dears, for they like us to be neatly labelled. An artist of the calibre of Peggy Ashcroft cannot be labelled and because she has consciously set out to preserve a dignified silence about her private life she is often grossly overlooked while lesser talents make the headlines. With his usual perception Richard Findlater has also sensed this; he has written that 'at the heart of her mystery there is, it seems, as profound a simplicity and humility as any professional actress can afford and sustain'.

*   *   *   *

Beyond Sybil Thorndike, Edith Evans, Flora Robson and Peggy Ashcroft we can list many fine actresses who have kept alive the glories and eccentricities of our acting tradition from the nineteen thirties to the present day. Some, alas, once household names, are no longer with us or else are spending the twilight of their years in obscurity or, worse still, in obscurity *and* poverty. The fate of an actress who is past her prime is often more pitiful than that of her male colleagues in the same position. There are many reasons for this. Male roles have always been more plentiful and the magnet of a stage career attracts more women then men. Surveys have revealed that one in three actresses can expect to be out of work for six months of the year, and over half of them seldom earn more than £1,000 a year; a temporary typist can earn that amount within three months. Even when established the majority of actresses have to search for something worthy of their talents, for the number of major roles written for women in this century can be counted on two hands. We have seen how in the past, with women barred from the stage, this pattern came to be established. The small total of great classical roles that do exist demand a maturity and breadth of experience that is beyond the younger actress. Dramatists as a whole have done little to redress the balance in recent years: Osborne, to take one example, has not devoted his talents to a female role as powerful as that made famous by Nicol Williamson in *Inadmissible Evidence*. Pinter has produced a whole new dramatic form in which women play their enigmatic part, but again it is the men who come off best. The same can be said of the screenwriter in the film industry and although the occasional Glenda Jackson or Jane Fonda thunders through, it is the male superstars who flourish. Coward could write wonderfully eccentric women, or good roles for elegant women capable of delivering his clipped epigrams, but the Coward school of acting appeared to die with him and nobody has yet stepped into his breech. Only Enid Bagnold can be said to have consistently laboured on behalf of her own sex; from *Lottie Dundass*, through *The Chalk Garden* to her latest, *A Matter of Gravity*, written when she was well into her eighties. Christopher Fry, more or less in isolation, wrote *The Dark is Light Enough* for Edith Evans, but it has not become part of any subsequent repertoire. Emlyn Williams, that superb natural dramatist who understood his craft as well as anybody in this century, provided Miss Moffat in *The Corn is Green* for Sybil Thorndike, and this is a role that has attracted a number of leading ladies right up to the present day, for in 1979 Katharine Hepburn played her in Cukor's version filmed expressly for television. Williams could always write wonderful *character* roles for women and we have never lacked for character actresses. (Names such as Margaret Rutherford, Kathleen Harrison, Beryl Reid and Joyce Barbour immediately come to mind.) But we have never had a modern dramatist of the calibre of Tennessee Williams writing a series of major female roles in plays that must, eventually, prove the classical revivals of the next generation. It was, after all *A Streetcar Named Desire* that afforded Vivien Leigh her most challenging contemporary stage role, and it is a curious footnote to her career that her greatest triumphs came when she played Americans, either on stage or in the cinema. That in itself is an indictment of our home-grown dramatists, for at the time when Olivier and Vivien Leigh stood head and shoulders above the crowd, truly theatrical royalty, it seems incredible that dramatists did not fall over themselves to create complementary leading roles for such an illustrious pair. Only Rattigan, with his Coronation offering *The Sleeping Prince*, made the token gesture and this, we are reliably told, only came the way of the Oliviers by chance. For the rest the wife of our leading player, with a film career and international reputation that few could challenge, had to be content with foreign imports—*The Skin of Our Teeth*, Thornton Wilder's satire that failed to grip London audiences, two productions of Giraudoux' *Duel of Angels* and a motley assortment of translations from Feydeau, Deval and Maurice Druon. Given the eminence of the Oliviers such a situation would have been unthinkable at the turn of the century, if we compare their situation with the Ellen Terry-Irving partnership that filled the Lyceum for so many years. Admittedly Ellen Terry did not divide her time between the stage and the cinema as did Vivien Leigh, but there was never any shortage of dramatists willing to submit their offerings to her. Vivien Leigh was, in many ways, an under-estimated stage actress whose greatest disadvantage was her extraordinary beauty. She never lacked the courage to tackle roles that many felt were beyond her range, and inevitably she could not avoid the manufactured conflict inherent in a marriage to a man of Olivier's unique standing. Olivier was able to grasp Osborne's nettle, *The Entertainer*, but Vivien Leigh was never given the counter choice. And she was not alone; there were many fine actresses around in the forties and fifties who could have met any challenge a courageous dramatist cared to throw at them. But for the most part, while a new generation of young actors came charging through the class barriers, giving theatregoers a new breed of leading men, the actresses had to be content with second best. It was left to television to make new female stars and provide the roles that the theatre so shamefully avoided. Actresses cannot live by the classics alone, for many of the more enduring female roles provided by Shaw, Ibsen and Chekhov are not commercially viable outside the subsidised theatres. For a young actress of today a career such as Edith Evans and Peggy Ashcroft so painstakingly plotted for themselves is virtually an impossibility. There are few impresarios with real flair and courage or the necessary basic artistic judgement to delegate in those areas where they are pathetically bereft. Managements mostly lack the moral sense to put back into the commercial theatre what they take out; as a general rule everything is sacrificed for expediency and in a gold-rush to satisfy the tourist trade they ensure that mediocrity is given pride of place.

It is only in the subsidised theatres, notably The National, The Royal Shakespeare and the Young Vic that inexperienced talent can be brought forward at the proper pace, yet as a nation we exhibit a mean reluctance to pay for the preservation of our heritage. Penal taxation and the political philosophy of spite played out between the two major ruling parties have successfully stamped out patronage on the scale needed. I once made myself extremely unpopular as a guest speaker at the Conservative Party Conference by suggesting that we should establish a Ministry of Taste with Cabinet rank, deliberately seeking to over-state my argument in an effort to make one small point: namely, that whereas we can apparently afford to finance whole armies of civil servants and local authority worthies whose sole function is to ensure that the average citizen is allowed to live in dwellings that would appear to have been designed by a child in nursery school, any attempt to provide adequate funds for the Arts is met with anguished cries of Rape. In our decline as an industrial society the Arts could become one of our most valuable national assets for there are rich deposits everywhere waiting to be mined. Money, modest sums of money in comparison to the funds squandered on less pleasurable activities, could ensure that in the years ahead, when technology will create a vacuum of leisure for great masses of our population, our lives are enriched rather than further impoverished. It is curious that whereas thosands of millions of pounds can be provided overnight from the national purse to prop up an industry making obsolete motor cars that will in turn further erode the declining supply of mineral fuel, not one fraction of such sums can be extracted for the Arts without a protracted and anguished debate. Even if the vast amounts of money yearly being spent to advertise nationalised monopolies (i.e. the Postal Services, Gas and Electricity) could be diverted towards the Arts the difference in value would be incalculable. To urge people to use a service or a facility for which no alternative exists is so obviously an exercise in futility that anybody of normal intelligence must despair. Money spent on the Arts does not go to monopolies, but is used to give a choice of entertainment. The live theatre, and by that I include the literature of the theatre, is our most enduring artistic heritage, and it is from the living theatre that the talent is drawn to provide the entertainment demanded by the mass mediums of television and the cinema. By giving pittances successive governments have ensured that a snobbish exclusivity is perpetuated since it is inevitable that the major proportion of the funds available flows to London and is thus denied to the majority of the population. This very exclusivity, deliberately brought about, is then used as an argument against the provision of a larger allocation. The Arts should never be used as a political pawn by any society that boasts of being civilised. It is always argued that public money spent on the Arts must be carefully policed. We who go with the begging bowl are constantly asked, How will it be spent? You may lose it all, we are told, and we shall see no return. What will the balance sheet show at the end of the financial year? The unanswerable questions are put to us like tales told to an idiot. I have not observed that the same objections are put so forcibly to those who solicit public funds for the ultimate impoverishment of mankind. There is no great outcry when a £30,000,000 fighter plane spins to flaming destruction, or a government building costed at £4,000,000, eventually rockets to £40,000,000. It took us a hundred years to get a home on the South Bank, yet we could build three National Theatres for either of these items and have money to spare for a symphony orchestra or a modest-sized art gallery. We spend more money on National Health aspirins and sedatives in any one year than we do on the living arts, paying cheerfully for the removal of minor pains but loth to forke out for a modicum of pleasure.

The wonder of it is, therefore, that we still have an acting tradition to be proud of, for although the actor may be an irritant to society he has seldom been a burden on society. He has survived because he is determined to survive and is one of the least parasitic species that inhabit our land. The notional conception of the actor as a preening layabout forever crying that the world owes him a living is not, in my experience, justified. The true actor wants to act: i.e. he wants to work. He does not enjoy the inevitable periods of unemployment any more than the out-of-work docker, ship builder or miner, but whereas when the shipbuilders, dockers and miners are thrown on to the dole society rightly feels great concern, the plight of the unemployed actor passes with little or no comment—if anything he is the object of humour rather than pity. Why should this be so? It is because the average unknown actor has still not attained any real status, even after four centuries. When he is out of sight he is out of the public mind. During the protracted ITV strike of technicians in 1979 the actors thrown out of work were hardly consulted or indeed seldom mentioned.

As the war ended, England underwent a profound social revolution which continues in fits and starts to the present day. The social changes were reflected throughout the Arts as they were in all other areas of our society. A new breed of young actors emerged, some of whom returned home from the armed forces, many of them with regional accents and none of them conventional West End material. The re-emergence of the Old Vic, not in Waterloo Road but at the New Theatre in St Martin's Lane had triumphantly demonstrated that there was an audience avid to be shown the best. It would be difficult to over-value the contribution made to their fellows by Olivier, Richardson and John Burrell, for by their combined efforts they brought a feeling of excitement back to the theatre. Olivier had, of course, proved that Shakespeare was not the dull academic exampaper writer of the schoolroom; the world-wide success of his film of *Henry V*, made under extreme difficulties during the war, had created a new audience. It was a rare case of the cinema driving people back into the theatre. There were some who carped at *Henry V*'s blatant appeal to patriotism, forgetting that the spirit of the times demanded it and Olivier was satisfying a need. Then came the venture at the New Theatre, which not only introduced an actress of the calibre of Margaret Leighton to London, a new play by Priestley and four or five totally stunning theatrical experiences that have gone into the history books, but also gave a fillip to the entire, jaded West End scene. London was still pitted with bomb sites, rubble and dirt; rationing was still in force and the population defiantly shabby—victory as well as defeat has its sullen aspects for it is by definition an anti-climax; we had gone fifteen rounds to the last bell and the final round had been confusing. We were now in the atomic age, relieved to be alive but beginning to question the method that had proved our salvation. Everything was changing and yet nothing had changed. There was no sudden Red Sea opening and our Moses wore an austerity-quality pin-striped suit. The New Theatre was an oasis of hope, a glimpse of culture in the same old desert. Whether by instinct or by luck, Olivier and Richardson headed a company that gave us something sacred as well as profane; the theatre suddenly became something more than a place of entertainment, it became a temple again. Here was a gathering together of four hundred years of tradition, and the New seemed alive with distinguished ghosts. Here was Olivier conjuring up the spirits of Garrick and Kean—his *Richard III* walked hand in hand with past giants. Here was Richardson evoking the qualities we sensed that Burbage must have had; Tynan felt it for he wrote that Richardson as Peer Gynt suggested 'Bottom bewitched'. The very fact that *Peer Gynt* had been chosen as the opening play in the repertory meant that those in control had nailed their colours to the mast. This was not going to be the mixture as before. The company surrounding Richardson in the central role underlined the authority of the enterprise, for it included Sybil Thorndike, Joyce Redman, Vida Hope, George Relph, Michael Warre, Harcourt Williams (a nice gesture) and of course Margaret Leighton, with Olivier contenting himself with the small role of the Button Moulder. Eight days later he unveiled his historic *Richard III*.

Half a mile away in the Theatre Royal, Haymarket, Gielgud was preparing his own seasons, and thus by October 1944 our three greatest living actors were engaged in amiable competition and London had two repertory programmes to choose from. In addition to giving us a new and more mature reading of his *Hamlet*, Gielgud revived Maugham's *The Circle, The Duchess of Malfi, A Midsummer Night's Dream* and, most notably, Congreve's earthy *Love for Love*. It is worth quoting W. A. Darlington's evocation of that glorious period. Comparing the two seasons he makes the valid point that Gielgud's choice of Congreve's play 'belonged in spirit and in fact to the war-time and not the post-war theatre. The crowds who flocked to see it were not impelled by a sudden realization of Congreve's excellence as a writer, but by his bawdiness. Everybody in London, civilians as well as those members of the forces, women as well as men, had had in those days ... the experience of seeing war-clouds that had long hung directly overhead recede to the horizon. The general mood was that of troops on leave whose traditional need in the theatre is for a good laugh, the smuttier the better. It was astonishing, and uplifting to one's hopes, that so many of them could find fulfilment of this need at a highly literate comedy, no matter how brilliantly produced and acted. . . . The long run of *Love for Love* did certainly show that the post-war theatre would have a new public to cater for, and one of temper very different from that of the old. It did not give any evidence how serious that temper was likely to be.'

It is also worth noting that Gielgud was working within the *subsidised commercial* theatre, a curious anomaly brought about by a revolutionary concession of the Treasury whereby a play judged to be of sufficient artistic importance could be excused the onerous entertainment tax. The ever-shrewd Hugh Beaumont was quick to spot the advantages of this scheme, and formed a non-profit-making company which enabled a season such as Gielgud's to weather the economic risks that a semi-classic repertoire usually involved. It would be naive to suppose that Beaumont and his parent company, H. M. Tennent derived no indirect benefit from the Treasury largesse, but at the same time justice demands that he be given credit for using public money in such a creative fashion. It was open to anybody to follow his lead, but other commercial managements lacked his flair and the enormous influence he exercised over many of the leading players of the day.

If Gielgud aimed his season at the more conventional theatregoing public as W. A.

Darlington, without disapproval, suggests, then by his logic we must allow that Olivier, Richardson and Burrell judged with more daring. In the second and immediately post-war season at the New they introduced a memorable *Henry IV, Parts I and II* with Richardson giving us a Falstaff that transcended buffoonery; not the conventional sweaty fat man with the Cox's Orange Pippin cheeks and George Robey eyebrows, all belches and lewdness, but a dignified and often heartrendingly melancholy nobleman—a majestic figure, rotund with humanity. I choose Tynan, writing with precocious brilliance, to convey the spirit of that production. Describing the scenes in Shallow's orchard he painted them as having 'a golden autumnal veil. . . . There was a sharp scent of plucked crab-apples, and of pork in the larder: one got the sense of life-going-on-in-the-background, of rustling twigs underfoot and the large accusing eyes of cows, staring through the twilight'. In depicting Olivier's Shallow he caught the performance with the exactness of Cartier Bresson—'a crapulous, paltering scarecrow of a man, withered up like the slough of a snake' who nibbled at his lines 'as a parrot biting on a nut'.

I compare Olivier and Richardson to figures in a Swiss clock, circling to our delight; as Richardson's Falstaff disappeared Olivier's *Oedipus Rex* swung into view, and behind that came, as if by sleight of hand, Mr Puff from Sheridan's *The Critic*. We became gluttons for excellence, and those of us fortunate to be present during those performances when the double bill of *Oedipus* and Sheridan was given were numbed by the experience. It was an amazing *tour de force* from Olivier, like going to an arena where the matador first demonstrates the awesome ballet of death in the afternoon, and immediately follows this with a knockabout comedy routine. It must be added that the combination dismayed some, mortally offended others, but gave the majority, myself among them, unalloyed pleasure.

It was during these two momentous seasons that Beatrix Lehmann, an actress of no mean distinction, said to a friend, 'Don't you feel as if the *great* days have come again?' The profession as a whole felt that the cause had been advanced; particles of the glory rubbed off on the humblest player; acting of this order engenders a collective pride and in some curious way, unexplainable to the general public, spurs new hopes in us all.

There is one name, one actor contemporary with Olivier, Gielgud, Richardson and Redgrave, who missed greatness as it is generally understood yet did as much as anybody in this century to carry Shakespeare to the far corners of this island. That actor was the late Sir Donald Wolfit. In his time he was often under-estimated, for he was not always *of* his time, being more of a throw-back to the age of Kean. Perhaps he was his own worst enemy, a man difficult to advise, for he had a personal vision that left little room for outsiders. In real life he was warm and often funny, with an earthy sense of humour strangely at variance with the image he presented to those who only knew him from across the footlights. He had a real actor's face; a piece of worked clay in a sculptor's studio that had been well-thumbed but left unfinished, the features coarse but human, very human. He always reminded me of a figure by Blake and in a sense his whole life, which was never easy, was a pilgrimage. Always operating on slender resources, proud of his independence, he made repeated tours throughout England consumed with a passion for Shakespeare. In the end he outlived his critics, demanding respect through selfless dedication. Although he was often the target for ill-informed and inaccurate gossip, he passed the acid test time and time again: his colleagues knew his real worth. Those who understood acting did not mock.

Olivier, for instance, had this to say: 'At the time when I first began to think about *Richard III*, I didn't want to play the part at all. Donald Wolfit had made an enormous success in the role only eighteen months previously. I had seen him and when I was learning it I could hear nothing but Donald's voice in my mind's ear, and see nothing but him in my mind's eye. And I thought, "This won't do, I've just got to think of something else." And it was the childishly approached differences, really, that started me on a characterisation that, without comparing it with Donald's at all, at least made it different. I think any actor would understand this desire on my part not to look the same as another actor. Now this can get you very wrong sometimes, and land you in very hot water indeed; at other times it may land you on to a nice fertile beach. First of all, I had heard imitations of old actors imitating Irving; and so I did, right away, an imitation of these old actors imitating Irving's voice—that's why I took a rather narrow kind of vocal address. Then I thought about looks. And I thought about the Big Bad Wolf, and I thought about Jed Harris, a director under whom I had suffered in extremis in New York. The physiognomy of Disney's original Big Bad Wolf was said to have been founded upon Jed Harris—hence the nose, which originally was very much bigger than it was finally in the film. And so, with one or two extraneous externals, I began to build up a character, a characterization. I may be quite wrong, but I fancy I possibly filled it out, possibly enriched it a bit with a little more humour than a lot of other people had done . . . I'd been on the stage for twenty years. I'd just finished making *Henry V* and, I don't know how or why, I just went into it with the same distrust of the critics, the same fear of public opinion as I had always experienced. I went on to the stage frightened, heart beating; came on, locked the door behind me, approached the footlights and started. I was just, once more, going to 'have a bash' as we say. One had Hitler over the way, one was playing it definitely as a paranoiac, so that there was a core of something to which audiences could respond. . . . I just simply went through it. I only know that I read a few notices, stayed up till three and drank a little bit too much. My next performance was the matinee the following day, for which I was all too ill-prepared. But there was something in the atmosphere. There is a phrase—'the sweet smell of success'—and I can only tell you I've had experiences of that: it smells just like Brighton and oyster bars and things like that. I felt for the first time that the critics had approved, that the public had approved, and they created a kind of grapevine, and that particular audience had felt impelled to come and see me.'

About this time Tynan was saying of Wolfit that his basic error lay 'in cherishing what I can only describe as a provincial inferiority complex to the extent of being unable or unwilling to work for anyone but himself. If he can overcome that, the West End will acquire an actor of greater technical power than it currently possesses; but there is not much time left'.

Ernest Milton felt that Wolfit's *Hamlet* was memorable, 'heroic in physique, which one doesn't associate with Hamlet, forgetting that after all the first Hamlet, the man who

DONALD WOLFIT as King Lear, 1942

created it, Burbage, was likewise heroic in physique'.

This gives us the chain, the elusive tradition—Olivier seeking to avoid comparison with a contemporary he admired, but borrowing a little from further back, from Irving; Ernest Milton reminding us that Wolfit, in his turn, reached further back still to assume some affinity with Burbage. Acting on this scale is like a message passed from cell to cell in a prison where the inmates never glimpse each other but share a common bond. Because of course all actors ultimately work in isolation; no matter what help they may receive in rehearsal, be it from their director or a colleague living or dead, the actual performance is a lonely walk to the scaffold. Wolfit isolated himself more than most and he did so by choice, in my opinion to the detriment of his career and his undoubted talents. He was a Tudor with a gargantuan appetite for the great roles, thundering down on them, vizor open, lance lowered for the killing tilt. He took on all-comers: Lear, Macbeth, Hamlet, Shylock, Volpone, Benedick, Bottom, Malvolio, Touchstone and Falstaff. It was fashionable, but false, to label him 'ham' because in this century naked emotion embarrasses many people. Donald Sinden, another admirer, called him 'the voice of God in Job. With his *Lear*, when he cursed Goneril, one trembled. I trembled in the theatre. I was petrified what was going to happen, because he certainly had influence with the gods. He really had an influence up there, and I thought: there will be a flash of smoke and Goneril will disappear. Astonishing. I'd never believed an actor could be that big'.

Wolfit himself acknowledged his own debts: 'Anything I've ever done as Lear I learned in the first place from Randle Ayrton. He did two wonderful things for me. On my first night of *Hamlet* he came into my dressing room with that terrible, sour-vinegar face which could break into the most enchanting smile and said, "Give'em a bit of the old!" It was the most wonderful feeling that this man, who had been such a great tradition at Stratford should do that for an up and coming young actor who was making his first attempt in the part of Hamlet.'

Ernest Milton, who admired Wolfit, was not somebody who scattered praise indiscriminately, nor was he remotely like Wolfit in temperament or personality. A genuine eccentric, capable of giving the most extraordinary readings in a voice that defied imitation. One of the most endearing of theatrical anecdotes is told of Milton when he was appearing in a small London fringe theatre. On the first night, just after the half had been called, a distraught stage manager knocked at his door and broke the news that the juvenile lead had been arrested. Since the play had not yet opened, the understudy was ill-prepared to take over on the very first night. Mr Milton did not succumb to panic. On the contrary he continued applying his make-up with calm, sure strokes. The stage manager repeated his dire news. 'I don't think you understand, Mr Milton', he said. 'The juvenile lead will not appear tonight. He has been arrested and is in custody. The understudy is quite incapable of taking over. We can't take the curtain up, Mr Milton. We can't open.' Ernest studied his own face in the dressing room mirror and finessed his eye-shadow. Then he spoke for the first time. 'Go bid his cap-tors release him', he said, in a voice made for parody.

Milton was one of a long line of English eccentrics. I can think of others: Ernest Thesiger, who used to sit and do needlepoint with old Queen Mary and almost grew to look like her; Nancy Price, who started the People's Theatre and was inseparable from her parrot. Then there was the tragic Hazel Terry, who once set light to herself in Gielgud's production of *The Winter's Tale* at the Phoenix. She was extinguished by the late John Whiting and Norman Bird, who were both playing small roles at the time. When Gielgud came down to the stage for his next entrance, he remarked: 'I hear cousin Hazel caught fire. The Terrys have always been combustible', before stepping out from the wings to resume playing Leontes. Again, one remembers Martita Hunt, wonderfully talented in the right role (as in *The Madwoman of Chaillot*) who provided her own funeral pyre by igniting herself with a cigarette in bed. Robert Newton, Alastair Sim. A. E. Matthews, Esme Percy, Jack Minster, Alfred Drayton, Ronnie Squire, Harold Scott—all characters capable of brightening the dullest company and who are still remembered whenever actors swop anecdotes. But pride of place in my own hall of eccentrics must go to Wilfrid Lawson with whom I worked on several occasions, both as fellow actor and as his director. He had the reputation of being a notable drunk who survived on a diet of alcohol and eel pies. Perhaps best remembered now for his Doolittle in the film of *Pygmalion*, he was, by any standards, an extraordinary actor. Olivier once told me that Lawson could have been one of the greatest actors of this century, and certainly anybody who saw his performance in *The Father* would not dispute this claim. To the best of my knowledge his last appearance was in a film I directed called *The Wrong Box*. He was a dying man when the film started but we all nursed him through it, and I recall that Sir Ralph Richardson behaved towards him with a courtesy and gentleness that was most touching to observe. 'Willie', as he was always affectionately called, gave readings of individual lines in a language that only he spoke; the director could only roll the camera and wait for the unexpected, and the unexpected was usually, in my experience, pure gold. His characterisation of the aged butler in *The Wrong Box* was a not unfitting swan song, and in America at least, it became a cult performance. Strangers still stop me in the streets of New York and ask, 'Who was the old guy who played the butler in your film?' The name Wilfrid Lawson, when I give it, means little to them, but there on the pavement they smile with remembered pleasure, as I do, for I had the privilege of knowing him.

⟦ 22 ⟧

THE NEW ELIZABETHANS

NOW we approach the new Elizabethan age of acting, first typified by Sir Alec Guinness, who at one time appeared to be heir apparent to at least two thrones. I use the word 'typified' because he was the first major actor to desert his classical origins for the more immediate rewards of international fame as a film star. It was a path followed by several of our most talented younger actors—notably Richard Burton, Peter O'Toole, Albert Finney, Anthony Hopkins and John Neville. Only Paul Scofield seems content to adopt a take-it-or-leave-it attitude towards the enticements of Hollywood and this despite the fact that he received the Academy Award for his film recreation of Sir Thomas More in Bolt's *A Man For All Seasons*.

One must quickly add that Guinness is a consummate film actor, able to take his performances down to the more exacting requirements of that difficult medium. He served

ALEC GUINNESS as the Fool in *King Lear*, New Theatre, 1946

In *The Prisoner*, ALEC GUINNESS with WILFRID LAWSON, Globe Theatre, 1954 his stage apprenticeship in what Findlater has tellingly dubbed 'the extraordinary theatrical forcing-house' of the 1930s, and survived being summarily fired from the Old Vic's production of *The Country Wife* at the instigation of the American actress Ruth Gordon. He went on to carve out a career which always contained evidence of greatness, and by the time he was twenty-four he was back at the Old Vic and playing Hamlet in a modern dress production which aroused much controversy. If Olivier paints in oil on the scale of Goya, and if Gielgud gives us the pastel water-colours of Turner, then Guinness is a master miniaturist. His first film performance in David Lean's *Great Expectations* was a revelation, for he seemed immediately at home, as though everything else had been a preparation for this debut. Once he had followed *Great Expectations* with his Fagin in *Oliver Twist* for the same director there was no escaping his celluloid destiny. His name became synonymous with the halcyon days of Ealing Studios; there it seemed as though Sir Michael Balcon's family of writers, directors and designers had found their prodigal son. Guinness is at his happiest when portraying self-effacing men who conceal base thoughts beneath the chameleon mask, and this was never better demonstrated than in the classic *The Lavender Hill Mob* in which he was teamed with Stanley Holloway.

We should have detected this quality earlier, of course, for his Fool to Olivier's *Lear* in the 1946–47 Old Vic season at the New was painted with the same brush. He likes nothing better than to hide his own personality within men who also have something to hide; men tortured with self-doubt, men searching for some Holy Grail—these he does to perfection, suggesting the torment with the minimum of histrionics. Without in any way regretting the contributions he has made to the cinema, one cannot help bemoaning the loss to the stage. He was never at home with the orthodox Shakespearean traditions, but in contemporary plays such as Bridget Boland's *The Prisoner, Ross* and *The Cocktail Party* his unique qualities were never less than impressive. His acting always reminded me of an autumn fire: it seems inert and then suddenly there is a sharp, brief flame; it burns fiercely and then dies away again, the heart of the fire hidden beneath the gathered leaves. His Colonel in *The Bridge on the River Kwai* contained the pure essence of his acting style: a kind of mania smouldering, bordering on the comic, but always kept under control. His critics complain that he is over-wary in the theatre, that he never 'lets himself go', that his understatement has become an irritating vice. This seems to me particularly arid criticism, for it implies that there can only be one style of acting that merits the superlatives. It is true that for some time now he has forsaken Shakespeare and the great classical roles and this is what is complained of, more in sorrow than in scorn. Within his self-imposed limits he is unsurpassed; an actor who has staked his claim in an anti-heroic way if, in the terms of reference used throughout this book, heroic acting is used to describe the greatest of our players, but nevertheless a career forged with integrity and intelligence.

Integrity is also a word that comes naturally when writing of Paul Scofield's career. I have attempted throughout this book to conceal my prejudices about individual players and to remain reasonably objective about my personal favourites. But as we approach the actors of my own generation, colleagues I grew up with and sometimes worked with, such impartiality as I have so far maintained becomes increasingly difficult. I said at the

PAUL SCOFIELD as Hamlet, Stratford-on-Avon, 1948 *Right* In *A Man For All Seasons* as
Sir Thomas More, Globe Theatre, 1960

very beginning of this book that I am not a professional historian and therefore my objectivity must, on occasion, become corrupted by personal experience. I will try and keep my enthusiasms within decent bounds and not over-state my case, but I must readily confess that Paul Scofield seems to me the most consistently brilliant actor of my generation who, if justice prevails, and his good health continues, should in time rightfully stand as the leader of the English stage. When we examine his entire career to date we see how slowly and methodically he attacked the West Face of his particular Everest; in the beginning an unspectacular ascent, but always making progress, securing each foothold before moving further up, securely roped to his ideals.

Base camp was the London Mask Theatre School, and he made his first stage appearance at the Theatre Royal Brighton in 1936 while still studying. His professional debut took place four years later at the Westminster Theatre in *Desire Under The Elms*. He was in repertory at Bideford when the war came, then joined an E.N.S.A. company for a tour of *The Taming of the Shrew*. His basic training was done with the Birmingham Repertory Theatre before being invited to become a member of the Shakespeare

PAUL SCOFIELD as King Lear Statford-on-Avon and Aldwych, 1962

Opposite RICHARD BURTON (*right*) and HARRY ANDREWS as the dying King in *Henry IV*, Part 2, Statford-on-Avon, 1951

Memorial Theatre for the 1946–47 seasons. There was no sudden rush to the glory of stardom; he did not plant that flag on the West End summit until he appeared in Rattigan's *Adventure Story* in 1949 and by then he was a veteran of some ten years, who had already given us his first and compelling *Hamlet* at Stratford in the previous year.

He is the least known of all our younger leading actors and has succeeded where others have notably failed in keeping his private life private. Such reticence in a public figure has been known to spur Grub Street to frenzied bouts of conjecture, but his sincere dislike of publicity and his determination to remove himself from all such temptations has so far thwarted most attempts to penetrate his lair. As and when he is judged he insists on being judged by his work and not by his views on marriage, women's liberation, politics, disco dancing, abortion, the cost of dog licences or any other subjects which constitute the basis for instant wisdom in the popular Press. Instead he saves his intellectual strength for his carefully spaced appearances on our stages. With his grief-frozen face he sometimes seems to have stepped from the pages of a Graham Greene novel and I believe it was not by accident that one of his greatest performances was as the tortured whisky-priest in Denis Cannan's adaptation of Greene's *The Power and The Glory* which Peter Brook directed. He has an affinity with men of conscience, an ability to convey the endless patience that such men possess, what Sir Harold Hobson once described as 'a deep, though sometimes masked, distress'. The most individual of actors, his deliberately

flattened delivery grates on some people, and he has been called monotonous. I do not find him so. His voice never fails to excite me, and I know it to be an instrument capable of a wide variety of tones. If we take two of his performances, Sir Thomas More in *A Man For All Seasons* and his beautifully judged homosexual hairdresser in *Staircase*, it would be patently absurd to contend that he used the same notes in both. Or again, if we take his superb King Lear in 1962 and contrast this with the extrovert, quick-talking character he portrayed in John Osborne's *The Hotel in Amsterdam*, we are looking at an actor who has infinite range. Yes, he is enigmatic, both in real life and in many of the characters he presents to us on stage; yes, we are kept at a distance, as I believe we should be, for that is part of the true actor's mystique. In Scofield's case it is not affectation, but a matter of necessity, a question of survival deliberately planned and deliberately executed. I know him to be a most articulate and amusing companion when he is relaxed and amongst friends, but he does not socialize easily. He is a man who feels deeply about those causes closest to him and who reserves his energies to fight for them, excluding all extraneous matter. He is an actor first and last and has shown no ambition to become a director or go into management. My respect for him is not to the exclusion of all others, for my generation produced at least half a dozen potential contenders for the crown, but it has been Scofield's singleminded quest that has set him apart. Others with equal or superior talents have squandered them carelessly, allowing themselves to be diverted and

275

exploited. Scofield has chosen his roles and his directors carefully and much of his best work has been done for either Peter Brook or Sir Peter Hall. He is not a trendy actor given to sudden bursts of experiment, nor does he subscribe to the school of total naturalism, but for all his remoteness from the changing contemporary scene he remains consistently in touch with modern audiences. Perhaps they have more perception than they are generally given credit for and recognise in Scofield a talent that does not trade on tricks or surprises, but moves steadily forward in a straight line. He has not burdened his life with extraneous preoccupations and audiences sense this; they sense they are getting their full money's worth, the whole man.

Scofield's comparatively few screen performances have followed the same pattern. He is on record as saying that he would like to work more often in films, but needs to feel complete confidence in his director. Outside the theatre his preference is for radio drama. I find that in arriving at my own conclusions as to his past and his future, I am as one with that wise elder statesman of criticism, W. A. Darlington. Darlington paired Scofield with Irving, stating that in both men 'there is a force which transcends argument. When he plays Shakespeare, however oddly, Shakespeare is there to meet him'. Scofield has not arrived at this point in his career from a psychological approach to his art, but from an intuitive understanding of what makes an actor what he is. He has demonstrated time and time again that he is not prepared to worship false gods, preferring the lonelier search for self-dependence. His detachment from the mainstreams of our theatrical life has sometimes provoked inaccurate criticism of his motives. His overriding motive has been to discover a purity of method and a purity of performance, and it is my belief that his total dedication merits the sparing use of the word 'greatness'.

*   *   *   *

There are some actors, and I am not sure whether they are blessed or damned, who appear perfectly equipped for eventual greatness the very first time they step on to a stage. Such an actor is Richard Burton who, with all the insolent aplomb and physical agility of a Welsh forward, arrived on the English touchline and plonked the ball down for a try before the natives were aware that the game had started.

In many ways his early life mirrored Emlyn Williams' fictional Morgan Evans, the central figure in his celebrated play *The Corn is Green*. Burton was the twelfth of thirteen children. He was christened Richard Jenkins, and took his stage name from the first of two surrogate fathers, a perceptive schoolteacher named Philip Burton who befriended and shaped his life during the all-important formative years. His real father bequeathed Burton 'a love for beer. He was a man of extraordinary eloquence, tremendous passion, great violence'. Burton might have added that he also inherited a quick, poetic intelligence, so characteristic of his fellow-countrymen; and with that rich dark seam of Welsh romanticism running through his veins he was obviously destined to follow either Dylan Thomas or Edmund Kean. He chose acting after (like Williams' hero) going to Oxford and serving in the R.A.F. and ever since has spoken poetry instead of writing it, though he has shown evidence that he is fully capable of turning to a literary career if he so chooses.

Emlyn Williams proved to be the second father figure in his life and cast him as a young boy in *The Druid's Rest* at the Royal Court Theatre in Liverpool in November 1943, a performance which he subsequently repeated when the play came to the St Martin's the following January. Service in the R.A.F. interrupted further progress until 1947, but the moment he was demobilised he was taken under the wing of a remarkable lady who befriended many of us at the start of our careers. This was Daphne Rye, the then casting director for H.M. Tennent, who deserves more credit than she has been accorded for nurturing a score of young players. She had a very keen eye for potential talent and was indefatigable in her search for new faces, travelling extensively to every repertory theatre in the country and always willing to fight for unknowns if she believed in them. Many of us have reason to be grateful to her for she not only brought us to London but even acted as landlady to a chosen few who, she felt, should not be allowed to roam homeless in the streets. Richard Burton and I were two of 'Daphne's lodgers' at the start of our careers and we shared many of the vicissitudes that came our way in the theatreland of the late 1940s and early 1950s. Burton appeared in three of Christopher Fry's plays in succession — *The Lady's Not For Burning, The Boy With A Cart* and *A Phoenix Too Frequent*, while I was lucky enough to appear with Gertrude Lawrence in her last appearance in this country (Daphne du Maurier's *September Tide*) and Wynyard Browne's haunting *The Holly and the Ivy*, in which Herbert Lomas gave such a memorable performance. From the very beginning Burton gave notice that he was, in Tynan's words, soon to turn 'interested speculation to awe'. He seemed to me, and I observed him at close quarters, to be brimming over with talent and enthusiasm, a contemporary one could admire without reservation or professional jealousy. This quality of excitement that he generated on and off stage, allied to the right proportion of luck, Daphne Rye's motherly concern for her brood and the fact that he got the right roles and the right directors at the right time, ensured that his career roared away.

By 1951, writing of his performance as Prince Hal in *Henry IV, Part One* at Stratford (to which he had quickly progressed) Tynan had this to say: 'Burton is a still, brimming pool, running disturbingly deep; at twenty-five he commands repose and can make silence garrulous. . . . If he can sustain and vary this performance through to the end of *Henry V*, we can safely send him along to swell the thin company of living actors who have shown us the mystery and the power of which heroes are capable.'

When eventually he did play *Henry V* at Stratford that austere but reliable critic T. C. Worsley made the prediction that 'if he works at his art long and humbly, he has every chance of becoming a great actor by the age of forty. But he risks at the same time losing that very naturalness which makes for his present success. And the Tempters beckon alluringly; Hollywood and Ealing, I have no doubt, will offer him fabulous rewards to stay just as he is; they will willingly exploit his personality, on the single condition that he doesn't develop it. The question for him, of course, is how long a lease of life this youthful sulky Welsh charmer has. Success in the twenties may be purchased at too high a price if it means being thrown on the dust heap at forty'. Although, happily, the last part of Worsley's fortune-telling did not come true, it is a surprisingly accurate piece of crystal gazing. The Tempters did make an early appearance in Burton's career — first Korda, then

Hollywood in the shape of Twentieth Century Fox who signed him to the then untold wealth of $50,000 a film and starred him in *My Cousin Rachel* opposite Olivia de Havilland. He enjoyed Hollywood and for a period Hollywood enjoyed him, he was dubbed 'a born male coquette' and went from strength to strength, securing the plum role in the first CinemaScope film *The Robe*, based on Lloyd C. Douglas' turgid Biblical best seller. He was nominated for his first and second Academy Awards and over the years has added several more, though so far failing to get an actual Oscar. As with Olivier and Redgrave before him he was given the standard publicity treatment: the studios smelt success and were anxious to exploit it to the hilt. He was offered double his initial salary to stay tied to a ten year contract after he had completed *The Desert Rats*, but by then he was tired of burning the Hollywood candle at both ends and returned to the Old Vic for the 1954 season at a fraction of his film salary but with the carrots of *Hamlet, King John, Coriolanus* and *The Tempest*. At that time he seemed to stand unchallenged; fame and certainly riches were within his natural orbit and more than any other young actor of this century he combined great natural talent with a physical presence that audiences admired and flocked to.

That perceptive lover of the theatre Ronald Bryden once wrote 'no one who saw Burton at Stratford-upon-Avon and the Old Vic in the early fifties can have much doubt that here was . . . the next wearer of the mantle of Edmund Kean. He was the Prince Hal and Hamlet of his generation and should have gone on to become its Macbeth, Oedipus and Othello—Macbeth is the part he was born for, I suspect'. But Burton chose a different destiny, believing, publicly stating, that 'the fundamental basis of being an actor is not the desire to be the curate's son, but simply to make money. . . . I do it because I rather like being famous, I rather like being given the best seat on the plane, the best seat in the restaurant, the best food in that particular restaurant'. He followed no trends for such an alleged trendy figure; he refused to be disciplined and had nothing but contempt for that most-idolized of twentieth century dramatists, Brecht. Yet, perversely, he clung to the conviction that the theatre is essentially a writer's theatre (no one has ever accused him of lacking in respect for language) and that the majority of theatre directors are 'jumped-up stage managers'. Surprisingly, he at one time felt (and may still do for all we know) that he cannot act with girls in the traditional romantic sense. 'I think I'm recognised as a sort of sexual actor in some senses of the word, but Romeo, for instance, I've never played; it's beyond my capacity. Because the urge, the acting urge to kiss somebody on the stage, is beyond me, I can't do it, I can't bear to be touched, physically touched on the stage or on the screen; it has to be very carefully arranged. And I very rarely allow myself to touch other people, physically touch them I mean.'

These are odd and unconventional admissions from an actor who in many people's minds epitomizes the romantic lover. He counts his Ferdinand in *The Tempest* as his greatest failure for just this reason, applying the same ruthless candour to himself that he sometimes unleashes on others. 'It's an unplayable role. If you happen to be rather shortish as I am, tottering about, with nothing to say of any real moment, bloodless, liverless, kidneyless, a useless member of the human race—well, I found myself incapable of playing such a role.' This facility for self-analysis, which has the ring of truth about it rather than something invented for the sake of being contentious, is something he applied to all aspects of his art. He felt that because he was the son of a Welsh miner people would expect him to be at his happiest playing peasants, people of the earth; 'but in actual fact I'm much happier playing princes and kings. Now whether this is a kind of sublimation of what I would like to be, or something like that, I don't know, but certainly I'm never really very comfortable playing people from the working class'.

Regarding the demands made on a leading actor he had this to say: 'I think that particular loneliness, solitude, the idea of carrying your own private room, is not unique to actors; though all actors have it. I have it perhaps, or sometimes have it, a little more than most. When I get out there on the stage I'm battling the world, I have to be the best as far as I can. . . . I have to have a lot of space on the stage, a lot of space that I can move about in, without being bothered by too many people.' There are distinct echoes of Edmund Kean in this and a kind of fatalism that crops up again and again in his recorded theories about the craft of acting as it applies to his own personality. 'I think the only kind of interesting parts to play are defeated men. That's why the great tragedies are so attractive to actors. One must always play a defeated man. The hero, the one who succeeds, is always faintly boring. Hamlet is a defeated man, Macbeth is a defeated man, Lear is a defeated man, they're all defeated men. Othello is, Iago is; Antony fascinated me for that particular reason.'

Mention of Antony draws us closer to that watershed in his life when his entire career changed direction for a second time. When Olivier's crown and Gielgud's orb were his for the claiming he embarked upon a period of self-destruction, or so it seemed to most. Everything he touched grew stale, flat, but not necessarily unprofitable in a material sense. By nature a heretic, he became the great absentee from the theatre. His return to Hollywood brought only a series of average or undistinguished films which made little or no impact on public or critics. To Ronald Bryden this renunciation was 'as painful as watching a tennis champion grow competent at pingpong, an organist of genius work wonders with a concertina'. His decision distressed his friends and dismayed his admirers, for the waste of talent was so patently obvious. He had the honesty to admit that he was doing what he was doing for the money and that he derived little artistic pleasure from his acts. Occasionally, as in the film version of *Look Back in Anger*, his material was worthy of him—too worthy, perhaps, for the mass audience conditioned to shadow rather than substance—and he was able to dredge his authority back to the surface. He tasted the backlash that is invariably handed out to those who have been lavishly praised too early, and doubtless it was as bitter and rank for him as for others. Never missing an opportunity to stab yesterday's heroes in the back, Hollywood's publicity machine went into reverse; the once-golden-boy became a shared target for all the character assassins. Then his luck turned again. Lerner and Loewe selected him to play King Arthur in *Camelot* on Broadway opposite Julie Andrews and although, inexplicably, the score and the book came in for savage handling, Burton, 'rediscovered' by those who a few months previously had been writing him off as a has-been, made an enormous personal triumph. Before the run of the play ended he had many offers to choose from. The one he accepted was the role of Mark Antony in the would-be epic production of *Cleopatra* with Elizabeth Taylor in the title part. Twentieth Century Fox paid $50,000 to obtain his early release from *Camelot*, the first down payment on a film that was destined to bring the studios to its knees. It was a long-drawn-out experience that changed the lives of many of the people connected with it and has been the subject of a dozen or more books, mostly written like post-mortem reports and vastly more entertaining than the film itself. Burton's emotional involvement with Elizabeth Taylor was to wreck his marriage to Sybil Burton and relaunch him on a free-spending, headline-making voyage with his new superstar wife. Their subsequent life together, their films, their first divorce and subsequent remarriage, followed by a second divorce, has been detailed in the world's Press with all the thoroughness of a KGB dossier re-written by a sub-editor of *Private Eye*, and I do not propose to add to the mountain of literary dross that already exists on the subject. What does concern me in this account is how Burton's progress as an artist was affected by this episode in his life. It merits attention because his talents are sufficiently unique to inspire regret that events conspired to remove him from what is thought to be his rightful place in the living theatre. In the deliberately manufactured hysteria that attended his every movement during the time he was married to Elizabeth, over-reaction was the order of the day. As Burton himself said, 'You'd think we were out to destroy Western civilization or something'. Certainly few actors throughout the centuries have acquired such instant notoriety, or been feasted upon by more leeches. Alongside this we had the spectacle of an actor of classic stature forcing T. C. Worsley's prophecy to come true: to those closest to Burton it was like watching a friend court artistic anorexia. That he survived at all was a tribute not only to his physical stamina, but also to his basic intelligence. He did survive as an actor and in recent years has set about an artistic rehabilitation. He gave a compelling *Hamlet* in New York in 1964, which unfortunately was not exported to these shores; later he took a brave decision to attempt a modern role which had already been played with great distinction by several other actors—the psychiatrist in Peter Shaffer's *Equus*. It is a long and demanding role, one that needs a deliberate balance; a strange mixture in fact, part Chorus, part the stage-manager (as in Thornton Wilder's *Our Town*) and part leading man. Burton triumphed in it, exercising his old powers of mesmeric charm but sublimating some of the tricks he had, from personal necessity, acquired during his days in the wilderness. Anybody who cares for the theatre must share the hope that these few portents will one day result in his return home to either the National or the Royal Shakespeare, for there is still time, and the need, 'to swell the thin company of living actors who have shown us the mystery and power of which heroes are capable'.

*   *   *   *

We, who have always had such a rich store of talent to draw upon, have sometimes failed to observe how quickly the seed corn disappears. We are so careless of our heritage, so confident that the future will take care of itself, so indoctrinated to the philosophy that the State will provide everything from the cradle to the grave without any effort on our own part, so brain-washed by the media to the belief that anything that is not commonly shared is a waste of time, that we have become indifferent to standards of quality. Private patronage having been taxed out of existence we have turned, instead, to the tyranny of the committee, that slow-moving complacent dinosaur which wears the mask of sympathy to conceal its basic stupidity. The wonder of it is that we have any Art left at all and the fact that there are still pockets of resistance is due more to the resilience of the artist rather than the efforts of those who pay lip-service to the task of conserving what is left.

Beyond Richard Burton there have been other defectors, some who absented themselves by choice, others who left because of indifference, lack of opportunity, our tax laws or general disenchantment. Star actors alone do not ensure a healthy theatre; what they do provide is a focal point around which can be built a chain of excellence. When that chain is weakened the continuity of excellence falters. The great actor dares more, attempts more, fails more spectacularly, soars when he succeeds and at all times adds the adrenalin of controversy without which no art form can survive. Audiences, do not flock to a theatre, any more than football fans flock to Wembley, to be lulled by a goal-less draw. They want excitement, the opportunity to applaud, a chance to worship heroes and to be spectators of something that is outside their normal ken. In a word, they want blood. Ensemble playing is the purist's ideal, a great dovetailing of equal talents, but great art is seldom a collaboration; it is the product of the individual vision, the interpretation of the soloist, the renegade. Human nature always makes a physical choice, mental appreciation comes later, for the great majority of us feel before we think. The star actor ensures the continuity of his art just as sexual attraction ensures the perpetuation of the human race. He canalizes the playwright's view of life into tangible and immediately recognizable human form, constantly seeking new meanings to familiar words and, if he has genius, transforming them. Those who decry the star system ignore the basic human need for heroes, since the first function of any art form is to lift us beyond the ordinary tribulations of everyday existence for a few brief hours and give us a glimpse of immortality. To state otherwise is as banal as the belief, often voiced, that any child can produce a Picasso drawing. Star actors, like great painters, do not follow, they lead; by proximity to their genius others are encouraged to dare more and in turn germinate the seed for the next generation.

Let us take the case of John Neville, that most elegant and wonderfully versatile actor, who in recent years has no longer graced our stages, having forged a new career abroad. Penelope Gilliatt once described him as 'a handsome evacuee' and events have since proved her to be uncannily accurate. His training for the stage took a conventional route—the Royal Academy of Dramatic Art, walk-ons at the Old Vic, a season in Regent's Park with Robert Atkins' company, weekly repertory in a provincial backwater, then to Birmingham and eventually to the Bristol Old Vic. He said of his days at R.A.D.A., 'There was nothing that they could do with me; I came in with the first wave of ex-Servicemen, which blew a wave of fresh air through the building; it badly needed it at that time. I was one of many, and I didn't shine.' After modest success in Bristol he progressed from the junior branch to the London Old Vic, in all spending ten years as an actor in permanent companies and was thus shielded from many of the compromises that a purely freelance actor has to embrace. He has gone on record that the biggest influence in his career was the director Michael Benthall who took over the running of the Old Vic at the moment when Neville's talents began to open out and who undoubtedly rescued the Vic from what would have been oblivion. Benthall's salvage operation was a bold one; he announced his intention of producing all of Shakespeare's plays over a five year period. Neville was an invaluable member of that company during the whole campaign, playing twenty-two different Shakespearean roles, ending with what became known as 'Hamlet-in-jeans'. ('When Benthall said, "You've gone right through the whole thing, I think your apotheosis ought to be Hamlet—how do you see it?" I said, "I'd like to be in a pair of jeans and a white shirt." I'd been through a lot of plays in those six years, and I'd been inflicted with a number of designers who were trying to rule the theatre at that time; it was a sort of natural reaction. Anyway, that was how we did it. . . . I started off with a black hussar's jacket; that came off very soon, and I was in a white shirt and tight black trousers nearly all the rest of the play.')

During the 1956 season Neville and Richard Burton experimented with a variation of the earlier Gielgud-Olivier partnership; they alternated the roles of Othello and Iago with only six weeks to rehearse the play both ways round. 'What made it even more difficult', Neville recalled, 'is that we had one first night, and we did it the other way round the very next night. Initially, we rehearsed it quite separately, so that we both got our ways of doing each character quite clearly defined. I was particularly fortunate in that we rehearsed it with me playing Iago first, and I was for ever after very grateful, because it's a fiendishly difficult part to learn. It's difficult because the major part of it is in prose, so you don't have the help of the poetry rhythm to help you. I got all that under my belt and poor Richard was left in the second period of rehearsal having to learn Iago, which was very, very hard. Incidentally, it's one of the largest parts in Shakespeare.'.

Neville's presence at the Vic ensured a legion of young and (some felt) over-enthusiastic fans. He became a matinee idol and when Burton was also in the company they jointly inspired what Ronald Bryden has termed 'a war of Mods and Rockers' with Neville as the champion of the Mods. This was a return to tradition with a vengeance; not only would it have delighted Lilian Baylis, who liked her audiences to make their presence felt, but it reached farther back to the days when the London theatres were rowdy cockpits. It was all in glorious contrast to the sedate, tea-and-wholemeal-biscuits-during-the-interval atmosphere of Shaftesbury Avenue, where the occasional patron might be forgiven for thinking he had stumbled upon a religious service for the dead. Benthall was a benevolent dictator who allowed his star generals to shine on the parade ground; he encouraged them to make the crowds cheer as the parade went by.

When Neville finally left the shelter of the Waterloo Road he carried away with him some of Benthall's contempt for the theatrical establishment, and a desire to continue experimenting, testing himself in an American comedy, *Once More With Feeling*, and then slightly confusing his fans by taking over a singing and dancing role in the long-running *Irma La Douce*. Then he went back to one of his early foster homes, the Bristol Old Vic, to try his hand at directing, selecting not the expected classical revival but a remarkably adept and tough play by a new Australian playwright, Ray Lawler's *Summer of The Seventeenth Doll*. 'Secretly', he admitted, 'what I'd always wanted to do was to run a theatre rather than just direct plays. . . . I don't hold with the mystique of the director. . . . I believe in the author, and I believe that his interpreter is the actor: that's the way it has always been. There are two people, the author and the actor, who are working with the audience, a live audience. I think the director can be very talented, but his job is to interpret the author to the audience and not interpret his own vanity or his own arrogance to the audience. What you won't ever do away with is the actor getting up and telling a story that the author has given him. You can do without the director'.

He realised his ambition to have a theatre of his own following an association with Frank Dunlop at the Nottingham Playhouse. There he was able to test out many of his theories when the old playhouse was rebuilt and he was appointed theatre director of the new building. A defender of having a repertoire of plays, this was the system he insisted upon from the start. 'The advantages are that it's much more interesting for a company of actors to play: you're doing something different every night, you don't get stale, it's not like doing a long run of a play. But perhaps, more important, it's very good for the audience. You can begin to widen your audience. If you give people the right surroundings, the right conditions, then it's likely you will attract more people into the theatre. . . . It's the basic reason why one wants to act, and it's the basic reason why one wants to run a theatre: to attain the widest possible audience, and to attract those people who don't yet come.'

It is a philosophy devoutly to be wished, but difficult, in today's economic climate, to sustain. Sir Peter Hall and Peter Brook and the brilliant young directors who have clustered around the Royal Court in Sloane Square like anxious wasps would all echo Neville's sentiments, and have done their level best to emulate his example. But a permanent theatre is now a strange hybrid—an industrial complex grafted on to an artistic endeavour, and the resulting animal has not yet been tamed. Peter Hall is unique in that he has claimed to enjoy his Jekyll and Hyde existence as a committee man and an artist, but I doubt whether he found much cause for celebration in the realisation that his National Theatre could be blacked out by the dismissal of a single plumber at the height of the Jubilee season. Therein lies the continuing problem, the unsolved equation of how the artist reconciles his vision with the day to day necessities of our industrial society.

Neville's achievements at Nottingham were considerable and it is a tragedy that we are now denied his vitality and down-to-earth intelligence. In Neville we had an actor capable of playing *Hamlet* or *Alfie* with equal verve, a renegade who never sought to destroy tradition but always to improve and enlarge it. With the face of a romantic hero, he was able to transform himself into the common man. Whether playing prince or pauper he never lost sight of the need to establish contact with his audiences, a physical presence that the living theatre alone can provide.

*　　*　　*　　*

Two hundred years after Garrick and Johnson set out from Lichfield another young man and his companion undertook a similar journey from Stratford upon Avon to London. The name of one of them is Peter O'Toole and the story is best told in his own words.

'We had twenty-five shillings between us, just enough to see *Macbeth*, Redgrave's Macbeth. I think that cost us 11/6d each, which left exactly two bob. We went into a working men's cafe and had two dinners each, then made a run for it. We slept in a haystack, or what we thought was a haystack. I started to build a bivouac, taking great armfuls of straw to build a little house for the night. But it wasn't straw. It was dung. We had picked a dung heap and they had put the straw on it to keep it warm and alive. But nothing could shift us by then, we were too tired, and the following morning we were also very warm and "alive". No one would speak to us. We got as far as Oxford and then managed to get a lift on a lorry to London. The driver dropped us off at Euston station, still reeking the while, and we went to the YMCA because we could get a bed there. Now to get to the YMCA from Euston we walked down Gower Street and there was the Royal Academy of Dramatic Art. I was dungy and very hairy. We walked in. Sir Kenneth Barnes, God rest his soul, came out and said, "What's the problem?" I explained our situation to him and he was very sympathetic. He told me that if I came back in the afternoon he would give me a personal, private audition. Well, I auditioned, and I came out of it with a scholarship, and the whole course of my life changed.'

It was a fitting beginning for a career that has never lacked notoriety of one sort or another. Peter O'Toole has always been the most extrovert of actors; flamboyant, a *jeune premier* in the classical mould, a tough matinee idol, a compelling and elegant *actorish* actor. He may have arrived at Sir Kenneth Barnes' door smelling less than a rose, but many of his subsequent adventures in the theatre have been charmed. After R.A.D.A. he served a long apprenticeship with the Bristol Old Vic, making his first London appearance in 1956 with that company when they brought a production of *Major Barbara* to the Old Vic in which he played Peter Shirley. He was then twenty-four and had already tackled a wide variety of roles; rumours of his abilities had preceded him to London, but it was his performance as Private Bamforth in Willis Hall's *The Long and The Short and The Tall* (the best anti-war war play since *Journey's End* in my opinion) in January 1959 at the Royal Court that set him firmly on top of his erstwhile dung heap. When the play subsequently transferred to the New he went with it, and inevitably his talents were eagerly bartered for by a film industry desperately short of romantic leading men. O'Toole, although ambitious, played hard to get; his sights were set on a more classical career and he had no intention of selling himself cheaply. He joined the Shakespeare Memorial Company and set about consolidating his position in a number of leading roles—Shylock, Petruchio, Thersites and ultimately Hamlet. Critics found it difficult to pin him down. Some found him part Gielgud, part Olivier, part Redgrave; others merely a one-off Irish original. Certainly off-stage he was decidedly, determinedly himself, enjoying a reputation as a renegade and a hell-raiser, thus encouraging a number of people to the belief that he did not take his work seriously enough. Because he is a natural actor, born with those attributes that must lead, with a reasonable amount of luck, to stardom, he possibly did treat himself and his talents with a certain amount of disrespect.

He was a throwback, if you like, to the days when theatricality was an accepted part of an actor's personality and a disregard for convention all part of the game.

When he did sign a film contract it was on his own terms; he chose wisely, taking the name role in David Lean's *Lawrence of Arabia*. It was a gruelling baptism, requiring physical stamina and the highest degree of discipline, for the film took the best part of two years to complete. The finished product launched him as an international name, but with an instinct for self-preservation he did not abandon the theatre for the increasingly lucrative spoils of the cinema. There is always the danger that when a young actor makes so great an impact at the beginning of a career he is forever trapped by the initial image. After *Lawrence* he might have been condemned to play a series of mystics, but although like most Irishmen he is drawn towards mysticism he is also a realist, and he was determined to survive on his own terms. He alternated between the cinema and the theatre and it was in the theatre that he dared most. Partly under his own management he presented and appeared in an ambitious production of Brecht's *Baal* at the Phoenix Theatre, gave a fascinating *Hamlet* at the Vic, then returned to his origins with O'Casey's *Pictures in The Hallway* and *Juno and The Paycock* which he played in both London and Dublin.

He is an actor who needs firm handling, and there are not too many David Leans around in the film industry. Perhaps next to *Lawrence* his most compelling screen performance was given in *The Lion in Winter*, directed by Anthony Harvey, where he slugged it out in a feast of old-style acting with Katharine Hepburn, a lady who quickly earned O'Toole's lasting respect. Like Richard Burton, he is good at playing kings, for he has a natural regal manner, an aura of being somebody set apart. In addition to the two films mentioned above, he gave a quite extraordinary performance in one that more or less vanished without trace—*The Ruling Class*. It was a film ahead of its time and was thus unfairly dismissed; in it O'Toole showed that his talents are as diverse as they are unique.

Perhaps his very flamboyance worked against his best interests. In many ways he was too big for the cinema, dwarfing those around him. The trend was towards neo-realism and the production scene shifted back to Hollywood from Europe; in Hollywood the graduates of the mumble-mumble school of acting were in the ascent, European leading men of O'Toole's calibre became less fashionable.

At his best, which is very good indeed, he is an actor of great presence and power, constantly swimming against the tide. A romantic by nature, he finds much to criticise in the contemporary theatrical scene and can unleash laser beams of invective against the citadels of mediocrity. In recent years he has been tested in other ways, fighting ill-health with all the panache and tenacity that characterises his best performances. Happily he is now braced to return to his first love and by the end of 1980 he will be back at the Old Vic and in command of his own destiny. As well as the classical roles he is so finely equipped to play, he needs a contemporary dramatist who can write specifically for him, somebody who has the courage to pick up the glove that O'Toole has flung in the face of convention. There is passion and violence beneath the handsome mask, for the face as well as the man has matured. His destiny lies not in the mundane but the heroic—and heroism is thought reactionary these days, more's the pity.

[23]

THE ROYAL COURT

'The greatest actors in the world do more than hold the mirror up to Nature, they hold what you might describe as the crystal ball up to Nature; that imaginative, hypnotic glass in which perhaps one can glimpse heaven and hell.' The words of Ralph Richardson, who believes that the actor works by hypnotic suggestion. 'No one can show, no one can really act what the audience sees a great actor do. He doesn't in point of fact do it. He suggests to you and you do the work in your own imagination. This is complete contact with the deep imaginative sub-conscious inside the mind of the beholder.'

Richardson, the elder statesman, can perhaps afford such bold refinement of his work—what Dame Edith used to call 'tearing away', reducing everything to the bare bone, a line drawing by Matisse, something which forces the audience to use its imagination. There is always this problem facing the young actor: how to fuse emotion with technique in such a way as to give to the audience what is by right a shared experience that transcends ordinary existence.

It was a problem which particularly exercised the next generation of young actors, graduates of a wandering academy that had no set curriculum, and on whom privilege of birth or education bestowed no extra favours. They came, it seemed, from nowhere, appearing overnight and carrying satchels of surprises. Two decades earlier many of them would not have progressed beyond a West End audition. This is no reflection on their merits, for they arrived with excess baggage where talent was concerned; it was simply they did not look or talk like leading men, nor were they interested in following in their elders' footsteps. Equally, had they come on the scene at an earlier date they would have been starved of anything to say, since the playwrights who provided them with the right words to fit their view of life and their provincial accents did not exist. But by some curious alchemy once this new breed of actors made their first entrances, the playwrights were not far behind. Two names pushed their way into the front of the classical ranks while others, equally talented, were content to march in step with the contemporary drama. Instead of being condemned to a life of spear-carrying and lower-deck, low-comedy characterisations that would have sufficed as a career in previous decades, they came as rebels with a cause looking for the nearest soap-box from which to spread the new gospel.

It was the formation of the English Stage Society with its battle headquarters at the

Royal Court in Sloane Square that provided the platform—an arsenal barely disguised as a theatre. The Pied Piper in charge was that remarkable yet still shadowy figure, George Devine. He and his colleagues did not want to bring off an experiment in management, they wanted a revolution. Like Granville-Barker, Devine had a vision of discontent; he wanted change and he shared his young company's impatience to sweep away the old order and re-establish the theatre of ideas. In a sense Devine was the Philby of theatreland, working from within the establishment and with an incredible grasp of the complexities of such dangerous subterfuge. He carried with him all the code books passed down from Komisarjevsky, the Compagnie des Quinze, Gielgud and Michel Saint-Denis, it being his intention to establish a theatre that would become part of the intellectual life of the country. The theatre had always been his religion, and he shared with John Neville the conviction that in the beginning is the word. Once convinced that his defection was permanent the establishment became patronising and the intellectuals proved too narrow and carping for a man of his bigness of heart. It is said with telling cynicism that it is the ultimate fate of all revolutionaries to be absorbed, and when Devine died, worn out by years of 'prodigious, hopeful effort' he counted himself, too harshly, as an utter failure. He may have been defeated, but he was no failure. For a few brief years he raised the tattered standard and gave encouragement, hope and a home to a score of unknown playwrights headed, of course, by John Osborne. Since everything has to be reduced to simplistic terms in order that our daily pap proves digestible to every taste, the Royal Court became known as the haven of the Angry Young Men (Translator's Note: *Look Back In Anger* = Militancy. Q.E.D.) To the popular imagination it was bracketed with Carnaby Street, Jean Shrimpton, Mary Quant; a place where Clement Freud ran a restaurant and to which the debs and Hooray-Harrys flocked for an evening's slumming. Devine was too intelligent, too keenly aware of external events not to realise that much of his dream had already evaporated when he died at the early age of fifty-five. Those who wish to follow the intricate life of a man who brought to our theatre the same selfless devotion as Lilian Baylis should make it a point of honour to read Irving Wardle's definitive study of *The Theatres of George Devine*. Few books about the theatre have been written with more compassionate understanding about what makes a man who believed 'intensely in the creative value of struggle' carry on when dissatisfaction with himself and with the cause to which he had committed his life was a constant threat to his health and sanity.

In Peggy Ashcroft's view Devine 'was essentially an actor's director and an actor's actor. He knew absolutely the importance of acting. It was called a writer's theatre, because he felt the writers were not having the opportunity he wanted for them. But I don't think that was ever intended at the expense of the actors, particularly where young actors were concerned'.

The opening production of the English Stage Society was *The Mulberry Tree*, by novelist Angus Wilson. Lindsay Anderson, a pioneer of enormous influence in both theatre and films, was there to witness the first night: 'I remember going as a friend and sympathiser, though I had only met George very briefly. But I remember being struck by something that I would later know was the result of his personality—and that was the

Look Back in Anger by John Osborne, Royal Court Theatre, 1956, with (*l to r*)
MARY URE, ALAN BATES, HELENA HUGHES and KENNETH HAIGH

whole feeling of the play and the production. It was direct and honest and done with great intelligence and respect for the text; it had a feeling and relationship to people as I knew them, not generally experienced in the theatre. There was also what I think was very important: a kind of wholeness about the presentation, so that not merely was it an intelligent play, well acted, but it was also well designed. The whole look of the stage, the whole feeling of the evening had a kind of integrity about it which to me was very much part of George Devine and one of the most important things he brought to the theatre. Certainly to those of us who were fortunate enough to work at the Court it was the thing he made us most conscious of.'

In historical terms, although the Angus Wilson play provided an auspicious debut for the new venture, it was the selection by Devine of Osborne's unsolicited manuscript from some 700 submissions (most of them inevitably from the lunatic fringe) that placed the Royal Court firmly on the map. The first night of *Look Back In Anger* on May 8th 1956 was the turning point for a great number of people; for Osborne, obviously, for Kenneth Haigh, Mary Ure and Alan Bates, the director Tony Richardson and designer Alan Tagg. Kenneth Tynan, very much the Cardinal Richelieu of the British theatre at that period, was amongst the first to recognise the significance of Osborne's inspired tirade.

'At the first interval I can remember saying to the girl I was with, "They are going to hate this. They are going to loathe it. I can see that fixed look—it isn't boredom, it's a faint derision—on the faces of a great many of my colleagues." One could almost have written their notices for them to a certain extent; phrases like "young pup" and "arrogant upstart" dropped into one's mind. There were things about the play that I thought were wrong. I thought it was too long, about a quarter of an hour too long. But the great thing that leapt off the stage and buttonholed you was that, for the first time, I was recognising people on stage that I'd lived with, that I shared bed-sitting rooms with, that I queued for buses with, that I'd been in the local amateur dramatic society with in my home town, Birmingham. For the first time my own generation was on stage, not by tolerance but by right, saying the kind of things that we'd spent nights at the University arguing about; but now saying them in public to an audience that wasn't used to hearing them. And it was painfully obvious as the evening went on that they were not laughing as they expected to at the escapades of a group of young people. This was a challenge, a confrontation with a generation that was saying to them, "What kind of a mess have you made and what are you going to do about it?" And not saying it self-pityingly either, or tragically; saying it with a cocksure, derisive self-confidence. I've often wondered since how John put that character on stage without making him a whiner or a tearful self-pitier. I think he did it because he came from a generation that had a lot to do with the Education Act of 1944. They were a fully educated generation. They'd been in their early teens, I suppose, during the first post-war Labour governments, and they'd come to maturity with no doubt in their minds that they had a stake in the country's future. They had a stake in what society meant and was going to do, and they were no longer prepared to be admitted to the arts on sufferance; the arts were their business and their business was the arts.'

Until that first night Osborne had been an unknown actor with aspirations to be a playwright. He woke up the next morning to find himself securely labelled and packaged, a 'product' rather than a playwright, something to be marketed by the media like some new stain-remover that had to be handled with care. If his play changed the life of many others, it certainly changed his own, committing him to the counter-attack, the endless charges over the top into that no-man's land where there is always a sniper's sight trained on those who dare to question the wisdom of their elders. He responded with all the explosive invective of his most famous creation, Jimmy Porter. If they wanted a fight, he could reply in kind, eye-gouging with his pen, putting the literary knee into the soft groin of his inferiors in talent. But thereafter he could never afford to relax his guard. Unprepared for the furore that his play would produce, he learnt quickly, taking a crash course, self-taught, in unarmed combat, swinging his typewriter like a bazooka and blasting away at those who, from that moment onwards, sought to reduce him to their size.

'When the notices came out the following day', he said, 'the reception was very tepid. I remember the first-night house was half empty and there wasn't a great deal of prior interest. In a rather simple-minded way I think I was rather surprised at the response. And George said to me, not unkindly, "What did you expect, dear boy?" He was astonished and I was astonished, and we were all delighted when the Sunday papers came out and there was a completely different response.' In that Sunday's *Observer* Tynan had written 'It is the best young play of its decade . . . to have done it in a first play is a minor miracle. All the qualities are there, qualities one had despaired of ever seeing on the stage. . . . I doubt if I could love anyone who did not wish to see *Look Back in Anger*.' It was brave of Tynan to bare his emotional life in this fashion and the passion that saturated his review, and his subsequent follow-up pieces, forced many who would otherwise have remained unimpressed, to journey to the Court to see for themselves. One distinguished figure who made the pilgrimage was Olivier.

Olivier confessed later that 'I saw it the first time and I didn't like it. Then I saw it the second time and was completely won round by it. I felt quite foolish about it, and it was then that I met John Osborne and asked him if he could think of me sometime in writing a play. It looked as if *The Entertdiner* emerged from that moment, but I think he had *The Entertainer* up his sleeve anyhow. The Court adjusted our ideas completely. In my own case, it changed my career as an actor very much just at a time when I needed a shot in the arm. My career was getting awfully predictable and solid and rather established and dull, and he changed that. He changed it for so many people. He gave me a chance that I wouldn't have found otherwise. I wasn't able to bring out anything from any bag of tricks that was going to be a surprise to anybody, and *The Entertainer* changed this. It enabled me to feel like a modern actor again.'

If Devine was a visionary from the old school willing to learn new tricks, his counterpart from the younger generation was Peter Hall, who conducted his own revolution in a different way, working from respectability back to notoriety of a different kind. Once again it was the playwrights who guided him to the theatre of his imagination, notably Beckett and Pinter. *Waiting For Godot* startled the West End, not so much by its content but the fact that it transferred from a private club of a public theatre and was a success. Peter Hall's association with Pinter extends back to that supremely gifted writer's emergence as a major force in the theatre. *The Caretaker*, with Donald Pleasance and Alan Bates, was a cogent example of Ralph Richardson's theory: audiences were forced to use their imagination to find a personal solution to the writer's crossword puzzle. Pinter has proved to be the most original British dramatist of this century in terms of form. Inevitably he has inspired a number of inferior imitations and is not without his detractors. Actors love him because he makes them extend themselves: nobody can lazily freewheel in a Pinter play. Most importantly he is able, without recourse to smut or four-letter words, to suggest a smouldering sexuality in passages that, on the page, seem as bare of innuendo as the withered elms that now festoon our countryside. In this respect he has often been brilliantly served by Vivien Merchant.

Peter Hall came to London as Assistant Director of the Arts Theatre, after an apprenticeship that commenced with the Cambridge Amateur Dramatic Club and various repertory companies. *Waiting For Godot* came to him very early in his time at the Arts and he freely acknowledges that this was a matter of luck rather than the product of a long search. The controversy which surrounded the play ensured that his services would be sought by a number of managements who might otherwise have ignored him. Like Devine his first loyalties were to his actors and, Pinter apart, he did not profess any slavish devotion to the sanctity of texts. He looked ridiculously young for the burdens he shortly assumed, for five years after *Godot*, having sampled the tribulations of running his own production company, he was appointed Managing Director of the Stratford Memorial Theatre, a post he filled from 1960–68. His sights were always fixed on something larger, and it was no secret that he felt that Stratford was in danger of becoming merely an old curiosity shop tourist attraction. The conception and creation of the Royal Shakespeare

PETER WOODTHORPE (*left*) and PAUL DANEMAN in Samuel Beckett's *Waiting for Godot*,
Criterion, 1954

Company was the eventual outcome of his thinking; he wanted to greatly enlarge the range of the company and provide it with a London annexe where modern as well as classical productions could be mounted. Now, twenty years after the event, the RSC seems a logical step in the development of our theatre, but at the time he had many critics who felt that this was the thin end of the wedge. They were quite right. The wedge needed inserting and Hall had the courage and the resilience as well as the administrative and artistic talent to push it into place. From the very beginning he realised that he would need some equally stalwart allies and with this in mind the first person he attempted to recruit was Peggy Ashcroft.

'I drove her round Trafalgar Square in mid 1958 after having taken her out to dinner. I thought, if I could persuade her to come in on this mad plan of actually trying to make a group of people more or less permanent, I would have one of the leaders of the profession—a great actress and a great person. And to my absolute amazement, she said yes. And she stayed with the company right through all its difficult, early years, giving a series of amazing performances.'

Hall is one of our most accomplished speakers on the subject of the theatre. He confesses that he is basically a shy person who has made himself articulate as a spokesman for the profession. Certainly he has needed some form of permanent armour in recent years as Director of the National Theatre, concealing his shyness, but not his passionately held convictions, in a most articulate way.

While he was still at the RSC he gave an interview in which he explained his view of our theatrical heritage, emphasising that he had been impressed how extraordinarily alive the Shakespearean tradition is. He felt that it was not 'something highbrow, classical, cliquish. It is in the very broad sense still popular. We could not fill a 1,400-seat theatre from April until December each year if it was a highbrow Art Festival, or something that ought to be done, or peddling culture for schools, or a tourist attraction. A convention in the theatre is a living means of expressing an imaginative act to an audience of now. But if the next generation come along and say, "Shakespeare is done like this, Gilbert and Sullivan is done like this—as D'Oyly Carte always did it, Moscow Arts say Chekhov must be done like this because this is the way Stanislavsky did it," then there is a great danger that you get a museum art which is rather dead, rather respectable, technically very adroit, but is not fully meaningful because the conditions which produced it have vanished. This is mainly why I felt that the Shakespearean problem was bedevilled with a number of contradictory conventions—Victorian word music, reciting. Pre-Raphaelite conception of poetry on the one hand, on another hand a feeling that our naturalistic style of acting in this century, which of course has been very much influenced by the cinema and the smallness of playing in the cinema, was resulting in a kind of acting which relied more on the sub-text rather than the text itself. In Shakespeare, although the images reverberate in their meaning, Shakespeare says what he means and he says it very explicitly and very concretely. The young actor is so much part of the personality cult of our time, where he feels that his native accent is an inviolate part of his personality, that blank verse is an imposition, that he must therefore re-write Shakespeare in his own terms. It seemed to me that in order to make a proper examination of all these points, first of all you have to have a company. This gives a certain basis to the work so that you can get on with the actual craft. Without a continuity in a company you cannot do all the things that I've tried to sketch. Yet you can't have a company doing nothing but Shakespeare. An actor who is a Shakespearean actor and that alone is generally somewhat coarse-grained, somewhat rhetorical. He's got to be able to test his technique on other things.'

So, as all these different forces gathered together there was a quickening of the artistic pulse, a feeling of renaissance that embraced the whole spectrum of the arts. In the mass popular sense the Beatles went beyond entertainment to become a religion; British films suddenly came of age; the theatre, with its cross-pollinisation of the new Elizabethans and open-minded figures such as Ashcroft and Olivier produced a hybrid that blossomed time and time again. It was the best of times to be working in the theatre or in films and now one wonders why it all evaporated so quickly. The answer possibly lies somewhere outside the theatre in the national exhaustion, the tired, grubby and increasingly irritable attitude towards everything that involves any effort, either mental or physical.

To me the actor I automatically associate with the Sixties is Albert Finney. Born in Salford and yet another honours graduate of the Birmingham Repertory, he seemed as topical and as brash as a Beatles lyric. When he played Macbeth in 1958, at the age of twenty-one, there was a smell of cordite in the air as heady and intoxicating as Chanel No. 5. Entirely in keeping with the times, if somewhat improbably, it was Charles Laughton who brought him to London. Laughton, too, had been a prodigy and he saw to it that his discovery accompanied him to Stratford the following season. There Finney played Edgar to Laughton's *Lear* and Lysander in *A Midsummer Night's Dream* when Laughton found some of his old genius as Bottom. They made an odd couple—Laughton the

ALBERT FINNEY and CHARLES LAUGHTON in *The Party*, New Theatre, 1958

legendary figure who had gone from early brilliance to years of self-parody that bordered on buffoonery, coming home in the twilight of his career to show a new generation of theatregoers some old magic, but also finding, in Albert Finney, somebody to whom he could hand on the baton.

In the beginning while a student at the R.A.D.A. Finney, one of the new breed, was a strange mixture of ambition and awkwardness. 'I felt I wanted a great career, like Garrick and Kean and Irving . . . but I was very self-conscious in the beginning because I felt very unattractive, kind of podgy. . . . And with my thick North Country speech, I did feel very awkward and shy and self-conscious.' Later, at Birmingham, he began to find his feet, and in retrospect defended the repertory system: '. . . it's from acting in front of the punters in the flesh, from that contact and that working on a performance and then playing it, that you understand the demands made by the theatre. There's also the experience of playing parts for which you're totally wrong, but which you get away with. We did an adaptation of *Jekyll and Hyde*, and I played an inspector. I was nineteen, twenty, totally wrong—just eligible to be a police cadet and there I was playing an inspector on this big case: I wouldn't do that now, but that's what you can do in rep.; you can make glorious errors and get through a performance when you're playing a character part, by putting on a beard with enough hair in it for twenty. . . .'

When he was invited to play Macbeth at his coming of age he realised that he was miscast and has since cherished a newspaper quote which described him as 'a juvenile delinquent in a kilt'. But he persisted, he accepted the challenge and tried to make it work despite the very obvious lack of experience. 'At first I used to take two hours over the make-up . . . and I used to come out looking twenty-one. But I spent two hours doing it with moustaches and beards and things; because I was thinking, now you're Macbeth, and I created it all to myself in the mirror. By the time I walked on stage I was dead; I'd exhausted myself. Then one matinee I thought, don't spend two hours on it, you're killing yourself making-up. Today just go in, throw the make-up on and run on stage and do it. And I did. . . . So that was one of the things I learnt, that you can exhaust yourself before you get on stage, if you get too intense in the dressing room. . . .'

Although Laughton had an instinctive regard for Finney's potential talents, contrary to the more popular version, he did not admire this hairy-under-age Macbeth. Finney relates: 'He came round and said, "You were bloody awful" . . . He was the first kind of legend I had contact with professionally. . . . I admired him in his movies; I'd never seen him on the stage. I thought he was terrific in some of his films, there was such a sort of vulnerability in the man, such openness in his portrayal . . . the professionalism had kind of shattered off the vulnerability of his soul. It was extraordinary seeing him work in the theatre because he seemed to be less theatrical than he was in the films, he seemed to make it very tiny. . . . He talked to me an awful lot about acting . . . about Shakespeare, because he was going to play Lear and he wanted me to play Edgar. I didn't really want to go to Stratford, partly because I didn't respond to the roles I was offered, but I went because Charles wanted me to play them. . . . One of the things I remember very clearly, he said, when he was talking about insanity, acting madness, and also acting royalty, that if you're playing a madman or a king, you do less—what makes the audience believe you're mad is the reaction of others around you: which is absolutely true. I mean, a madman does not go around saying, "I'm potty, run away from me." He comes up to you, starts talking to you, and you believe he's sane until you realise that what he's actually saying isn't logical, then you think he's mad and it's you who gets away from him. . . . Charles just saying that to a young actor of twenty-two, you just felt, well that saves me ten years. It was a very valuable piece of observation to get from a master.'

The lesson of the master was well learnt. Finney, although a frequent absentee from the theatre, and for one sabbatical year when he took himself off to a tropical island to contemplate his navel an absentee from both theatre and films, has gone about shaping his career with infinite care. There was a time when he might have accepted becoming the local James Dean, for his success in *Saturday Night and Sunday Morning* was so complete, so totally accepted by both critics and public that he could easily have become typecast as a tearaway. His identification with Sillitoe's Arthur Seaton was total and it was one of the most remarkable film performances ever given by a young actor, far superior in my mind to Dean's in *Rebel Without A Cause*. One must allow that Dean's film was glossy and bogus, a manufactured view of youth in rebellion, expertly done but without any real heart. *Saturday Night and Sunday Morning* on the other hand was an observation of life transformed into art and it had at its core Finney's rock-like characterisation. He wasn't just impressive, he was overwhelmingly impressive in a cast that fought him toe to toe; they all slugged it out until the last bell went.

The truth of it is (and shorn of the grotesqueries, we can see the influence of Laughton) Finney is basically a character actor who, because of his physical appearance, has to masquerade as a perennial juvenile. But he has adapted himself to this, never taking the easy route, always pacing himself, choosing divers roles—Billy Liar, Luther, Tom Jones, John Armstrong in *Armstrong's Last Goodnight,* Don Pedro in *Much Ado About Nothing*, Jean in *Miss Julie*; alternating between the theatre and films but always conscious that 'if one wants to do serious work in the theatre, and play the great parts, I don't think you can do the pictures and just go back to the theatre for a year, you need more than that. The instrument needs more work than it does in the movies; you've got to be able to share it with people a hundred yards away. You've got to be physically fit to get through two and a half hours. If you play Macbeth you cover an awful distance on stage; you cover miles, going up and down the boulders, on and off for exits, up to your dressing room at the interval for a smoke and a cup of tea'.

While at Stratford he lived the plot beloved by every novelist who tackles a theatrical subject: the understudy who goes on for the star. In Finney's case the star was Olivier and the role was Coriolanus. 'It's terrible to hear that announcement—you know, you're in your dressing room putting on the make-up—Sir Laurence won't be playing tonight: terrible groan throughout the auditorium. His part will be played by Al—Albert Finney. And then I came on, and I had the costume on, and so they immediately think I'm talented because I've actually got into the clothes. . . . If you're an understudy and you go on, the card you've actually got in your hand is that they think you might not be able to get through at all, and if you can get through with any degree of professionalism, they think you're very good. I felt a kind of freedom , , , because I had no responsibility; I was his understudy, it didn't matter what happened. It didn't matter if I dried; they'd expect it. If I fainted, well it's a lot of pressure on the lad, you know. So I didn't worry. All the clouds which were around the rest of my performances at Stratford, all the rubbish, the tunnel I felt in with my work, all the difficulties blew out of the window. . . . There is one scene where Coriolanus is outside the gates of Rome and about to invade, and his mother comes out and pleads with him not to. Dame Edith Evans had a speech of Shakespearean verse which goes on, I suppose, for two and a half sides. I did six performances of the part, and every time while Dame Edith was doing the speech, I wept. I had my back to her for the second half of it—Coriolanus turns away in the middle of the speech, and I just used to feel that all one had to do was just listen to Dame Edith. . . . When you hear Sir Laurence's tones ringing in your ears it's very difficult for you not to be similar, because you're working on his blue-print. What is interesting, what one did learn from that is how a great actor can take the peaks and valleys of a performance, the ups and downs of a character as written and push them even further apart. He makes the climaxes higher and the depths lower than you feel is possible in the text.'

Finney may have been lucky, first with Laughton, then with Olivier and Dame Edith, in coming to the realisation of what great acting is all about when his own personality was still malleable, but it was his triumph to use that knowledge in a wholly individual way. He is very much a physical actor who knows the extent of his own inherent charm and works to control it. At the start of his career he spoke of playing to and for the punters, and the punters still have their money on him, for with Scofield, he looks like a thoroughbred, an outsider but still a thoroughbred and capable of winning any race he enters. He is far more complex than his cherubic face suggests. 'A certain amount of loneliness is inevitable for a person who is like myself', he has told us. 'You're not lonely for people or for company, but there's a loneliness because of one's life, one's thoughts . . . what I want to do in the theatre. . . . One can only communicate it by doing, by acting it.'

This is a recurring theme that many actors voice. Dorothy Tutin expressed it in a different way, but the meaning was the same. She said that she felt the last night of any play was like 'life going by, each moment was never, never going to be recaptured again, and it gave one a feeling of death . . . sometimes when you're acting it's a sort of death. It's as though you were dying to be the part. I mean, that you yourself would no longer wish to exist, you only want the person you're playing to exist. So there is a sort of death in that every now and then it comes to this strange feeling of almost being on the edge of yourself and the edge of a part.'

I can remember seeing Dorothy Tutin for the first time when she was still a R.A.D.A. student appearing in an end-of-term production of *Cradle Song* in the little theatre at Gower Street. She seemed minute, a scaled-down version of Celia Johnson, but even on that bare stage one could discern the actress she was to become. I cannot claim to have 'discovered' her, but I can credit myself with the perception to urge my then agent, Olive Harding, who looked after so many young players of my generation, to sign her up. Actors and actresses do not always get the roles they deserve at the time when they are most capable of fully realising them. Tutin was the exception, for early in her career she was cast as Rose Pemberton in Graham Greene's *The Living Room*. The part of Rose is a familiar figure in Greene's fictions; we find traces of her in *Brighton Rock*, *England Made Me* and *The Heart of The Matter*, the child-wife figure broken by the demands of those older than her. In retrospect Dorothy Tutin seemed to have been born for the role, though she was not handed it on a plate: she gave three auditions before it was hers.

She now stands at the head of a generation of actresses, many of them supremely gifted, who have had to meet different, and in general, more difficult challenges than their male contemporaries. On the whole they have dared more; if the chances were there to be taken, they took them. By no means the weaker sex and well aware that traditionally the men have been better served by the dramatists, their quest for proper recognition outside the sparse classical roles has only been accomplished by talent and perseverance. Where the actresses have come to the fore in the past two decades has been on television. In that medium the writers and for that matter the producers and directors have enjoyed greater freedoms than they could find in the live theatre. They are not so craven, for instance, in demanding that they must have acknowledged star names. Now admittedly the television audience makes no physical commitment—other than sitting in an easy chair—when watching television drama. They are spared a journey to the West End, the struggle to obtain decent seats at ever-rising prices, the problems of parking or using unreliable public transport; they are therefore in a more relaxed mood and prepared to give newcomers a hearing. Television drama, and in particular BBC television drama, frequently attains a very high standard: at any given night of the week there is usually a programme far superior, both in the writing and the performance, to the average West

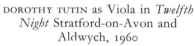

DOROTHY TUTIN as Viola in *Twelfth Night* Stratford-on-Avon and Aldwych, 1960

MAGGIE SMITH and JEREMY BRETT in *Hedda Gabler*, Cambridge Theatre, 1970

End offering. New young dramatists with something to say and a vital way of saying it have been commissioned to write directly for the small screen; in many instances they have chosen to create leading female characters and as a result a great number of young actresses who would otherwise never have achieved the acclaim their talents deserve have been brought to public and critical notice. This in turn has led to an enhanced reputation in the theatre, for that is their spiritual home and the place to which most of them yearn to succeed. One can instance several examples—Diana Rigg obtained her grounding with the Royal Shakespeare Company, but it wasn't until she made a spectacular success in television's *The Avengers* series that she was able to exploit her real worth in the theatre. I have no doubt that she was offered further television and film contracts at salaries that the RSC and the National could not match, but she has elected to concentrate on the theatre, with occasional sorties into films and television. She has proved herself to be an actress of style and stature in the theatre, alternating between classical and modern plays in a way that suggests that her career will be long and distinguished. Dorothy Tutin herself has given some memorable performances on television, notably in the adaptation of *South Riding*. Susan Hampshire is another young lady who, as a result of attracting much attention by her television appearances, has been able to forge a more rewarding career in the theatre.

Television is, of course, a monster, with the ability to destroy careers as quickly as it makes them. This is particularly true of comedians for whereas in the old days when there were sufficient theatres to sustain a year's tour without repetition, a single comedy routine could suffice for the entire period; today that same comedy routine will only survive for one night on television. The situation comedy series, a far cry from the early

ALEC McCOWEN and DIANA RIGG in *The Misanthrope*

VANESSA REDGRAVE in *The Lady from the Sea* Round House, 1979

soap operas, have made particular use of young actresses. *The Good Life* clearly established both Felicity Kendal and Penelope Keith as major talents, though neither of them could have been accounted unknowns when the series first commenced. We should also recall the extraordinary impact made by Carol White in *Cathy Come Home*, though Miss White's subsequent career has been mainly concentrated on films.

The more established younger actresses such as Maggie Smith, Glenda Jackson, Vanessa Redgrave, Judi Dench, Zena Walker, Janet Suzman, Joan Plowright, Gwen Watford, Jill Bennett, Anna Massey and Jennie Linden, to name a representative few, have used television and films when the opportunity for experiment has presented itself, but are basically creatures of the theatre. Maggie Smith, Glenda Jackson and Vanessa Redgrave have gained international reputations through their films, all three having won the Academy Award, but have never deserted the theatre. Maggie Smith with her then husband Robert Stephens were two of the most consistently excellent members of Olivier's National company and at one time seemed set fair to become the Lunts of the sixties. Maggie Smith is a delicious comedienne in the tradition of Kay Hammond, yet her range is such that she can encompass Desdemona and Jean Brodie in *The Prime of Miss Jean Brodie*. Her comic invention is an object lesson for other young actresses; there is a sexual spontaneity, a freshness, about her; her face, voice and gestures all combine to suggest a lack of inhibitions, a down-to-earth, completely feminine approach to whatever she tackles. Some of this may stem from her early experiences in revue and cabaret and she has revealed that comedy was forced on her rather than something she turned to by choice. She has also told us that she does enjoy the mechanics of film acting, though the results belie this. She dislikes 'the lack of contact, the fact that there isn't an audience. . . .

You get so inhibited, at least I do, that I tend not to do anything. I'm fine in a film if I'm acting a small part, a neurotic person, or a shy person; then it's not quite so difficult'. Her graduation to the classic roles was a slow process and she dismisses her initial attempts, yet when she came to tackle her first tragic role, that of Desdemona, she seemed the most obvious choice to set beside Olivier's controversial Othello. 'I didn't see myself in it', she said. . . . 'Why should John Dexter have seen me as Desdemona? I doubt if many other people would. I was very nervous of Sir Laurence. It's unfair on him, but it's bound to happen. You are in awe of him, very much so. He has enormous self-discipline and control as an actor. I've learnt a lot from him about discipline. Or rather, I haven't learnt—but I wish I had. You don't learn specific things from other actors.'

Glenda Jackson surprised her audiences by moving in the reverse direction; from being associated with serious, not to say heavy roles, she displayed an equal talent for comedy. Although now primarily thought of as a film actress, she came up through the ranks in conventional fashion: first R.A.D.A., then repertory in Worthing before making her mark in *Alfie*. She then joined the Royal Shakespeare company and appeared in the experimental Theatre of Cruelty season before attempting Ophelia in 1965, and later attracted much comment with her electrifying portrayal of Charlotte Corday in Peter Brook's production of *Marat/Sade*. As a result she might well have become type-cast had such fame come to her a decade or so earlier. Curiously it was films and not theatre that allowed her the greatest freedom of expression. Her performance as one of D. H. Lawrence's most completely realised female characters in *Women in Love* established her reputation on an international level. Without, I hope, any condescension, but more in homage to her talents, I have to record that to many people she appeared an unlikely candidate for screen stardom: not since Bette Davis had the screen been given an actress of her calibre; she has the strength, the versatility, and the individuality of Miss Davis— the outward appearance of toughness that suddenly melts into feminine vulnerability. It is a malleable, urchin face, with a touch of Edith Piaf about it. She uses it carelessly, for she is not in the least concerned with the glamour privileges usually associated with female film stars. Because of the position she has deservedly reached she has cast herself boldly, choosing *content* in her selected scripts rather than follow the conventional film star route of choosing the mixture as before. We can contrast her performances in *Sunday Bloody Sunday, The Triple Echo* and *A Touch of Class*, and set these against her Vittoria Corombona in *The White Devil*, and it is difficult to believe that we are seeing the same actress. As with Paul Scofield, she does not court spurious publicity, yet is devoid of any Garboisms, thinking of herself as a working actress who has been fortunate enough to be given a wide variety of opportunities. She appears to have no illusions about herself or about the profession she follows. She is the first to admit that she is not everybody's cup of tea, but even her most ungenerous detractors allow that she has never compromised. There is a rare, unvarnished honesty about her acting that reminds me of Edith Evans, and it is to be hoped that eventually a major dramatist will pick up the glove, just as James Bridie picked it up for Edith, and provide her with a role as exceptional as Lady Pitts in *Daphne Laureola*. Glenda Jackson conveys to me the feeling that the peaks she has so far scaled are but the hills before the distant mountain ranges she will, in time, attempt.

The name we must bracket with Glenda Jackson is Vanessa Redgrave, for again we have an actress with a passport that takes her across the frontiers of theatre, film and television with no discernible break in excellence. Yet in many ways Miss Redgrave is the most difficult artist to place in proper perspective. Whereas her contemporaries can be judged on their performances alone, Vanessa Redgrave has obliged her public to evaluate her in two quite separate guises. There is the luminous Vanessa Redgrave they have seen in *As You Like It* and there is the Vanessa Redgrave of the political hustings. This is where the dichotomy begins. Now it can be argued that the two identities should never be mentioned in the same breath, yet if an actor, by his or her continued public actions, makes it impossible for audiences to divorce one from the other, then it is inevitable that a measure of the private personality will come between the audience and any character that actor portrays.

The Redgraves are a completely theatrical family and the three children—Vanessa, Lynn and Corin—have all separately, and on their individual merits, extended the fame of their parents. In Vanessa's case fame touched her from the very beginning. It sometimes happens that a whole career seems to be set by a single performance, and such a moment can come at the start, the middle or even, occasionally, towards the end of a career.* Vanessa's triumph in the Royal Shakespeare's production of *As You Like It* in 1961 was as complete as had been Edith Evans' when she played the same role opposite Michael Redgrave twenty-five years previously. The main difference was that where Edith was forty-eight when she played it, Vanessa was a fledgling of twenty-four.

The problem with such an overwhelming success at the very beginning of a career is how to sustain it. It is particularly hard for a young actress simply because of the lack of suitable roles in the classical repertory. Many of Shakespeare's heroines demand a technique that is beyond the reach of the average young actress; traditionally they have therefore been played by ladies from whom the bloom of youth has been brushed away (an added factor being that the leading men were also usually of mature years and unwilling to promote a Juliet, Ophelia or Desdemona likely to make them appear as octogenarian cradle-snatchers). Thus many promising or indeed spectacular debuts have been blighted by this very lack of opportunity. Added to which all the Redgrave children carried the added burden of following in their parents' footsteps. This is always a mixed blessing since more is expected of the children of famous parents. Such talents as they possess are often cynically discounted as the spoils that stem from nepotism. Vanessa was luckier than most in that she was able to stabilize her emotional and professional development through the influence of her husband, Tony Richardson. He was at the centre of George Devine's revolution at the Royal Court, and although he stopped short at dispatching all tradition to the tumbrils, he nevertheless displayed a languid disdain for the established hierarchy. Directly and indirectly he exercised a forcible influence on the new playwrights and carried that influence through into British films by the formation of his production company, Woodfall. After a modest start, the huge commercial success of *Tom Jones*, directed by Richardson from a screenplay by Osborne, gave all concerned the

* Witness Katie Johnson who achieved fame in *The Ladykillers* two years before her death after a lifetime in supporting roles.

freedom of choice that comes from a solid financial base, and gave it at the very time when their creative urges were most fertile. Solvency is always of great assistance to any revolution.

Vanessa triumphed again as Nina in her husband's production of *The Seagull* in 1964, and then two years later consolidated her position with two widely different roles—the enigmatic girl in Antonioni's film *Blow Up* and the title part in *The Prime of Miss Jean Brodie* in the theatre. She had already made her mark in films with Karel Reisz's *Morgan, A Suitable Case for Treatment* opposite David Warner and Robert Stephens and the timing of her emergence as a leading actress coincided with the birth of the youth cult. Because of the type of roles she played she came to be identified with that movement—the shifting, restless surges of young people the world over in search of Jimmy Porter's lost great causes. What had begun as a gentle and non-violent rebellion of the Flower Children in San Francisco gradually distorted into violence. Europe witnessed the student revolts of 1968 as the lava of discontent that had been boiling up ever since the earlier CND campaigns finally erupted. Hungary, Suez and Vietnam all combined to give young people of conscience an outlet for their general discontent with the old order of things.

The effect on the theatre was two-fold: world events gave a whole flock of new dramatists an impetus to express what I can only describe, paradoxically, as passive anger, and the actors who had been denied any platform for their energies formed themselves into a number of splinter groups. This was the confused genesis of the Alternative Theatre, a theatre that borrowed its clothes from a dozen different sources. An American comedian of undisciplined but undoubted genius—Lenny Bruce—had evolved a new comedic art form in which nothing was sacred. Death, religion, birth, motherhood, all the hitherto preserved species became targets for his withering satire. He used savage language, taboo words, kicking respectability into the aisles as he shocked his audiences into surprised laughter. Eventually and tragically his own fire consumed him, but not before he had shown others how to rub two tired old conventions together and make sparks. In England we produced gentler blazes: the *Beyond The Fringe* quartet and the larger group of talents that operated within the framework of *That Was The Week That Was* gave theatre and television audiences glimpses of the bonfires to come. Political satire which had been muted since the middle of the nineteenth century suddenly became all the vogue. It was as audacious as the mini-skirt, welcomed by youth and frowned upon by the older generation brought up in the belief that public idols never have feet of clay. Bad taste became good news at the box office and one by one the sacred cows were taken to the knacker's yard. It was the best of times for young people, a time of confusion for the elders whom they no longer considered their betters.

While the Alternative Theatre remained a hundred different characters in search of an author, a small army of new dramatists, composers and performers occupied whole areas in the West End. The musical *Hair* pushed all the old maids back into the mountains, though for my money the new wave of talent came of age two years previously, on August 9th 1972, when *Jesus Christ Superstar* opened at the Palace Theatre. Tim Rice and Andrew Lloyd Webber gave back to the English theatre a vitality, both intellectual and physical, that had been missing for over a century. Their retelling of the events leading to the crucifixion had been anticipated by *Godspell* in 1971 when that play with music was first presented at the Roundhouse, and while *Godspell* remains a remarkable piece of theatre, it perhaps lacks that final touch of inspired audacity that sets *Jesus Christ Superstar* in a class of its own. Brilliant in conception and executed with breathtaking panache, it fuses all the elements of classic opera to straight drama but presents the resulting whole in the idiom of today.

In the straight theatre, Joe Orton translated the gospel according to Lenny Bruce into three acts, producing some of the most remarkable black comedies in the English language before emulating Bruce by becoming the victim of his own philosophy. There were others, notably Willis Hall, Edward Bond, David Hare, David Mercer, Shelagh Delaney, Christopher Hampton, Arnold Wesker, Brendan Behan, Ann Jellicoe and John Arden, who also extended the frontiers of the drama, and for a few years there was reason to believe that things would never be the same again. There was controlled anger, turbulence, disrespect, a questioning of sterile values from all these pens. There was Joan Littlewood with her genius for dragooning raw, unproven recruits into still raw, but now disciplined troops, capable of giving a savage account of themselves in *Oh, What A Lovely War—Cavalcade* turned inside out. Joan Littlewood was a blaspheming Lilian Baylis and her transformation of the derelict Theatre Royal in Stratford-atte-Bow akin to producing water out of the rock. Her reign, while it lasted, had an electrifying effect on everybody who came within range; her departure from the scene like some Lady Hester Stanhope to the wilder shores of love is greatly to be regretted.

Meanwhile the Alternative Theatre was getting organised. One of the first and most enduring groups was Red Ladder and they still flourish. These off-shoots from the legitimate theatre have made an important contribution to the drama of ideas and while improvised plays sometimes have little or no staying power (for it is well nigh impossible for revivals to reproduce the burning sincerity of the original casts) they act as a purgative on the constipated imaginations of actors and audiences alike. Their offerings are sometimes great theatre, but not necessarily great drama. What is interesting about the whole alternative movement is that it leads the actors back to their origins, and as we near the end of this account, we find evidence that everything is different yet everything is the same. The nomadic instincts that every actor carries within his personality, those instincts that have been sublimated as he gained more social respectability, are always there just beneath the surface. It is my conviction that the actor should at all times remain distanced from the mob, the interpreter of human failings; if he joins those who wish to flatten-out human nature then he relinquishes his prime function. Obviously the artist cannot be totally divorced from the political climate of the times he lives in, but he must remain sufficiently aloof to make his judgements impartial, seeing both sides of the question but leaving the final answer to posterity. I have not observed that great art flourishes when umbilically tied to any political philosophy. The whole point of being an artist is to be free, and the rule is without exception.

'TO TEACH THE HUMAN HEART . . .'

THROUGHOUT the writing of this book I have been seeking for one anecdote
that would unlock the complex mechanism of an actor's personality. Perhaps there
is no Houdini answer, but one incident comes to mind. It is a scene from a famous pre-
war French film, *La Fin du Jour*, a story built around a collection of old actors and
actresses living out their memories in a home for the aged. The last scene in that film takes
place in a graveyard where one of the old actors is being buried. A famous colleague, still
in his prime, reads a eulogy at the graveside. It is a eulogy written in over-generous terms
by the dead man himself, the last conceit if you will. The famous actor, played by Victor
Francen, suddenly pauses. He looks around at the mourning faces and says: 'No, I can't
read this. It isn't true. I can't say he was a great actor . . . he wasn't, but he loved the
theatre.'

It is an inescapable truth that for most who choose the profession of actor there are no
great rewards. Through the centuries countless numbers of them have spent their lives in
the service of the theatre and caused not a ripple. They have died in unmarked graves in
cities far from their homes, un-mourned, soon forgotten completely. Only the most
dedicated theatrical historian can find the barest traces of them; just a name on a faded
playbill in a play that is now never performed. The lives that many of them have led are
almost beyond the comprehension of outsiders, for their existence was as bleak and as ill-
paid as coal-miners at the turn of this century. We have seen how some clawed their way
into society's favour, but these were the few; the majority were never accepted once they
stepped beyond the range of the footlights.

I have attempted to illuminate some of the dark corners of our theatrical heritage and
to bring back to life on these pages what Sir Lewis Casson once described as the 'animal
smell' of the theatre. He once said: 'The theatre can't die. It will never die, because people
need the ensemble experience of the animal smell which binds them together. That is the
whole secret of the circus and the essence of all theatre.'

Well, now there is a new generation seeking to give continuity to a profession that has
never been an economic necessity, a despicable race, half accepted, sometimes 'out even
to a full disgrace'. I can pick a few names at random, scattered through the ranks—
Donald Sinden, Derek Jacobi, Ian McKellen, Kate Nelligan, Tom Conti, John Wood,
Nicol Williamson, Helen Mirren, Colin Blakely, Denis Quilley, Jonathan Pryce, Ian
Holm, Jane Lapotaire—who stand at the threshold of possible greatness. It is an

IAN McKELLEN and JUDI DENCH in *Macbeth*

incomplete list, taking no account of those who are just starting and those who have so far laboured without recognition. And while this book is being set into print there will be others knocking at the door. Tonight, tomorrow night, in Shaftesbury Avenue, at the South Bank, on television, or in some obscure fringe theatre, a young unknown will suddenly ignite the popular imagination. There will be others still giving auditions, waiting outside agents' offices, writing those hopeful letters to casting directors, learning roles they will never play. Some are more favoured than most, but all can tumble from grace within the space of a curtain's rise and fall. It seems it was ever so, from the sawdust of the pit in Burbage's Globe to the concrete calm of the National. Perhaps the first and only tradition of the actor is courage?

Let Olivier have the centre of the stage to speak the Epilogue. He once said: 'As long as the actor has been in existence he has been an extremely underrated person. I believe that the importance of his work measures up with the work of the doctor, of the psychologist or even of the minister. I think his work is so important, because he is in the position of one who is able to teach the human heart the knowledge of itself.'

ACKNOWLEDGEMENTS

This book originated from a series of four BBC Radio 4 programmes conceived and produced by John Knight, which I wrote and narrated under the same title and which were first broadcast in November 1977. The series proved to have wide popular appeal and was subsequently rebroadcast on two occasions.

Limited by the time allocated to us, John Knight and I took David Garrick's journey to London in the company of Samuel Johnson as our starting point: what followed was not the complete story, but it enabled us to build towards the heart of the matter in radio terms—the beginning of the present century where the BBC's superb library of recorded archive material could come into its own. The last two programmes made extensive use of the actual voices of many of our greatest theatrical personalities.

The field of theatrical literature is vast: the admirable bibliography published by The Society For Theatre Research, edited by James Fullarton Arnott and John William Robinson (London 1970) lists over four and a half thousand titles published during the period 1559–1900. Since the turn of the century the total must have doubled. My own library runs to many hundreds of volumes and I was fortunate enough to be able to draw upon the papers and books of the late Dame Edith Evans. In addition I consulted many living authorities and interviewed a great number of our most eminent actors and actresses. The opinions I have put forward and the conclusions I have drawn are my own and unless otherwise attributed I must take whatever blame (or possibly praise) is placed upon my words.

In the earlier chapters the written rather than the spoken word became my main source and drawing upon my own experience as an actor I attempted to force my way through the labyrinth of conflicting opinions, some critical, some sycophantic, others merely vicious, that necessarily, human nature being what it is, surround the lives of those who live in the public spotlight. My aim was to try and give a balanced view of lives lived in turbulence.

As the story grew closer to the last century I was able to use much of the spoken testimony which came through so vividly in the radio series. I would like to record my unstinted admiration of the BBC, for from the day it was granted its Charter it has never neglected to collect, to store and to evaluate the very stuff of history in a way that no other broadcasting organisation has ever approached. I am most grateful to the BBC for allowing me to draw so extensively on their archive material, and also to the actors, actresses and others who have generously given permission for extracts from their broadcasts to be quoted here.

Bryan Forbes
April 1980

SOURCES
1. Textual Material

p. 9   Charles Churchill, English satirist and poet, 1731–1764 *Apology, 1*—1761, quoted in Stevenson.

p. 9   'Peel'd, patch'd and piebald . . .'—Pope, *The Dunciad*, Book iii, 1.—1712.

p. 17   *Paul Hentzner's Travels in England During the Reign of Elizabeth*, translated by Richard Bentley, 1797 and quoted in Professor Schoenbaum's *William Shakespeare* (Oxford University Press 1977). Hentzner was a tutor from Brandenburg who came to London in 1598.

p. 17   Anthony Burgess—*Shakespeare* (Jonathan Cape, 1970) pps. 71–2

p. 20   Ernest Schanzer, *Thomas Platter's Observations on the Elizabethan Stage*—Notes and Queries (1956)

p. 21   *Ex Observationibus Londinensibus Johannis de Witt*, translated from the Latin. De Witt was a priest from Utrecht who is thought to have visited London in 1596 where he made architectural drawings of the theatres he found there, in addition to recording his observations of the London scene. The originals disappeared, though fortunately a friend, Arend van Buchell, made copies now to be seen in the University Library, Utrecht. Again my source is Professor Schoenbaum's masterpiece of documentary research on the life of Shakespeare, a work no student of the plays can afford to overlook.

p. 21   Stephen Gosson. Quoted in Dr. Doran's invaluable *Their Majesties Servants* or *Annals of the English Stage*, second edition, Wm. H. Allen, London 1865. Doran writes of Gosson as the 'parson' of St. Botolph's who in 1579 'discharged the first shot against stage plays in a book entitled *A School of Abuse*, self-described as a 'pleasant investive against poets, players, jesters, and such like caterpillars of a Commonwealth.'

p. 24   Description of Betterton: Doran, Ibid.

p. 25   John Evelyn, *The Diaries*, 1659

pps. 26–7   The reference to the female impersonators: Doran, Ibid.

p. 37   Description of Christopher Rich: from Colley Cibber's *Apology*

p. 46   Description of Cibber as Richard III: Doran, Ibid.

pps. 68–9   Garrick as Abel Drugger: Richard Findlater, *The Player Kings*, Stein and Day NY 1971.

pps. 78–9   Description of Susannah Cibber from *Memoirs of the Life of David Garrick*, 2 vols. (Boston 1818)

pps. 88–94   Roger Manvell, *Sarah Siddons*, p. 243.

pps. 88–94   *Reminiscences of Sarah Siddons*.

pps. 88–94   Hazlitt: Collected Works, Vol. 8., p. 312. (1903).

p. 93   Findlater: *The Player Queens*, p. 91 (1976).

p. 97   *The Diaries of Henry Crabb Robinson*, p. 12. Published by the Society for Theatre Research 1966, edited by Eluned Brown.

p. 100   Donald Sinden, quoted from BBC archive material.

p. 100   Sheridan on Sarah Siddons, quoted by Roger Manvell, *Sarah Siddons*, p. 342.

p. 103   George Colman, the younger 1796. Quoted in *Drury Lane Journal—Selections from James Winston's Diaries* 1819–1827. Edited by Alfred L. Nelson and Gilbert B. Cross (Society for Theatre Research 1974).

p. 104   Crab Robinson, Ibid. pps. 45 & 46.

p. 112   Kemble on Kean's Othello: quoted from *Old Drury Lane—Fifty Years' Recollections by Edward Stirling* (1881) p. 148.

306

p. 113   Hazlitt: quoted by Richard Findlater, *The Player Kings*.

p. 117   *Journals of William Charles Macready*, Abridged & Edited by J. C. Trewin (1967).

p. 120   Findlater, *The Player Kings*.

pps. 125–73   Irving on his physical handicaps: this appears in many biographies but in all references to Irving I have usually been guided by *Henry Irving* (Faber and Faber, 1961), his grandson Laurence Irving's definitive biography, checked against Gordon Craig and James Agate. All three seem to agree on the important issues and Laurence Irving's masterly understanding of his illustrious ancestor can seldom be faulted. It is one of the greatest theatrical biographies ever published.

pps. 140   Ellen Terry *The Story of My Life*, (Hutchinson, London 1908).

p. 143   Ellen Terry *The Story of My Life*, Edited by Edith Craig (G. P. Putnam, NY 1932).

pps. 146–7   Reade's description of Ellen Terry quoted from Tom Prideaux's *Love or Nothing, The Life and Times of Ellen Terry*, page 189 (Scribner, NY 1975).

p. 150   Sir John Gielgud: BBC archive material.

pps. 158–161   Edward Gordon Craig on Irving in *The Bells*: Gordon Craig *Henry Irving*, (J. M. Dent & Sons Ltd, London 1930)

p. 164   Henry James on the differences between the London and Paris stages is taken from Leon Edel's mammoth and definitive biography.

p. 168   Gielgud: told in private conversation with the author.

p. 170   Henry James: see above.

p. 172   Athene Seyler: BBC archives.

p. 172   Irving to Russell Thorndike: BBC archives.

p. 173   Gordon Craig on Ellen Terry & Irving: BBC

p. 176   Sir Max Beerbohn on Sir Herbert Beerbohm Tree: BBC archives.

p. 179   Ben Travers on Tree: BBC archives

p. 180   'Never hit a back cloth when it's down'—Richard Huggett: BBC archives.

p. 100   Clifford Mollison on Tree: BBC archives.

p. 180   Prometheus story: Huggett: BBC archives.

p. 180   Robert Atkins: BBC archives.

p. 181   William Armstrong: BBC archives.

p. 181   Richard Huggett: BBC archives.

p. 182   Constance Collier: *Harlequinade—The Story of My Life* (John Lane The Bodley Head Ltd, London 1929)

p. 185   Sir Ralph Richardson on Mrs Campbell: BBC archives.

p. 196   Richard Huggett: BBC archives.

p. 186   Gielgud on Mrs Campbell: BBC archives.

pps. 186–7   Forbes-Robertson on himself: from his autobiography mentioned in the text.

p. 187   Richard Findlater: *The Player Kings*, Ibid.

p. 190   Machugh on Martin-Harvey: BBC archives.

p. 191   Sir Harold Hobson: BBC archives.

p. 191   Robertson Hare: BBC archives.

pps. 192–3   Sir Lewis Casson on Poel: BBC archives.

pps. 194–5   Casson on Granville-Barker: BBC archives.

pps. 195–6   Dame Sybil Thorndike on Barker: BBC archives.

p. 196   Casson on Shaw and Barker: BBC archives

pps. 197–9   Sir Tyrone Guthrie on Sir Frank Benson and on the Old Vic: BBC archives.

pps. 199–200   Sybil Thorndike on Lilian Baylis: BBC archives.

p. 200   Robert Atkins on Baylis: BBC archives.

p. 200   Ernest Milton on Baylis: BBC archives.

p. 204   Gielgud on *The Vortex*: BBC archives.

p. 205   Sir Noël Coward on Charles Hawtrey: BBC archives.

pps. 205–6   Olivier and Gielgud, Angela du Maurier and Sir Felix Aylmer on du Maurier: BBC archives.

p. 207   Gielgud on his Romeo: BBC archives.

p. 208   Hal Burton on the Old Vic: *Great Acting* (BBC, 1967)

p. 208   Richardson on Gielgud, Olivier on Coward: BBC archives.

p. 210   Sir John Gielgud on style in acting—BBC archives.

p. 212   Billy Wilder: told to the author in Hollywood.

pp. 216–18   Gielgud: *Early Stages*, Page 31, revised edition Taplinger Publishing Company, NY, 1976

pps. 217–18   Letter from Akerman May: quoted in Ronald Hayman's *Gielgud*, Page 27, Heinemann 1971.

p. 218   Gielgud on rehearsing Romeo: *Early Stages*, Ibid, Page 50.

p. 218   Ivor Brown: review in *The New Age*, May 1924.

p. 218   Sir Harold Hobson: quoted in Ronald Hayman's *Gielgud*, Page 29.

pp. 219–20   Ivor Brown on Gielgud's 1929 *Hamlet*: The *Observer*.

p. 220   Gielgud speaking of his own *Richard II*: BBC archives.

pps. 221–2   Gielgud speaking of his own *Hamlet*: BBC archives.

p. 222   E. A. Baughan reviewing *Noah*: *News Chronicle* 1934.

p. 222   Gielgud and Sir John Martin-Harvey during the time when Gielgud was contemplating a new production of *A Tale of Two Cities*: quoted in Ronald Hayman's *Gielgud*, Ibid.

p. 223   Gielgud on Granville-Barker: quoted in Ronald Hayman's *Gielgud*, Page 124, Ibid.

p. 228   Letter from Dame Edith Evans: taken from her letters in the author's possession.

p. 229   Dame Sybil Thorndike on Father Heald: BBC archives.

p. 230   John Cottrell *Laurence Olivier*, Weidenfeld & Nicolson, 1975.

p. 232   Olivier: 'the most difficult equation . . . etc': BBC archives.

p. 232   Dame Sybil Thorndike on the young Olivier: BBC archives.

pps. 232–3   Denys Blakelock: *Round the Next Corner*, Gollancz 1967.

pps. 239–40   Olivier and Gielgud discussing their exchange of roles in *Romeo & Juliet*: BBC archives.

p. 240   Olivier on Elisabeth Bergner: quoted in John Cottrell's *Laurence Olivier*, Page 101, Ibid.

p. 242   Sir Ralph Richardson on himself; BBC archives.

p. 243   Richardson discussing Harcourt Williams: BBC archives.

p. 243   Richardson on Shaw: BBC archives.

p. 245   Richard Findlater on Richardson: *The Player Kings*, p. 265.

p. 246   Tynan on Richardson's Falstaff: *He That Plays The King*, p. 49 (Longmans 1950).

p. 246   Richardson on the gasworks: BBC archives.

p. 247   Richard Findlater: *The Player Kings*, page 267.

p. 249   Sir Michael Redgrave on Compagnie des Quinze: BBC archives.

pps. 249–50   Redgrave on Lilian Baylis and William Armstrong: BBC archives.

p. 251   Dame Edith Evans on herself as Rosalind: *Ned's Girl* p. 184 (Elm Tree Books, 1977).

p. 251   Redgrave on 'without moral values': taken from a BBC taped interview conducted by the author on Sir Michael's 70th birthday.

p. 251   Dame Edith Evans to Redgrave—'What sort of actor do you want to be?' There appears to be several versions on this. Richard Findlater quotes one in his *Michael Redgrave, Actor*, p. 31, (Heinemann 1956). Sir Michael gave a slightly different version to Lilian Ross during an interview for *The New Yorker* and Dame Edith herself told me her version, and was obviously proud that she had given this advice to this particular player.

p. 252   Redgrave on Stanislavsky: BBC archives.

p. 253   Rupert Hart-Davis: *Collected Letters*.

p. 255   Ashley Dukes on Redgrave in *The Family Reunion*: Richard Findlater, *Michael Redgrave, Actor*, p. 50, Ibid.

p. 256   Dame Peggy Ashcroft on Edith Evans: BBC archives.

p. 259   Gielgud on Dame Peggy Ashcroft's Desdemona in the Paul Robeson *Othello*: BBC archives.

p. 267   Tynan on *Henry IV*: *He That Plays The King*, p. 51, Ibid.

p. 268   Olivier on Wolfit's *Richard III*: BBC archives.

p. 268   Tynan on Wolfit: *He That Plays The King*, p. 40, Ibid.

p. 268   Ernest Milton on Wolfit's *Hamlet*: BBC archives.

p. 269   Donald Sinden on Wolfit: BBC archives.

p. 269   Wolfit on Randle Ayrton: BBC Archives.

p. 276   W. A. Darlington on Paul Scofield: *Six Thousand and One Nights, Harrap*, 1960.

p. 277   Tynan on Richard Burton: *Curtains*, Pages 11–12, Longmans, 1961.

p. 277   T. C. Worsley on Burton: *The Fugitive Art*, p. 238, John Lehmann, 1952.

p. 278   Ronald Bryden on Burton: Introduction to *Acting in The Sixties*, p. 13, BBC Publications 1970.

pps. 278–9   Burton on himself: BBC archives.

p. 282   John Neville on Burton: BBC archives.

p. 283   John Neville on himself: BBC archives.

p. 284   Peter O'Toole on himself: BBC archives.

p. 286   Richardson on 'what the actor does': BBC archives.

p. 287   Peggy Ashcroft, also Lindsay Anderson, on George Devine: from *The Theatres of George Devine* by Irving Wardle (Cape, 1978).

pps. 288–90   Tynan, Osborne and Olivier on *Look Back in Anger*: BBC archives.

p. 291–2   Sir Peter Hall on Peggy Ashcroft: BBC archives. On our theatrical heritage: BBC archives.

pps. 293–4   Albert Finney on himself and Charles Laughton: on Olivier and Edith Evans: BBC archives.

p. 296   Dorothy Tutin: BBC archives.

pps. 298–9   Maggie Smith: BBC archives.

p. 303   Sir Lewis Casson on 'the animal smell': BBC archives.

p. 304   Olivier on 'to touch the human heart:' BBC archives.

2. Black and White Illustrations

See list of numbered plates, pp. 7 and 8.

BBC Hulton Picture Library: 15, 25, 33, 34, 36, 40, 43, 47, 48, 49, 50, 51, 59, 60, 69, 72, 73, 88, 94, 95
British Theatre Museum: 2, 3, 4, 5, 6, 10, 11, 12, 13, 14, 16, 17, 18, 21, 24, 26, 27, 28, 31, 45, 46, 52, 53, 54, 55, 74, 75, 80, 81, 82, 85, 89, 90, 91, 92, 95, 96
Joe Cocks Studio: 102
Zoe Dominic: 83, 87, 93, 97, 98, 99, 100
Dulwich College Picture Gallery: 1
The Garrick Club: 8, 19, 29
Pamela Hansford Johnson: 44
Raymond Mander & Joe Mitchenson Theatre Collection: 7, 9, 20, 23, 30, 32, 58, 61, 62, 63, 64, 65, 66, 67, 68, 70, 71, 76, 77, 78, 79, 84, 86
Alastair Muir: 101
National Portrait Gallery: 22, 39, 56
Royal Photographic Society: 35
Tate Gallery: 37

SELECT BIBLIOGRAPHY

ADDENBROOKE, David *The Royal Shakespeare Company—The Peter Hall Years*, William Kimber & Co. Ltd, 1974

AGATE, James *Alarums and Excursions*, Grant Richards Ltd, 1922

——*The Amazing Theatre*, George C. Harrap & Co. Ltd, 1939

——*Buzz, Buzz! Essays of the Theatre*, W. Collins Sons & Co. Ltd

——*The Contemporary Theatre*, 1926 Chapman & Hall Ltd, 1927

——*Ego*, Hamish Hamilton, 1935

——*Ego 2*, Victor Gollancz Ltd, 1936

——*Ego 8*, George C. Harrap & Co. Ltd, 1947

——*Ego 9*, George C. Harrap & Co. Ltd, 1948

——*First Nights*, Ivor Nicholson & Watson, 1934

——*More First Nights*, Victor Gollancz Ltd, 1937

——*My Theatre Talks*, Arthur Barker Ltd

ALBANESI, E. M. *Meggie Albanesi*, Hodder & Stoughton

James Fullarton Arnott, & John William ROBINSON, *English Theatrical Literature 1559–1900*, The Society for Theatre Research 1970

BAKER, Michael *The Rise of the Victorian Actor* Crom Helm Ltd, 1978

BANCROFT, Sir Squire & Lady *The Bancrofts—Recollections of Sixty Years*, Thomas Nelson & Sons Ltd, 1911

BANNISTER, Winifred *James Bridie and His Theatre*, Rockliff Publishing Corporation Ltd, 1955

BARRAULT, Jean-Louis *Reflections on the Theatre*, Rockliff Publishing Corporation Ltd, 1951

BARTON, Margaret *Garrick*, Faber and Faber Ltd, 1948

BEERBOHM, Max *Around Theatres*, Rupert Hart-Davis, 1953

BENTLEY, Nicolas, *The Victorian Scene: 1837–1901*, Weidenfeld & Nicolson Ltd, 1968

BERNHARDT, Sarah, *The Art of the Theatre*, Geoffrey Bles

BINGHAM, Madeleine *The 'Great Lover'—The Life and Art of Herbert Beerbohm Tree*, Hamish Hamilton Ltd, 1978

BINGHAM, Madeleine *Sheridan—The Track of a Comet*, George Allen & Unwin Ltd, 1972

BOLITHO, Hector *Marie Tempest*, J. B. Lippincott Co., 1937

BRIDIE, James *One Way of Living—James Bridie's Autobiography*, Constable & Co. Ltd, 1939

BROWN, Eluned (ed. by) *The London Theatre 1811–1866—Selections from the diary of Henry Crabb Robinson*, The Society for Theatre Research, 1966

BROWN, Ivor *Theatre 1955–6*, Max Reinhardt, 1956

BURTON, Hal (ed. by) *Great Acting*, BBC, 1967

CHARQUES, R. D. (ed. by) *Footnotes to the Theatre*, Peter Davies Ltd, 1938

CHUTE, Marchette, *Shakespeare of London*, Souvenir Press (Educational & Academic) Ltd, 1977

COCHRAN, Charles B. *I Had Almost Forgotten*, Hutchinson & Co. (Publishers) Ltd, 1932

COLLIER, Constance *Harlequinade—The Story of My Life*, John Lane The Bodley Head Ltd, 1929

COLLINS, Charles W. *Great Love Stories of the Theatre*, Duffield & Co., 1911

CORNELL, Katharine *I Wanted to Be An Actress—The Autobiography of Katharine Cornell*, Random House, 1938

COTTRELL, John *Laurence Olivier*, Weidenfeld & Nicholson, 1975

COWARD, Noel *Future Indefinite*, William Heinemann Ltd, 1954

CRAIG, Edward Gordon *Ellen Terry and Her Secret Self*, Sampson Low, Marston & Co. Ltd

——*Index To The Story Of My Days—Some Memoirs of Edward Gordon Craig*, Hulton Press Ltd, 1957

CROSBY, John *With Love and Loathing*, McGraw-Hill Book Co., Inc., 1963

CURTIS Anthony (ed. by) *The Rise and Fall of the Matinee Idol*, Weidenfeld & Nicolson Ltd, 1974

——*Somerset Maugham*, Weidenfeld & Nicolson

DARLINGTON, W. A. *Laurence Olivier*, Morgan Grampian Books Ltd, 1968

——*Six Thousand and One Nights*, George C. Harrap & Co. Ltd, 1960

DAUBERRY, Peter *My World of Theatre*, Jonathan Cape Ltd, 1971

DEAN, Basil *Seven Ages—An Autobiography 1888–1927*, Hutchinson & Co. (Publishers) Ltd, 1970

——*Mind's Eye—An Autobiography 1927–1972*, Hutchinson & Co. (Publishers) Ltd, 1973

DENT, Alan *Mrs Patrick Campbell*, Museum Press Ltd, 1961

——*Preludes and Studies*, Macmillan & Co. Ltd, 1942

——*Vivien Leigh—A Bouquet*, Hamish Hamilton Ltd, 1969

DU MAURIER, Daphne *Gerald—A Portrait*, Victor Gollancz, 1934

DUNBAR, Janet *J. M. Barrie—The Man Behind The Image*, Houghton Mifflin Company, 1970

——*Mrs G.B.S.—A Biographical Portrait of Charlotte Shaw*, George C. Harrap & Co. Ltd, 1963

DUNLOP, Ian *Palaces and Progresses of Elizabeth I*, Jonathan Cape, 1962

EDWARDS, Anne *Vivien Leigh—A Biography*, Simon and Schuster, 1977

ELSOM, John *Post-War British Theatre*, Routledge & Kegan Paul Ltd, 1976

EMBODEN, William *Sarah Bernhardt*, Studio Vista, 1974

ERLANGER, Philippe *The Age of Courts and Kings—Manners and Morals 1558–1715*, Weidenfeld and Nicolson Ltd, 1967

ESSLIN, Martin (ed. by) *Illustrated Encyclopaedia of World Theatre*, Thames & Hudson Ltd, 1977

FAIRWEATHER, Virginia *Cry God for Larry*, Calder & Boyars Ltd, 1969

FARJEON, Herbert *The Shakespearean Scene*, Hutchinson & Co. (Publishers) Ltd   *date* ?

FFRENCH, Yvonne *Mrs Siddons—Tragic Actress*, Derek Verschoyle Ltd, 1936

FINDLATER, Richard *Michael Redgrave—Actor*, William Heinemann Ltd, 1956

——*The Player Kings*, Stein & Day, 1971

——*The Player Queens*, George Weidenfeld & Nicolson Ltd, 1976

——*The Unholy Trade*, Victor Gollancz Ltd, 1952

FITZSIMONS, Raymund *Edmund Kean—Fire From Heaven*, Hamish Hamilton Ltd, 1976

FORDHAM, Hallam *John Gielgud—An Actor's Biography in Pictures*, John Lehmann Ltd, 1952

FORSYTH, James *Tyrone Guthrie*, Hamish Hamilton Ltd, 1976

GASCOIGNE, Bamber *World Theatre*, Ebury Press, 1968

GIELGUD, John *John Gielgud—Early Stages 1921–1936*, Taplinger Publishing Co., Inc., 1974

GIELGUD, Kate Terry *An Autobiography*, Max Reinhardt, 1953

GLASSTONE, Victor *Victorian and Edwardian Theatres*, Thames & Hudson Ltd, 1975

GOURLAY, Logan (ed. by) *Olivier*, Weidenfeld & Nicolson, 1973

GRANVILLE-BARKER, Harley *A Companion to Shakespeare Studies*, & G. B. HARRISON (ed. by) Cambridge University Press, 1934

GRANVILLE-BARKER, Harley *Prefaces to Shakespeare*, Sidgwick & Jackson Ltd, 1930

GREENE, Graham *Lord Rochester's Monkey*, The Bodley Head Ltd, 1974

GUERNSEY, Otis L. Jr (ed. by) *Playwrights, Lyricists, Composers on Theater*, Dodd, Mead & Company, 1964

GUTHRIE, Sir Tyrone *A Life in the Theatre*, Hamish Hamilton Ltd, 1960

HACKETT, James H. (as recorded by) *King Richard III—Edmund Kean's performance*, The Society for Theatre Research, 1958

HANLEY, Tullah Innes *The Strange Title of G.B.S.*, Bruce Humphries, Inc., 1959

HARDWICKE, Sir Cedric *A Victorian In Orbit*, Methuen & Co. Ltd, 1961

HARRIS, Frank *Bernard Shaw*, Victor Gollancz Ltd, 1931

——*Frank Harris—His Life and Adventures*, The Richards Press Ltd, 1947

HARVEY, Sir Paul (compiled & ed. by) *The Oxford Companion to English Literature*, Oxford University Press, 1932

HASSALL, Christopher (arranged by) *Ambrosia and Small Beer—The Record of Correspondence between Edward Marsh and Christopher Hassall*, Longmans, Green & Co. Ltd, 1964

HAYMAN, Ronald *British Theatre Since 1955—A Reassessment*, Oxford University Press, 1979

——*John Gielgud*, Heinemann, 1971

HELBURN, Theresa *A Wayward Quest—The Autobiography of Theresa Helburn*, Little, Brown & Company (Inc.), 1960

HIBBERT, Christopher *The Court at Windsor—A Domestic History*, Longmans Green & Co. Ltd, 1964

——*The Personal History of Samuel Johnson*, Longman Group Ltd, 1971

HOBSON, Harold *The Theatre Now*, Longmans, Green & Co. Ltd, 1953

——*Verdict At Midnight*, Longmans, Green & Co. Ltd, 1952

HODGKINSON, J. L. & Rex POGSON *The Early Manchester Theatre*, The Society for Theatre Research, 1960

HOLROYD, Michael (ed. by) *The Genius of Shaw*, Hodder & Stoughton, 1979

HUGGETT, Richard *The Truth About 'Pygmalion'*, William Heinemann Ltd, 1969

IRVING, Laurence *Henry Irving: The Actor and His World*, Faber & Faber, 1951

——*The Successors*, Rupert Hart-Davis Ltd, 1967

ISAAC, Winifred F. E. C. *Ben Greet and The Old Vic*, Winifred F. E. C. Isaac, 1964

LANE, Margaret *Samuel Johnson and His World*, Hamish Hamilton Ltd, 1975

LANGNER, Lawrence, *G.B.S. and The Lunatic*, Atheneum, 1963

LAWRENCE, W. J. *Old Theatre Days and Ways*, George C. Harrap & Co. Ltd, 1935

LLOYD EVANS, Gareth & Barbara *Everyman's Companion to Shakespeare*, J. M. Dent & Sons Ltd, 1978

Lom, Herbert *Enter A Spy—The Double Life of Christopher Marlowe*, The Merlin Press, 1978
Loraine, Winifred *Robert Loraine*, Collins, 1938
Lucey, Janet Camden *Lovely Peggy—The Life and Times of Margaret Woffington*, Hurst & Blackett, 1952

MacCarthy, Desmond *Drama*, Putnam, 1940
Macdermott, Norman *Everymania—The History of The Everyman Theatre, Hampstead 1920–1926*, The Society for Theatre Research, 1975
MacQueen-Pope, W. *Ladies First*, W. H. Allen & Co. Ltd, 1952
——*St James's—Theatre of Distinction*, W. H. Allen & Co. Ltd, 1958
Malleson, Constance *After Ten Years*, Jonathan Cape Ltd, 1931
Mander, Raymond & Joe Mitchenson *The Theatres of London*, Rupert Hart-Davis Ltd, 1961
——*Theatrical Companion to Coward*, Rockliff Publishing Corporation, 1957
Manvell, Roger *Ellen Terry*, G. P. Putnam's Sons, 1968
Marshall, Dorothy *Fanny Kemble*, Weidenfeld & Nicolson Ltd, 1977
Matlaw, Myron *Modern World Drama—An Encyclopedia*, Martin Secker & Warburg Ld, 1972
Maude, Cyril *The Haymarket Theatre*, Grant Richards, 1903
Maugham, W. Somerset *The Summing Up*, William Heinemann Ltd, 1938
Munby, A. N. L. (ed. by) *Poets and Men of Letters, Volume 1*, Mansell Information/Publishing Ltd, 1971
Murray, Christopher *Robert William Elliston*, The Society for Theatre Research, 1975

Nalbach, Daniel *The King's Theatre 1704–1867*, The Society for Theatre Research, 1972
Nash, Mary *The Provoked Wife*, Little, Brown & Company, 1977
Nelson, Alfred L. & Gilbert B. Cross (ed. by) *Drury Lane Journal—Selections from James Winston's Diaries 1819–1827*, The Society for Theatre Research, 1974
Nemirovitch-Dantchenko, Vladimir *My Life In The Russian Theatre*, Geoffrey Bles, 1937
Nicoll, Allardyce *British Drama*, George C. Harrap & Co. Ltd, 1925
——*The English Theatre*, Thomas Nelson & Sons Ltd, 1936
Noble, Peter *Ivor Novello—Man Of The Theatre*, White Lion Publishers Ltd, 1975

O'Casey, Sean *Drums Under The Window*, Macmillan & Co. Ltd, 1945
Oman, Carola *David Garrick*, Hodder & Stoughton, 1958

Parker, John (compiled & ed. by) *Who's Who In The Theatre, 10th Edition*, Sir Isaac Pitman & Sons Ltd, 1947
Pearson, Hesketh *Beerbohm Tree—His Life and Laughter*, Methuen & Co. Ltd, 1956
——*G.B.S.—A Postscript*, Collins, 1951
——*Lives of the Wits*, William Heinemann Ltd, 1962
Poel, William *Monthly Letters*, T. Werner Laurie Ltd, 1929
Preston, Kerrison (ed. by) *Letters from Graham Robertson*, Hamish Hamilton Ltd, 1953
Prideaux, Tom *Love Or Nothing—The Life and Times of Ellen Terry*, Charles Scribner's Sons, 1975
Priestley, J. B. *Victoria's Heyday*, William Heinemann Ltd, 1972

Quennell, Peter (ed. by) *Memoirs of William Hickey*, Routledge & Kegan Paul Ltd, 1960

RANSOME, Eleanor (ed. by) *The Terrific Kemble*, Hamish Hamilton Ltd, 1978

RICHARDSON, Joanna *Sarah Bernhardt*, Max Reinhardt Ltd, 1959

ROBERTS, Peter *The Old Vic Story*, W. H. Allen, 1976

ROSS, Lillian & Helen ROSS *The Player—A Profile of an Art*, Simon & Schuster, Inc., 1962

ROWELL, George (selected & introd. by) *Victorian Dramatic Criticism*, Methuen & Co. Ltd, 1971

SCHOENBAUM, S. *William Shakespeare—A Compact Documentary Life*, Oxford University Press, 1977

SCOTT, W. S. The Georgian Theatre, John Westhouse (Publishers) Ltd, 1946

SENIOR, F. Dorothy *The Life and Times of Colley Cibber*, Rae D. Henkle Co., Inc.

SHAW, Bernard *Sixteen Self Sketches*, Constable & Co. Ltd, 1949

SHEPPARD, Dick *Elizabeth—The Life and Career of Elizabeth Taylor*, W. H. Allen & Co. Ltd, 1975

SHORT, Ernest *Introducing The Theatre*, Eyre & Spottiswoode, 1949

——*Theatrical Cavalcade*, Eyre & Spottiswoode (Publishers) London, 1942

SKINNER, Otis *Footlights and Spotlights*, The Curtis Publishing Company, 1923

SMITH, Lacey Baldwin, *The Elizabethan Epic*, Jonathan Cape, 1966

SMYTH, Ethel *Streaks of Life*, Longmans, Green & Co., 1921

SPEAIGHT, Robert (ed. by) *A. Bridges-Adams Letter Book*, The Society for Theatre Research, 1971

——*William Poel and the Elizabethan Revival*, William Heinemann Ltd, 1954

STEEN, Marguerite *A Pride of Terrys*, Longmans Green & Co. Ltd, 1962

STIRLING, Edward *Old Drury Lane*, Chatto & Windus, 1881

TAYLOR, John Russell *Anger and After*, Methuen & Co. Ltd, 1962

TERRY, Ellen *Ellen Terry's Memoirs*, G. P. Putnam's Sons, 1932

TREWIN, J. C. *Drama 1945–1950*, Longmans Green & Co. Ltd, 1951

——(ed. by) *The Journal of William Charles Macready 1932–1851*, Longmans, Green & Co. Ltd, 1967

——*The Theatre Since 1900*, Andrew Dakers Ltd, 1951

TYNAN, Kenneth *Curtains*, Longmans, Green & Co. Ltd, 1961

——*He That Plays The King*, Longmans, Green & Co. Ltd, 1950

——*Tynan Right and Left*, Longmans, Green & Co. Ltd 1967

——*A View of the English Stage 1944–63*, Davis-Poynter Ltd, 1975

VALENCY, Maurice *The Cart and The Trumpet—The Plays of George Bernard Shaw*, New York Oxford University Press, 1973

VALLANCE, Rosalind & John Hampden (ed. by) *William Hazlitt—Essays*, Folio Society, 1964

WAIN, John *Samuel Johnson*, Macmillan Ltd, 1974

WALDMAN, Milton *Elizabeth and Leicester*, Collins, 1944

WARDLE, Irving *The Theatres of George Devine*, Jonathan Cape Ltd, 1978

WARREN, Neilla (ed. by) *The Letters of Ruth Draper 1920–1956* Hamish Hamilton, 1979

WEBSTER, Margaret, *Don't Put Your Daughter On The Stage*, Alfred A. Knopf, Inc., 1962

——*The Same Only Different*, Alfred A. Knopf, Inc. 1969

WEINTRAUB, Stanley *Bernard Shaw 1914–1918—Journey to Heartbreak*, Routledge & Kegan Paul Ltd, 1973

WILLIAMS, Emlyn, *Emlyn—An Early Autobiography 1927–1935*, The Bodley Head Ltd, 1973

WILLIAMS, Harcourt *Old Vic Saga*, Winchester Publications Ltd, 1949

——*Vic-Wells—The Work of Lilian Baylis*, Cobden-Sanderson, 1938

WILLIAMSON, Audrey *Theatre of Two Decades*, Rockliff Publishing Corporation Ltd, 1951

WINSTEN, S. *Days With Bernard Shaw*, Hutchinson & Co. (Publishers), Ltd

WINTLE, Justin & Richard KENIN (ed. by) *The Dictionary of Biographical Quotation*, Routledge & Kegan Paul Ltd, 1978

WORSLEY, T. C. *The Fugitive Art—Dramatic Commentaries, 1947–1951*, John Lehmann Ltd, 1952

YOUNG, G. M. (ed. by) *Early Victorian England 1830–1865*, Oxford University Press, 1934

YOUNG, Vernon *On Film*, Quadrangle Books, Inc., 1972

ZOLOTOW, Maurice *Stagestruck—The Romance of Alfred Lunt and Lynne Fontanne*, Harcourt, Brace & World, Inc., 1964

Five Seasons of The Old Vic Theatre Company 1944–1949, The Saturn Press

The Royal Shakespeare Theatre Company 1960–1963, Max Reinhardt Ltd, 1964

Studies in English Theatre History, The Society for Theatre Research, 1952

INDEX

References to actors are in bold type